CHINESE POWER AND ARTIFICIAL INTELLIGENCE

T0386428

This book provides a comprehensive account of Chinese AI in its various facets, based on primary Chinese-language sources.

China's rise as an AI power is an event of importance to the world and a potential challenge to liberal democracies. Filling a gap in the literature, this volume is fully documented, data-driven, and presented in a scholarly format suitable for citation and for supporting downstream research, while also remaining accessible to laypersons. It brings together 15 recognized international experts to present a full treatment of Chinese artificial intelligence. The volume contains chapters on state, commercial, and foreign sources of China's AI power; China's AI talent, scholarship, and global standing; the impact of AI on China's development of cutting-edge disciplines; China's use of AI in military, cyber, and surveillance applications; AI safety, threat mitigation, and the technology's likely trajectory. The book ends with recommendations drawn from the authors' interactions with policymakers and specialists worldwide, aimed at encouraging AI's healthy development in China and preparing the rest of the world to engage with it.

This book will be of much interest to students of Chinese politics, science and technology studies, security studies, and international relations.

William C. Hannas is a Georgetown professor and CSET's lead analyst. Prior to this, he was a member of the Central Intelligence Agency's Senior Intelligence Service and a three-time recipient of its McCone Award. He is the lead author of *Chinese Industrial Espionage* (2013) and co-editor of *China's Quest for Foreign Technology* (2020).

Huey-Meei Chang is a Research Analyst at Georgetown University and is CSET's senior China S&T Specialist. She began her career as a data analyst at Taiwan's Academia Sinica, Institute of Biomedical Sciences and taught document analysis for more than a decade to researchers at U.S. Government agencies.

Asian Security Studies

Series Editors: Sumit Ganguly, *Indiana University, USA*, Andrew Scobell, *United States Institute of Peace, USA,* and Alice Ba, *University of Delaware, USA.*

Few regions of the world are fraught with as many security questions as Asia. Within this region it is possible to study great power rivalries, irredentist conflicts, nuclear and ballistic missile proliferation, secessionist movements, ethnoreligious conflicts and inter-state wars. This book series publishes the best possible scholarship on the security issues affecting the region, and includes detailed empirical studies, theoretically oriented case studies and policy-relevant analyses as well as more general works.

India's Nuclear Proliferation Policy
The Impact of Secrecy on Decision Making, 1980–2010
Gaurav Kampani

China's Quest for Foreign Technology
Beyond Espionage
Edited by William C. Hannas and Didi Kirsten Tatlow

US–China Foreign Relations
Power Transition and its Implications for Europe and Asia
Edited by Robert S. Ross, Øystein Tunsjø and Wang Dong

Explaining Contemporary Asian Military Modernization
The Myth of Asia's Arms Race
Sheryn Lee

The Covid-19 Crisis in South Asia
Coping with the Pandemic
Edited by Sumit Ganguly and Dinsha Mistree

Chinese Power and Artificial Intelligence
Perspectives and Challenges
Edited by William C. Hannas and Huey-Meei Chang

CHINESE POWER AND ARTIFICIAL INTELLIGENCE

Perspectives and Challenges

William C. Hannas and Huey-Meei Chang

Routledge
Taylor & Francis Group

LONDON AND NEW YORK

Cover image: © Igor Kutyaev

First published 2023
by Routledge
4 Park Square, Milton Park, Abingdon, Oxon OX14 4RN

and by Routledge
605 Third Avenue, New York, NY 10158

Routledge is an imprint of the Taylor & Francis Group, an informa business

© 2023 selection and editorial matter, William C. Hannas and Huey-
Meei Chang; individual chapters, the contributors

British Library Cataloguing-in-Publication Data
A catalogue record for this book is available from the British Library

Library of Congress Cataloging-in-Publication Data
Names: Hannas, Wm. C., 1946- editor.
Title: Chinese power and artificial intelligence : perspectives and
challenges / William C. Hannas and Huey-Meei Chang.
Description: First edition. | Abingdon, Oxon ; New York, NY :
Routledge, 2022. | Series: Asian security studies | Includes
bibliographical references and index. |
Identifiers: LCCN 2022003783 (print) | LCCN 2022003784 (ebook) |
ISBN 9781032081106 (hbk) | ISBN 9781032081090 (pbk) | ISBN
9781003212980 (ebk)
Subjects: LCSH: Artificial intelligence. | Artificial
intelligence--Engineering applications--China.
Classification: LCC Q335 .C4854 2022 (print) | LCC Q335 (ebook) |
DDC 006.3--dc23 /eng20220525
LC record available at https://lccn.loc.gov/2022003783
LC ebook record available at https://lccn.loc.gov/2022003784

ISBN: 978-1-032-08110-6 (hbk)
ISBN: 978-1-032-08109-0 (pbk)
ISBN: 978-1-003-21298-0 (ebk)

DOI: 10.4324/9781003212980

Typeset in Bembo
by KnowledgeWorks Global Ltd.

CONTENTS

ILLUSTRATIONS

Figures

Tables

ABBREVIATIONS

Acronym	Term
973 Plan	National Basic Research Program
AGI	artificial general intelligence
AI	artificial intelligence
AIDP	Artificial Intelligence Development Plan
AIIA	AI Industry and Technology Innovation Alliance of China
ANN	artificial neural network
ASI	artificial superintelligence
ATR	automated target recognition
AUV	autonomous underwater vehicles
AVIC	Aviation Industry Corporation of China
BAAI	Beijing Academy of Artificial Intelligence
BAIIA	Beijing AI Industrial Alliance
BAT	Baidu, Alibaba, and Tencent
BATH	Baidu, Alibaba, Tencent, and Huawei
BCI	Brain-computer interfaces
BI-AI	brain-inspired artificial intelligence
BIS	Bureau of Industry and Security
BQP	Baidu Quantum Plan
C4ISR	Command, control, communications, computers, intelligence, surveillance, and reconnaissance
CAAI	Chinese Association for Artificial Intelligence
CAE	Chinese Academy of Engineering
CAICT	China Academy of Information and Communications Technology
CAJ	Chinese Academic Journal(s)
CANZUK	Canada, Australia, New Zealand, and the United Kingdom

CAS	Chinese Academies of Science
CASC	China Aerospace Science and Technology Corporation
CASIA	Institute of Automation, CAS
CASIC	China Aerospace Science and Industry Corporation
CCP	Chinese Communist Party
CDSTIC	China Defense Science and Technology Information Center
CEC	China Electronics Corporation
CSET	Center for Security and Emerging Technology
CETC	China Electronics Technology Group Corporation
CLC	Chinese Library Classification
CNITSEC	China Information Technology Security Evaluation Center
CNKI	Chinese National Knowledge Infrastructure
CNN	convolutional neural networks
COSTIND	Commission on Science, Technology and Industry for National Defense
CPC	Communist Party of China
DGA	domain generation algorithms
DOD	Department of Defense (US)
DSR	Digital Silk Road
EDMR	electrically-detected magnetic resonance
ESR	electron spin resonance
EU	European Union
GAN	generative adversarial networks
GDPR	General Data Protection Regulation
GGF	government guidance funds
GIGA	Global and Innovation Gateway for All
GIS	Geographic Information System
GPU	graphics processing unit
I&W	indications and warning
IARPA	Intelligence Advanced Research Projects Activity
ICT	Internet, communications, and telecommunications
IJOP	Integrated Joint Operations Platform
IoT	Internet of Things
IP	intellectual property
ISO	International Organization for Standardization
ISR	intelligence, surveillance, and reconnaissance
ISTIC	Institute of Scientific and Technical Information of China
KNN	K-nearest neighbor
LAWS	lethal autonomous weapons systems
LSAM	Long short-term memory
MAC	media access control
MCF	Military-Civil Fusion
MHRSS	Ministry of Human Resources and Social Security
MIIT	Ministry of Industry and Information Technology

ML	machine learning
MLP	Medium- and Long-Term Plan for S&T Development
MOE	Ministry of Education
MOF	Ministry of Finance
MOST	Ministry of Science and Technology
MOU	memorandum of understanding
MPS	Ministry of Public Security
MRFM	magnetic resonance force microscopy
MSIRC	Military Science Information Research Center
MSS	Ministry of State Security
NBC	nuclear, biological, and chemical
NDRC	National Development and Reform Commission
NFTTC	National Fund for Technology Transfer and Commercialization
NGAI	New Generation AI
NHP	non-human primates
NIH	National Institutes of Health (US)
NKPs	National Key R&D Programs
NMR	nuclear magnetic resonance
NNSF	National Natural Science Foundation of China
NSTAC	National Science and Technology Analysis Center
OCAO	Overseas Chinese Affairs Office
ODMR	optically detected magnetic resonance
OODA	Observe-Orient-Decide-Act
OSINT	open-source intelligence
PE	private equity
PIPL	Personal Information Protection Law
PLA	People's Liberation Army
PRC	People's Republic of China
Program 111	Program of Introducing Innovative Talents of Disciplines to Universities
QAAA	quantum AI, quantum algorithm, and quantum architecture
R&D	research and development
RDT&E	research, development, test, and evaluation
RNN	recurrent neural networks
S&T	science and technology
SAFEA	State Administration of Foreign Experts Affairs
SC	State Council
SDIC	State Development Investment Corporation
SEI	Strategic Emerging Industries
SIA	Shenyang Institute of Automation
SKLs	State Key Laboratories
SOEs	state-owned enterprises

SPOT	Screening Passengers by Observation Technique
SSF	Strategic Support Force
STEM	science, technology, engineering, and mathematics
STI	science and technology intelligence
TAAC	Tsinghua Alumni Academic Club of North America
UAV	unmanned aerial vehicle
USIC	United States Intelligence Community
UUV	unmanned undersea vehicle
VAE	variational autoencoders
VC	venture capital
VPN	virtual private network
VQC	variational quantum circuit
VSM	Vector Space Model
WBE	whole brain emulation
ZGC	Zhongguancun

PREFACE

On behalf of our contributors, co-editor Huey-Meei Chang and I are pleased to offer this first comprehensive account of Chinese artificial intelligence, a distillation of 18 months of research by a cadre of talented specialists of varied backgrounds. The book is distinguished by its use of primary (Chinese-language) sources and by the acquaintance of many of its authors with U.S. and allied policymakers, whose concerns this book seeks to address. We also hope to promote awareness of China's approach to AI among other constituencies in government, academia, and industry, where engagement with China is sometimes driven by fear or naiveté.

We start with a brief summary of AI's history, generally and in China, as background for this book's genesis.

"Artificial intelligence" (AI) began life as a term and object of research at a conference at Dartmouth in 1956, attended by Claude Shannon (information theory), Marvin Minsky (MIT's AI lab), Ray Solomonoff (algorithmic probability), and eight other computing visionaries. The basic idea had surfaced six years earlier in Alan Turing's paper "Computing Machinery and Intelligence" in which he defined criteria for determining whether a machine can "think" based on its ability to convincingly manipulate linguistic symbols.[1] The conference's agenda in part reflected this approach:

> "The study is to proceed on the basis of the conjecture that every aspect of learning or any other feature of intelligence can in principle be so precisely described that a machine can be made to simulate it. An attempt will be made to find how to make machines use language, form abstractions and concepts, solve kinds of problems now reserved for humans, and improve themselves."[2]

If these goals resemble modern definitions of artificial *general* intelligence (AGI), for example,

> "the capacity of an engineered system to display the same rough sort of general intelligence as humans"[3] or
> "the representation of generalized human cognitive abilities in software"[4]

it is not coincidental. Early AI scientists saw their discipline as a machine-based proxy for human thought. Their failure to realize this goal or explore intermediate applications led to the so-called "AI winters" of reduced funding and interest.[5] This problem, where hype and expectations outpace reality,[6] was compounded by a phenomenon known as the "AI effect" of shifting goal posts, such that when AI succeeded, it lost its label.[7]

Undeterred, AI followed its own dynamic with more subtle, real-world uses that sustained it into the first decade of this century,[8] when machine learning (ML) and its derivatives[9] elevated AI to its present high-level of interest. Although a shared definition of "AI" has been elusive,[10] the term itself is now a household word—and a source of hope or anxiety for many.

If "artificial intelligence" is a major focus of scientific and popular attention outside China, it is no less so today in China where the term 人工智能 (réngōng zhìnéng)[11] is found in media of all genres, spawning some 56 million Google hits in late 2021—not to mention dedicated journals, academic societies, university departments, megalabs, unicorn companies,[12] and the government plans and proclamations detailed in this volume.

This was not always the case. AI was slow to catch on in China, where it was seen in the 1950s as a figment of bourgeoisie pseudoscience, and in the 1960s and beyond as a symbol of Soviet revisionism and an impossible fantasy.[13] A 1974 Chinese Academic Journal (CAJ) article titled "Does AI Exist?" summarized AI's state of acceptance in China: "Can 'intelligence' be created artificially? No."[14] Perhaps on some metaphysical level, these events in China equate to the "AI winters" seen elsewhere.

Three watershed events changed China's involvement with AI—and in the long term, as a likely consequence, the world itself. In March 1978, Chinese leader Deng Xiaoping (邓小平) delivered a landmark speech at a national science conference in Beijing titled "Science and Technology Are Productive Forces" (科学技术是生产力) credited as marking the "coming spring" (春天来临) of China's (re)emergence as an S&T power.[15] While banal in today's context, the statement was revolutionary in a country whose intellectuals had been persecuted for a decade (1966–1976).

A second catalyst were China's intellectuals themselves. Three in particular are regarded in Chinese sources as early pioneers, including mathematician Wu Wenjun (吴文俊, 1919–2017) known for his contributions to automated theorem proving[16]; Zhang Bo (张钹, 1935–), computer scientist, artificial neural network theorist, dean of Tsinghua University's Institute of Artificial

Intelligence, and proclaimed "founder of artificial intelligence in China"[17]; and Qian Xuesen (钱学森, 1911–2009), returned scientist, epistemologist, leader of China's ballistic missile program, progenitor of the world's largest and most successful open source S&T monitoring program,[18] and early 1980s advocate of AI research in China.[19]

The third element in China's acceptance of AI was the impact of returnees in general, who in Cai Zixing's words became "the academic leaders and backbones in the research, development, and application of artificial intelligence in China."[20] We documented the importance of returnees to China's AI development in earlier work[21]; it is taken up below in the context of talent programs, so we will not belabor it here. Cai also mentions early AI-predecessor research in China on automation, natural language processing, biological cybernetics, pattern recognition, and fuzzy logic dating from the late 1970s, noting however, as we do later (Chapter 7), that the emergence of AI *as a standalone discipline* in China was late to receive formal backing.[22]

A few other markers stand out. In 1979, a Chinese delegation headed by Tsinghua University computer scientist Lin Yaorui (林尧瑞, 1933–) participated in the International Joint Conference on Artificial Intelligence, held that year in Tokyo, the first to do so.[23] In 1981, the Chinese Association for Artificial Intelligence (中国人工智能学会) was stood up, now celebrating its 40th anniversary.[24] And in 1987, Chinese-born American computer scientist King-Sun Fu (傅京孙, 1930–1985) and Cai Zixing (蔡自兴, 1938–), then professor of Central South University's Center for Intelligent Systems and Intelligent Control (中南大学智能系统与智能控制研究所), published 人工智能及其应用 (*Artificial Intelligence and Its Applications*),[25] China's "first domestic monograph on AI."[26]

Significant later developments are noted in the chapters that follow.

My own "history" with AI grew from Robert Heinlein's novel *The Moon is a Harsh Mistress* read circa 1976.[27] For many of that generation, it was HAL 9000 (heuristically programmed algorithmic computer) in Arthur Clark's *Space Odyssey* series,[28] which came to epitomize malevolent AI, but my personal introduction to AI was more auspicious. Mycroft Holmes, Heinlein's mainframe, achieved consciousness when enough hardware was attached to meet a threshold. "Mike" and its programmer went on to lead a revolution against their oppressive government, inspirational even today. This positive attitude was reinforced by Ray Kurzweil's books, beginning with *The Age of Intelligent Machines* read in 1990[29] and ending with *The Singularity Is Near*, a non-fiction work read in 2005 that some regard as fiction.[30]

While this was running in the background, my working life from 2005 onward consisted of pouring through Chinese academic journals—obtuse, publicly available scholarly compilations in Chinese, which we treated as a barometer of China's progress in science and technology (S&T). The challenge was less with the technical Chinese (which is easier for foreigners than creative literature) and more with understanding the concepts—a chore even for disciplinary experts, which we mostly were not—compounded by errors, plagiarism, and disinformation to throw off foreign analysts (they need not have bothered). Since my "account" included what passed then for computing, I got an early dose of what would later become Chinese AI.

Fast forward a decade. If the CAJ literature was the fuel, the appearance of Nick Bostrom's *Superintelligence* in 2014[31] was the catalyst that caused me to take this work seriously. It also wrecked my Utopian vision of how AI would liberate us from everything. At this point, alarms were already sounding elsewhere in the "community." Prompted by a request from Assistant to the President for National Security Affairs Susan Rice for information on AI's impact on U.S. security, Director of National Intelligence James Clapper tasked the community's technical arm—the Intelligence Advanced Research Projects Activity (IARPA)—for a paper on the topic. That task fell on Dr. Jason Matheny who, atypically for someone in this position, continued the study personally after assuming IARPA's directorship in August 2015, with my support, that of (present) director of Georgetown's Center for Security and Emerging Technology (CSET) Dr. Dewey Murdick, and a former National Intelligence Officer. The result, published internally in September, was the U.S. Government's first assessment of global AI progress.[32]

Dr. Matheny carried this baton into the private sector in autumn of 2018, when he laid out with support from Dr. Murdick, myself, and others the framework for a think tank aimed at detecting and mitigating national security challenges posed by emerging technologies, AI chief among them. The project was realized in early 2019 with the inauguration of CSET. As is evident from the biographies, CSET analysts played the dominant role in this book's creation—11 of its 15 authors—who came together to produce this account. Although not its product per se, we have benefitted greatly from CSET's research and the opportunities it has afforded us to interact with AI scholars and practitioners worldwide.

The book is divided into five parts, each with three chapters of equal length (if we learned nothing else from our China studies, it is the Great Han penchant for universal order). Part I discusses state (Chapter 1) and private sector (Chapter 2) inputs into China's AI enterprise. The third chapter takes up an overlooked—albeit not by China itself—aspect of that country's AI development, namely foreign dependencies. Part II views China AI from a global perspective: China's domestic and international quests for talent (Chapter 4), China's academic research in the context of worldwide AI scholarship (Chapter 5),[33] and China's AI strengths and weaknesses relative to the rest of the world (Chapter 6).

AI, like steam power and electricity, is an *enabler* of technologies. Part III examines the impact of AI on Chinese work in three representative disciplines: neuroscience (Chapter 7), biology (Chapter 8), and quantum science (Chapter 9). In Part IV, we enter the netherworld of AI used in military (Chapter 10), cyber (Chapter 11), and surveillance applications (Chapter 12). Part V guesses where China AI may be headed (Chapter 13), and what China (Chapter 14) and the rest of the world (Chapter 15) are doing, or can do, to nurture its healthy development. We conclude with a list of policy recommendations from the book's contributors.

Co-editor H.-M. Chang and I are grateful to this volume's authors, who found time from their busy schedules to contribute. We thank Georgetown University's School of Foreign Service and our directors—Drs. Dewey Murdick, Igor Mikolic-Torreira, and Catherine Aiken in particular—for the latitude to engage in this project. Thanks are also due to SOSi's Defense Group Inc. and its former director Dr. James Mulvenon, whose staff authored two technical chapters and supported the book with their trademark speed and professionalism.

We acknowledge with gratitude Brian Fleeger, Glenn Tiffert, Jeffrey Ding, Matt Sheehan, Michael Sulmeyer, Morgan Clemens, Norm Kahn, Scott Livingston, Sean Eddy, Steven Block, and Will Hunt, who commented on parts of the manuscript; cadre who contributed narrative beyond their own significant chapters, including Daniel Chou, Helen Toner, Jeffrey Stoff, John Chen, Jonathan Ray, and Karen M. Sutter; and—as always—senior editor Andrew Humphrys and the Routledge staff for bringing another of our books to print.

We also thank Acclaim Technical Services and Joumana Sleiman for supporting one of us in our transition to academia. Our deepest gratitude is to Dr. Jason Matheny, who was there at the start of this journey, and to our spouses and families for their forbearance.

Many contributors are or were in government service. Accordingly, we disclaim any use of classified information in this book's preparation—the uncomfortable truth is that the path of enlightenment is almost always in the opposite direction. Those with standing requirements for official review completed that process. Even where such formal requirements are lacking, we endeavored to maintain the standards of our sponsoring institutions. The views expressed here are ours alone and not necessarily those of current and past employers.

Similarly, this book makes no use of proprietary data sources beyond those that were first published at CSET under license by Georgetown University. We thank GU/CSET for permission to cite papers, graphs, and data published previously under CSET auspices.

A final disclaimer: there are no sinophobes here. If you are looking for another screed about the impending "Yellow Peril," you won't find it here. Nor do many of us qualify as sinophiles. We call things as we see them—a legacy of the "speaking truth to power" maxim we were taught to follow—and wherever possible let the data and people making AI policy and doing the science speak for us. All of us have lots to complain about in our home countries and prefer to invest what spare cycles we have in narrative aimed at making the world more livable for everyone, now and into the future. Hence our focus on artificial intelligence.

William C. Hannas
Georgetown University

Notes

1 *Mind*, 1950. That is, the famous Turing Test. Descartes (1637) is credited in the *Stanford Encyclopedia of Philosophy* as his intellectual forerunner. "Artificial Intelligence," July 12, 2018.
2 J. McCarthy et al., "A Proposal for the Dartmouth Summer Research Project on Artificial Intelligence," August 31, 1955, http://www-formal.stanford.edu/jmc/history/dartmouth/dartmouth.html.
3 http://www.scholarpedia.org/article/Artificial_General_Intelligence.
4 https://searchenterpriseai.techtarget.com/definition/artificial-general-intelligence-AGI.
5 https://en.wikipedia.org/wiki/AI_winter#cite_note-FOOTNOTEKurzweil2005264-5.
6 Chris Smith, Introduction to "The History of Artificial Intelligence," December 2006, p. 4.
7 Michael Haenlein and Andreas Kaplan, "A Brief History of Artificial Intelligence: On the Past, Present, and Future of Artificial Intelligence," *California Management Review* 61.4, August 2019, pp. 5–14.
8 David Marshall, "Artificial Intelligence (AI): Controversies and Myths," *Vmblog.com*, March 30, 2018. Remarks attributed to Rodney Brooks in 2002 and Ray Kurzweil in 2005.
9 Computer algorithms that self-improve with experience and access to data.
10 Pei Wang, "The Logic of Intelligence," in Ben Goertzel and Cassio Pennachin, eds., *Artificial General Intelligence*, Springer, Berlin Heidelberg, 2007.
11 A calque or "loan translation" from the English "artificial" (人工) + "intelligence" (智能).
12 A privately held company valued at over $1 billion.
13 Cai Zixing (蔡自兴), "中国人工智能40年" (40 Years of Artificial Intelligence in China), 科技导报 (*Science and Technology Review*), 34.25, 2016; "人工智能在中国曾被当成伪科学" (Artificial Intelligence Was Once Regarded as Pseudoscience in China), *Gugong.net* (故宫历史网), October 27, 2018.
14 "人工造得出'智能'吗? 造不出." Lu Lou (路娄), "有没有'人工智能'?" 摘译外国自然科学哲学 (Excerpts of Foreign Natural Science Philosophy), 上海人民出版社 (Shanghai People's Publishing House.), 2, 1974, p. 26.
15 "新中国档案: 邓小平提出科学技术是第一生产力" (New China Archives: Deng Xiaoping Proposed that Science and Technology Are the Primary Productive Forces), *China Government Net*, October 10, 2009.
16 Cai, op cit.
17 "中国人工智能奠基者." He Yingchun (贺迎春) and Ding Yixin (丁亦鑫), "坚守三尺讲台逾一甲子醉心AI创新超40年" (Holding Fast to the Podium for More Than 60 Years, Fascinated by AI Innovation for Over 40 Years), *People's Daily* (Overseas Edition), August 30, 2021.
18 William C. Hannas and Huey-Meei Chang, "China's STI Operations," Georgetown University, Center for Security and Emerging Technology, January 2021.
19 Cai, op cit.
20 Ibid.
21 William C. Hannas and Huey-Meei Chang, "China's 'Artificial' Intelligence," in William C. Hannas and Didi Kirsten-Tatlow, eds., *China's Quest for Foreign Technology: Beyond Espionage*, Routledge, London and New York, 2021.
22 Cai, op cit.
23 "对话 IJCAI「中国参会第一人」林尧瑞教授:回首从零开始的中国AI 研究之路" (Dialog with Professor Lin Yaorui, the IJCAI's First Participant from China: Looking Back on the Path of China's AI Research from the Start), Sohu.com, March 31, 2019.
24 https://www.caai.cn/

25 清华大学出版社 (Tsinghua University Publishing Co.), 1987. Available through Google Books. A co-authored 5th edition was released by the Tsinghua house in 2016.
26 Cai, op cit.
27 Robert A. Heinlein, *The Moon is a Harsh Mistress*, Putnam's Sons, New York, NY, 1966.
28 Arthur C. Clark, *2001: A Space Odyssey*, Hutchinson, London, 1968.
29 Ray Kurzweil, *The Age of Intelligent Machines*, MIT Press, Cambridge MA, 1990.
30 Ray Kurzweil, *The Singularity Is Near*, Viking Penguin, New York, NY, 2005.
31 Nick Bostrom, *Superintelligence: Paths, Dangers, Strategies*, Oxford University Press, Oxford, UK, 1994.
32 Jason Matheny, personal communication, November 13, 2021. Matheny's paper led to creation of an AI working group within the White House's National Science and Technology Council and a "National Artificial Intelligence Research and Development Strategic Plan" in October 2016 (https://obamawhitehouse.archives.gov/sites/default/files/whitehouse_files/microsites/ostp/NSTC/national_ai_rd_strategic_plan.pdf).
33 We acknowledge and appreciate co-authors Ashwin Acharya's and Daniel Chou's extraordinary ability to combine their complementary approaches to data analytics into a compelling narrative. Elements of both efforts were preceded by papers published previously by GU/CSET, reproduced here with gratitude.

PART I
Foundations of Chinese AI power

1

State plans, research, and funding

Ngor Luong and Ryan Fedasiuk

The Chinese government documents its artificial intelligence (AI) ambitions in formal and transparent plans and policies, which are drafted and promulgated by the highest echelons of its government and ruling Communist Party (CCP). Chinese policymakers have consistently emphasized AI as a pillar of China's aim to become a technology superpower.

This chapter introduces the Chinese state's plans, government-led funding mechanisms, and research efforts that underpin China's AI development. The first section explores high-level policies that form the blueprint for China's AI development, including specific strategies and benchmarks for industry growth. The second section discusses the structure of China's science and technology (S&T) ecosystem and illustrates the government's role in financing AI research, especially basic research and development (R&D). The final section discusses a key element of China's approach to AI that gives it unique advantages: the role of industrial policies. Leveraging the market to meet the state's AI ambition is integral to Xi Jinping's philosophy on economic governance in China.[1] By leaning on traditional and new industrial policy tools, the CCP under Xi is incentivizing private firms to align themselves with the state's AI development objectives.[2]

The blueprint for China's AI development

The first official Chinese government plan to mention "artificial intelligence" was published in 2015.[3] But China's interest in advanced technology dates back much further. In the 1950s, the then-Chairman Mao Zedong popularized the propaganda slogan "Surpass Britain and catch up to America" (超英赶美) through technology development. Deng Xiaoping, the then-leader of China, continued the country's pursuit of key technological development by importing $80 billion of advanced technology in 1978.[4]

DOI: 10.4324/9781003212980-2

In 1986, the CCP crystallized its first series of S&T plans, which were designed to fill China's strategic gaps and "leapfrog" the United States technologically and economically.[5] Major strategic initiatives such as the 863 Program (863计划) and 973 Program (973计划) accelerated China's technological progress in the 1980s and 1990s, and contributed to the country's advances in aerospace and telecommunications.[6] By the mid-2000s, Chinese leaders had begun to recognize the importance of "intelligent" (智能) systems and equipment alongside digital technologies.[7] The 2010s' boom in deep learning research—the key to AI's recent and explosive growth—has attracted significant attention from the Chinese government.

Several of the CCP's guiding S&T policies emphasize the role of AI in amassing comprehensive national power, as shown in Table 1.1. These policies map out China's ambition to become an AI global superpower and often include specific targets for China's AI market, development of core AI technologies, and budget for AI R&D.

Three-year Action Plans for AI

Four Chinese ministries jointly released the 2016 "Internet + Three-year Action Plan for Artificial Intelligence," a continuation of China's Internet plus policy with a focus on AI industry development. With a goal to scale up China's AI market to $15 billion (100 billion RMB) and to cultivate leading AI firms, the plan called for a rapid development of nine major AI technologies such as smart home appliances, intelligent automotive, unmanned systems, and smart terminals, among others.[16]

In December 2017, China's Ministry of Industry and Information Technology (MIIT) issued a "Three-year Action Plan for Promoting Development of a New Generation Artificial Intelligence Industry (2018–2020)" to reaffirm commitments made in the previous three-year plan.[17] Released five months after the "New Generation AI Development Plan," the Action Plan was also set to implement this massive AI initiative. It prioritized specific product categories for AI industry development previously named in the 2016 Internet + Three-year Action Plan and identified pattern recognition, intelligent semantic understanding, and intelligent analysis and decision-making as core AI technologies.[18]

The New Generation AI Development Plan

Released in 2017, the State Council's New Generation Artificial Intelligence Development Plan (AIDP) signaled a major shift to focus on AI as a core aspect of China's national economic development strategy.[19] China's leaders see AI as key to the nation's technological development, stating in the plan that "AI is a strategic technology that will lead in the future."[20] The plan calls for both relevant state and non-state actors to support the central government in pursuing global leadership in AI and using the technology to achieve the next phase of economic growth.[21]

TABLE 1.1 Chinese AI-related national planning documents

Policy	Year issued	Significance for AI development
"Internet +" Action Plan[8]	2015	Includes first formal mention of AI, identifies 11 specific actions for technological transformation, and sets to grow the market size of China's AI industry to hundreds of billions of RMB.
"Internet +" Three-year Action Plan for Artificial Intelligence (2016–2018)[9]	2016	Lays out commitments in building China's AI industry ecosystem with a market size of $15.26 billion (100 billion RMB) and cultivating leading global AI companies by 2018.
National Science and Technology Programs for 13th Five-year Plan (2016–2020)[10]	2016	Defines AI goals in terms of human-centric intelligent computation.
13th Five-year Plan for the Development of Strategic Emerging Industries[11]	2016	Sets goals to accelerate AI development by promoting basic research and application of the technology in various fields.
New Generation AI Development Plan[12]	2017	Major shift toward AI promotion; AI as an "engine for economic development," but acknowledges China's significant technological bottlenecks.
Three-year Action Plan to Promote Development of a New Generation Artificial Intelligence Industry (2018–2020)[13]	2017	Reaffirms the commitments in the "Internet +" Three-year Action Plan for Artificial Intelligence; sets out specific targets for AI industry development in a range of product categories such as intelligent service robots, data processing, and intelligent unmanned aerial vehicles, among others.
Strategic Emerging Industries Strategy[14]	2020	Looks to strengthen and reform public-private investment vehicles to support strategically important technology clusters, including AI.
14th Five-year Plan (2021–2025)[15]	2021	Enumerates new "frontier industries," AI chief among them, and emphasizes basic research funding and high-quality patent production.

Broadly, the AIDP focuses on progressing toward intelligentized systems, establishing supporting policies and regulations, and mobilizing talent and resources around the nation's innovation ambitions. In particular, the plan identifies shortcomings and develops benchmarks for basic and applied research to meet China's technological ambitions. AIDP sets different targets for AI core and AI-related industries. By 2030, it aims for China's AI core industries to exceed $150.8 billion (1 trillion RMB) in market size, a ninefold increase from the 2018 target, and the country's AI-related industries to surpass $1.48 trillion (10 trillion RMB). At the same time, Chinese leaders recognize areas where China is lacking, such as original AI algorithms, high-end computer chips, and foundational materials. The plan further assesses that Chinese research institutions and companies lack the global influence, basic R&D infrastructure, and talent required to pursue China's AI ambition.

To address these shortcomings, Chinese leaders continue to prioritize AI as a vital component of China's global technological leadership and support the integration of AI in governance and industry. It has mobilized government personnel, state-owned enterprises, and private companies to develop AI-related software and hardware.[22]

Strategic Emerging Industries strategy

Initiated by the National Development and Reform Commission (NDRC) in 2020, the Strategic Emerging Industries (战略性新兴产业, SEI) strategy guides Chinese investment in several "key industrial investment domains"—chief among them being "information technology," which includes AI.[23] The plan specifically calls on Chinese enterprises to "Steadily advance the integrated innovation and combined application of the industrial Internet, artificial intelligence (AI), Internet of Things (IoT), Internet of Vehicles, big data, cloud computing, blockchain, and other technologies."[24] Chinese leaders also hope to accelerate the country's progress in AI by channeling more investment into related, data-heavy fields such as urban infrastructure and telecommunications.

The SEI calls for local governments and private investors to jointly fund projects essential to China's long-term economic growth.[25] Specifically, it tasks the NDRC, Ministry of S&T (MOST), MIIT, and Ministry of Finance (MOF) with mobilizing funding and resources for emerging industries.[26] Beyond the national strategy, "most provinces and cities have also actively introduced policies such as artificial intelligence development plans," thereby "accelerating the deep integration of artificial intelligence with the economy, society, and industry."[27] SEI also encourages small and micro enterprises to accelerate the adoption of AI in all sectors of the Chinese economy by integrating data analysis into their day-to-day operations. This ambition is also reflected in plans like the "'Internet+' Three-year Action Plan for AI."

The 14th Five-year Plan (2021–2025)

China's national five-year economic development plans are the most visible and consequential products of Chinese central planning. Issued in 2021, the 14th Five-year Plan (14th FYP) is particularly significant. The plan was developed and approved on the eve of the centennial of the founding of the CCP. It reaffirms China's mission to become a global S&T power, setting measurable goals and gesturing toward the tools it will use to achieve them. The plan also identifies weaknesses within China's national S&T ecosystem and prescribes specific remedies. These include the creation of new national "megaprojects" (重大项目) in strategically important industries, new tax preferences for institutions engaged in basic research, and the designation of "chief scientists" who are to take charge and lead major research projects.[28]

Beyond its broad focus on S&T, the 14th FYP reaffirmed AI as the CCP's top S&T research priority.[29] China's leaders consider new generation AI to be crucial for national security and overall development, and they aim to "make breakthroughs in cutting-edge basic theories, develop dedicated chips, and construct open-source algorithm platforms such as deep learning frameworks."[30] AI is ranked first among "frontier industries" the Chinese government will focus on through 2035.

State support for AI research in China

The state is responsible for funding significant portions of S&T in China, especially basic R&D. According to China's MOST, some 90 percent of worldwide AI innovation stems from basic research, which has enabled other countries to gain a "technology monopoly" in this sector that China has traditionally neglected.[31] Breaking that monopoly is a focus of China's S&T ambition. Remedies will be achieved through new R&D funding mechanisms and by reforming old ones.[32]

One such mechanism is the "2030 Science and Technology Innovation—'New Generation Artificial Intelligence' (NGAI) Megaproject" (科技创新 2030—'新一代人工智能'重大项目). Begun in 2018 as part of the New Generation AI Development Plan (2017), the NGAI megaproject amasses contributions from, and distributes support for, AI development among a wide array of Chinese universities, companies, and research labs. MOST, NDRC, and MOF jointly administer NGAI megaproject funding, and in 2018 authorized $134 million (870 million RMB) across 39 research projects.[33] In 2020, MOST's AI megaproject grant application guidelines were related to theoretical AI research such as brain-inspired spiking neural networks, semantic understanding, and advanced machine learning theory; and other key areas such as natural-language processing, autonomous driving, and smart chip technology.[34] The following year, MOST reiterated its call for projects that address issues in basic AI theory, such as causal reasoning and decision theory, theory of continuous learning, memristors (感存算一体化), and cross-domain (跨域异质) analytical reasoning.[35]

MOST sees the NGAI megaproject as a core component of China's broader S&T aims in the 2020s.[36] The ultimate goal is to overcome "bottlenecks" to China's S&T development, fill strategic gaps, and accelerate China's progress as an "innovative country" (创新国家). Several other government megaprojects dedicated to big data, quantum computing, and brain-inspired research will also benefit AI development in China.[37]

A second government effort that aims to reduce China's R&D deficit involves the progressive reform of existing funding mechanisms, which focus more on applied research. China's 863 Program, for example, was personally launched by the then-leader Deng Xiaoping to develop information infrastructure, the bioeconomy, and new materials and advanced manufacturing.[38] By 1997, Chinese leaders began to recognize the importance of *basic* research in advancing China's status as a world power, and initiated the National Basic Research Program (973 Plan).[39] Both plans have since been absorbed into new mechanisms outlined below, although their authorizations continue to sustain many research projects undertaken by government-sponsored laboratories and universities.[40] Examples are as follows:

- National Key R&D Programs (NKPs) are a new category created after the 2014 reform of the national S&T funding system, jointly administered by MOST and MOF, through which the state awards research grants to universities, laboratories, and enterprises. Of 1,036 publicly disclosed NKP research projects awarded in 2018, 97 (9 percent) appear related to AI.[41] Examples include supply chain process control for intelligent manufacturing, data mining and analysis, and new cloud computing architectures for big data processing. AI-related projects amounted to $3 billion (20 billion RMB) in value, with the largest recipients of AI-related NKP funding being Tsinghua, Zhejiang, and Shanghai Jiaotong Universities.
- The National Natural Science Foundation (NNSF) of China is China's largest funder of basic research and is generally considered an analog to the National Science Foundation in the United States. NNSF supports more than 18,000 research projects each year. In 2019, AI projects bearing specific AI-related funding codes (F06) totaled 537 with a combined value of $41 million (268 million RMB).[42] These projects ranging from "AI fundamentals" (F0601) through "cognitive and neuroscience-inspired AI" (F0607) all pertain to AI as its own discipline.[43] An analysis by the authors of project titles, where AI is likely to play some role—e.g. autonomous vehicles, and adaptive learning for modeling and recognition—identified some 1,300 (7 percent) of the NNSF's publicly disclosed projects as potentially germane, yielding an outer bound of $1.7 billion (11.1 billion RMB).[44]

These mechanisms are illustrative but not an exhaustive account of state funding, neither for AI (in all its manifestations) nor for S&T in China, some of which is unavailable for public scrutiny. However, it is evident that among China's largest research funding programs, AI has emerged as a priority—in 2018, amounting to at least $4.7 billion—to say nothing of the private sector's own investments (see Chapter 2).

China's AI research doers

Organizations such as the Chinese Academy of Science (CAS) and NNSF are China's largest funders of basic research, dedicating $5.4 billion (36 billion RMB) and $4.8 billion (32 billion RMB), respectively, to basic research programs—across all fields—in 2019.[45] Many of these grants are executed by faculty and staff at elite universities as well as researchers at laboratories managed directly or indirectly by the Chinese government.[46] It is therefore important to distinguish between the *funders* and *doers* of China's public-sector AI research portfolio.

Among China's state-run research centers, China's State Key Laboratories (国家重点实验室, SKLs) are the most prestigious and consequential. Numbering some 550 institutions nationwide, they are primarily managed by MOST, the CAS, and the Ministry of Education—while other "Enterprise SKLs" are managed by private and state-owned corporations.[47] While some of these labs are multidisciplinary, others specialize in a certain industry or technology area.[48]

Several SKLs are involved in AI R&D in China. Since 2007, the Chinese government has built at least two publicly disclosed AI laboratories, focused on brain science and virtual reality systems, respectively. CAS research institutes operate several of the SKLs at the forefront of AI research in China. The CAS Shenyang Institute of Automation (SIA), for example, is a leader in autonomous vehicles, whereas the CAS Institute of Automation (CASIA) focuses on data analysis and pattern recognition. Several others are supportive of China's nationwide AI enterprise owing to the nature of their research, as shown in Table 1.2.

Distinct from SKLs are AI research institutes within Chinese universities, which numbered 34 as of 2021.[49] Their primary mission is to train undergraduate students in machine learning techniques. These university institutes draft academic curricula and work with Chinese and foreign enterprises to learn about cutting-edge developments in the field of AI.[50] Each AI institute has a specific research specialization "which range from natural language processing to robotics, medical imaging, smart green technology, and unmanned systems."[51]

Beginning in 2018, AI institutes have been established at China's premier universities, such as Tsinghua and Shanghai Jiaotong Universities, as well as at defense-affiliated institutions, such as Harbin Institute of Technology and Nanjing University of Aeronautics and Astronautics. Moreover, universities sometimes establish these centers jointly with Chinese AI companies. For example, in 2018, Chongqing University of Posts and Telecommunications jointly set up an institute with the AI unicorn iFlytek (科大讯飞), while Tencent Cloud struck similar partnerships with Shandong University of Science and Technology and Liaoning Technical University.[52]

The heart of China's AI advantages: industrial policies

China's government uses industrial policies to promote industries integral to the country's technological development and to close gaps with other industrialized states.[53] Xi Jinping's speech to MOST in 2013 typifies this mindset.[54]

> Our technology still generally lags that of developed countries, and we must adopt an asymmetrical strategy of catching up and surpassing, bringing our own advantages to bear.

TABLE 1.2 Select state key laboratories involved in AI research

State key lab	Responsible institution	Founded	Research focus
Pattern Recognition (模式识别国家重点实验室)	Institute of Automation, CAS	1984	Visual information processing, biometric voice language information and security
Software Development Environments (软件开发环境国家重点实验室)	Beijing University of Aeronautics and Astronautics	1988	Social brain computing theory and software engineering group, big data computing theory
Network and Exchange Technology (网络与交换技术国家重点实验室)	Beijing University of Posts and Telecommunications	1988	Network services, network management and security
Automotive Simulation and Control (汽车仿真与控制国家重点实验室)	Jilin University	1989	Automobile design and theory, vehicle power transmission system
Robotics (机器人学国家重点实验室)	Shenyang Institute of Automation, CAS	1989	Theoretical acclimatization and autonomous behavior, robotic behavior mechanisms
Information Security (信息安全国家重点实验室)	Institute of Information Engineering, CAS	1989	Cryptography theory, related mathematical algorithm design theory
Complex System Management and Control (复杂系统管理与控制国家重点实验室)	Institute of Automation, CAS	1991	Intelligence science, complex systems theory and applications
Computer Science (计算机科学国家重点实验室)	Institute of Software, CAS	1993	Theoretical foundations of computer science, formal methods of software development
Brain and Cognitive Science (脑与认知科学国家重点实验室)	Institute of Biophysics, CAS	2007	Protein science, brain and cognitive sciences
Virtual Reality Technology and Systems (虚拟现实技术与系统国家重点实验室)	Beijing University of Aeronautics and Astronautics	2007	Modeling theory and methods, virtual reality, augmented reality, and natural human-computer interaction
Robot Technology Systems (机器人技术与系统国家重点实验室)	Harbin Institute of Technology	2007	Optimization of advanced and innovative robot system design, robot dynamics and control methods

As a disruptive, emerging technology, AI is a natural focus for China's ambition to catch up to the world's most advanced technology powers. In an effort to realize its AI ambitions, the Chinese government enlisted both traditional mechanisms such as subsidies and preferential tax treatments to provide direct financial support to Chinese AI companies, as well as emerging mechanisms such as government guidance funds to mobilize both public and private support for China's AI industry development.

Direct state financial support to Chinese AI-related companies

Developing AI capabilities requires large capital investments. With its control over key aspects of China's economy, the Chinese government is willing and able to pay a high cost in pursuit of global leadership in emerging technologies. The state has crafted aggressive industrial policies as tools to help mobilize and allocate state and private capital into emerging industries.

China's government provides key funding to ease market barriers to entry for domestic companies in emerging sectors such as AI. The government is showering homegrown national champions with subsidies and cash handouts—directly from government outlays—to speed up AI innovation. To "pick winners" in AI, the Chinese government establishes public-private collaboration platforms, such as China's Artificial Intelligence Industry Alliance (人工智能产业联盟), which distribute subsidies and cash to promising AI companies.[55] For example, a brain-inspired and deep learning company, iDeepWise (深思考人工智), participated in the 2018 medical AI competition organized by the alliance, won first place, and went on to receive $75,400 (500,000 RMB) in cash rewards and $3 million (20 million RMB) in R&D subsidies over three years. While these sums are not huge, they may prove decisive for early stage companies to raise their profile and commercialize. The following year, iDeepWise became the first AI company invested by Huawei's venture capital arm, Hubble Technology Investment Co. Ltd (哈勃科技投资有限公司).[56]

In addition to direct state funding, the Chinese government has tax alleviation tools at its disposal and is not hesitant to use them.[57] For example, in Shanghai's Changning district alone, the district Taxation Bureau spent more than $90 million (570 million RMB) in tax preferential treatment on 47 high-tech companies in 2020.[58] Shanghai-based WestWell Lab (西井科技), an AI company specializing in neuromorphic circuits, has reportedly received more than $9.5 million (60 million RMB) in R&D expenditure and tax cuts.[59] In 2020, WestWell Lab went on to raise over $15.7 million (100 million RMB) from investors, including Shanghai Military Civil Industry Investment Fund (上海军民融合产业投资基金), an emerging funding vehicle.[60]

Notwithstanding these efforts, the government's financial support for China's AI-related technology faces deadweight losses and in some cases, corruption and fraud. The two cases below exemplify China's difficulties in overcoming its technology chokepoints, not just in the semiconductor industry but potentially in other emerging industries such as AI.

- Chinese policymakers recognize that advanced semiconductors are needed to train AI algorithms. China's pursuit of advanced chip development was promising at the start. In 2003, Chen Jin (陈进), a dean at Jiaotong University in Shanghai, received more than $14 million in government R&D funding to develop China's first homegrown digital signal processing (DSP) microchip, called Hanxin (汉芯).[61] In 2005, Chen was unmasked as a fraud, who had simply scratched away the label on foreign chips and replaced it with his own.[62]
- Hanxin was a national embarrassment and a cautionary tale for state direct capital allocation in pursuit of advanced chips, but it was not the last. A more recent chip scheme involving Wuhan Hongxin Semiconductor Manufacturing (HSMC) lasted almost three years and cost the Wuhan government $2.4 billion (15.3 billion RMB) of wasted investment.[63]

It is clear that money cannot buy everything.[64] But with some waste tolerance from the Chinese government, the outpour of money into China's AI-related industry may yield some results. For instance, massive government investment in semiconductors has made China more competitive in market segments such as memory, mature node logic foundries, and fabless chip design.[65]

An emerging industrial policy tool: government guidance funds

In addition to funneling capital directly into China's AI companies, the Chinese government is also trying to introduce profit motive into an industrial policy to gain financial returns and achieve its strategic objectives. The aim is to mobilize capital and other resources for emerging technologies through public-private investment vehicles, also known as government guidance funds (政府引导基金).[66]

The first known guidance fund was the Zhongguancun Venture Capital Guidance Fund established in 2002 to support venture capital companies. In 2016, the number of guidance funds peaked at more than 500 (Figure 1.1). This rapid growth was fueled by central government policies, trend-chasing among provincial and local bureaucrats, and relatively loose regulation of guidance funds coupled with new restrictions on other types of local government spending. The number of funds began to fall in 2017 and stagnated at about 100 annually as China's economy slowed down and the government imposed tighter regulations.

Guidance funds use the limited partnership structure common in equity finance worldwide. But the Chinese government's presence can be found at various stages of the fund's development. Most importantly, the government sets up the fund's target size, allocates 20–30 percent of the target, and raises the rest from "social capital" (社会资本) investors.[67] The latter are limited partners who contribute capital raised from private-motivated investors not connected to the

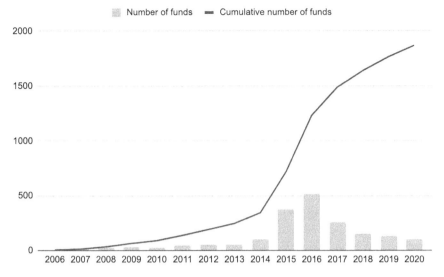

FIGURE 1.1 Growth of guidance funds, 2006–2020

Source: Authors' research and compilation of data provided by Zero2IPO research center.

government. But in practice, most social capital investors are state-owned enterprises and state-run banks in disguise. Yet, by allocating initial capital to part of the funds' target, government sponsors may attract investors who have too little appetite for risk to invest in emerging technologies.[68]

Through guidance funds, the government can offer patient capital to emerging industries, such as AI, where stable, long-term investment capital is potentially decisive for early stage companies to innovate and grow. Even promising AI startups with strong initial funding may not cross the "valley of death" where innovation and the opportunity to scale up and commercialize go to die. Guidance funds can fill the gap.

The Tianjin Municipal Government set up an AI-focused guidance fund worth $16 billion (100 billion RMB) in 2018.[69] The fund has invested in Hwatsing (华海清科),[70] a semiconductor company that produces cutting-edge chemical-mechanical planarization (CMP) equipment.[71] The Tianjin Municipal Government's financial support was directly responsible for Hwatsing's rise, transforming a startup company of some ten people into a mature company.[72]

Guangzhou-based Cloudwalk Technology (云从科技), one of China's four AI dragons (AI四小龙)—a collection that also includes SenseTime, Megvii, and Yitu—was born from Guangdong Province's guidance funds.[73] After receiving $310 million (2 billion RMB) directly from the Guangzhou Municipal Government in 2017, Cloudwalk raised $160 million (1 billion RMB) from Guangzhou Industry Investment Fund (广州产业投资基金) and other financing groups in 2018.[74] In 2020, the company raised another $280 million (1.8 billion RMB) from state-owned investment institutions such as Guangzhou Nansha

Financial Holdings (广州南沙金控), which manages a guidance fund established to promote Strategic Emerging Industries.[75]

Similarly, iFlytek received $2.9 million (18.5 million RMB) investment from Hefei Venture Capital Guidance Fund (合肥市创业投资引导基金). This state-sponsored funding accounts for nearly 8 percent of the company's equity shares.[76]

However, despite enormous political and financial support from the Chinese government, guidance funds often raise less money than intended. By the end of 2020, 1,851 guidance funds had only raised $873 billion (5.65 trillion RMB), which is less than half of the registered target size of $1.78 trillion (11.53 trillion RMB), from public and private sources.[77] Even when guidance funds manage to raise money, much of the capital is never actually deployed, in large part due to the investment hype cycle of emerging technologies including AI. One independent market research firm reported that "many regions have jumped on the bandwagon of establishing AI industry development funds, even though there are few local companies in the AI field."[78] Government guidance funds are still relatively new. It remains uncertain whether these state-sponsored private equity funds will push China ahead to become a global leader in AI.

Conclusion

This chapter identified the main government policies, edicts, and funding mechanisms that underpin China's development of AI. While these policy tools are limited by market forces and the bounds of China's political economy, there is no denying that some of China's AI initiatives have been met with success. With at least $4.7 billion in direct, annual government funding, no other country holds a candle to China's public-sector support for AI-specific R&D—and additional laboratories and research institutes are beginning to proliferate nationwide. Moreover, through traditional policy levers such as direct state subsidies, and new ones such as guidance funds, China aspires to bend the private sector to invest in what it cannot reap from abroad.

As the following chapter makes clear, China's for-profit companies, ranging from publicly traded tech giants, privately held companies, to obscure startups, are leading the charge in AI and are most responsible for the country's rapid AI growth. That said, the line between state and private enterprises is blurring still further as China's government leads a convergence of state and market forces.

Notes

1 PRC State Council, The New Generation AI Development Plan, 2017.
2 中共中央办公厅印发关于加强新时代民营经济统战工作的意见 (The General Office of the Central Committee of the CCP Issued Opinions on Strengthening the United Front Work of the Private Economy in the New Era), *Xinhua News* (新华社), September 15, 2020.
3 PRC State Council, "State Council's Guidelines on Positively Promoting the 'Internet +' Action," 2015.

4 Frederick C. Teiwes and Warren Sun, "China's New Economic Policy under Hua Guofeng: Party Consensus and Party Myths," *The China Journal*, 66, July 2011, p. 11.
5 Denis Fred Simon and Merle Goldman, *Science and Technology in Post-Mao China*, Cambridge MA: Harvard University Asia Center, 1989. See also William C. Hannas and Huey-Meei Chang, "Chinese Technology Transfer—An Introduction," in *China's Quest for Foreign Technology: Beyond Espionage*, Routledge, London, 2021.
6 Karen M. Sutter, "Foreign Technology Transfer through Commerce" in *China's Quest for Foreign Technology*; see also Alex Rubin, Alan Omar Loera Martinez, Jake Dow, and Anna B. Puglisi, "The Huawei Moment," Georgetown University, Center for Security and Emerging Technology, July 2021.
7 As early as 2006, China's Medium- and Long-Term Plan for Economic Development (2006–2020) had listed "intelligent" traffic control systems, information processing, and design and manufacturing as priority S&T development areas.
8 PRC State Council, "State Council's Guidelines on Positively Promoting 'Internet +' Action," July 4, 2015.
9 NDRC et al., "Notice of the Four Departments on the Issuance of the 'Internet +' Artificial Intelligence Three-year Action Implementation Plan," May 23, 2016.
10 PRC State Council, "Notice of the State Council on Issuing the National 13th Five-year Plan for Science and Technology Innovation," July 28, 2016.
11 PRC State Council, "Notice of the State Council on Issuing the National 13th Five-year Plan for the Development of Strategic Emerging Industries," November 29, 2016.
12 PRC State Council, "The New Generation AI Development Plan," July 8, 2017.
13 PRC MIIT, "Three-year Action Plan to Promote the Development of New Generation Artificial Intelligence Industry 2018-2020," December 26, 2017.
14 PRC NDRC, "Guiding Opinions on Expanding Investment in Strategic Emerging Industries and Cultivating Strengthened New Growth Points and Growth Poles," September 8, 2020.
15 National People's Congress and Chinese People's Political Consultative Conference, "The 14th Five-year Plan for the National Economic and Social Development of the People's Republic of China and Outline of Long-term Goals for 2035," March 11, 2021.
16 NDRC et al., "Notice of the Four Departments on the Issuance of the 'Internet +' Artificial Intelligence Three-year Action Implementation Plan," May 23, 2016.
17 MIIT, 2017.
18 Ibid.
19 PRC State Council, "The New Generation AI Development Plan," 2017.
20 人工智能是引领未来的战略技术
21 Ibid.
22 Ibid.
23 NDRC, Guiding Opinions, 2020.
24 Ibid.
25 Frank Tang, "China Unveils 'Strategic Emerging Industries' Plan in Fresh Push to Get Away from U.S. Technologies," *South China Morning Post*, September 24, 2020.
26 NDRC, Guiding Opinions, 2020.
27 2020 新兴产业政策法规白皮书 (*2020 Emerging Industry Policies and Regulations White Paper*), 赛迪智库 (CCID Think Tank), Beijing, 2020, p. 151, https://perma.cc/4CZW-98JE.
28 Mu-ming Poo, "Innovation and Reform: China's 14th Five-year Plan Unfolds," *National Science Review*, 8.1, January 2021.
29 "The 14th Five-year Plan," Artificial Intelligence Is Listed First in the Table of Prioritized "Cutting-edge S&T Fields (科技前沿领域攻关)," 2021.
30 Ibid.
31 MOST, Department of International Cooperation, "Science & Technology Newsletter 17," September 15, 2017.

32 MOST, "'国家重点研发计划启动实施'新闻发布会:文字摘要" (Press Conference on the 'Launch and Implementation of the National Key R&D Program': Summary Transcript), February 16, 2016.

33 MOST, 科技部关于发布科技创新2030—"新一代人工智能"重大项目2018年度项目申报指南的通知(MOST on the Release of 2030 Science and Technology Innovation—Notice on the 2018 Project Application Guidelines for 'New Generation Artificial Intelligence' Megaproject), October 12, 2018. Grants sometimes include obligatory "matching +" provisions from the sponsoring institution.

34 MOST, 科技创新 2030—"新一代人工智能" 重大项目 2020 年度项目申报指南 (Science and Technology Innovation 2030—'Next Generation Artificial Intelligence' Application Guideline for Major Projects in 2020), March 25, 2020.

35 MOST, 科技创新 2030—"新一代人工智能" 重大项目 2021 年度项目申报指南 (Science and Technology Innovation 2030—'Next Generation Artificial Intelligence' Application Guideline for Major Projects in 2021), July 30, 2021.

36 "Science & Technology Newsletter 17."

37 William C. Hannas and Huey-Meei Chang, et al., "China AI-Brain Research," Georgetown University, Center for Security and Emerging Technology (CSET), September 2020.

38 Qiang Zhi and Margaret M. Pearson, "China's Hybrid Adaptive Bureaucracy: The Case of the 863 Program for Science and Technology," *Governance* 30.3, September 27, 2016, pp. 407–424.

39 "国家重点基础研究发展计划(973计划)简介" (Introduction to the National Key Basic Research and Development Program (973 Program)), November 12, 2012, http://www.wfcms.org/973Project/ShowFSpecialTopic!toFSpecialTopicDetail.action?st_id=8.

40 "'973' '863' 取消后科研咋办? 国家重点研发计划正式启动" (What about Scientific Research after '973' '863' Were Cancelled? The National Key Research and Development Program was Officially Launched), *Xinhua Net* (新化网), February 16, 2016.

41 Authors' analysis based on project titles. Source data at "2018年国家重点研发计划已公示项目汇总" (Summary Table of Publicized Projects in the National Key Research and Development Plan in 2018), December 6, 2018, https://www.sciping.com/23261.html.

42 Wu Guozheng (吴国政), Wu Yunkai (吴云凯), Zhang Zhaotian (张兆田), Han Junwei (韩军伟), "浅析人工智能学科基金项目申请资助情况及展望" (Review of the Applications and Grants of the National Natural Science Foundation on Artificial Intelligence and Its Prospects), 自动化学报 (*Acta Automatica Sinica*), 46.12, 2020, pp. 2711–2718.

43 Hannas and Chang, 2020.

44 "2019年面上项目名单公布" (Announcement of the List of General Projects in 2019), 科塔学术, August 19, 2019, https://www.sciping.com/29892.html.

45 Ryan Fedasiuk, Emily Weinstein, Ben Murphy, and Alan Omar Loera Martinez, "Chinese State Council Budget Tracker," Georgetown University, Center for Security and Emerging Technology, February 2021.

46 Emily Weinstein, Ryan Fedasiuk, Channing Lee, and Anna B. Puglisi, "China's State Key Laboratory System: An Overview," Georgetown University, Center for Security and Emerging Technology, forthcoming.

47 Ibid.

48 Weinstein, Fedasiuk, Lee, and Puglisi, op. cit.

49 Dahlia Peterson, Kayla Goode, and Diana Gehlhaus, "AI Education in China and the United States: A Comparative Assessment," Georgetown University, Center for Security and Emerging Technology, September 2021.

50 Ryan Fedasiuk and Emily Weinstein, "Universities and the Chinese Defense Technology Workforce," Georgetown University, Center for Security and Emerging Technology, December 2020.

51 Peterson, Goode, and Gehlhaus, op. cit.

52 Ibid., p. 13.

53 Barry Naughton, *The Rise of China's Industrial Policy 1978 to 2020*, Centro de Estudios China-México, 2021.

54 "习近平论科技赶超战略:应该有非对称性'杀手锏'" (Xi Jinping on Technological Catch-up Strategy: There Should be an Asymmetric 'Assassin's Mace'), *People's Daily* (人民网), March 22, 2016.

55 Ngor Luong and Zachary Arnold, "China's Artificial Intelligence Industry Alliance," Georgetown University, Center for Security and Emerging Technology, May 2021.

56 Doris Yu, "Huawei-Linked Fund Hubble Makes Its First AI Company Investment In iDeepWise," *China Money Network*, October 28, 2019.

57 "创新创业促进产业升级人工智能等新产业吸引投资趋势将持续" (Innovation and Entrepreneurship Promote Industrial Upgrading, New Industries Such As Artificial Intelligence Will Continue to Attract Investment), *Xinmin Evening News* (新民晚报), October 29, 2017.

58 "减税降费助企顶住疫情冲击!中国制造在创新中赢得海外市场" (Cut Taxes and Fees to Help Companies Withstand the Impact of the Pandemic! Made in China Wins Overseas Market through Innovation), *China State Taxation Administration News* (国家税务总局新媒体), January 26, 2021.

59 Ibid.

60 https://www.chinaventure.com.cn/news/80-20200415-354171.html.

61 Henry Rowen, "China's Quest for Independent Innovation," Shorenstein Asia-Pacific Research Center, August 2005.

62 "Chip Scandal Hurts High-tech Push" *China's Daily*, May 15, 2006.

63 Su Jianxun (苏建勋) and Qiu Xiaofen (邱晓芬), "深度调查: '武汉弘芯半导体'千亿芯片大骗局" (In-depth Investigation: 'Wuhan Hongxin Semiconductor' 100 Billion Chip Scam), *Sina Finance* (新浪财经), January 28, 2021.

64 Experts in the semiconductor industry express little confidence in the role of state financial support in accelerating China's position in the global semiconductor competition. Will Hunt, Saif M. Khan, and Dahlia Peterson, "China's Progress in Semiconductor Manufacturing Equipment: Accelerants and Policy Implications," Georgetown University, Center for Security and Emerging Technology, March 2021.

65 "SIA Whitepaper: Taking Stock of China's Semiconductor Industry," Semiconductor Industry Association, July 2021.

66 Luong, Arnold, and Murphy, "Understanding Chinese Government Guidance Funds," op. cit.

67 "2019 年中国政府引导基发展研究报告(上篇)" (Report on the Development of Chinese Government Guidance Funds 2019 (Part 1)), *Zero2IPO* (情科研究中心), October 17, 2019.

68 Ibid.

69 Meng Jing, "Tianjin City in China Eyes US$16 Billion Fund for AI Work, Dwarfing EU's Plan to Spend US$1.78 Billion," *SCMP*, May 16, 2018.

70 http://www.hwatsing.com/.

71 "海河产业基金搭台我市打造半导体芯片全产业链" (Haihe Industry Fund to Build the City's Semiconductor Industry Chip Industry Chain), *Tianjin Daily* (天津日报), April 14, 2020.

72 "区领导参加华海清科新厂区启用仪式并开展调研服务" (District Leaders Participated in the Opening Ceremony of the New Factory of Hwatsing and Launched the Research Service), *Rong Media Center* (融媒体中心), July 21, 2021.

73 Huang Haobo (黄浩博), "广州财政资金从补到投: 3年撬动86亿社会资本, 培育小鹏云从等15家上市企业" (Guangzhou Financial Funds from Subsidy to Investment: Leveraging 8.6 Billion Private Capital in Three Years, Cultivating 15 Listed Companies Such As Xpeng and Cloudwalk), *Sina Finance* (新浪财经), July 21, 2020.

74 Ibid.

75 Ibid; Nansha Financial Holdings (南沙金控), "广州南沙创业投资引导基金" (Guangzhou Nansha Venture Capital Guidance Fund), November 12, 2021, https://www.ns-jrkg.com/nd.jsp?id=225#_np=2_474.

76 "关于科大讯飞股份有限公司非公开发行股票申请文件反馈意见回复报告" (About 'Report on Feedback of Application Documents for Non-Public Offering of iFlytek Co., Ltd.'), April 1, 2021.
77 "2020年引导金设立放缓, 有基金一年投出十几支子基金" (The Establishment of Guidance Funds Slows Down in 2020, There Are Funds Investing in a Dozen Sub-funds in a Year), *Zero2IPO*, February 4, 2021.
78 Luong, Arnold, and Murphy, "Understanding Government Guidance Funds," op. cit.

Bibliography

"'973' '863'取消后科研咋办? 国家重点研发计划正式启动" (What about Scientific Research After '973' '863' were Cancelled? The National Key Research and Development Program was Officially Launched), Xinhua, February 16, 2016.

"2019 年中国政府引导基发展研究报告(上篇)" (Report on the Development of Chinese Government Guidance Funds 2019 (Part 1), *Zero2IPO* (情科研究中心), October 17, 2019.

Luong, Ngor, Zachary Arnold, and Ben Murphy, "Understanding Chinese Government Guidance Funds: An Analysis of Chinese-Language Sources," Georgetown University, Center for Security and Emerging Technology, March 2021.

Peterson, Dahlia, Kayla Goode, and Diana Gehlhaus, "AI Education in China and the United States: A Comparative Assessment," Georgetown University, Center for Security and Emerging Technology, September 2021.

PRC Ministry of Industry and Information Technology, 促进新一代人工智能产业发展三年行动 计划 2018-2020年 (Three-year Action Plan to Promote the Development of New Generation Artificial Intelligence Industry 2018-2020), MIIT 315, 2017.

PRC Ministry of Science and Technology, 2018年我国R&D 人员发展状况分析 (Analysis of the Development Status of R&D Personnel in China in 2018), November 2, 2020.

PRC National Development and Reform Commission et al., 四部门关于印发"互联网+" 人工智能三年行动实施方案的通知 (Notice of the Four Departments on Issuance of the Three-year Action Implementation Plan for 'Internet +' Artificial Intelligence), NDRC 1078, 2016.

PRC National Development and Reform Commission et al., 四部门联合印发关于扩大战略性新兴产业投资培养壮大新增长点增长极的指导意见 (Notice of the Four Departments on Guiding Opinions on Expanding Investment in Strategic Emerging Industries, and Cultivating New Growth Points and Poles), NDRC 1409, 2020.

PRC State Council, 国务院关于积极推进"互联网+"行动的指导意见 (State Council's Guidelines on Positively Promoting the 'Internet +' Action), SC 40, 2015.

PRC State Council, 国务院关于印发"十三五"国家科技创新规划的通知 (Notice of the State Council on Issuing the National 13th Five-year Plan for Science and Technology Innovation), SC 43, 2016.

PRC State Council, 国务院关于印发"十三五"国家战略性新兴产业发展规划的通知 (Notice of the State Council on Issuing the National 13th Five-year Plan for the Development of Strategic Emerging Industries), SC 67, 2016.

PRC State Council, 国务院关于印发新一代人工智能发展规划的通知 (The New Generation AI Development Plan), SC 35, 2017.

PRC National People's Congress and Chinese People's Political Consultative Conference, 中华人民共和国国民经济和社会发展第十四个五年规划和 2035 年远景目标纲要 (The 14th Five-year Plan for the National Economic and Social Development of the People's Republic of China and Outline of Long-term Goals for 2035), 2021.

2

China's AI companies

Hybrid players

Karen M. Sutter[1] and Zachary Arnold

Introduction

China sees AI as a new area of global competition that will drive the next industrial revolution, upgrade and transform China's economy and industry, promote social development, and protect domestic order. The government has prioritized the development of AI as a strategic capability and fundamental enabling technology that supports its broader national technology, economic, and geostrategic goals. It emphasizes breakthroughs in AI research and development (R&D) and deployment and calls for leaning on foreign ties to develop China's capabilities.[2] China's government assesses that AI could provide a first mover advantage that allows China to leapfrog technologically, disrupt the current global paradigm of U.S. economic and technology leadership, and narrow the military power gap vis-a-vis the United States.

To realize its goal of AI leadership, the Chinese government is leaning on its companies and research institutes to lead the development of China's capabilities. The government seeks to meld state planning and control while allowing some operational flexibility for firms.[3] In this context, China's AI firms are hybrid players. The state guides their activity, funds, and shields them from foreign competition through domestic market protections, creating asymmetric advantages as they expand offshore.

While China seeks to become a global center for AI innovation by 2030, the United States remains the global leader. China lags the United States in AI talent, basic research, and software, and is seeking to address these gaps through foreign collaboration, particularly with U.S. firms and universities. Ties to U.S. and other foreign AI hubs have played a central role in developing China's capabilities. Many of China's top AI professionals were trained in the United States and worked for U.S. companies and labs. To secure foreign partnerships, China

DOI: 10.4324/9781003212980-3

has offered funding, access to data, and promises of future market access. China's emerging strengths in AI data generation and technology adoption also appear to be attracting U.S. companies and investors.[4]

The state's interests and role implicate regulatory, corporate, and university actors in China. Recent moves by the Chinese government to enhance control over its AI firms' data, financial, and offshore operations raise concerns about the state's reach into AI firms' global operations. China's companies also pose unique ethical concerns, including China's use of AI capabilities at home and abroad for surveillance, propaganda, espionage, and military purposes. Ties between PRC AI companies and foreign business, research, and financial institutions may be nurturing a competitor and potential adversary.

An overview of China's corporate AI sector

China's corporate AI sector is diverse, with a wide variety of firms driving innovation and deployment. Generally, these firms can be grouped into five categories.[5]

- First, China's diversified digital giants, such as the "BAT" firms (Baidu, Alibaba, Tencent) and Huawei. These companies maintain significant AI operations in China and overseas. They use AI in a range of products, from AI-centric services like speech recognition, to other areas where AI is a less pervasive but still vital component, such as gaming, banking, logistics, and health.
- Second, large firms that are developing AI-related technologies as their core product line. Prominent examples are iFLYTEK, which largely focuses on natural language processing applications; CloudWalk, which focuses on facial recognition; and Cambricon, which develops AI-optimized computer chips.
- Third, large state-owned enterprises (SOEs)[6] that provide national infrastructure for China's AI applications, lead AI applications prioritized by the government, and fund other AI firms.[7] Many of these firms also have their own AI business lines. They operate in areas such as energy, insurance, manufacturing, telecommunications, and transportation. Examples include State Grid (国家电网), China Railway Rolling Stock Corporation (中国中车, CRRC), and China Telecom (中国电信).
- Fourth, state and state-tied technology firms associated with the military and security services and active in AI research and deployment. Examples are the Aviation Industry Corporation of China (中国航空工业集团, AVIC), Datang Telecom (大唐电信)[8], China Aerospace Science and Industry Corporation (中国航天科工集团, CASIC), China Aerospace Science and Technology Corporation (中国航天科技集团, CASC), China Electronics Technology Group (中国电子科技集团, CETC),[9] and Qihoo360.[10]
- Fifth, startups and small- to medium-sized firms active across a range of AI input and application areas. Reliable estimates of their numbers are challenging, given the volatile nature of startups and data gaps. In 2018, a Chinese government report estimated that 2,167 small to medium AI-related firms

were active in China.[11] These firms—such as Uisee, Tianrang, and XYZ Robotics—often receive seed funding and other support from China's research institutes, state firms, and AI champions.[12]

China's hybrid corporate model

China's AI companies are hybrid players: they operate as commercial entities, but are subject to the influence, guidance, and control of the Chinese state.[13] China's *Medium- and Long-Term Plan for S&T Development* (MLP), enacted in 2006, elevated the role of China's companies as central to national innovation and technology development. In establishing this role for China's firms, the government sought to maximize the benefits of market flexibilities—including greater operating agility in recruiting talent, fundraising, acquiring foreign technology, and operating offshore—while retaining state controls.[14]

As China has positioned its AI industry at the center of national innovation, the government seeks to direct the development and rollout of AI in China, manage competition among its firms, and ensure state control, including as firms expand offshore. China's AI plans call for the development of leading global AI "backbone enterprises." China's "national team" (see below) and other AI firms receive substantial state funding, preferences, and support, and follow central government guidance. The government uses industrial policies—including government plans, projects, funding, policy preferences, industrial alliances, and relevant laws and regulations—to shape corporate behavior. Many AI companies also have state investors, shareholders, directors, supervisors, and advisors as another avenue for the state to influence firms.[15] In response to CPC requirements, companies also maintain internal Party committees whose members often have senior management or board roles.[16]

China's hybrid economic strategy to develop critical technologies and strategic industries is not limited to AI, but the AI sector provides rich and diverse examples of the strategy in practice.

This section explores the main ways "state capitalism" shapes Chinese AI firms, their behavior, and their prospects for success.

State plans and funding

China's national industrial plans establish AI development priorities which, in turn, direct state funding for AI firms through programs and projects, financing from state-controlled banks, government guidance funds (GGFs), and direct equity investments. State-tied capital supports the research, development, and commercialization stages.

The government's national S&T and R&D programs drive the development of targeted sectors such as AI. China's National Natural Science Foundation supports basic research and China's S&T Megaprojects develop strategic technologies prioritized in the plans. China's 13th Five-year Plan for Science, Technology, and Innovation (2016–2020) designated 15 "megaprojects," in AI-related areas such as brain science, smart grid, quantum, space-ground networks, big data, robotics, smart manufacturing, and cybersecurity. These and other projects offer firms key revenue and support.[17] The government's Technology Innovation Guidance Fund (技术创新引导专项基金), the National Fund for Technology Transfer and Commercialization (国家科技成果转化引导基金, NFTTC), and the State Development Investment Corporation (国家开发投资集团有限公司, SDIC) support the commercialization of government-funded research and directly or indirectly invest in AI firms.[18]

Increasingly, the government is funding firms through GGFs and their sub-funds, which use a private equity (PE) model to channel investment from the Ministry of Finance to strategic industries such as AI. The government also routes monies through SOEs, pensions, state banks, state venture capital (VC) funds, and capital market investments. The GGFs seek to attract funding from a wide range of "social capital," such as other state-tied companies, banks, and VC firms.[19] In this model, state funding pathways are complex; state, corporate, and foreign investments are commingled, opaque, and difficult to disaggregate.[20]

As it seeks agile financing and corporate structures, since 2019, the Ministry of Science and Technology (MOST) has begun using innovation vouchers to fund R&D, including AI-related services, for technology firms and research entities that are state-directed but legally independent.[21] The model allows greater operational flexibility, including to attract investment and talent. The government also offers land, facilities, and preferential treatment in procurement, research, and talent recruitment.[22]

AI firms also work with China's state security services and the PLA, providing these AI firms important sources of revenue.[23] This collaboration appears to be two-way: the government provides a market for AI firms, and, in turn, uses them to censor, conduct surveillance, and support other state functions in China and offshore.[24] For example, Tencent and ByteDance use AI algorithms to police social media content, and China's security agencies reportedly commandeer infrastructure and staff from Alibaba to process intelligence datasets.[25] These activities have caused pushback overseas against Chinese firms' involvement in telecommunications and infrastructure projects.[26]

Industrial parks

The Chinese government uses technology zones and industrial parks to promote AI. It has created several pilot zones, including in Beijing, Shanghai, and Hefei, and aims to create 20 such zones by 2023.[27] These zones partner with local governments to provide infrastructure, funding, and tax incentives, and to recruit talent. Often, the zones have their own government-tied investment vehicle to invest in AI firms. Large property developers both develop these zones and invest in AI firms themselves. China Evergrande, for example, has a $16 billion MOU with CAS to invest in AI, semiconductors, electric vehicles, and quantum

BOX 2.1

INTELLECTUAL PROPERTY

Intellectual property is a fundamental building block that will allow Chinese AI firms to develop products and services and influence standard setting. Baidu reportedly holds the most AI-related patents of any firm or institute in China. As of 2021, Baidu claimed to have 3,652 AI-related patents and 13,007 pending AI-related patent applications.[31] China's Ministry of Industry and Information Technology (MIIT) reports that Tencent, Huawei, Inspur, State Grid, and Tsinghua University have significant AI-related patent holdings.[32] China's AI firms have gained patents from their overseas acquisitions. Securitization of IP is a major focus of China's 14th Five-year Plan (2021–2025). The government prioritizes domestic listings for AI firms and promotes IP securitization to facilitate listings. Industrial zones and local governments subsidize the interest on loans, provide collateral, and offer lending and leasing services to incentivize banks to invest in startups with IP of strategic value.[33] China's new 15-year plan for IP prioritizes developing IP related to semiconductors, algorithms, and AI products.[34]

computing.[28] Greenland is a large shareholder in AI "unicorn" DeepBlue.[29] Country Gardens is building a robotics park in Guangdong province and partners with Tsinghua University.[30]

Industrial alliances

The Chinese government has created over 190 AI industry alliances, including the national AI Industry and Technology Innovation Alliance of China (中国人工智能产业发展联盟, AIIA),[35] which boasted 567 members in 2021.[36] These alliances seek to align government, corporate, and university work in AI research, standards, IP, and policy. In addition to China's top AI firms, the alliances include state telecom carriers, equipment providers, and a few foreign firms.[37] Regional alliances include the Beijing AI Industrial Alliance (北京人工智能产业联盟, BAIIA), which is led by Baidu and includes other major firms such as ByteDance, Cambricon, BOE Technology Group, Didi Chuxing, Huawei, JD.com, Kuaishou, Megvii, Meituan, and 360 Vision.[38] The Shanghai AI alliance promotes China's AI applications with foreign firms.[39]

Government institutes and universities

Government AI research institutes—such as the Beijing Institute of Big Data Research[40] and the Beijing Academy of Artificial Intelligence (北京智源人工智能研究院, BAAI)[41]—also seek to align China's AI efforts, set standards, and provide government data and computational power. In some cases, prominent foreign AI experts serve as advisors.[42] The institutes work closely with China's AI companies, alliances, and research bodies, such as the China Academy of Information and Communications Technology (中国信息通信研究院, CAICT), and the China Electronics Standardization Institute (中国电子技术标准化研究院, CESI).[43] The Chinese Academy of Engineering, the drafter of China's *Standards 2030* plan, chairs the government's AI Strategy Advisory Committee and is a deputy chair of the China Association for Artificial Intelligence through the overlapping roles of its senior engineer Pan Yunhe (潘云鹤).[44]

CAS and Tsinghua University work closely with China's AI companies. CAS has a leadership role in the AI industrial alliances, and the CAS Institute of Automation (CASIA) produces research that is commercialized by China's firms.[45] Alibaba and Baidu have leveraged CASIA's speech technologies. State security applications utilize CASIA's intelligent video surveillance and face recognition technologies; Chinese petrochemical companies have used its AI software.[46] CAS also directly owns AI firms, including Hanwang Technology (electronic surveillance systems) and Sciample (intelligent manufacturing equipment and systems). AI "unicorn" CloudWalk is a CAS spinoff.[47] Table 2.1 includes additional examples of ties among Chinese AI companies, government research institutes, and universities.

The national team: open AI platforms

The Chinese government has designated certain companies "national champions" in specific AI capabilities and applications. The State Council's July 2017 *New Generation AI Development Plan* called for creating "innovation platforms" (创新平台) to "strengthen the foundational support for AI R&D and applications."[54]

TABLE 2.1 Collaborations among Chinese AI companies, universities, and state institutes

AI company	Institute	Nature of collaboration
Baidu	Tsinghua University Institute for AI Research	Develop and connect Baidu's Apollo autonomous driving system to China's 5G networks[48]
Tencent	Tsinghua University	Support scientific research by providing AI and cloud computing services[49]
Alibaba	CAS Institute of Physics	Provide cloud platforms, algorithms, software, and consulting services[50]
Tencent	CAS National Astronomical Observatories and Department of High Energy Physics	Develop AI applications for an aperture spherical radio telescope and gamma-ray burst polarimeter[51]
Alibaba	University of Science and Technology in Hefei	Partner with advanced computing program[52]
Alibaba and Cambricon	CAS Supercomputing Testbed in Shenzhen	Provide data analytic support[53]

TABLE 2.2 China's AI "National Team"[57]

Company	Designated focus area
Alibaba Cloud (Aliyun)	Smart cities
Baidu	Autonomous driving
Hikvision	Video sensing
Huawei	Software and hardware infrastructure
iFLYTEK	Smart audio
JD.com	Smart supply chain
Megvii	Image sensing
MiningLamp Technology	Intelligent marketing
Ping An Insurance	Inclusive finance
Qihoo360	Cyber security
SenseTime	Smart vision
TAL Education Group	Smart education
Tencent	Medical imaging
Yitu Technology	Visual computing
Xiaomi	Smart home

A MOST-held meeting in November 2017 designated the "BAT" companies—Baidu, Alibaba, and Tencent—and iFLYTEK as leaders of these national platforms. The government tasked Baidu to focus on autonomous driving, Alibaba to develop platforms for smart city applications, Tencent to develop medical applications, and iFLYTEK to lead on voice and intelligence applications.[55] Fifteen Chinese companies (Table 2.2) are now part of the "open AI platform" model; they are referred to as China's AI "national team."[56]

By assigning companies to different AI application areas, the government seeks to direct commercial activity toward its priorities and minimize competition it sees as duplicative. The state hopes that these firms will lead development and testing of targeted AI technologies, share data and algorithm libraries, and foster innovation in their respective areas.[58] In exchange, these firms receive government funding and policy preferences. They may benefit from being the first to market and related preferential or protected leadership status in certain market segments they have been called to develop. Reinforcing the "open platform" model, in 2020, the Chinese government required its AI national champions and other leading AI firms to open their proprietary services to one another in order to disrupt emerging technology fiefdoms and maintain state control.[59]

Global footprint and foreign ties

China's policies encourage AI firms to "go out" and leverage global capabilities, and Chinese AI firms have benefitted significantly from foreign research, commercial, and financial ties. Their growing global presence covers R&D, talent recruitment and development, business development, two-way investing, and data, technology, and corporate acquisitions.

BOX 2.2

MARKET PROTECTIONS AND BARRIERS[60]

Barriers to foreign entry into China's technology market—particularly in software and Internet-tied businesses—have prevented many foreign companies and universities from accessing opportunities in China, and have required others to partner with Chinese institutions as a condition of market access. Chinese government subsidies, domestic market protectionism, and data access restrictions insulate Chinese firms from foreign competition, allowing them to develop to the point that they are capable of competing globally. Since 2020, the government has enhanced controls and protections in the AI sector and related data and technological areas. The government has enacted laws that restrict dual-use exports (e.g. exports of algorithms) and require additional scrutiny of foreign investment and data transfers. These measures have extraterritorial reach, raising concerns about China's ability and intentions to control certain aspects of its AI firms' offshore operations. These concerns are fueling debates outside China about whether Chinese firms should be blocked from certain AI-related markets and activities. To date, however, much Chinese offshore AI activity has escaped scrutiny by U.S. and other governments, in part because it is often structured through research collaboration and centers that fall outside the current scope of foreign investment review and export control authorities.

Research and talent ties

China's 14th Five-year Plan (2021–2025) incentivizes AI firms to establish overseas R&D centers and recruit foreign talent. Many of China's large AI firms already have R&D centers outside China, including in the United States.[61] Researchers from China's firms collaborate with foreign AI scientists and have research partnerships with top global university AI programs (see Table 2.3).[62] Some of these ties have come under scrutiny.[63]

Similarly, U.S. academic ties and corporate labs in China are developing China's AI capabilities, including talent. Ten percent of the known AI research labs of Facebook, Google, IBM, and Microsoft (considered collectively) were located in China at the end of 2020.[74] Microsoft's Beijing-based Research Asia lab is its largest lab outside of the United States and has had an enormous impact on China's ability to cultivate AI "talent."[75]

China's talent programs incentivize overseas Chinese and foreign experts to work in China and share AI expertise. China's AI firms also recruit overseas and are hiring China-born and foreign-educated AI talent. There is a lack of detailed data on cross-border talent flows, however, and available indicators

TABLE 2.3 Examples of Chinese AI firms' foreign research activities

AI firm	Foreign partnerships	Activity
Tencent	Partnership with University of Hong Kong	Collaboration on block chain technologies[64]
Alibaba	Labs in San Mateo, California; and Bellevue, Washington Partnership with University of California at Berkeley	R&D on quantum computing and AI algorithms[65, 66]
JD.com	Lab in Seattle, Washington	AI R&D[67]
Alibaba, Huawei, and others	Partnership with RISC-V (Silicon Valley and Switzerland)	Collaboration on open source technology AI semiconductor chip design[68]
Baidu Research	Labs in Silicon Valley; Seattle, Washington Partnership with MILA in Montreal, Canada	AI research[69]
Huawei	R&D centers in Cambridge, United Kingdom and Grenoble, France	Optoelectronics, sensors, and software research[70]
Huawei and Tencent	Partnerships with Oxford University and the University of Edinburgh	AI research collaboration; provision of cloud services[71]
CRRC	Partnership with University of Illinois	Intelligent manufacturing collaboration with departments also associated with Argonne National Lab[72]
SenseTime	Singapore Institute of Technical Education	AI hub and talent partnership[73]

show potentially divergent trends. China's state-run Thousand Talents Program attracted thousands of scientists and engineers back to China between 2008 and 2018, but one study found that over 90 percent of China-born U.S.-educated AI PhDs remained in the United States five years after graduating.[76] Factors influencing talent flows include U.S. and PRC government visa policies, state talent program funding, vibrancy of China's AI sector,[77] and travel challenges during the COVID-19 pandemic. Even though PRC AI talent may remain in the United States, researchers have other ways to support China's AI development, including through PRC-tied research partnerships, academic exchanges, and professional associations. China's state talent programs call for participating researchers to "serve the country" (为国服务) while working abroad, which can involve the transfer of capabilities to China.[78]

Business development and acquisitions

China's AI firms are rapidly expanding offshore and investing in foreign startups. This includes AI hardware manufacturers, such as Huawei and Hikvision, and service-oriented firms like DiDi, which has a large share of the Latin American ridesharing market.[79] Software-tied businesses such as ByteDance's TikTok social media platform, Tencent's WeChat, and Alibaba and Huawei cloud services have expanded significantly and are globally popular.[80] With 689 million global active users, TikTok in 2020 was the seventh most used social network in the world; Tencent's WeChat was sixth.[81] AI algorithms used for these platforms are developed in China, and their Chinese parent organizations may control operations even if offshore operations are said to be separate.[82] Southeast Asia is a first and important foreign market for many firms; Alibaba, Tencent, TikTok, and SenseTime have hubs in Singapore.[83] PRC companies are also funding U.S. AI research centers. For example, Alibaba co-CEO Joe Tsai (蔡崇信) and Hong Kong tycoon Li Kai Shing (李嘉诚) are investing in brain research at Stanford University and the University of California at Berkeley.[84]

Foreign acquisitions, investments, and partnerships have facilitated the overseas expansion of many Chinese AI firms. In some instances, through these investments, China's AI firms have acquired technological capabilities in a wide range of areas that include biotechnology, genetics, facial recognition, sensors, semiconductors, and gaming. For example:

- Tencent has developed its global network through a series of investments in foreign gaming firms.[85] Its investments in mobile payment app Lydia and the B2B bank Qonto allowed it to enter the European financial market without having to secure a license.[86] Similarly, Tencent has entered Latin America through a joint investment with SoftBank in the Argentina-headquartered fintech company Uala.[87]
- ByteDance's acquisition of Musical.ly in November 2017 added an estimated 80 million U.S. users to TikTok's platform.[88]
- BGI Group (formerly Beijing Genomics Institute) acquired its DNA sequencing capabilities through its 2012 acquisition of U.S.-headquartered Complete Genomics.[89]
- Pharmaceutical technology company WuxiAppTech has used acquisitions to build a U.S. and European presence.[90]
- Alibaba is operating cloud services in the United States and has a payment systems joint venture with Walgreens.[91]
- Baidu's Apollo autonomous driving system has over 95 partners (including foreign auto firms), uses Microsoft's Azure Cloud services, and is testing in California.[92]

Overseas projects

As the Chinese government seeks to expand China's technology infrastructure overseas through its *One Belt, One Road* and related *Digital Silk Road* initiatives, large AI firms such as Alibaba and Huawei have developed infrastructure and business solutions in developing countries, often as part of government agreements and supported by government financing. In Malaysia, Alibaba is building backbone IT infrastructure that will run the company's cloud, financial, and retail services; Yitu is operating an AI facial recognition system.[93] Huawei is building and operating smart city projects around the world.[94] DeepBlue has AI labs in Europe that promote its AI technologies in smart cities, biotechnology, autonomous driving, and robotics.[95] Zimbabwe is working with Hikvision on smart cites, and its agreement with CloudWalk reportedly sends data to China for processing, allowing the firm to develop facial algorithm processing for different ethnicities.[96]

Fundraising and investment

Foreign investment flows to China's AI companies through their overseas and domestic public listings, as well as PE and VC investments.[97] Early stage funding from foreign VC firms and strategic investors like SoftBank has been critical for well-known Chinese AI firms such as Alibaba, Tencent, and SenseTime.[98] Similarly, Chinese AI firms use these same pathways for their own investments. China's larger companies, such as Alibaba, Huawei, and Tencent, are investing heavily in Chinese and foreign AI companies in the United States, Europe, India, and Southeast Asia.[99] The United States has attracted most of Chinese AI firms' disclosed overseas PE investment to date. Between 2015 and 2019, Chinese investors were involved in an estimated $7 billion of disclosed VC, PE, and M&A investments in non-Chinese AI companies, compared to about $100 billion in global deals that did not involve Chinese AI investors.[100] Some analysts assess that China's AI-related equity investments in the United States have dropped since 2016, in part due to increased scrutiny by the U.S. and PRC governments.[101] Much of this investment is not publicly disclosed, however, and significant aspects of two-way technology collaboration and investment are not captured in many investment datasets.[102]

Conclusion

China's AI firms are advancing China's interests domestically and globally. While China's firms have their own interests and competitive strategies, the Chinese government is intent on aligning corporate activities with state objectives. This alignment raises questions about how U.S. and foreign research and commercial ties with these companies in AI—and related areas such as semiconductors, advanced computing, and quantum—are helping the Chinese state develop AI capabilities that can be deployed across a range of commercial, security, and military applications. There are growing concerns about how China is deploying these capabilities for political surveillance and in other ways that contravene U.S. interests and global values. China's firms may also use the gains they are making through foreign ties to compete with these partners, as has happened in other industries.

State support and coordination—together with a restricted domestic market—position China's AI firms to develop in China while they push offshore, potentially crowding out other market participants over time. Global adoption of China's AI-related technology and systems may, in turn, give China greater leeway to set de facto and formal standards and control the global value chain in ways that could challenge U.S. economic, political, and security interests. Despite privacy and security concerns, many developing countries are adopting Chinese infrastructure that supports its related AI products and services. In developed markets, policy stasis on how to address the role of the state in China's AI firms, risks in research ties, and China's market barriers is allowing China to develop capabilities and gain a market foothold.

Notes

1 The views expressed in this chapter are those of its authors and are not presented as those of the Congressional Research Service or the Library of Congress.
2 PRC State Council. 国务院关于印发新一代人工智能发展规划的通知 (The New Generation AI Development Plan), SC 35, 2017.
3 The authors use the term "state" to describe the combined role of the Communist Party of China (CPC), the government, and the military.
4 Daniel Castro and Michael McLaughlin, "Who Is Winning the AI Race: China, the EU, or the United States?" Center for Data Innovation, January 2021.
5 Zachary Arnold, Testimony at Hearing on U.S. Investment in China's Capital Markets and Military-Industrial Complex, U.S. China Economic and Security Review Commission (USCC), March 19, 2021.
6 This term refers to the 96 national-level firms owned and managed by the State Council's Assets Supervision and Administration Commission of 国务院国有资产监督管理委员会. http://en.sasac.gov.cn/directory.html.
7 For instance, China's state telecom providers are shareholders in iFLYTEK. See Kevin Zheng Zhou, "State Ownership and Firm Innovation in China: An Integrated View of Institutional and Efficiency Logics," *Administrative Science Quarterly*, 62.2, October 10, 2016, p. 375.
8 Datang is active in government and military telecommunications. See "Occupying the Information High Ground: Chinese Capabilities for Computer Network Operations and Cyber Espionage," Northrop Grumman Submission to the USCC, March 7, 2012.
9 CETC is a defense contractor, specializing in microelectronics. It has developed AI surveillance applications and is a majority shareholder of Hikvision. See Charles Rollet, "In China's Far West, Companies Cash in on Surveillance Program that Targets Muslims," *Foreign Policy*, June 13, 2018.
10 Elsa B. Kania, "Chinese Military Innovation in Artificial Intelligence," testimony before the USCC, June 7, 2019. Qihoo360 is associated with the Central Military Commission's Cyberspace Security Military-Civil Fusion Innovation Center. See Elsa Kania, "China's Quest for Political Control and Military Supremacy in the Cyber Domain," Australian Strategic Policy Institute, March 16, 2018.
11 Ministry of Human Resources and Social Security (人社部), "新职业-人工智能工程技术人员就业景气现状分析报告" (A New Occupation—An Analytical Report on Current Employment Prospects for AI Engineers and Technicians), April 30, 2020; Zachary Arnold et al., "Tracking AI Investment: Initial Findings from the Private Markets," Georgetown University, Center for Security and Emerging Technology, September 2020.
12 See AI Startups in China, updated on June 13, 2021, https://www.ai-startups.org/country/China/.
13 Curtis J. Milhaupt and Wentong Zheng. "Beyond Ownership: State Capitalism and the Chinese Firm," *Georgetown Law Journal*, 2015.

14 Cong Cao, Richard P. Suttmeier, and Denis Fred Simon, "China's 15-year Science and Technology Plan," *Physics Today*, December 2006.

15 Some of China's leading AI firms were founded by the state or incubated in China's universities and research centers.

16 Scott Livingston, "The New Challenge of Communist Corporate Governance," CSIS, January 15, 2021; Emily Feng, "Chinese Tech Giants like Baidu and Sina Set up Communist Party Committees," *Financial Review*, October 11, 2017; "Alibaba Beijing Office Sets Up a CPC Committee," *Global Times*, March 25, 2021; Lauren Yu-Hsin Yin and Curtis J. Milhaupt. "Party Building or Noisy Signaling? The Contours of Political Conformity in Chinese Corporate Governance," *Journal of Legal Studies*, Vol. 50, No.1, 2021, pp. 187–217.

17 MOST, 国家新一代人工智能创新发展试验区建设工作指引 (Work Guidelines on the Establishment of National New Generation Artificial Intelligence Innovation Development Experimental Zones), MOST 298, 2019; Fei Dian, "Investors Flee Artificial Intelligence."

18 MOST, "2019 年度国家科技成果转化引导基金拟设立创业投资子基金名单" (Establishment of 9 New National Venture Capital Guidance Funds), https://chinainnovation-funding.eu/establishment-of-9-new-national-venture-capital-guidance-funds/.

19 Ngor Luong et al., "Understanding Chinese Government Guidance Funds: An Analysis of Chinese-Language Sources," Georgetown University, Center for Security and Emerging Technology, March 2021.

20 VC firms that appear to have state ties include Hillhouse Capital, IDG Capital, Sequoia Capital China, GGV, GSR, Pine Capital, Shunwei Capital, Tsinghua, Sinovation, and Zhen Fund.

21 "关于印发汾湖高新区科技创新券管理办法(试行)的通知" (Measures for the Administration of Science and Technology Innovation Vouchers in Fenhu High-tech Zone (for Trial Implementation)), December 12, 2020. https://yqtong.com/front/policyCenterDetail/57.

22 See MOST, "关于促进新型研发机构发展的指导意见" (Guiding Opinions on Promoting the Development of New Type R&D Organizations) MOST 313, September 2019; Tong Wangyue, "Enterprises Benefit from Voucher Scheme in Jiading," *Shine*, May 26, 2020.

23 "Examples of Chinese Military Ties to Alibaba, Tencent, and Baidu," RWR Advisory Group, LLC, January 12, 2021; Fei Dian, "Investors Flee Artificial Intelligence."

24 Liza Lin and Josh Chin, "China's Tech Giants Have a Second Job: Helping Beijing Spy on Its People," *The Wall Street Journal*, November 30, 2017.

25 Catherine Shu, "China's Government Will Embed Police in Its Largest Tech Firms," *TechCrunch*, August 5, 2015; Zach Dorfman, "Tech Giants Are Giving China a Vital Edge in Espionage," *Foreign Policy*, December 23, 2020.

26 Stuart Lau, "Alibaba and the 40 Spies? Belgium Frets over Chinese Mega Project," *Politico*, May 12, 2021.

27 MOST 298, 2019; MOST "国家新一代人工智能创新发展试验区建设工作指引" (Establishment of New National New Generation AI Developmental Experimental Zones). Some 15 were created as of July 2021. "解码人工智能'国家队': 15个试验区'落子'13省份, 城市'智治'场景牵动产业创新," *21st Century Business Herald*, July 10, 2021.

28 "恒大'牵手'中科院为高科技产业引最强智库," *ScienceNet.cn*, April 4, 2018; Summer Zhen, "China Evergrande Raises a Further US$9 Billion to Cut Debt Ahead of Shenzhen Listing," *South China Morning Post*, November 6, 2017.

29 Tang Shihua, "China's DeepBlue Technology, Greek University to Set Up Smart City AI Lab," *Yicai Global*, June 28, 2019.

30 Wang Xiaoming, "China's Property Giant Country Garden to Build USD11.7 Billion Robot Valley," *Yicai Global*, September 10, 2018; "Country Garden's 80 Billion Robot Dream Has Been Burned for Two Years and Is in a Dilemma," *DayDayNews*, March 30, 2020.

31 "CIC Report," China National Industrial Cyber Security Development Center, October 2020, as referenced in Baidu's 6-K filing to the SEC, March 2021.

32 "The National Center for Industry and Information Security and MIIT Released the *Report on China's Artificial Intelligence High-Value Patent and Innovation Drivers*," (国家工信安全中心, 工信部电子知识产权中心发布中国人工智能高价值专利及创新驱动力分析报告), *IPR Daily*, October 15, 2021.

33 China Bank Insurance Regulatory Commission, the National Intellectual Property Administration and the National Trademark Administration, "关于进一步加强知识产权质押融资工作的通知" (Notice on Further Strengthening IP Pledge Financing Work), 34, 2019; Zhongguancun S&T Park Management Committee, the People's Bank of China Business Management Department, the Beijing Regulatory Authority of the Bank of China Insurance Regulatory Committee, and the Beijing Intellectual Property Office, "关于进一步促进中关村知识产权质押融资发展的若干措施" (Several Measures for Further Boosting the Development of IP Pledge Financing in Zhongguancun), 66, 2019.

34 Central Committee of the Communist Party of China and the State Council, "知识产权强国建设纲要" (Outline for Building a Powerful Country with Intellectual Property Rights 2021-2035), September 22, 2021.

35 See http://www.aiiaorg.cn/uploadfile/2020/0721/20200721031100933.pdf and MOST, "Vice Minister Li Meng Attended and Addressed the Inaugural Meeting of China's Artificial Intelligence Industry Alliance," October 17, 2017; Liu Gang, "新挑战和机遇下的中国人工智能科技产业发展" (China's Artificial Intelligence Technology Industry Development under New Challenges and Opportunities), Chinese Institute of New Generation Artificial Intelligence Development Strategies, June 24, 2020.

36 Ngor Luong and Zachary Arnold, "China's Artificial Intelligence Industry Alliance: Understanding China's AI Strategy through Industry Alliances," Georgetown University, Center for Security and Emerging Technology, May 2021.

37 China Mobile, China Telecom, China Unicom's Digital Tech, and Xiaomi are BAIIA members.

38 "重磅!北京人工智能产业联盟正式成立, 百度牵头发起, 任理事长单位," (Breaking! Beijing Artificial Intelligence Industry Alliance Formally Established, Baidu Takes lead, Serves As chairing unit) *China Daily*, June 10, 2021.

39 "Shanghai Forms AI Industrial Alliance," *Xinhua*, May 10, 2019.

40 http://www.bibdr.org/.

41 "China Tech Digest: Beijing AI Industry Alliance Established," *China Money AI*, June 10, 2021.

42 AI experts from Cornell, Princeton, University of California Berkeley, UCLA, and the University of Manchester serve as advisors to BAAI. https://www.baai.ac.cn/en.

43 Jeffrey Ding, "Balancing Standards: U.S. and Chinese Strategies for Developing Technical Standards in AI," National Bureau of Asian Research, July 1, 2020.

44 "AI Policy – China," Future of Life Institute, accessed November 16, 2021.

45 http://english.ia.cas.cn/.

46 Ibid.

47 https://www.hanvon.com/list-10-1.html; http://www.sciample.com/index.php?catid=30.

48 Eric Walz, "China's Baidu Announces 'Apollo Air' Which Supports Self-driving Vehicles Using Real-time Data From 5G-Connected Roadside Units," *FutureCar*, May 14, 2021.

49 Fan Feifei, "Tsinghua University, Tencent Sign In-depth Cooperation Agreement," *China Daily*, September 28, 2020.

50 Chen Na, "Aliyun and China Academy of Sciences Sign MOU for Quantum Computing Lab," CAS News Release, July 31, 2015.

51 Chi Jingyi and Deng Xiaoci, "Tencent's AI Technology to Find Pulsars 'FASTER'," *Global Times*, July 8, 2021.

52 Craig S. Smith, "Competing Visions Underpin China's Quantum Computer Race," *IEEE Spectrum*, September 15, 2021.
53 "China's National Supercomputing Center Launches AI Testbed," *Xinhua*, June 1, 2019.
54 PRC State Council, 国务院关于印发新一代人工智能发展规划的通知 (The New Generation AI Development Plan), SC 35, 2017.
55 "科技部召开新一代人工智能发展规划暨重大科技项目启动会" (MOST Holds Kick-off Meeting for the New Generation AI Development Plan and Major S&T Projects), http://www.cac.gov.cn/2017-11/16/c_1121964697.htm.
56 "人工智能'国家队'扩容 十家公司入选," *Xinhua*, August 30, 2019.
57 Sirui Zhou, "10 Companies Join China's National Open Platform for Next Generation AI," *Equal Ocean*, August 29, 2019.
58 MOST, 265, 2019.
59 Jing Yang and Keigh Zhai, "Alibaba and Tencent Consider Opening Up Their 'Walled Gardens'," *The Wall Street Journal*, July 14, 2021.
60 Karen M. Sutter, *China's Recent Trade Measures and Countermeasures: Issues for Congress*, Congressional Research Service (CRS), September 20, 2021; Stephen Ezell, *False Promises II: The Continuing Gap between China's WTO Commitments and Its Practices*, ITIF, July 26, 2021.
61 https://chinatechmap.aspi.org.au/#/map/.
62 William C. Hannas and Huey-Meei Chang, *China's Access to Foreign AI Technology*, Georgetown University, Center for Security and Emerging Technology, September 2019.
63 Alexandra Harney, "Risky Partner: Top U.S. Universities Took Funds from Chinese Firm Tied to Xinjiang Security," *Reuters*, June 12, 2019; Will Knight, "MIT Cuts Ties with a Chinese AI Firm Amid Human Rights Concerns," *Wired*, April 21, 2020.
64 Adrian Zmudzinski, "Chinese IT Giant Tencent and University of Hong Kong Collaborate on Fintech," *Cointelegraph*, March 7, 2019.
65 "Distinguished Scientist Mario Szegedy to Join Alibaba's DAMO Quantum Computing Lab," *Enterprise IT World*, January 18, 2018.
66 https://damo.alibaba.com/; Luke Stangel, "Chinese Retail Giant Alibaba Opening New R&D Lab in San Mateo," *Silicon Valley Business Journal*, October 11, 2017; Catherine Shu, "Alibaba Group Will Invest $15B into a New Global Research and Development Program," *TechCrunch*, October 11, 2017.
67 https://air.jd.com/people-detail.html?id=43.
68 RISC-V originated at the University of California and is now headquartered in Switzerland. See Karen M. Sutter, *China's New Semiconductor Policies: Issues for Congress*, CRS, April 20, 2021; Sutter, *China's Recent Trade Measures and Countermeasures*.
69 http://research.baidu.com/.
70 "Huawei to Build an Optoelectronics R&D and Manufacturing Center in Cambridge," Company Press Release, June 25, 2020; "China's Tech Giant Huawei Opens New Research Center in France, *Xinhua*, November 29, 2018.
71 Nic Fildes, "Huawei Buys Access to UK Innovation with Oxford Stake," *Financial Times*, October 1, 2019; Poppy Watson, "Scottish University Strikes Ties with Chinese Cloud Giant," *FutureScot*, May 26, 2021.
72 Brett Hansard, "Argonne Researchers Using Artificial Intelligence to Shape the Future of Science," Argonne National Laboratory, May 25, 2021.
73 Gigi Onag, "SenseTime Picks Singapore as AI Innovation Hub in Southeast Asia," *FutureIoT*, July 20, 2021.
74 Roxanne Heston and Remco Zwetsloot, "Mapping U.S. Multinationals' Global AI R&D Activity," Georgetown University, Center for Security and Emerging Technology, December 2020.
75 William C. Hannas and Huey-Meei Chang, "China's 'Artificial' Intelligence," in William C. Hannas and Didi Kirsten-Tatlow, eds., *China's Quest for Foreign Technology: Beyond Espionage*, Routledge, 2021, pp. 198–199.

76 Remco Zwetsloot et al., "Keeping Top AI Talent in the United States," Georgetown University, Center for Security and Emerging Technology, December 2019.

77 Meng Jing, "China's Top Talent Now Wants to Work for Rising Domestic Tech Stars, Not Big Brand Multinationals," *South China Morning Post*, June 21, 2019.

78 See, e.g., William C. Hannas, James Mulvenon, and Anna B. Puglisi, Chinese Industrial Espionage, pp. 171–174; David Zweig, Chung Siu Fung, and Donglin Han, "Redefining the Brain Drain: China's 'Diaspora Option'," *Science, Technology and Society* 13.1, May 2008, 1–33.

79 Fan Yiying, "China's Didi Eyeing Africa, Europe en Route to Global Expansion," *Sixth Tone*, March 23, 2021.

80 Jonathan E. Hillman and Maesea McCalpin, "Huawei's Global Cloud Strategy: Economic and Strategic Implications," Center for Strategic and International Studies, May 17, 2021. Alibaba Cloud operates in Australia, Germany, India, Indonesia, Japan, Malaysia, Singapore, UAE, the UK, and the United States. https://www.alibaba cloud.com/global-locations.

81 Katie Sehl, "23 Important TikTok Stats Marketers Need to Know in 2021," *Hootsuite*, May 5, 2021.

82 Salvador Rodriguez, "TikTok Insiders Say Social Media Company Is Tightly Controlled by Chinese Parent ByteDance," *CNBC*, June 25, 2021.

83 "China's Tencent to Open Southeast Asia Regional Hub in Singapore," *Reuters*, September 15, 2020.

84 Lisa Trei and Nathan Collins, "With Significant Philanthropic Investments, Stanford Makes Major Leap Forward in the Neurosciences," Stanford University, October 10, 2018; Jose Rodriguez, "Campus Dedicates Li Ka Shing Center for Biomedical and Health Sciences, Philanthropist Receives Berkeley Medal," University of California at Berkeley, October 21, 2011.

85 Pieter Haeck, "China's Tencent Goes on a European Shopping Spree," *Politico*, August 18, 2021.

86 Matteo Giovannin, "Tencent Is Betting Heavy on European Fintech Companies," *China Daily*, February 24, 2020.

87 "Tencent, SoftBank-led Funding Pushes Argentina's Uala to $2.45 bln Valuation," *Reuters*, August 13, 2021.

88 Mansoor Iqbal, "TikTok Revenue and Usage Statistics (2021)," *Business of Apps*, September 28, 2021.

89 "BGI-Shenzhen Completes Acquisition of Complete Genomics," *PR Newswire*, May 18, 2013.

90 In the United States, the company acquired AppTech Lab Services (2008), Medkey (2011), Xeno Biotech Laboratories (2014), HD Biosciences (2017), Research Point Global (2017), and Pharmspace (2019). In Europe, the firm acquired Crelux (2016), Bristol Myers Squibb production facilities (2021), and Oxgene (2021). See https://www.wuxiapptec.com/about/history.

91 Rita Liao, "China's Alipay Digital Wallet is Entering 7,000 Walgreens Stores," *TechCrunch*, February 13, 2019.

92 "Baidu Partners with German Auto Suppliers to Develop Autonomous Driving," *Xinhua*, June 3, 2017; Rita Liao, "After Baidu Tie-up, BMW Taps Tencent for Autonomous Driving in China," *TechCrunch*, July 19, 2019; "Rise of China's Big Tech In AI: What Baidu, Alibaba, and Tencent Are Working On," *CB Insights*, April 26, 2018.

93 Barry Naughton, "Chinese Industrial Policy and the Digital Silk Road: The Case of Alibaba in Malaysia," *Asia Policy*, January 28, 2020.

94 Katherine Atha et al., "China's Smart Cities Development," Research paper prepared for USCC, January 2020.

95 Tang Shihua, "China's DeepBlue Technology, Greek University to Set Up Smart City AI Lab," *Yicai Global*, June 28, 2019.

96 Problem Masau, "Chinese Tech Revolution Comes to Zimbabwe," *The Herald*, October 9, 2019.

97 Zachary Arnold Testimony, March 19, 2021.
98 Jon Russell, "Tencent Confirms Deal to Buy Majority Stake in Supercell from Soft-Bank for $8.6 Billion," *TechCrunch*, June 21, 2021; "HOPU-ARM Innovation Fund Officially Launched," ARM Newsroom, February 9, 2017.
99 Rebecca Kagan et al., "Corporate Investors in Top AI Startups," Georgetown University, Center for Security and Emerging Technology, February 2021; Paolo Cervini and Mark J. Greeven, "Digital China Is Coming to Europe," *LSE Business Review*, April 24, 2018; Aditi Shah and Sumeet Chatterjee, "Exclusive: Alibaba Puts India Investment Plan on Hold Amid China Tensions, Sources Say," *Reuters,* August 26, 2020.
100 Zachary Arnold et al., "Tracking AI Investment."
101 Ibid; Thilo Hanemann et al., "Two-Way Street: 2021 Update – US-China Investment Trends," Rhodium Group, May 2021.
102 Hanemann et al., Kate O'Keefe, Heather Somerville, and Yang Jie, "U.S. Companies Aid China's Bid for Chip Dominance despite Security Concerns," *The Wall Street Journal*, November 12, 2021, pp. 26–27.

Bibliography

CAICT and AIIA, 人工智能治理白皮书 (White Paper on Artificial Intelligence), September 2020.
China Electronics Standardization Institute (中国电子技术标准化研究院), 人工智能标准化白皮书 (White Paper on Artificial Intelligence Standardization), 2018.
Curtis J. Milhaupt and Wentong Zheng, "Beyond Ownership: State Capitalism and the Chinese Firm," *The Georgetown Law Journal*, 103(3): 665–772, 2015.
Fei Dian (斐典), "Investors Flee Artificial Intelligence" (投资人逃离人工智能), *36Kr*, September 26, 2019.
Ngor Luong and Zachary Arnold, "China's Artificial Intelligence Industry Alliance: Understanding China's AI Strategy through Industry Alliances," Georgetown University, Center for Security and Emerging Technology, May 2021.
PRC Ministry of Science and Technology, 国家新一代人工智能开放创新平台建设工作指引 (Instructions for Building the National Open Platform for Next Generation Artificial Intelligence), MOST 265, 2019.
PRC National People's Congress and Chinese People's Political Consultative Conference, 中华人民共和国国民经济和社会发展第十四个五年规划和2035年远景目标纲要 (The 14th Five-year Plan for the National Economic and Social Development of the People's Republic of China and Outline of Long-term Goals for 2035), March 11, 2021.
PRC State Council, 国务院关于印发《中国制造2025》的通知 (Made in China 2025), SC 28, 2015.
PRC State Council, 国家中长期科学和技术发展规划纲要(2006-2020年) (National Medium- and Long-term S&T Development Plan (2006-2020)), SC 9, 2006.
PRC State Council. 国务院关于积极推进"互联网+"行动的指导意见 (State Council Guiding Opinions on Positively Promoting 'Internet +' Action), SC 40, July 2015.
Thilo Hanemann et al., "Two-Way Street: 2021 Update – US-China Investment Trends," *Rhodium Group*, May 2021.

3

Foreign support, alliances, and technology transfer

Huey-Meei Chang and William C. Hannas

Chapters 1 and 2 describe state and corporate aspects of Chinese AI power. Given the relationship between the PRC government and commercial enterprises, this distinction is somewhat artificial, rendering cross-country calculations of public versus private investment difficult. Complicating China and ROW comparisons further are the effects of massive state-supported technology transfers, of which China has been the beneficiary for decades.

Without belittling China's indigenous accomplishments, in practical areas especially, this "informal" dimension of AI power merits equal treatment as a measure of China's composite AI strength. Accordingly, the present chapter updates previous work done by its authors on Chinese gray zone technology transfer in general[1] and as applied to AI.[2] We cover this in sufficient detail to acquaint the reader with its basic role and operation.

The final sections break new ground by focusing on a neglected aspect of technology transfer, namely, *legal* transactions by Chinese state and corporate entities abroad, by multinationals in China, and through academic alliances, which likely outweigh the impact on host countries of illegal and extralegal transfers combined.

Chinese tech transfer: an overview—and a choice

We begin with a thought experiment, a self-test, inspired by an apocryphal quote attributed to James Jesus Angleton that "There are two, five, seven ways of looking at any given set of facts,"[3] and by reactions to our efforts over the past decade to convey the import of China's foreign technology transfer operations to sympathetic, skeptical, and even hostile audiences. The reader is invited to identify with one scenario, the other, or an intermediate interpretation.

> **Scenario 1**: Owing to circumstances beyond China's control, in particular, Western aggression (the "unequal treaties"),[4] the Japanese occupation

DOI: 10.4324/9781003212980-4

(1931–1945), and a civil war (1927–1949) abetted by foreign antagonisms played out on Chinese soil, China began the 20th century at a disadvantage. These extrinsic challenges were built on—indeed, were a consequence of—China's own pre-Communist legacy of semi-feudal and petit-bourgeoisie inertia, against which the new progressive society continues to struggle.

Add to these political obstacles a bias toward practical achievement[5] that serves China well in normal times but delayed its participation in the scientific revolution,[6] coupled with the West's refusal to share with China the fruits of the world's technology, and it is obvious that China had no choice but to follow the path taken by developing nations everywhere—post-war Japan, South Korea, the United States itself[7]—and look to its privileged competitors for inspiration and guidance.

Thanks to self-strengthening, China overcame these obstacles, is reaching parity with the West, and is poised to overtake it in some key areas. America's obsession with economic espionage—a form of racism[8]—and its bogus construct of "extralegal" transfers[9] meant to stigmatize behavior disliked by foreign monopolies and their stooge governments are the last gasps of a dying civilization reduced to substituting blame for initiative. China's work to engage its diaspora population and reverse a brain drain are the normal activities of a developing nation, which in any case have largely abated.

Scenario 2: China for six decades has savaged intellectual property (IP) through a state-backed program of technology appropriation. The cost to its victims of cyber theft alone represents "the greatest transfer of wealth in history."[10] Traditional espionage by insiders, students, scientists abroad, and through patent theft, reverse engineering, and grants to naive or complicit academics account for another part of the score. A third element includes gray zone (extralegal) practices that net China even more misbegotten gains.[11]

Arguments normalizing this behavior are disingenuous. The problem can be traced to a creativity deficit caused by multiple interlocking factors, such as a distaste for abstract thinking,[12] a political tradition adverse to change,[13] the lack of competition for most of its history,[14] elite disdain for technical skills,[15] rote memory-based education, a culture of obedience, a writing system absent analytic cues,[16] psychological[17] and philosophical[18] predispositions to holistic thought, and a genetic surfeit of serotonin that biases Chinese to collectivism and the status quo.[19]

China's predatory practices will not end when it achieves parity, because the causes of the behavior predate the problem. Its penchant for co-opting foreign achievements to counter foreign challenges also dates to antiquity,[20] expressed in the so-called *ti-yong* (体用) modernization formula[21] meant to preserve the country's dysfunctional political core. The upshot is a unique system that avoids blind alleys and allows China to "leap ahead" on technologies important to China—while skirting liberalization.

The two scenarios are polar positions and represent an evolution in our approach to the problem. Mindful of the passions surrounding the matter, we prefer to present the facts and let others interpret them. Toward that end, we offer below an abbreviated *Wertfrei* list of China's transfer practices as an introduction to the system and the chapter's AI focus.[22]

State enactments

Some two-dozen major "notifications" were issued by the State Council, Communist Party Central Committee, and national ministries between 1994 and 2020 to facilitate access to foreign technology "by various means" (以多种方式).[23] Included are subsidies for "short term" returnees and "dual base" operations, where research abroad is mirrored in China; indigenization enclaves; "talent" programs; and incentives to transfer "patents, scientific research results, and proprietary technology."[24] The directives are backed by local measures. Tech-specific development plans have their own provisions for foreign access.

Transfer offices

The number of Chinese government offices pursuing technology transfer ranges from a dozen high-level units to several hundred, since central management is replicated locally. The top ones are the State Administration of Foreign Experts Affairs (国家外国专家局, SAFEA),[25] the Overseas Chinese Affairs Office (国务院侨务办公室, OCAO),[26] the Ministry of Human Resources and Social Security (人力资源和社会保障部, MHRSS),[27] Ministry of Science and Technology (科学技术部, MOST), Ministry of Education (教育部, MOE), the Chinese Academy of Sciences (中国科学院, CAS),[28] and China's clandestine services.[29]

NGOs and front organizations

A parallel "unofficial" bureaucracy executes programs while offering plausible deniability to foreign participants. The China Association for Science and Technology (中国科学技术协会)[30] runs a "Help Our Motherland through Elite Intellectual Resources from Overseas."[31] China's United Front Work Department (统一战线工作部) and Western Returned Scholars Association (欧美同学会) support transfers in multiple ways.[32] Other shadow organizations share staff and offices with their ministry counterparts, such as the China Overseas Exchange Association (中国海外交流学会), which fronts for OCAO, and SAFEA's "China International Talent Exchange Association" (中国国际人才交流协会)[33] with multiple branches overseas.

Outreach and incentive programs

China's central and local governments offer incentives for "skilled persons" living, studying, or with connections abroad to contribute to China's scientific and technological progress, including cash, research grants, soft loans, tax breaks, academic sinecures, government posts, lab subsidies, free travel, dependent care, and so on. Duration can be a few days at a debriefing facility, two-year renewable contracts, or lifelong tenure. The best-known vehicle is the so-called "Thousand Talents Plan" (千人计划)[34] but this is not the first, only, or even best example.

Open source monitoring

China has operated a science and technology intelligence (STI) program since 1958 to identify useful technologies and facilitate their transfer. Insiders put the number of workers at 100,000,[35] up from 60,000 in 1985.[36] Its budget can exceed state expenditure on R&D.[37] These figures are matched by a level of professionalization among "STI workers" (科技情报工作人员) unrivaled elsewhere.[38] Its accomplishments, heralded in book-length accounts, include support for nuclear weapons, missile, and satellite programs.[39]

Diaspora guilds

Some 200 ethnic Chinese professional associations abroad accumulate the science, engineering, and enabling skills sought by China.[40] Many of these guilds were created quasi-independently by expatriates, while others were launched at the PRC's behest. Some 61 percent, conservatively estimated, "exchange technical information, bring scientists to China, or contribute to specific Chinese talent plans."[41] Half advertise their support for China on the Chinese language parts of their websites only,[42] and many acknowledge their raison d'être as "serving China" (为国服务).

Indigenization enclaves

Foreign technologies brought "back" to China achieve their Chinese characteristics at enclaves ranging from modest offices to multi-acre, multi-story megacenters. Known as Technology Transfer Centers, or Overseas Chinese Scholar Pioneering Parks, National Innovation Centers for New and High Technology, etc.,[43] they are subsidized clearinghouses for IP transitioning to China from abroad. Studies done in 2010,[44] 2016,[45] and 2019[46] traced their growth from fewer than 300 through roughly 900 to its present number of some 2,000 facilities.

Gray zone transfers of foreign AI technology

The above sketch omits some practices we described elsewhere,[47] including covert operations that shape most of the public's awareness.[48] We now examine how these venues apply to AI.[49]

China's earliest state notifications on artificial intelligence included appeals for foreign support. In May 2016, less than a year after the PRC government's first formal mention of AI,[50] a consortium of ministries issued a "Three-year

Action Implementation Plan for 'Internet +' Artificial Intelligence"[51] that counseled going global (走出去), "integrating domestic and foreign innovative resources," and building a service platform for foreign AI cooperation. Two months later, its State Council issued a "Notification on National Science and Technology Innovation Programs for the 13th Five-year Plan," that highlighted brain-computer intelligence (see Chapter 7) and called for foreign access to facilitate its development.[52]

Foreign support came up again in a November 2016 State Council memo that cited "international cooperation" 13 times and outlined a dozen venues through which accesses could be achieved.[53] In July 2017, the council addressed AI specifically in a "New Generation AI Development Plan,"[54] whose Section 4 reads like a recitation of the techniques described in this chapter's first section.[55] Subsequently, three Chinese ministries each issued programs for AI development calling for:

• Full use of international cooperation mechanisms and attracting high-level talent through the "Thousand" and "Ten Thousand Talents" Plans (MIIT)[56];
• "Foreign intellect recruitment innovation bases" (创新引智基地, "Program 111"), joint AI laboratories, importing top scholars, and organizing international AI forums (MOE)[57];
• Use of foreign scientists employed concurrently by foreign and Chinese employers as AI project leaders (MOST).[58]

China's 14th Five-year Plan (2021–2025), in which AI looms large, indicates that foreign "talent" will continue to support progress into the future. Heralded by *Nature* as "scientific self-reliance,"[59] the plan mandates the following:

Chapter 6 Stimulate the creative vitality of talent[60]

"Cultivate, draw in (引进), and make good use of talent in an all-round way, giving full play to the role of talent as the first resource (充分发挥人才第一资源的作用)… Implement a more open talent policy and build a scientific research and innovation highland that gathers outstanding talent at home and abroad."

"Improve the permanent residence system for foreigners in China and explore the establishment of a skilled immigration system.[61] Improve salary and welfare, children's education, social security, tax incentives and other systems to provide an internationally competitive and attractive environment for overseas scientists to work in China."

Chapter 7 Improve the system and mechanism of S&T innovation[62]

"Launch a number of major scientific and technological cooperation projects, study the establishment of global scientific research funds, and implement scientist exchange plans. Support the establishment of international

S&T organizations in China, and foreign scientists [ability] to hold posts in our S&T academic organizations."

This pattern of state support for AI development is reflected in the priorities of China's foreign technology "outreach" organizations. Research done in 2019 and reconfirmed by the authors 18 months later showed each of the Ministry of Science and Technology's seven transfer offices engaged in AI-related promotion and "exchanges." The State Administration of Foreign Experts Affairs (now also under the science ministry) registered 90,300 Google hits when searched with "人工智能" (artificial intelligence) in December 2019; that figure doubled to 186,000 in April 2021.[63]

Meanwhile, China's Ministry of Education in January 2020 promulgated measures aimed at addressing endemic shortcomings (noted elsewhere in this volume) in China's AI development, namely, "basic AI theory, original (原创) algorithms, and high-end microchips" by building the so-called "double first-class" (双一流) institutes of higher education—world-class universities and world-class disciplines.[64] Article 4.11 lays out its foreign agenda:

Strengthen international exchanges and collaboration[65]

> "Aiming at the international cutting edge of AI and at weaknesses in domestic development, increase support for joint training of doctoral students in AI-related fields at home and abroad. Actively encourage high-level talent to carry out international exchanges and expand the depth and breadth of cooperation. Hold internationally influential AI academic conferences and forums and create high-level academic journals. Build a number of AI international cooperative scientific research platforms and bases and strengthen the development and training of international high-end talent. Encourage universities to initiate and organize AI international big science projects (大科学计划) and create international academic organizations and university cooperation alliances. Promote the formation of relevant international standards and ethical norms in the field of AI. Vigorously cultivate internationalized talent to participate in its global governance."

The CAS Institute of Automation (自动化研究所), a key driver of AI innovation, dispatches some 320 staffers abroad annually for "short term" exchanges and hosts "more than 700 overseas guests for scientific visits."[66] As of April 2021, its website had a breakdown of the institute's "talent corps" of 179 people, at least 39 of whom were recruited through one of three outward-facing talent programs.[67]

That figure barely scratches the surface. Prior research by the authors in 2020 elicited specific information on more than one hundred Thousand Talents Plan (千人计划) foreign co-optees supporting China's AI programs, chiefly from the United States and Europe, despite efforts by the sponsor to obscure their identities.[68] In 2021, we widened the search to include the major "active" plans listed in CSET's "Chinese Program Talent Tracker,"[69] including the Changjiang

Scholars Award Program (长江学者奖励计划), Chunhui Program[70] (春晖计划), Hundred Talents Program (百人计划), National Science Fund for Distinguished Young Scholars (国家杰出青年科学基金), the Homeland Serving Action Plan for Overseas Chinese (海外赤子为国服务行动计划), and subcategories of the reconstituted Thousand Talents Plan.[71] Each program without exception included several dozens to thousands of unique references to "artificial intelligence."

These foreign AI talent initiatives are mirrored in the work of China's overseas technical support guilds. Groups early to respond to China's AI talent calls included the Silicon Valley Chinese Engineers Association (硅谷华人工程师协会), Virginia's North American Chinese Scholars International Exchange Center (北美洲中国学人国际交流中心), the Federation of Associations of Chinese Professionals in Southern USA (美南中国专家协会联合会) based in Atlanta, Houston's Chinese Association of Professionals in Science and Technology (中国旅美专家协会), the Association of Chinese-American Scientists and Engineers (旅美中国科学家工程师专业人士协会) out of Chicago, and, of course, the Chinese Association for Science and Technology USA (中国留美科技协会) and its engineering counterpart, the Chinese Institute of Engineers USA (美洲中国工程师学会). Meanwhile, entirely new support guilds were founded in Japan, Germany, and the United Kingdom that, unlike these former groups, focus on AI exclusively.[72]

China's sprawling network of home-based indigenization enclaves—incubation hubs for foreign technology—also rose to the AI challenge. In late 2019, we pinpointed AI-related initiatives at transfer centers and returnee parks in 21 Chinese cities.[73] Google searches in April 2021 on four Chinese language name variants of these centers and "人工智能" (artificial intelligence) yielded over ¾ of a million hits. A Baidu search went off the charts.

Scope and impact of legal AI transfers

In the preceding section, we rehearsed and updated original research on China's extralegal—essentially *unsupervised*—access to foreign AI technology. The motivation for this research dates from our support for U.S. efforts to counter illicit acquisition of proprietary technology, which we determined to be an inadequate measure of the challenge, and hence began a decade-long crusade to expand the "threat space" to include this large, intermediate area.[74] Success at propagating this meme, however, was a mixed blessing since by defining the problem from a counterintelligence perspective, we *endorsed by default* the legal hemorrhaging of technology that benefits China more than the informal techniques we wrote about.

Accordingly, these final sections highlight some "normal" venues of AI technology transfer, beginning with Chinese investment abroad.

A landmark study by CSET analysts Kagan, Gelles, and Arnold found that China's stake in top U.S. AI startups *doubles* that of other foreign investors, that "Chinese investors are more likely to invest in U.S. AI startups than in other industries," and similarly that "U.S. AI startups are likely to have a greater number of Chinese investors than startups in other industries."[75] China's lopsided interest in U.S. AI technology is also evidenced in funding value, with 15 percent of (traceable) investment in top U.S. AI startups involving China, compared to 6 percent for non-AI startups.[76] The CSET study is complemented by other analysis that shows "around one-third" of Silicon Valley's AI startups having Chinese founders.[77]

Startups are not the only venue. China's top AI companies themselves are present in the tech corridor from Silicon Valley to Seattle. The list includes Alibaba, Baidu, iFlytek, JD, Tencent—and sundry other firms subsidized by China's state-backed ZGC Innovation Center (中关村硅谷创新中心) in Santa Clara.[78] Baidu's Silicon Valley AI Lab, to cite one famous example, was founded in 2013 by the former head of Google Brain.[79]

The United States is not the only target. Britain's Cambridge Science Park, home to 120 tech firms, is combed for investment opportunities by Chinese firms like Huawei and China's local scouting services.[80] A recent example is an "investment pitch session with Chinese investors" focused on AI and biotech:

> "To help connect Chinese investors with emerging and innovative Cambridge and UK-based businesses, Cambridge China Centre is curating an exclusive venture-capital pitch event with a carefully selected panel of Chinese investors in Cambridge."[81]

Interested U.K. companies are asked to sign a "letter of engagement." Elisabeth Braw, author of the *Foreign Policy* study, adds an important observation that casts doubt on our ability to gauge China's actual penetration of startup venture capital (VC):

> "But public investments by Chinese venture-capital groups in Western companies are only the visible tip of an iceberg. Chinese entities also invest in Western start-ups through Western firms, in which they participate as limited partners. Those limited partnerships allow the Chinese entities to get access to the technology in which they invest without having their names touted anywhere in the process... Because these firms are not obliged to disclose their limited partners, nobody knows how many Western start-ups have received Chinese venture-capital funding—much less what those start-ups are."[82]

Danhua Capital (now Digital Horizon Capital), a Silicon Valley VC firm that invests in AI startups, is backed by Beijing's Zhongguancun (ZGC) Development Group and is a standout example of indirect Chinese investment in foreign high-tech sectors.[83] Q Bay Center (钱塘中心) in San Jose, backed by China's Hangzhou city government, is another.[84] Oriza Ventures (Santa Clara) owned by the Suzhou municipal government and SAIC Capital (上汽创投, Menlo Park) owned by Shanghai's SAIC Motor with an interest in self-driving autos are two more. A Reuters article claimed that more than 20 such Silicon Valley VC firms have "close ties" with PRC state entities,[85] driving home Braw's point about the obscurity created through "funds of funds." Our earlier observation about shell organizations fronting extralegal transfers apparently applies to the open sector as well.[86]

This sketch of China's AI investment abroad is one part of the picture.[87] Another part is R&D done in China by AI multinationals. We documented the creation of AI labs in China by U.S.-based companies in earlier studies, noting the advantages for China and questioning how these corporate gains benefit the United States as a whole.[88] A subsequent study by CSET analysts on U.S. AI labs' global presence found China to be their second most popular location for overseas research, after Europe, and access to "talent" to be the prime driver.[89]

Examples are easy to find. Shanghai's "Zhangjiang AI Island" (张江人工智能岛) is host to more than 90 domestic and international companies[90] focused on AI, 5G, the Internet of things, cloud computing, blockchain, quantum computing, and virtual reality. Shanghai itself has more than 1,000 AI companies.[91] Among foreign multinationals, IBM was first to put roots there in 2019.[92] Microsoft's AI lab in Shanghai is its world's largest,[93] and reportedly has partnerships with 30 local enterprises.[94]

The same combination of AI, brain science, and quantum sciences is driving the expansion of Beijing's R&D establishment.[95] This is consistent with China's 14th Five-year Plan, which puts "new generation AI, quantum information, integrated circuits, and brain science/brain-inspired research" at the apex of its development priorities.[96] The municipality, ranked top "science city" in the world,[97] is building a "Beijing International S&T Innovation Hub" for "international talent, who can contribute to China's drive to become a global power in S&T development."[98] Google, IBM, Microsoft, and Intel are already there.

Intel, whose China portfolio includes AI, self-driving cars, 5G, and virtual reality,[99] formed an alliance in 2017 with Guiyang's government to develop an AI "innovation accelerator" (创新加速器). The provincial capital is a national big data zone[100]—a staple of machine learning and AI success. Other AI involvement by the chipmaker includes a partnership with Tik Tok owner Bytedance for a lab in Beijing,[101] and an "FPGA Innovation Center"—the world's largest—in Chongqing.[102] Field programmable gate arrays are key hardware in AI applications.

Meanwhile, Dell, the U.S. computer company, committed in 2015 to build "in China, for China" (在中国、为中国) an AI and advanced computing lab with CAS's Institute of Automation.[103] Research at the lab includes "cognitive function simulation" and brain-inspired information processing.[104] Market entry was the draw.[105]

The impact of multinationals on China's ability to do AI goes much deeper than the utility gained by joint development of marketable products. Rather, much of the resident talent sought by foreign companies was trained by these companies themselves. We noted earlier Microsoft Research Asia's outsized role in training a generation of skilled Chinese technical workers.[106] Let's look at IBM's contribution to the comparative advantage of America's workforce.

Big Blue's partnership with China began in 1984, with the donation of hard- and software to Chinese universities, and crystallized in a 1995 pact with China's MOE to enhance IT-related curricula development at over 60 Chinese universities to "nurture talent in China."[107] In 2014, the company committed to providing expertise in big data analysis to 100 Chinese universities.[108] In 2018, IBM was organizing sabbaticals at American universities for Chinese university software majors[109]; supporting a Chinese student innovation competition for "new generation information technology" in AI and blockchain[110]; sponsoring with MIIT and 11 leading Chinese universities an "AI and Cognitive Computing Education Working Committee"[111]; discussing "how to deepen the integration of production and education" with 40 Chinese institutes of higher education[112]; providing "84 high-quality online technical courses and 115 experimental case tutorials" to PRC universities on AI, quantum, cognitive and cloud computing, blockchain, etc.[113]; teaching AI and blockchain to "120 professors from 62 Chinese universities[114]; and reaffirming its commitment to "nurturing STEM talent in China."[115]

In 2019, IBM's efforts attained the following milestones:

> "In the whole year, more than a million students learned IBM-related technical courses through online and offline methods, 120 teachers received various training organized by IBM, and more than 80 IBM campus report lectures were organized. There were 20 student innovation experimental projects, and four campus competitions in which more than 30,000 students participated. A total of 640 graduates were recruited throughout the year, and the total investment in education was worth over 50 million yuan."[116]

Intel, for its part, committed in 2019 to training "10,000 FPGA professionals in China within three years."[117] The logic of multinational firms willingly— eagerly it seems—creating their own competition is mystifying. As citizens of a nation challenged by China's mercantilist practices, we struggle to see a positive link between domestic security and the actions of U.S. companies invested in China's access-for-technology model. If these reservations haunt us in the sphere of business, our anxieties are tested further in the academic arena.

The academic dimension

Examples of Sino-foreign academic cooperation in S&T fill volumes and we are hard-pressed to condense just those pertaining to AI into the remaining space. Here are a few cases to illustrate the forms these transactions can take.

1. *Training by "international" scientists.* Microsoft and IBM are not alone here. In April 2018, Peking University and China's MOE teamed with entrepreneur

Kai-Fu Lee and other world-class AI experts, including Cornell's John Hopcroft (deep learning) and Toronto's Geoffrey Hinton (neural networks), to launch an "International AI Training Program for Chinese Universities" (中国高校人工智能人才国际培养计划). Initial goals are 100 teachers and 300 students, projected to reach 500 and 5,000 in five years.[118]

2. *Multinational alliances.* In 2018, a "Global Artificial Intelligence Academic Alliance" was stood up, as it happened, in Shanghai to "streamline academic exchanges and collaboration." The usual Chinese players—MOST, MIIT, and CAS—met with "the world's most influential AI scientists and academics," including MIT's Eric Grimson (computer vision) and CMU's Raj Reddy (AI) and Tom Mitchell (machine learning),[119] to implement the "NGO's" vision of "academic communications and cooperation among world leading AI research institutes."[120]

3. *Bilateral associations.* These groups consist of scholars whose scientific or humanitarian interests "transcend" national politics. Examples include the Sino-French "AI Alliance" (AI 联盟) joined by Fields medalist Cedric Villani (Sorbonne)[121]; the "Brain and Intelligence Science Alliance" established in 2019 with Australia[122]; the "Sussex AI Institute" run with Zhejiang Gongshang University (浙江工商大学)[123]; and the "China-UK Research Centre for AI Ethics and Governance" (中英人工智能伦理与治理研究中心).[124]

4. *School-to-school partnerships.* Tsinghua University and the University of Washington in Seattle manage a "Global Innovation Exchange" focused on AI/ML and 5G products, with a $40 million grant from Microsoft.[125] China's National Defense University studies quantum information exchange with Cambridge University.[126] Wuhan University of Science and Technology offers MS degrees in AI with Vrije Universiteit Amsterdam.[127] Leiden and Xi'an Jiaotong Universities do joint research on AI and data science.[128] The list is endless.

5. *Foreign-based alumni groups.* The Tsinghua Alumni Academic Club of North America (北美清华教授协会, TAAC), an expatriate group of 500 graduates headed by USC's S. Joe Qin (秦泗钊), hosted an "Artificial Intelligence Everywhere" event in Seattle in 2018 to "discuss and popularize the latest research results in the field of AI," attended by experts and scholars from North America and China, including MIT, CMU, and Peking University.[129] TAAC has a long-term "strategic cooperation agreement" with Shenzhen's Tsinghua branch for tech transfer.[130]

6. *Academic forums.* In May 2018, experts from top universities participated in a "China-Canada Artificial Intelligence and Robot Research Cooperation Seminar" sponsored by China's MOST and the Ontario provincial government. Some 200 scholars represented 30 universities and institutes, including Shi Luping (施路平), director of Tsinghua's Center for Brain-inspired Computing Research,[131] leader of the Tsinghua group that invented China's first neuromorphic computing chip, and a leading advocate of artificial general intelligence (AGI).[132]

7. *Academic sponsorship of commercial ventures.* Yu Shui (余水), professor at Sydney's University of Technology, in 2019 set up a "China–Australia AI and Big Data Research Center" with China's Southeast Digital Economy Development Research Institute in Quzhou to supply the latter with "top international talent."[133] Meanwhile, an alliance of international scientists established a "Deutsche Forschungszentrum für Künstliche Intelligenz" (德国人工智能研究中心) in Shanghai "to facilitate the transformation and upgrading of the manufacturing industry."[134]

8. *Co-authorship of academic papers.* A 2019 MOST report proclaimed that "cooperation in AI research papers between China and the United States is the largest, and is the center of the global AI cooperation network."[135] A third of Australia's AI papers are co-authored by Chinese scholars.[136] Cooperation extends to ownership of the journals themselves, for example, the *Journal of Artificial Intelligence for Medical Sciences*, edited by Huang Zhisheng (黄智生) at Vrije Universiteit Amsterdam (computer science),[137] with offices in Beijing and Zhengzhou.

9. *"Using foreigners to draw in foreigners"* (以洋引洋). Dr. John Hopcroft, whose support for China's AI higher education is legendary, directed Shanghai Jiaotong University's computer science global recruitment committee and arranged tenureships for 11 "internationally renowned computer scientists."[138] University of Hamburg robotics and ML professor Zhang Jianwei (张建伟) chairs sundry China talent recruitment committees.[139] Foreign co-optees of China's "talent" programs upon reaching a certain level transition to recruiters themselves.[140]

10. *Chinese AI students abroad.* At present, some 97,000 Chinese students are studying AI-related disciplines at U.S. universities and still more at institutions outside China.[141] Host country retention rates vary depending on the level of degree obtained. The jury is out on the relative advantages to China and host nations: undoubtedly, China benefits directly and indirectly from transfers through this venue, just as host countries benefit from their expertise.

Academic cooperation across national boundaries is regarded by its practitioners as an absolute good, exemplified in the following statement by a Boston University physicist, whose lab has attracted some 75 Chinese scientists:

> "I'm not interested at all in politics. I'm a scientist. If a person anywhere in the world wants to come to my group, and they have the money to come, I say why not?"[142]

The pecuniary caveat is telling, as it removes idealism from the equation and puts the enterprise on the same moral footing as any other business transaction. The authors recognize the benefits of cooperation but at the same time counsel scrutiny and full disclosure[143] in the interest of AI safety and the security of sovereign nations, which at times conflict with personal gain.

However one feels about the matter, foreign technology transfers of all types account for much of China's AI power and must be part of any assessment of its overall strength.

Notes

1 Hannas, Mulvenon, Puglisi, *Chinese Industrial Espionage*, 2013. Hannas and Chang, "China's STI Operations," January 2021.
2 Hannas and Chang, "China's Access to Foreign AI Technology," September 2019; Hannas and Chang, "China's Artificial Intelligence," in Hannas and Tatlow, eds., 2021.
3 Robert Littell, *The Company*, New York: The Overlook Press, p. 242. Angleton was the CIA's counterintelligence chief from 1954 to 1975.
4 Chinese: 不平等条约, i.e. treaties forced on China during the 19th and early 20th centuries resulting in loss of national sovereignty.
5 Kai-Fu Lee, *AI Superpowers*, Boston: Houghton Mifflin Harcourt, 2018.
6 Joseph Needham, *The Grand Titration: Science and Society in East and West*, London: George Allen & Unwin, 1969.
7 Christopher Klein, "The Spies Who Launched America's Industrial Revolution," January 10, 2019, https://www.history.com/news/industrial-revolution-spies-europe.
8 "Committee of 100 Releases White Paper Analyzing Economic Espionage Act Cases," May 26, 2017, https://www.committee100.org/press_release/committee-of-100-releases-white-paper-analyzing-economic-espionage-act-cases/.
9 Acts and venues not scrutinized by sanctioning authorities, whose legality is therefore unknown.
10 Attributed to former NSA Director Keith Alexander, https://www.zdnet.com/article/nsa-cybercrime-is-the-greatest-transfer-of-wealth-in-history/.
11 Hannas, Mulvenon, Puglisi, 2013.
12 Hajime Nakamura, *Ways of Thinking of Eastern Peoples: India, China, Tibet, Japan*, Honolulu: University of Hawaii Press, 1964, pp. 189–190.
13 Exemplified in the "dynastic cycle" (朝代循环).
14 Mark Elvin, *The Pattern of the Chinese Past*, Stanford University Press, Redwood City, California,1973.
15 Disparaged as "small skills" (小技).
16 William C. Hannas, *The Writing on the Wall*, Philadelphia: University of Pennsylvania Press, 2003.
17 Richard E. Nisbett, The *Geography of Thought: How Asians and Westerners Think Differently … and Why*, New York: The Free Press, 2003.
18 Leonard Schlain, *The Alphabet Versus the Goddess*, New York, Penguin Putnam, 1999.
19 Joan Y. Chiao and Katherine D. Blizinsky, "Culture-Gene Coevolution of Individualism-Collectivism and the Serotonin Transporter Gene (5-HTTLPR)," *Proceedings of the Royal Society B: Biological Sciences* 277, no. 1681, 2010, 529–537.
20 Chinese: 以夷治夷, "using barbarians to control barbarians."
21 Chinese: 中学为体, 西学为用, "Chinese learning as substance, Western learning for application" attributed to Zhang Zhidong (张之洞, 1837–1909).
22 A more complete typology can be found in Hannas and Chang, September 2019, pp. 4–5.
23 Hannas and Tatlow, eds., 2021, especially pp. 9–11.
24 Ibid., p. 10.
25 Formerly independent but now part of MOST.
26 Now a subordinate division of the Communist Party of China's United Front Work Department.
27 Formerly China's Ministry of Personnel.

28 CAS's status as an appendage of the PRC government was confirmed by a senior staff member in a letter to the editor of *Nature* magazine on October 20, 2019, www.nature.com/articles/d41586-019-03205-z.

29 Matthew Brazil and Peter Mattis, *Chinese Communist Espionage: an Intelligence Primer*, Naval Institute Press, Annapolis, Maryland, 2019.

30 CAST's formal affiliation with the PRC government is demonstrated in Hannas, Mulvenon, Puglisi, 2013, p. 97.

31 Hannas and Chang, "Chinese Technology Transfer—Introduction," in Hannas and Tatlow, eds., 2021, pp. 11–12.

32 Alex Joske and Jeffrey Stoff, "The United Front and Technology Transfer," in Ibid., pp. 258–274; Ryan Fedasiuk, "Putting Money in the Party's Mouth: How China Mobilizes Funding for United Front Work," *The Jamestown Foundation*, September 16, 2020.

33 Formerly the "China Association for the International Exchange of Personnel" (CAIEP).

34 Formally the Recruitment Program for Global Experts (海外高层次人才引进计划), begun in 2008 and later reconstituted as the High-end Foreign Expert Recruitment Program (高端外国专家引进计划) with eight divisions each aimed at different demographics.

35 Zeng Jianxun (曾建勋), "基于国家科技管理平台的科技情报事业发展思考 (Reflections on the Development of the Scientific and Technical Information Industry Based on the National Science and Technology Management Platform)," 情报学报 (*Journal of the China Society for Scientific and Technical Information*), 2019: 38 (3), 227–238.

36 Miao Qihao, "Technological and Industrial Intelligence in China: Development, Transition and Perspectives," John E. Prescott and Patrick T. Gibbons, eds., *Global Perspectives on Competitive Intelligence*, Alexandria, VA: Society of Competitive Intelligence Professionals, 1993, pp. 49–53.

37 Chen Jiugeng, "Actual Strength of S&T Information Service System in China," *China Information Review*, 2006: 10, 17–22.

38 Hannas and Chang, January 2021.

39 Huo Zhongwen (霍忠文) and Wang Zongxiao (王宗孝), 国防科技情报源及获取技术 (*Sources and Methods of Obtaining National Defense Science and Technology Intelligence*), Beijing: Kexue Jishu Wenxuan Publishing Company, 1991; 中国科学技术信息研究所 (ISTIC), 甲子辉煌—中国科学技术信息研究所成立60周年纪念 (*60 Years of Glory—The 60th Anniversary of the Founding of the Institute of Science and Technical Information of China*), Beijing, 2016.

40 Hannas, Mulvenon and Puglisi, 2013; Ryan Fedasiuk and Emily Weinstein, July 2020.

41 Fedasiuk and Weinstein, July 2020. Jeffrey Stoff, whose team studied the problem for the USG, argues that the actual figures are significantly higher (personal communication).

42 Ibid.

43 Hannas, Mulvenon, Puglisi, 2013, p. 176.

44 Ibid.

45 Internal USG whitepaper by the authors, 2017.

46 Ryan Fedasiuk, Georgetown University, unpublished CSET research.

47 Hannas and Tatlow, eds., 2021.

48 James Mulvenon, "Economic Espionage and Trade Secret Theft Cases in the U.S.," in Hannas and Tatlow, eds., 2021. Dr. Mulvenon compiled a 16-page closely typed chronology of Chinese technology theft cases dating from 2004 to 2019, omitted from the 2021 book for lack of space.

49 Parts of this section reference two of the authors' previous studies: Hannas and Chang, September 2019 and "China's Artificial Intelligence," in Hannas and Tatlow, eds., 2021.

50 国务院关于积极推进"互联网+"行动的指导意见, State Council 40, 2015.

51 "互联网+"人工智能三年行动实施方案的通知, NDRC 1078, MOST, MIIT, and CAC, 2016.

52 国务院关于印发"十三五"国家科技创新规划的通知. State Council 43, 2016.

53 国务院关于印发"十三五"国家战略性新兴产业发展规划的通知, State Council 67, 2016.

54 国务院关于印发新一代人工智能发展规划的通知, State Council 35, 2017.

55 Hannas and Chang, "China's Artificial Intelligence," in Hannas and Tatlow, eds., 2021, p. 189.

56 "促进新一代人工智能产业发展三年行动计划" (Three-year Action Plan to Promote the Development of New-Generation AI Industry), MIIT 315, 2017. Section 4, "Accelerate the cultivation of talent."

57 高等学校人工智能创新行动计划 (AI Innovation Action Plan for Institutes of Higher Education), MOE 3, 2018. See Andrew Spear, "Serving the Motherland while Working Overseas," in Hannas and Tatlow, eds., 2021, pp 31–32, for a description of Program 111.

58 科技部关于发布科技创新2030—"新一代人工智能"重大项目2018年度项目申报指南的通知 (Project Application Guidelines for S&T Innovation 2030-'New Generation Artificial Intelligence' 2018 Major Projects), MOST 208, 2018.

59 "China's Five-year Plan Focuses on Scientific Self-reliance," *Nature*, https://www.nature.com/articles/d41586-021-00638-3.

60 中华人民共和国国民经济和社会发展第十四个五年规划和2035年远景目标纲要, March 2021.

61 In fairness, these provisions sound a lot like CSET's own recommendations to attract and retain foreign "talent."

62 Ibid.

63 A parallel search on SAFEA's front organization, the China International Talent Exchange Foundation, returned 10,500 hits.

64 关于"双一流"建设高校促进学科融合,加快人工智能领域研究生培养的若干意见, MOE 4, NDRC, MOF, 2020.

65 Ibid.

66 http://english.ia.cas.cn/ic/introduction/.

67 https://app.mokahr.com/campus_apply/ia/2005#/. Several of the other talent programs on CAS's website recruit from both domestic and foreign pools, but details on origin are not provided.

68 Hannas and Chang, "China's Artificial Intelligence," in Hannas and Tatlow, eds., 2021, p. 193.

69 https://chinatalenttracker.cset.tech/.

70 Also called the "Spring Lights Program."

71 The count did not include hundreds of provincial and municipal programs.

72 Hannas and Chang, op. cit., 2021, pp. 194–195.

73 Ibid., p. 195.

74 Hannas, Mulvenon, Puglisi, 2013.

75 Rebecca Kagan, Rebecca Gelles, Zachary Arnold, "From China to San Francisco: The Location of Investors in Top U.S. AI Startups, CSET, February 2021.

76 Ibid.

77 Yizhou Gu and Linyan Feng, "The Vanguard in AI: Top 20 Startups in Silicon Valley," *Equal Ocean*, March 2, 2020.

78 Hannas and Chang, "China's Artificial Intelligence," in Hannas and Tatlow, eds., 2021, p. 196.

79 Daniel Alderman and Jonathan Ray, "Best Frenemies Forever: Artificial Intelligence, Emerging Technologies, and China-US Strategic Competition," Institute on Global Conflict and Cooperation, UC San Diego, 2017.

80 Elisabeth Braw, "How China Is Buying Up the West's High-Tech Sector," *Foreign Policy*, December 3, 2020.

81 https://www.cambridgechinacentre.org/events/investment-pitch-session-with-chinese-investors/.

82 Braw, op. cit.

83 United States Trade Representative, "Update Concerning China's Acts, Policies and Practices Related to Technology Transfer, Intellectual Property, and Innovation," November 20, 2018, pp. 46–49.

84 https://ori.hangzhou.com.cn/ornews/content/2019-12/15/content_7642239.htm.
85 "China's Penetration of Silicon Valley Creates Risks for Startups," *Reuters*, June 29, 2018.
86 The point is reinforced in a DNI/NCSC report "Foreign Economic Espionage in Cyberspace," 2018.
87 We have omitted for brevity an entire category of foreign-based AI transfers done through the so-called "startup competitions." See the authors' "China's Artificial Intelligence," in Hannas and Tatlow, eds., 2021, pp. 197–198.
88 Ibid., pp. 198–199. Also, Hannas and Chang, September 2019, pp. 13–14.
89 Roxanne Heston and Remco Zwetsloot, December 2020.
90 https://news.stcn.com/news/202011/t20201103_2501584.html.
91 http://www.chinadaily.com.cn/cndy/2019-07/04/content_37487859.htm.
92 https://www.yicaiglobal.com/news/shanghai-zhangjiang-ai-island-greets-ibm-as-its-first-resident.
93 https://pandaily.com/microsoft-china-sets-up-worlds-largest-ai-and-iot-lab-in-shanghai/.
94 http://english.pudong.gov.cn/2019-07/24/c_390311.htm.
95 http://global.chinadaily.com.cn/a/202101/26/WS600f54dea31024ad0baa4fc0.html.
96 http://www.xinhuanet.com/2021-03/13/c_1127205564_3.htm.
97 https://www.nature.com/articles/d41586-020-02577-x.
98 https://www.scmp.com/news/china/science/article/3118559/chinese-capital-beijing-sets-sights-building-trillion-yuan-hi.
99 https://www.yicaiglobal.com/news/intel-aims-to-cooperate-with-china-technology-enterprises-in-eight-fields-including-ai-robotics.
100 https://newsroom.intel.cn/news-releases/press-release-2017-aug-30/#gs.z6prma.
101 https://pandaily.com/intel-and-bytedance-join-hands-to-build-an-ai-lab/.
102 https://itpeernetwork.intel.com/intel-fpga-china-innovation-center/.
103 http://it.people.com.cn/n1/2016/0309/c1009-28183002.html.
104 http://www.ia.cas.cn/xwzx/ttxw/201511/t20151105_4454694.html.
105 https://global.chinadaily.com.cn/a/201911/15/WS5dcdfe3fa310cf3e355777f5.html.
106 Hannas and Chang, "China's Artificial Intelligence," in Hannas and Tatlow, eds., 2021, pp. 198–199.
107 https://www-03.ibm.com/press/us/en/pressrelease/44342.wss.
108 Ibid.
109 https://www-31.ibm.com/ibm/cn/university/aboutus/index.html.
110 Ibid.
111 https://www-31.ibm.com/ibm/cn/university/news/20180114.html.
112 https://www-31.ibm.com/ibm/cn/university/aboutus/index.html.
113 Ibid.
114 Ibid.
115 Ibid.
116 Ibid.
117 https://www.leiphone.com/category/chips/PEAhEit997dV56Mj.html.
118 http://pkunews.pku.edu.cn/xwzh/2018-04/04/content_301782.htm.
119 http://news.sciencenet.cn/htmlnews/2019/8/430040.shtm.
120 https://thegaiaa.org/web/#/.
121 http://www.amb-chine.fr/chn/zfjl/t1526081.htm.
122 https://istbi.fudan.edu.cn/lnen/info/1047/1888.htm.
123 http://www.sussex.ac.uk/broadcast/read/51875.
124 http://www.ia.cas.cn/xwzx/jryw/201911/t20191111_5428553.html.
125 https://www.geekwire.com/2018/microsoft-funded-u-s-china-tech-institute-gix-graduates-first-class-reveals-student-projects/.
126 http://www.chisa.edu.cn/rmtnews1/subject/201970zn/70znzdcj/201904/t20190412_224341.html.
127 http://www.huaue.com/zwhz2020/202031495508.htm.

128 https://www.universiteitleiden.nl/en/news/2017/11/a-rapidly-developing-international-friendship.
129 https://smart.huanqiu.com/article/9CaKrnK92uN.
130 https://www.sohu.com/a/237230440_688725.
131 https://news.tsinghua.edu.cn/info/1086/40918.htm.
132 *Tencent Net* (腾讯网), October 31, 2019, https://new.qq.com/omn/20191104/2019 1104A0BD9U00.html.
133 http://www.sohu.com/a/319292493_99977225.
134 https://finance.sina.com.cn/roll/2019-04-18/doc-ihvhiqax3660218.shtml.
135 http://www.xinhuanet.com/tech/2019-05/24/c_1124539084.htm.
136 https://www.australiachinarelations.org/content/cross-border-neural-networks-australia-china-collaboration-artificial-intelligence-research.
137 https://www.atlantis-press.com/journals/jaims/editorial-board.
138 http://www.sjtupmm.com/article-5406.html.
139 http://gsia.eu/?page_id=210. Professor Zhang was elected to the German National Academy of Engineering in October 2021, https://en.acatech.de/person/jianwei-zhang-universitat-hamburg/.
140 Jeffrey Stoff, personal communication, 2020.
141 Estimating the number of "AI" students is nearly impossible owing to its confluence with other disciplines. The 97,000 figures derive from totaling AI-relevant disciplines at all degree levels in Table 1 of Jacob Feldgoise and Remco Zwetsloot, "Estimating the Number of Chinese STEM Students in the United States," Georgetown University, Center for Security and Emerging Technology, October 2020.
142 Kate O'Keeffe and Aruna Viswanatha, "Chinese Military Turns to U.S. University to Conduct Covert Research," *Wall Street Journal*, February 23, 2020.
143 In Senator Patty Murray's words, "Successful collaboration requires trust, and trust requires transparency." https://www.aamc.org/advocacy-policy/washington-highlights/senate-help-committee-holds-hearing-foreign-influence-biomedical-research.

Bibliography

Braw, Elisabeth, "How China Is Buying Up the West's High-Tech Sector," *Foreign Policy*, December 3, 2020.

Fedasiuk, Ryan and Emily Weinstein, "Overseas Professionals and Technology Transfer to China," Georgetown University, CSET, July 2020.

Hannas, William C. and Huey-Meei Chang, "China's Access to Foreign AI Technology," Georgetown University, CSET, September 2019.

Hannas, William C. and Huey-Meei Chang, "China's STI Operations," Georgetown University, CSET, January 2021.

Hannas, William C. and Didi Kirsten Tatlow, eds., *China's Quest for Foreign Technology*, London and New York: Routledge, 2021.

Hannas, William C., James Mulvenon and Anna B. Puglisi, *Chinese Industrial Espionage*, London and New York: Routledge, 2013.

Heston, Roxanne and Remco Zwetsloot, "Mapping U.S. Multinationals' Global AI R&D Activity," Georgetown University, CSET, December 2020.

Kagan, Rebecca, Rebecca Gelles, Zachary Arnold, "From China to San Francisco: The Location of Investors in Top U.S. AI Startups, Georgetown University, CSET, February 2021.

PRC Ministry of Education, National Development Reform Commission, and Ministry of Finance, 关于"双一流"建设高校促进学科融合,加快人工智能领域研究生培养的若干意见 (Certain Opinions on Promoting Curricula Merging at 'Double First-Class' Institutes of Higher Education and on Accelerating the Cultivation of Graduate Students in the AI Field), MOE 4, 2020.

PRC National Development and Reform Commission, Ministry of Science and Technology, Ministry of Industry and Information Technology, and the Cyberspace Administration of China, 关于印发"互联网+"人工智能三年行动实施方案的通知. (Three-year Action Implementation Plan for 'Internet +' Artificial Intelligence), NDRC 1078, 2016.

PRC National People's Congress and Chinese People's Political Consultative Conference, 中华人民共和国国民经济和社会发展第十四个五年规划和2035年远景目标纲要 (The 14th Five-year Plan for the National Economic and Social Development of the People's Republic of China and Outline of Long-term Goals for 2035), March 11, 2021.

PRC State Council, "国务院关于积极推进'互联网+'行动的指导意见 (State Council Guiding Opinions on Positively Promoting 'Internet +' Action)," SC 40, 2015.

PRC State Council, "国务院关于印发'十三五'国家科技创新规划的通知 (State Council Notification on National Science and Technology Innovation Programs for the 13th Five-year Plan)," SC 43, 2016.

PRC State Council, "国务院关于印发'十三五'国家战略性新兴产业发展规划的通知 (Notification on National Strategic Emerging Industry Development Projects for the 13th Five-year Plan)," SC 67, 2016.

PRC State Council, "国务院关于印发新一代人工智能发展规划的通知 (The New Generation AI Development Plan)," SC 35, 2017.

Stoff, Jeffrey and Glenn Tiffert, "Eyes Wide Open: Ethical Risks in Research Collaboration with China," Hoover Institution, November 2021.

United States Trade Representative, "Update Concerning China's Acts, Policies and Practices Related to Technology Transfer, Intellectual Property, and Innovation," November 20, 2018.

PART II
China and the world

4

China's quest for AI talent

Emily Weinstein and Jeffrey Stoff

In 2016, Xi Jinping declared that the global "competition for comprehensive national strength is essentially a competition for talent."[1] Although not the first leader to call on the importance of talent for China's success, since his ascension to power in 2012, Xi has placed an even stronger emphasis on cultivating talent, particularly in emerging technology fields like AI, biotechnology, quantum computing, and more. These efforts have been twofold: on the one hand, ministries and offices across the Chinese Party-state have worked to reform primary, secondary, and higher education to equip the younger generation with the technical skills for the AI-era. On the other hand, China seeks to address long-standing concerns over a "brain drain" to the United States, Europe, and elsewhere, as these nations have the infrastructure, competitive advantage, resources, and notoriety to attract Chinese talent not only to go abroad to study, but also to stay for years afterward and postpone a return to China.

This chapter provides an overview of Chinese policies and reforms aimed at addressing both sides of the AI talent picture. It begins with an assessment of domestic AI training, followed by an analysis of gaps and outstanding issues. We then examine China's attempts to attract foreign talent, including members of the Chinese diaspora and non-ethnic Chinese experts abroad. The quest for AI talent is pursued globally and will be a focus of U.S.-China competition well into the future.

Training domestic talent

The Chinese education system—from primary through higher education—is centralized under the Ministry of Education (MOE). The MOE is responsible for setting the national curriculum, establishing standard syllabi for required subjects, evaluating and approving teaching materials, and supervising provincial and subordinate education departments, among other responsibilities.[2] More

DOI: 10.4324/9781003212980-6

recently, the MOE has ceded some responsibility to provincial and municipal counterparts, who are tasked to develop local curricula based on national guidelines and subject to the MOE's approval.[3] This context is important for understanding AI-specific education initiatives.

Overarching policies and plans

China has prioritized the modernization of domestic education at all levels since the 1990s, although some reforms began as early as the 1980s following Deng Xiaoping's "Reform and Opening Period" in 1978.[4] A more programmatic emphasis on talent came around the turn of the century, when Chinese leadership decided to move the country away from a dependence on cheap labor-based exports toward a "knowledge-based economy."[5] Within this new economic model, China has stressed the need to remedy high-skill labor shortages, particularly in emerging industries like AI, which are crucial to China's economic and social development goals.

Some of these policies and programs seek reform at the institutional level, such as the 211 and 985 Programs (211工程 and 985工程). Launched in 1993 by MOE, the 211 Program aimed to improve the global standing of Chinese universities by the early 21st century by focusing on the quality of education, scientific research, and management at a select 112 Chinese universities.[6] It also identified some 800 disciplines important to China's development.[7] Five years later, the 985 Program selected a subset of 39 universities slated to become "world-class leading universities."[8] In January 2017, MOE merged the 211 and 985 Programs into a "Double First-Class" (双一流) system[9] aimed at boosting China's elite universities to world-class status by 2050, and elevating the attention given to key disciplines, including AI, at the undergraduate level particularly.[10]

AI education looms large in China's 2017 "New Generation AI Development Plan" (新一代人工智能发展规划; hereafter "2017 AI Plan") on the premise that widespread use of AI in education, among other sectors, will greatly enhance the quality of public services and people's lives. Talent "cultivation" (培养), accordingly, is a primary focus of the plan to be achieved by improving AI education and introducing foreign AI talent to China.[11]

Domestically, the plan points out the need to strengthen professional and technical training in AI research at the basic, applied, and operations/maintenance levels. It encourages home enterprises and research institutions to support and develop additional AI talent. Pointers are given on how to build an AI academic discipline by establishing AI majors, AI institutes, conduits for training, and more. In April 2018, MOE followed up with an "Education Informatization 2.0 Action Plan" (教育信息化2.0行动计划) on modernizing education and "starting the new journey of education in the intelligent era."[12] That is, AI is seen not only as an object of learning but also as a tool to assist learning, for example, in improving adult education building "intelligent" educational aids, and using big data to create intelligent online learning platforms.

Primary and secondary education

The Chinese government is incorporating AI into primary and secondary education. At the highest levels, the 2017 edition of the MOE's "General High School Curriculum Plans and Standards for Chinese and Other Subject Curricula"[13] revised its national education requirements to include AI, Internet of Things (IoT), and big data processing.[14] This revision requires high school students to study AI in a compulsory IT course. At a more granular level, the program calls for building skills in data encoding; collecting, analyzing, and visualizing data; and learning a programming language—most often Python—to design simple algorithms.[15] In the fall of 2020, Beijing municipality organized two groups of elementary and middle school teachers (100 totally) to participate in the "National Evaluation of Artificial Intelligence Literacy Levels for Preschool Children and Adolescents" (全国幼儿及青少年人工智能素养等级测评). Over the next 3–5 years, the country will create some 100 experimental AI education schools and train a thousand or more so-called AI "seed teachers" (种子教师).[16]

Similar efforts are taking place globally, as countries look for ways to promote AI in the K-12 classroom. In 2018, the Japanese government announced its intention to develop a "Global and Innovation Gateway for All" (GIGA) School Program, to ensure that the country's nearly 13 million primary and secondary school students have high-speed internet, and that educators have the skills to teach students how to master digital tools and online learning.[17] The GIGA Program was born out of Japan's push toward a post-information "Society 5.0," which incorporates cyberspace, AI, big data, and the IoT. Although the program will not be fully implemented until 2024, some parts of Japan are already using AI-infused lessons.[18]

Higher education

China has bolstered AI course offerings and curricula at the undergraduate, graduate, and postgraduate levels. The MOE's "Innovative Action Plan for Artificial Intelligence in Higher Education Institutions" released in April 2018 aims at improving innovation, talent training, and international cooperation in AI.[19] The plan treats colleges and universities as the foundation of talent cultivation, S&T productivity, and basic research, thereby driving innovation in China. Here is the timeline[20]:

- By 2020: "The optimized layout of the university scientific and technological innovation and disciplinary system…will be basically completed… and the advantages of talent training and scientific research will be further enhanced."[21]
- By 2025: "Colleges and universities will have significantly improved their scientific and technological innovation capabilities and the quality of their talent training in new generation AI, achieving a number of original results

with international significance. Some theoretical research, innovative technologies, and applications will reach the world's leading level...."
- By 2030: "Colleges and universities will become the core forces in building
the world's major artificial intelligence innovation centers, as well as the
talent highlands leading the development of new generation AI...."

The plan also articulates specific steps that higher education institutions should take
to improve their AI capabilities. Notably, one of these is the construction of AI technology innovation bases designed to promote a collaborative interaction between
universities, research institutions, and enterprises.[22] Other measures include:

- promoting education in "AI+" composite fields, such as "new engineering"
(新工科),[23]
- establishing some 50 AI colleges and (cross-discipline) research institutes by
2020, and
- incorporating AI education at all levels, beginning in primary school.

As part of its "Double First-Class" program, the Chinese government released
"Certain Opinions on Promoting Curricula Merging at 'Double First-Class'
Institutes of Higher Education and on Accelerating the Cultivation of Graduate
Students in the AI Field" (hereinafter referred to as the 2020 Opinions on
AI Talent Cultivation) in January 2020.[24] Issued with the AI Plan in mind, this
document aims to improve the methods by which basic AI research and talent are
applied to S&T achievements in key industrial sectors. It lays out specific appli-
cations for AI in industrial innovation, social governance, and national security.
It also encourages collaboration between industry and academia wherein leading
AI companies provide both experimental and practical opportunities to train
university instructors in the latest developments.

Importantly, 2020 Opinions on AI Talent Cultivation stipulates that training experts in AI basic theory (基础理论), an area where China is relatively
weak, be given equal weight (并重) with training focused on practical "hybrid"
AI disciplines. The document referred specifically to machine learning, computer vision, pattern recognition, natural language processing, intelligent chips,
and systems, as areas where fundamental advances are needed.[25]

MOE is working to standardize an AI major across China's higher education system. In March 2019, it approved 35 colleges and universities to offer a four-year AI
major under the engineering degree category, including at four of the "Seven Sons
of National Defense" (国防七子) universities.[26] As of March 2021, 345 universities
had been approved to offer an AI major.[27] In both 2020 and 2021, the AI major
was the most popular new addition to university curricula, closely followed by
intelligent manufacturing and engineering, data science, and big data technology.[28]

China is also establishing AI institutes at several universities across the country, most of which preceded MOE's establishment of the AI major. By 2018,
some 34 institutions had AI institutes training both undergraduate and graduate

students. These AI institutes are more heterogeneous in their research foci, which range from natural language processing, medical imaging, unmanned systems, robotics, and more.[29] Some are established at universities in conjunction with well-known Chinese AI firms like Tencent and iFlytek. For example, the Zhejiang Lab (之江实验室) is run jointly by Alibaba, Zhejiang University, and the Zhejiang provincial government.[30]

Vocational training

China is also improving AI vocational training, which, according to the 2017 AI Plan, is a key piece of strengthening China's AI labor force.[31] This includes teaching more AI-relevant courses and skills and using AI to improve teaching methods. For example, the Hunan Automotive Engineering Institute launched a "smart campus system" in January 2019 to improve teaching process using AI.[32] The system collects relevant data during courses and utilizes AI to analyze and evaluate the teaching process to assist teachers in their professional development. In other instances, Chinese AI firms like SenseTime offer AI-related vocational training courses ranging from AI Foundations, Machine Learning, and Deep Learning, to Python Programming and other specific skills. SenseTime also offers training in autonomous driving, intelligent manufacturing, and more.[33] According to MOE statistics, as of early 2021, some 558 vocational colleges (高职院校) were approved by the ministry to host majors in either AI technology services (服务) or applications (应用).[34]

Outstanding issues

China's ability to cultivate AI talent faces several obstacles, in curriculum implementation especially. Children find the new AI-oriented curriculum difficult where background knowledge is needed to understand deep learning algorithms. There is also a lack of systematic and authoritative guidance on textbook development, little professional training for teachers, and a shortage of equipment in school AI labs in the K-12 AI system.[35] Moreover, China's 2015 census data shows that only 3 of 10 individuals in China's labor force attended high school, meaning that, according to Dr. Scott Rozelle, in China's 800 million-strong labor force, at least 500 million—mostly from rural communities—barely made it through junior high.[36] This will make the proliferation of AI education and technical literacy even more difficult.

At the higher education level, the difficulties are more complex. Since the mid-2000s, China has consistently produced more STEM PhDs than the United States and this trend is projected to continue, with China graduating more than 77,000 STEM PhDs per year compared to some 40,000 in the United States.[37] Similar trends exist at the undergraduate level. China has also been a top producer of science and engineering bachelor's degrees, with the number of graduates increasing from 359,000 in 2000, to 1.65 million in 2014.[38]

While enviable in one sense, China's economy is ill-prepared to absorb so many new graduates. In 2019, the government began articulating measures to assist recent graduates find work.[39] The COVID-19 pandemic has only worsened their prospects, with the unemployment rate for those 16–24 years of age at 16.2 percent as of July 2021.[40] These figures apply to college graduates in general. By contrast, for AI talent, China's Ministry of Industry and Information Technology in 2020 put domestic demand at 678,900 persons by 2022. This is 480,000 fewer than what China is expected to produce, meaning "the supply of talent from AI colleges will not meet the needs of Chinese industry."[41] Another official study the same year projected a shortage of "more than 5 million AI experts,"[42] a ten-fold difference, which may reflect different interpretations of what constitutes "AI."

Finally, China's acute lack of "talent" in basic sciences—in AI and scientific disciplines generally—is a well-known problem acknowledged in ministry pronouncements (see above), by China's top AI scientists (see this book's Chapter 7), and by AI pundits such as Kai-Fu Lee.[43]

Attracting international talent

China's efforts to attract international AI talent fall into three categories. China endeavors to attract ethnic Chinese talent, including non-returnees or members of the diaspora who have never been in China. These duties are relegated to party organs such as the United Front Work Department, the Organization Department, and sundry other offices, which work in tandem to recruit talent.[44] China also "draws in" (引进) foreign talent—of *any* ethnicity—to work in various capacities for varying durations. Finally, there are measures to use the "talent" who prefer to remain abroad but can be depended on to provide China needed skills while they "work in place" (就地工作).

Countries supplying expertise are often unaware at a regulatory level of the extent to which this sharing takes place. The preceding chapter provides an overview of the venues through which knowledge transfer is accomplished in general and the interested reader is invited to explore the literature.[45] The present chapter approaches talent acquisition in a stricter sense: cultivation and importation of the experts themselves. China achieves this in part through "talent programs"—state-sponsored recruitment run at national, provincial, municipal, and institutional levels,[46] the best known being Thousand Talents Plan (千人计划) and Changjiang Scholars (长江学者), although they may number some 300.[47] These programs function within a matrix of state-sponsored initiatives, some synergistic, some competing and duplicative.

Program 111 projects

The Program of Introducing Innovative Talents of Disciplines to Universities (高等学校学科创新引智计划), commonly known as Program 111 (111计划), was established in 2006 to create "foreign intellect recruitment innovation bases"

(创新引智基地), typically at universities. The bases are required to hire at least ten foreign experts, including an accomplished "academic master" (学术大师), who spends at least one month per year in China, and nine other tenured foreign experts there for varying durations.[48] The foreign-based teams are supported by domestic researchers who imbibe the expertise.[49] The following are typical examples.

- China's Northwestern Polytechnical University (西北工业大学) houses a Program 111 base that researches unmanned aerial vehicle (UAV) intelligent sensing technology, multi-source intelligent information processing technology, and swarm intelligence sensing and control—areas where AI has an outsized role. Staffing the "base" are experts who are residents in the United States, the U.K., Australia, Singapore, and Hong Kong and work with domestic PRC researchers, many of whom are selectees of other talent programs.[50] The university itself is one of China's "Seven Sons of National Defense" whose mission is to support China's defense industries.[51]
- Xidian University (西安电子科技大学) also houses a Program 111 base related to AI research, named the "National 111 Project Intelligent Information Processing Innovation and Intelligence Introduction Base" (国家 111 计划智能信息处理创新引智基地).[52] Xidian has extensive ties to the PLA and defense industries and is jointly administered by MOE, the State Administration for Science, Technology and Industry for National Defense, and the state-owned defense conglomerate China Electronics Technology Group Corporation.

Start-up contests

China sponsors several dozen start-up competitions that incentivize individuals (usually from overseas) to relocate or found new companies in China. Many hold initial contest rounds overseas to select finalists backed by PRC diplomatic missions and co-opted diaspora groups.[53] Final rounds are conducted in China and winners can expect low-cost financing, capital investment, free space in S&T parks, and other state-provided amenities. Here are a few examples.

- The Thousand Talents Program launched its own global start-up competition in 2012, rebadged in 2019 as the "Jinji Lake Start-Up Contest" (金鸡湖创业大赛), where its organizers—state-owned investment conglomerate Oriza Holdings and its affiliated Thousand Talents Venture Capital Center—are located as of October 2019; the contest had raised four billion RMB for finalists' projects.[54] The contest has a dedicated AI subcomponent known as the "Jinji Lake Start-up Competition AI Industry Finals" (金鸡湖创业大赛人工智能行业决赛). Winning projects included autonomous driving, intelligent security, augmented reality, and smart voice solutions.[55]
- The Chinese Association for Artificial Intelligence (中国人工智能学会) has had its own start-up contest since 2019, known as the "China 'AI+'

Innovation and Entrepreneurship Contest" (中国"AI+"创新创业大赛) with multiple tracks such as 5G, NLP, intelligent driving, and semi-supervised learning.[56] Each track appears to have its own co-organizers and supporting entities. For instance, the intelligent driving track is run by the Hangzhou municipal government with support from the Chinese Academy of Sciences (CAS) Institute of Automation, CAS Institute of Computing, and Tsinghua, Peking, Zhejiang, Beihang, and Beijing Post and Communications universities.[57]

AI talent recruited into PRC academia

China aggressively recruits AI talent from abroad to work at research institutions in the PRC. A non-exhaustive review of faculty pages and websites of PRC academic institutions doing AI research reveals many of their staff to be talent program selectees. Table 4.1 shows an illustrative sampling; all were trained overseas and recruited into institutions with significant defense R&D programs. An exhaustive account of all such selectees is beyond this chapter's scope.

TABLE 4.1 Some talent program selectees at PRC research institutions

Institution	AI expert	Talent program affiliation
CAS/ICT Key Laboratory of Intelligent Information Processing	Chen X.	CAS Hundred Talents Program
CAS Institute of Automation National Laboratory of Pattern Recognition	Wang L., Yang G.	CAS Hundred Talents Program
CAS Institute of Information Engineering	Cao X.	CAS 100 Talents; MOE New Century Outstanding Talent Support Program (新世纪优秀人才支持计划)
Wuhan University Computer Vision and Remote Sensing Laboratory	Yao J.	Hubei Province Chutian Scholar Specially-Appointed Professor (湖北省"楚天学者"特聘教授)
Nanjing University of Aeronautics and Astronautics	Wang J.	Jiangsu Province Double Innovation Program (双创计划)
Tianjin University School of Artificial Intelligence	Yu Q.	Tianjin Municipal High-level Overseas Experts Program (天津市海外高层次人才项目)
Harbin Institute of Technology Institute for Artificial Intelligence	Gao H., Jiang L., Liu H.	Changjiang Scholars Award Program
Xidian University School of Artificial Intelligence	Shi G.	Changjiang Scholars Award Program
Xidian University School of Artificial Intelligence	Li X.	Shaanxi Provincial Hundred Talents Program (陕西省"百人计划")

AI talent and Chinese AI firms

China's talent programs have also recruited individuals willing to commercialize their knowhow after receiving education and/or training overseas (see Box 4.1). For instance, entrepreneurial candidates applying to the flagship Thousand Talents Program require documentation of their intellectual property (such as patents they worked on or applied for) or knowhow they seek to further develop in China. The examples below are talent program selectees who obtained PhD degrees from U.S. universities—some of whom also worked at major technology firms—and subsequently founded AI companies in China. The following companies, including SenseTime, CloudWalk, Yitu, and DeepGlint, have been added to the Department of Commerce Entity List for their association with human rights abuses in China.

- Tang Xiao'ou (汤晓鸥) was recruited through the Thousand Talents Program after receiving a PhD from MIT. Tang co-founded SenseTime (商汤科技),[58] which develops computer vision solutions for facial recognition and remote sensing applications.
- Ke Yan (柯严) has a PhD degree from CMU, spent eight years at Microsoft, and was recruited through Shanghai's Thousand Talents Program. Ke is the founder and CTO of Clobotics (扩博智能技术), a computer vision and drone data analytics firm.[59]
- Zhou Xi (周曦) received a PhD from University of Illinois Urbana and is a CAS Hundred Talents Program selectee. Zhou founded CloudWalk (云从信息科技),[60] a PRC surveillance technology firm.
- Leo Zhu (aka Zhu Long, 朱珑) is a UCLA PhD and MIT postdoc, and Thousand Talents Program selectee.[61] Zhu founded Yitu Network Technology Co., Ltd. (依图网络科), a developer of facial recognition technologies.
- Zhao Yong (赵勇) has a PhD from Brown, worked at Google, and was recruited by the Thousand Talents Program.[62] Zhao is the co-founder of DeepGlint Technology Ltd. (格灵深瞳信息技术), a developer of computer vision systems for police and public security.

Ongoing challenges

China's investments in higher education have not eliminated the gap with foreign institutions in reputation and delivery. China's AI development policies continue to emphasize the need to tap foreign talent to address its deficiencies in expertise and will likely remain a priority as China's appetite for AI experts continues to grow.

A related challenge is attracting foreign talent to relocate to China to conduct research. A January 2021 survey of more than 500 international researchers found that only 10 percent of the respondents not currently in China assigned

BOX 4.1

HOW CHINA'S TALENT PROGRAMS SUBVERT U.S. AI TECH—THE CASE OF CHEN NING

Chen Ning (陈宁), a specialist in signal and video processing, received a PhD from Georgia Tech in 2012 and was the technology director of ZTE Corporation's U.S. operations. He returned to China through the Thousand Talents Program in 2014[63] and was subsequently selected by two other talent programs.[64]

This support enabled Chen to co-found Shenzhen-based Intellifusion (云天励飞), which produces AI software, neural network processing chips, and big data analytics solutions. The company partners with surveillance camera developers Hikvision and Dahua, sells its services to public security bureaus throughout China,[65] and provides facial recognition technology for AI-enhanced policework.[66]

Chen helped found the Tianjin University-Georgia Tech Shenzhen Institute (天津大学佐治亚理工深圳学院),[67] and employs its graduates at his firm.[68] The institute is slated to aid in recruiting new talent to Shenzhen under its Peacock Program (孔雀计划).[69]

Chen has served in leadership positions in PRC bodies that facilitate talent recruitment and technology transfer, including the State Administration of Foreign Experts Affairs, Western Returned Scholars Association (Overseas-educated Scholars Association of China) ((欧美同学会)中国留学人员联谊会),[70] Guangdong Overseas Chinese Innovation and Entrepreneurship Promotion Association (广东省华人华侨创新创业促进会), the Shenzhen High-level Talent Association (深圳市高层次人才联谊会),[71] and Shenzhen's Chinese People's Political Consultative Committee.[72]

more than a one-in-four probability they will move there within the next three years. Of those willing to migrate to China, most respondents were less concerned about visa or immigration issues and more wary of a mix of professional, cultural, and political stumbling blocks.[73] This may help explain China's increased efforts—particularly over the last decade—to modify or create new programs and incentives to recruit AI and other STEM talent to assist China without them having to relocate to China.

Conclusion

China is aware of the importance of developing its AI talent across the spectrum. As Chinese leadership has made efforts to incorporate AI into all aspects of life in China, so too has it set in place mechanisms to bolster its AI talent base to handle these changes, ranging from its youngest citizens to foreign AI experts.

Central policies like the 2017 AI Plan have set the stage for large-scale initiatives. Internally, the plan promotes the incorporation of AI into education at all levels. Looking outward, it puts heavy emphasis on recruiting foreign talent to bolster China's AI workforce. Additional AI-specific guidelines, like MOE's "Innovative Action Plan for Artificial Intelligence in Higher Education Institutions," work to complement the 2017 plan at a more granular level. Other long-standing policies create the foundation for China to improve its AI education and talent pipeline, such as the "Double First-Class Universities" program, which provides funding and incentives to modernize China's university system.

Chinese leaders have also hatched ambitious plans to attract (non-ethnic Chinese) "foreign nationals" (外籍) and members of the diaspora community to China. State-sponsored talent plans and start-up contests have grown at an unprecedented scale over the past decade, although a lack of scholarship on their scope and activities overseas makes it impossible empirically to measure the success of China's global talent recruitment efforts. Compounding this problem is the fact that these programs are well integrated into all aspects of China's technology acquisition apparatus, making efforts to isolate and measure them difficult.

Recently, Beijing has ramped up supervision of AI firms in China, ranging from hard-hitters like Alibaba and Didi, to smaller, lesser-known players in China's educational technology, or EdTech industry. A series of sweeping regulations beginning in late summer 2021 had catastrophic immediate outcomes for leading EdTech firms like New Oriental Education and Technology Group (新东方企业) and TAL Education Group (好未来), whose stocks have fallen 86 percent and 93 percent, respectively, as of September 2021.[74] Both entities have played a significant role in the development and funding of AI education across China.[75]

Policy ambitions do not necessarily equal outcomes. China's publicized aims for AI education await their realization. Finally, China's talent recruitment programs, now under global scrutiny, may need to adjust to keep pace with a rapidly changing technological ecosystem.

Notes

1 "综合国力的竞争说到底是人才的竞争." "习近平就深化人才发展体制机制改革作出重要指示强调" (Xi Jinping Made Important Instructions to Deepen the Reform of the Talent Development System and Mechanism), *Xinhua News*, May 6, 2016.
2 Center on International Education Benchmarking, "Shanghai-China: Governance and Accountability," *National Center on Education and the Economy*, https://ncee.org/what-we-do/center-on-international-education-benchmarking/top-performing-countries/shanghai-china/shanghai-china-system-and-school-organization.
3 Dahlia Peterson, Kayla Goode, and Diana Gelhaus, "AI Education in China and the United States: A Comparative Assessment," Georgetown University, Center for Security and Emerging Technology, September 2021.
4 Remco Zwetsloot, "China's Approach to Tech Talent Competition: Policies, Results, and the Developing Global Response," *Global China*, Brookings Institution, April 2020.

5 Ibid.

6 http://www.moe.gov.cn/jyb_hygq/hygq_zczx/moe_1346/moe_1366/201911/t20191128_409940.html.

7 PRC Ministry of Education, "211工程" 简介 (Introduction to the 211 Program), https://perma.cc/95RF-6HK5.

8 PRC Ministry of Education, "985工程" 简介, (Introduction to the 985 Program), https://perma.cc/Q2K4-VTKU.

9 For more information on the 211 and 985 Programs, see Denis Fred Simon and Cong Cao, *China's Emerging Technological Edge: Assessing the Role of High-End Talent*, Cambridge University Press, 2009.

10 Peterson, Goode, and Gelhaus, 2021.

11 PRC State Council, "国务院关于印发新一代人工智能发展规划的通知" (Notice of the State Council on Issuing the New Generation Artificial Intelligence Plan), 2017.

12 Yan Shouxuan (闫守轩) and Yang Yun (杨运), "Education Informatization 2.0 in China: Motivation, Framework, and Vision," *ECNU Review of Education* Volume 4, issue 2, 2021, pp 410–428.

13 PRC MOE, "教育部关于印发普通高中课程方案和语文等学科课程标准 (2017年版2020年修订)的通知," MOE 3, 2020.

14 引力波和人工智能写入高中课标 (Gravitational Waves and Artificial Intelligence Are Written into High School Curriculum Standards), *S&T Daily* (科技日报), January 1, 2018.

15 Peterson, Goode, and Gelhaus, 2021; 人工智能进入全国高中新课标, 2018秋季学期执行 (Artificial Intelligence Enters the New National High School Curriculum Standard, Implemented in 2018 Fall Semester), Sohu.com, January 23, 2018; Zou Shuo, "AI Now Most Favored Major at Universities," *China Daily*, March 3, 2021.

16 PRC MOE, 支撑青少年人工智能素养提升: 北京建百所人工智能教育实验校 (Support Young People's AI Literacy Improvement: Beijing Builds Hundreds of Artificial Intelligence Education Experimental Schools), November 10, 2020.

17 U.S. Department of Commerce, "Japan Educational Technology Opportunities," June 15, 2020.

18 "Japan's GIGA School Program Equips Students for Digital Society," *The Japan Times*, March 22, 2021.

19 PRC MOE, 教育部关于印发高等学校人工智能创新行动计划的通知(MOE Notification on Issuing the 'Innovative Action Plan for Artificial Intelligence in Higher Education Institutions'), MOE 3, 2018.

20 Ibid.

21 There is little evidence to show whether China achieved this 2020 goal. The COVID-19 pandemic likely delayed the timeline.

22 MOE 3, 2018.

23 Ibid. Examples provided in the Action Plan include computing, control, mathematics, statistics, physics, biology, psychology, sociology, and law.

24 Ministry of Education, National Development and Reform Commission, and Ministry of Finance, 关于"双一流"建设高校促进学科融合, 加快人工智能领域研究生培养的若干意见, MOE 4, 2020.

25 Ibid.

26 PRC MOE, 教育部关于公布2018年度普通高等学校本科专业备案和审批结果的通知 (MOE Announces Filing and Approval Results for Undergraduate Majors at Higher Education Institutions in 2018), MOE 7, 2019; Li Shifei (李帅飞), "全面出击! 我国180家高校新增 AI 本科专业, 研究生扩招也瞄准 AI" (Full Frontal Attack! 180 Chinese Colleges and Universities Add AI Undergraduate Majors, Graduate Enrollment Also Targets AI), *Leiphone* (雷锋网), March 4, 2020.

27 https://www.163.com/dy/article/GFR1ANG8053668T6.html.

28 MOE 7, 2019; 人工智能进入全国高中新课标, 2018秋季学期执行 (Artificial Intelligence Enters the New National High School Curriculum Standard, Implemented in 2018 Fall Semester), *Sohu.com*, April 24, 2018; Zou Shuo, 2021.

29 Peterson, Goode, and Gelhaus, 2021.

30 "Laboratory introduction (实验室简介), Zhejiang Lab," https://perma.cc/7K3B-2C9U. The lab's Chinese name (之江) is a historical allusion; the lab's (outward-facing) pinyin spelling is for modern "Zhejiang" and does not match the characters.

31 PRC State Council, New Generation AI Plan, 2017.

32 "人工智能催生职业教育新生态" (Artificial Intelligence Spawns a New Ecology of Vocational Education), *Xinhua News,* January 20, 2021.

33 "AI 职业教育" (AI Vocational Education), SenseTime, https://perma.cc/4DRR-4TBD.

34 https://www.163.com/dy/article/G9QGSJJS0532N2UB.html.

35 Peterson, Goode, and Gelhaus, "AI Education in China and the United States: A Comparative Assessment."

36 Heather Rahimi, Scott Rozelle, and Natalie Hell, "A Conversation with Scott Rozelle & Natalie Hell on their New Book, *Invisible China*," Stanford University, October 6, 2020.

37 Remco Zwetsloot et al., "China Is Fast Outpacing U.S. STEM PhD Growth," Georgetown University, Center for Security and Emerging Technology, August 2021.

38 "Rapid Rise of China's STEM Workforce Charted by National Science Board Report," American Institute of Physics, January 31, 2018.

39 "The Growing Ranks of Unemployed Graduates Worry China's Government," *The Economist*, August 3, 2019.

40 "China's Youth Unemployment Spikes as Students Graduate," *Bloomberg News*, August 16, 2021.

41 PRC Ministry of Industry and Information Technology, "人工智能领域人才需求预测报告" (Report on Forecast Demand for Talent in the AI Field), December 2020.

42 "我国人工智能人才目前缺口超过500万." PRC Ministry of Human Resources and Social Security, "新职业——人工智能工程技术人员就业景气现状分析报告" (New Occupation Analysis Report on the Employment Situation of AI Engineering the Technical Personnel), April 30, 2020.

43 https://www.voachinese.com/a/kai-fu-lee-on-ai-development-2018116/4662278.html.

44 Anne-Marie Brady, "Magic Weapons: China's Political Influence Activities under Xi Jinping," Wilson Center, September 18, 2017; Alex Joske and Jeffrey Stoff, "The United Front and Technology Transfer," in Hannas and Tatlow, eds., *China's Quest for Foreign Technology: Beyond Espionage*, London: Routledge, 2021.

45 The IP Commission Report, *The Theft of American Intellectual Property: Reassessments of the Challenge and United States Policy*, February 2019; William C. Hannas, James Mulvenon, and Anna B. Puglisi, *Chinese Industrial Espionage*, London and New York: Routledge, 2013; Michael Brown and Pavneet Singh, "China's Technology Transfer Strategy," Washington, DC: Defense Innovation Unit Experimental, February 2017; Office of the United States Trade Representative, "Section 301 Report into China's Acts, Policies, and Practices Related to Technology Transfer, Intellectual Property, and Innovation," March 27, 2018; U.S.-China Economic and Security Review Commission, "2019 Annual Report to Congress," November 2019; Hannas and Chang, "China's Access to Foreign AI Technology—an Assessment," Georgetown University, Center for Security and Emerging Technology, September 2019; Hannas and Tatlow, eds., *China's Quest for Foreign Technology: Beyond Espionage*, Routledge, 2020; Anastasya Lloyd-Damnjanovic and Alexander Bowe, "Overseas Chinese Students and Scholars in China's Drive for Innovation," U.S.-China Economic and Security Review Commission, October 7, 2020; and Jeffrey Stoff and Glenn Tiffert, "Eyes Wide Open: Ethical Risks in Research Collaboration with China," Hoover Institution, November 2021.

46 Jeffrey Stoff, "China's Talent Programs," in Hannas and Tatlow, eds., 2021.

47 Alex Joske, "Hunting the Phoenix: The Chinese Communist Party's Global Search for Technology and Talent," Australian Strategic Policy Institute, August 2020.

48 PRC Ministry of Education, 高等学校学科创新引智基地管理办法 (Administrative Measures for Bases for the Recruitment of Innovative Intellects in Academic Disciplines to Universities), MOE 4, 2006.

49 For more details on Program 111, see Andrew Spear, "Serve the Motherland While Working Overseas," *Beyond Espionage: China's Quest for Foreign Technology*, in Hannas and Tatlow, eds., New York: Routledge, 2021.

50 "高等学校学科创新引智计划:无人航行实时智能感知与计算技术创新引智基地" (Program of Introducing Talents of Disciplines to Universities: Foreign Intellect Recruitment Innovation Base for Instantly Intelligent Sensing and Computing Technology with Unmanned Navigation), Northwestern Polytechnical University, https://guoji.NPU.edu.cn/987654.pdf.

51 For a detailed discussion of China's "Seven Sons of National Defense" universities and the implications associated with U.S. collaboration with these schools, see Chapter 1 of Tiffert et al., *Global Engagement: Rethinking Risk in the Research Enterprise*, Hoover Institution, August 2020.

52 "人工智能学院组织机构介绍" (Introduction to the School of Artificial Intelligence Organizational Structure), Xidian University School of Artificial Intelligence, https://sai.xidian.edu.cn/xygk/zzjg.htm.

53 See Andrew Spear, "Serve the Motherland While Working Overseas" and Alex Joske and Jeffrey Stoff, "The United Front and Technology Transfer," in Hannas and Tatlow, eds., *China's Quest for Foreign Technology Beyond Espionage*, 2021.

54 www.zhitouwang.com/news/detail/70966.html.

55 http://1000.sandlake.com/dasaidongtai/newsStatus/2019-09-29/413.html.

56 "The Third Annual China AI+ Innovation and Entrepreneurship Contest (第三届中国 "AI+"创新创业大赛)," https://2021aichina.caai.cn/.

57 "赛道6专业赛:智能驾驶技术创新与应用大赛" (Track 6 Professional Competition: Intelligent Driving Technology Innovation and Applications Contest), https://2021aichina.caai.cn/track?id=1.

58 "汤晓鸥: 人脸识别的 '探路者' (Tang Xiao'ou: Facial Recognition 'Pathfinder')," *Communist Youth Daily* (中国青年报联), April 25, 2017, http://zqb.cyol.com/html/2017-04/25/nw.D110000zgqnb_20170425_1-03.htm.

59 "上海扩博智能技术有限公司 (Clobotics)," 新财网 (*Xincai Net*), September 26, 2021, http://www.xincainet.com/index.php/news/view?id=267975.

60 "云从人工智能视觉图像创新研发中心正式落户南沙" (Cloud AI Visual Images Innovation R&D Center Officially Settles is Nansha), http://www.china-nsftz.com/show.php?id=553.

61 喜报! 6人入选第十四批国家 "千人计划" 创业人才! (Good News! 6 People Selected into the 14th National Thousand Talents Entrepreneurs!)," http://1000.sandlake.com/dasaidongtai/2018-02-10/285.html.

62 "第十三批 "千人计划" 入选人员公示, 637人榜上有名 (The 13th Round 'Thousand Talents Plan' Selectees Announced, 637 People on the List)," https://news.pharmacodia.com/web/informationMobileController/getMobileNewInformationById?id=8a2d98375bec92cc015bf5e0efa80234.

63 "千人专家" 陈宁:胸怀中国"芯" 智享全世界" ('Thousand Talents Expert' Chen Ning: With China's 'Core' in Your Heart, We Can Enjoy the World with Wisdom), 神州学人, September 12, 2017, http://www.chisa.edu.cn/rmtnews1/chuangye/201709/t20170912_2765690.html.

64 "深圳三大人才新政打出创新创业组合拳" (Shenzhen's Three Major Talent Policies Play a Combination of Innovation and Entrepreneurship), 广东职工教育网 (Guangdong Employee Education Network), May 12, 2016, http://webcache.googleusercontent.com/search?q=cache:HmhWIZuRs7IJ:www.gdzgjy.com/%3Fs%3Dnews%26c%3Dshow%26id%3D9173+&cd=2&hl=en&ct=clnk&gl=us.

65 "Client in Partnership," https://web.archive.org/web/20180925172709/http://www.intellif.com/cases.

66 "云天励飞与中国人民公安大学侦查与反恐怖学院签署战略合作协议" (Intellifusion and the Peoples' Public Security University of China School of Investigation and Anti-Terrorism Sign Strategic Cooperation Agreement), Intellifusion Inc., October 25, 2018.

67 "天津大学佐治亚理工深圳学院第一届联合管理委员会第一次会议召开" (Tianjin University–Georgia Tech Shenzhen Institute – First Annual Unified Administration Committee's First Meeting Convenes), July 20, 2018.

68 "GT又出牛校友 – 陈宁，田第鸿让机器'看懂'世界" (GT Produces Another Alumni – Chen Ning, Tian Dihong Making Machines See the World), August 30, 2016.

69 "佐治亚理工学院加入深圳虚拟大学园" (Georgia Tech Joins the Shenzhen Virtual University Park), Shenzhen Virtual University Park, April 12, 2013.

70 http://www.chinaqw.com/qx/2020/01-06/242141.shtml.

71 https://www.scimall.org.cn/article/detail?id=303647.

72 "陈宁：建设人工智能基础系统生态，加速数字经济发展" (Chen Ning: Establish a Fundamental System Ecology for AI, Accelerate the Development of the Digital Economy), Shenzhen People's Political Consultative Conference, May 25, 2021.

73 Remco Zwetsloot et al., "The Immigration Preferences of Top AI Researchers: New Survey Evidence," Perry World House and the Future of Humanity Institute, January 2021.

74 Elliott Zaagman, "The Casualties of China's Education Crackdown," *TechCrunch*, September 22, 2021.

75 Xu Wei, "China's New Oriental Unveils AI-Related Education Initiatives," *YiCai Global*, October 31, 2018; and Georgina Lee, "TAL Education Uses Artificial Intelligence to Improve Online Tutoring As It Eyes New Markets," *South China Morning Post*, April 10, 2018.

Bibliography

Cao, Cong, "China's Brain Drain at the High End: Why Government Policies Have Failed to Attract First-rate Academics to Return," *Asian Population Studies*, November 2008.

Hannas, William C. and Didi Kirsten Tatlow, *Beyond Espionage: China's Quest for Foreign Technology*, New York: Routledge, 2020.

Hannas, William C., James Mulvenon, and Anna B. Puglisi, *Chinese Industrial Espionage: Technology Acquisition and Military Modernization*, New York: Routledge, 2013.

Joske, Alex, "Hunting the Phoenix: The Chinese Communist Party's Global Search for Technology and Talent," Australian Strategic Policy Institute, August 2020.

Leysdesdorff, Loet, Caroline S. Wagner, and Lin Zhang, "Are University Rankings Statistically Significant? A Comparison among Chinese Universities and with the USA," November 2017.

Ngok, Kinglun, "Chinese Education Policy in the Context of Decentralization and Marketization: Evolution and Impacts," *Asia Pacific Education Review* 8. 1, 2007, pp. 142–157.

Peterson, Dahlia, Kayla Goode, and Diana Gelhaus, "AI Education in China and the United States: A Comparative Assessment," Georgetown University, Center for Security and Emerging Technology, September 2021.

PRC Ministry of Education, National Development Reform Commission, and Ministry of Finance, 关于"双一流"建设高校促进学科融合，加快人工智能领域研究生培养的若干意见 (Certain Opinions on Promoting Curricula Merging at 'Double First-Class' Institutes of Higher Education and on Accelerating the Cultivation of Graduate Students in the AI Field), MOE 4, 2020.

PRC Ministry of Education, 支撑青少年人工智能素养提升: 北京建百所人工智能教育实验校 (Support Young People's AI Literacy Improvement: Beijing Builds Hundreds of Artificial Intelligence Education Experimental Schools), November 10, 2020.

PRC Ministry of Education, 教育部关于公布2018年度普通高等学校本科专业备案和审批结果的通知, (MOE Announces Filing and Approval Results for Undergraduate Majors at Higher Education Institutions in 2018), Ministry of Education, MOE 7, 2019.

PRC Ministry of Education, 教育部关于印发高等学校人工智能创新行动计划的通知 (MOE Notification on Issuing the 'Innovative Action Plan for Artificial Intelligence in Higher Education Institutions'), MOE 3, 2018.

PRC State Council. 国务院关于印发新一代人工智能发展规划的通知 (The New Generation AI Development Plan) SC 35, 2017.

Simon, Denis Fred and Cong Cao, *China's Emerging Technological Edge: Assessing the Role of High-End Talent*, UK: Cambridge University Press, 2009.

Spear, Andrew, "Serve the Motherland while Working Overseas," *Beyond Espionage: China's Quest for Foreign Technology*, eds., William C. Hannas and Didi Kirsten Tatlow, London and New York: Routledge, 2021.

Stoff, Jeffrey, "China's Talent Programs," *China's Quest for Foreign Technology: Beyond Espionage*, eds., William C. Hannas and Didi Kirsten Tatlow, London and New York: Routledge, 2021.

Stoff, Jeffrey and Glenn Tiffert, "Eyes Wide Open: Ethical Risks in Research Collaboration with China," Hoover Institution, November 2021.

Weinstein, Emily, "Chinese Talent Program Tracker," Georgetown University, Center for Security and Emerging Technology, November 2020.

Zwetsloot, Remco, "China's Approach to Tech Talent Competition: Policies, Results, and the Development Global Response," Brookings Institution, April 2020.

Zwetsloot, Remco, Baobao Zhang, Markus Anderljung, Michael C. Horowitz, Allan Dafoe, "The Immigration Preferences of Top AI Researchers: New Survey Evidence," Perry World House and the Future of Humanity Institute, January 2021.

Zwetsloot, Remco, Jack Corrigan, Emily Weinstein, Dahlia Peterson, Diana Gelhaus, and Ryan Fedasiuk, "China is Fast Outpacing U.S. STEM PhD Growth," Georgetown University, Center for Security and Emerging Technology, August 2021.

5

Academic literature

Quantitative and qualitative analyses

Daniel H. Chou and Ashwin Acharya

While Chapter 4 describes China's talent base, this chapter examines China's academic research, offering a complementary measure of China's strengths in artificial intelligence (AI). Academic publications serve as an indicator of a country's ability to use its talent, and as a pool of R&D knowledge that can lead to industrial applications. Accordingly, analyzing a nation's published scientific output provides a window into its present and future competitiveness, along with precious details on the nature of its research. This holds for all scientific disciplines but for AI especially, which has many characteristics of a general-purpose technology—one for which fundamental insights can lead to progress in many economic sectors.

AI has evolved over the years. Its latest incarnation is driven by methods for training artificial neural networks, including deep learning and reinforcement learning. Between 2010 and 2020, these new techniques achieved results far surpassing previous achievements for computer vision, autonomous navigation, and natural language processing. Over this same period, AI publications also rose rapidly, and China became a prolific source of AI research, leading the United States in overall publication count. At the same time, China improved the quality of its published research, as evidenced in highly cited papers and participation in top conferences.

The chapter begins with an overview of the bibliometric approach to Chinese document analysis followed by a high-level summary of its findings. Evidence is adduced from citation analysis to support an assessment that China has become a top AI publisher. We then look inward at China's AI infrastructure on the basis of what these publications provide, and at China's AI research hubs and collaboration networks. A final analytic section examines bibliometrics' ability to predict concrete outcomes.[1]

DOI: 10.4324/9781003212980-7

Bibliometric analysis of Chinese publications

AI research has grown quickly over the past decade, fueled by successes in machine learning (ML) and deep neural networks—a class of algorithms with applications in areas from computer vision to tactical decision-making to protein structure prediction. These developments aroused the interest of PRC research funders, academics, and state-run labs, reflected in a rapid rise in Chinese AI-related publications and conference attendance.[2] The upshot is that China today is competitive with the United States along various metrics of AI research.

Given the PRC's large and growing R&D budget,[3,4] and China's domestic[5] and international[6] talent pools, this rapid expansion in high-quality AI output is unsurprising. Although the data on which we base this assessment may be inflated by self-citation, the general trend of significant and increasing Chinese research strength holds when we consider different metrics and subsets of AI. Top Chinese publications are regularly cited by foreign papers and are common at Western AI conferences, indicating a growing body of Chinese AI research recognized as high-quality internationally.

In terms of raw numbers, prior estimates typically understate China's scholarly output, because they reference databases like Microsoft Academic and Web of Science, which do not capture all Chinese-language literature. Our analysis, which includes publications from the Chinese National Knowledge Infrastructure (CNKI, 中国知网), a major aggregator of Chinese scientific journals, finds that *most Chinese research on AI is published in Chinese*. These indigenous publications receive less interest and recognition from foreign researchers,[7] but they offer a sound indication of Chinese researchers' capabilities and of their funders' resources and interests.

Bibliometrics provide data about the scale and growth of important inputs to Chinese AI development as well: namely, R&D funding and its technical talent pool. The topics of research reflected in these tallies also suggest areas that interest China's state-run funding organizations, where downstream applications are likely to emerge. These areas include especially the broad AI subcategory of computer vision and its applied subfields such as remote sensing. They also include other topics of concern to the security state, where Chinese research has been particularly fruitful and intense. Focusing on publication counts and citations exclusively can distort an overall evaluation of AI competence by obscuring China's strengths in these prioritized areas.[8]

Bibliometric data has other limitations—it reflects material published and indexed by databases only. Our use of CNKI captures Chinese research unavailable in English, but more sensitive government research, as well as proprietary research at private institutions, may not be formally published anywhere. In addition, Chinese bibliometric data are prone to citation and count inflation, although we find China internationally competitive when we select for truly impactful papers, according to citation count.

There are also barriers between research ideas and deploying complete, reliable systems. AI has been described as a general-purpose technology; these technologies have transformative potential, but can take decades to yield widespread economic growth. Compared to other leading nations, China's AI research—to date—has been focused on incremental improvements that may yield better specialized AI systems in the near future, but Chinese researchers may undervalue efforts to make complex, independent AI systems viable in the longer term.

China as a top AI publisher

Mindful of these caveats, here follow salient takeaways from our and other bibliometric analyses of published Chinese AI research:

China publishes a large and growing share of the world's research in artificial intelligence, a fast-growing emerging technology area which the PRC has prioritized

AI is an emerging technology area of high importance—recognized by the Chinese government in the 2017 New Generation AI Development Plan.[9] While "AI research" can be operationalized in many ways, studies in the last few years have consistently found that China publishes at least as much AI research as the United States, and that its share of world AI research is growing. Moreover, these studies find that China is increasingly competitive with the United States not just in publication count, but in research impact.[10] These findings contradict the once-common perception that Chinese researchers are capable of copying others' innovations, but not of producing their own high-quality results.

China publishes as much highly cited AI research as the United States, and its share of such research is growing over time

A common metric of high-quality research is citation count, adjusted for publication year—as more recent papers have had less time to accrue citations, they are compared against other papers of similar age. A usual approach is simply to rank papers in a given research area and year of publication by their citation counts. Analysts then compare countries' output, e.g. the top 1% most highly cited AI papers published in a given year. Reports using these metrics have found that China's share of highly cited research is increasingly comparable to that of the United States.

For example, a 2019 study by the Allen Institute for Artificial Intelligence found that "China overtook the U.S. in the [total] number of AI research papers in 2006," and since 2010 has been increasingly competitive in highly cited papers.[11] By 2018, China was already closing in on the United States, which contributed 28% of the top 10% most highly cited AI papers, compared to 26.5% for China. The report predicted based on the two countries' shares of highly cited papers in 2013–2018 that China would soon overtake the United States: "If we fit a line to the trends of the last 5 years, we can see that China and the U.S. are set to converge in early 2020 for papers in the top 10% and in 2025 for papers in the top 1%."[12]

More recent analyses note similar trends and provide insight into China's areas of strength within AI.[13] A 2020 study by Georgetown University's Center for Security and Emerging Technology (CSET) focused on the top 1% of publications by citation count, both in AI overall and in three AI subfields: computer vision, natural language processing, and robotics.[14] It found that China led in computer vision, achieved parity with the United States in robotics, but lagged in natural language processing. Stanford's Institute for Human-Centered Artificial Intelligence's (HAI) AI Index 2021 likewise found that China had exceeded the United States in AI publications, and had overtaken it in journal citations in 2020, although the United States kept its lead in both number and citation rate of AI conference papers.[15]

China publishes a significant share of the research in top AI conferences, and its highly cited research is discussed internationally

To what extent do these data reflect genuine *quality*, as opposed to manipulation of citation metrics? That is, do Chinese authors perform well in highly regarded AI research venues? The "CSrankings.org" website, a practitioner-created analysis of institutional publications in top computer science venues, lists 13 conferences *and no journals* in its list of top AI venues, which suggests that this is the place to measure quality. Do the HAI conference ratings reflect China's inability to compete with the United States in these more highly regarded AI venues?[16]

Decidedly not. A recent analysis of the CSET Merged Corpus[17] found that Chinese researchers do perform well in top AI conferences. From 2015 to 2019, China's share of publications in the top 13 conferences rose from 16% to 30%, while the U.S. share was roughly constant at 50%.[18,19] CSRankings' analysis of institutions that contribute to top AI conferences also finds China becoming prominent: three PRC and six U.S. institutions were top contributors from 2011 to 2015; from 2016 to 2020, the figures were four Chinese and five U.S. institutions.[20]

Figure 5.1 illustrates the trend of increasing Chinese contributions to AI publications in the CSET Merged Corpus.[21] We see that China's share of overall AI research far outpaces the United States, and has for more than a decade. By contrast, China only recently caught up to the United States in highly cited publications, and still lags the United States in top-venue publications. In all areas, however, China's share of world AI research is growing steadily, while the U.S. share is stagnant.

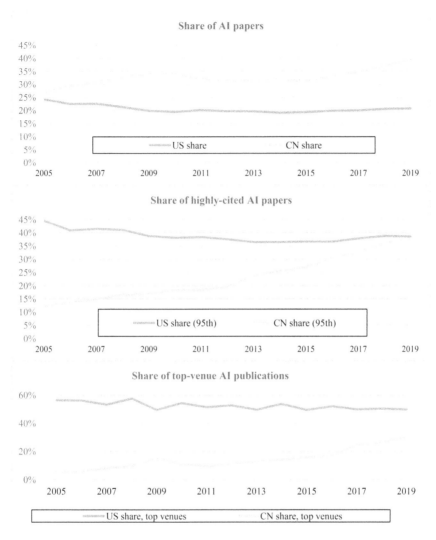

FIGURE 5.1   Chinese and U.S. shares of AI publications

Source: Acharya and Dunn, "Comparing U.S. and Chinese Contributions to High-Impact AI Research."

The evidence from citation analysis

Citations from international publications provide another way to estimate quality: do Chinese researchers attract the interest of foreign practitioners? Here, we find mixed results: highly cited Chinese publications receive a consistent share of their citations from non-Chinese publications, but this share is notably lower than for U.S. publications. In 2019, top Chinese AI publications (those in the top 5% of their field by citation count) received 38% of their citations from papers

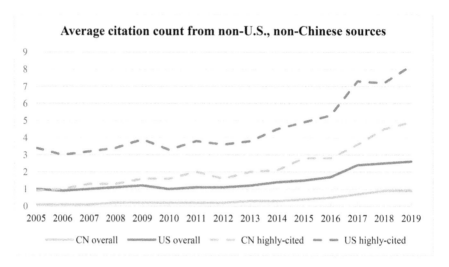

FIGURE 5.2   Third-party citations of Chinese and U.S. AI publications in their first year after publication

Source: Acharya and Dunn, "Comparing U.S. and Chinese Contributions to High-Impact AI Research."

without Chinese authors; the corresponding number for U.S. publications was 58%.[22] This suggests that China's growing output of highly cited research receives consistent international interest, but less than the U.S. output. Comparing U.S. and Chinese citations from third-country papers, the Chinese publications also received fewer citations than U.S. publications in their first year after being published. However, the number of international citations received by new AI publications in both countries is rapidly growing, as shown in Figure 5.2.

Multiple factors account for this disparity. A mix of researcher and funder interests may lead to much of the Chinese research being focused on areas of less interest to foreign scientists. U.S. publications are also more likely to be international collaborations, and their authors may be better connected with colleagues in other high-producing AI countries. Language barriers and differences in terminology may prevent foreign scientists from finding or appreciating relevant Chinese research. Although quantitative analysis does not distinguish the causes of this gap in Chinese and U.S. papers' ability to attract third-country attention, it almost certainly is due in part to the United States' greater degree of integration into the global research community.

China's increasing competitiveness in AI reflects its position as a significant producer of high-quality scientific research in general

The trends we observe in AI research mirror China's high-impact contributions to science, technology, engineering, and mathematics (STEM) overall, where it has risen to become a close competitor to the United States. An analysis by *Nature* found that China's rate of publication in 82 top science journals grew from 56% to 69% of the U.S. rate from 2017 to 2020.[23] China's growing international competitiveness is particularly notable in more applied research and development, a traditional focus of its S&T efforts—and a theme emphasized throughout this volume. A Nikkei-Elsevier study on highly cited publications found that China led the world in 23 of 30 emerging STEM areas with immediate technical applications.[24] China's rise as an STEM publisher has also been rapid, with its output growing far more over the past five years than that of other leading countries.[25]

Understanding China's AI infrastructure through academic publications

In this section, we zero in on what China's academic publications[26] tell us about Chinese AI research in a concrete sense: its topics, institutes, and sponsorship.

AI-related research in China

AI's status as a general-purpose technology and China's recognition of its potential role in multiple applications ("AI + 100") is reflected in the classification labels assigned by academic journals to article content. Table 5.1 lists Chinese Library Classification (CLC) subject topics jointly labeled with "Artificial Intelligence" sorted in descending order of AI share for papers published from 2010 to 2020 in the CNKI journals dataset.

The table shows raw paper counts of "AI papers" (identified by matching AI keywords) jointly listed with each CLC subject topic and the paper counts for each subject topic ("all papers") during the same period for reference. "AI share" is the ratio of these raw counts for each subject topic. We note that the AI keywords-based approach to identify AI papers has good but incomplete overlap with the "Artificial Intelligence" CLC label during the 2010–2020 period. Thus, CLC categorization criteria were found to be consistent with an AI keywords-based approach that we independently ran to identify Chinese-language AI papers, adding credibility to the exercise.

As expected, a high AI share is co-listed as a subject topic for publications in computer science-tangent fields like robotics, automation, and computing. Many emerging application fields, such as navigation and remote sensing, also made the list, validating impressionistic accounts of AI's spread through all areas of technology.

Where is China's AI research being done?

Commitment to the AI paradigm across Chinese research organizations can also be measured by the distribution of publications. Table 5.2 ranks PRC organizations by the number of AI academic publications in 2020; we include 2015 ranking stats for comparison. Some of these new leading organizations produced fewer than 400 AI research papers in 2015 as indicated by "N/A."

TABLE 5.1 AI applications according to subjects in CNKI journals

Topic	AI papers	All papers	AI share
Robot technology	36,621	38,787	0.9442
Artificial Intelligence	80,644	92,315	0.8736
Interpretation, recognition, and processing of remote sensing images	6,213	8,662	0.7173
General question—automation technology and equipment	1,551	2,411	0.6433
Automation device and equipment	1,220	2,069	0.5897
UAV (Unmanned aerial vehicle)	3,938	7,266	0.5420
Flight control system and navigation	4,060	8,050	0.5043
Computer application	178,068	380,957	0.4674
Application of remote sensing technology in agriculture	1,280	2,771	0.4619
Automatic control theory	3,399	7,956	0.4272
Surveying, mapping and remote sensing technology	3,881	9,298	0.4174
Fuzzy mathematics	1,763	4,262	0.4137
Guidance and control	2,165	5,324	0.4066
Application of electronic technology and computer technology in agriculture	1,779	4,550	0.3910
Game theory	1,325	3,499	0.3787
Computer applications in highway transportation and highway engineering	4,266	11,394	0.3744
Pump	2,609	7,022	0.3715
Information science	1,295	3,608	0.3589
Application of remote sensing technology	1,349	3,865	0.3490
Mechanical manufacturing process	6,075	18,638	0.3259
Nonlinear physics	1,120	3,881	0.2886
Teaching theory, teaching method	1,437	5,022	0.2861
Radar	7,964	27,836	0.2861
Optimal mathematical theory	1,017	3,608	0.2819
Circuit and network	4,614	16,485	0.2799
High voltage insulation technology	1,189	4,266	0.2787
Automated system	32,051	117,160	0.2736
Mental process and mental state	1,305	4,783	0.2728
Missile	2,894	10,848	0.2668
General question—computing and computer technology	17,989	68,105	0.2641

Source: Daniel H. Chou. "Counting AI Research," CSET, June 2022.

Rank order by volume, shown here, is one measure of an institute's contributions to AI and AI-related applications but not the only, or the best, guide for mapping an institute's importance, as it does not measure quality or innovativeness, and not all research is openly published. Some interesting phenomena stand out nonetheless, such as Wuhan University School of Information Science's commanding role, which does not surface elsewhere in this volume's chapters, and the rapid jump from 18th to 5th place by Sichuan University College of Computer Science, another provincial outpost typically neglected in analyses of China's AI progress that tend to focus on developments in Beijing and Shanghai.

TABLE 5.2 Organizations with top AI research output in CNKI journals

2020 rank	2020 papers	2015 rank	2015 papers	Organization
1	1,316	2	777	University of the Chinese Academy of Sciences (中国科学院大学)
2	1,249	1	1,037	Wuhan University School of Information Management (武汉大学信息管理学院)
3	1,132	4	713	Tsinghua University Institute of Automation (清华大学自动化系)
4	928	6	616	Shanghai Jiaotong University (上海交通大学)
5	889	18	502	Sichuan University College of Computer Science (四川大学计算机学院)
6	795	31	386	PKU School of Electronics Engineering and Computer Science (北京大学信息管理系)
7	770	80	221	Renmin University of China (中国人民大学)
8	770	5	680	Zhejiang University (浙江大学)
9	762	14	528	Tongji University (同济大学)
10	732	15	527	University of Shanghai for Science and Technology (上海理工大学)
11	718	46	311	Beijing Normal University (北京师范大学)
12	715	27	435	Nanjing University (南京大学)
13	701	3	748	NUAA (南京航天航空大学)
14	688	16	522	Jilin University (吉林大学)
15	686	12	531	Southeast University (东南大学)
16	658	10	567	Tianjin University (天津大学)
17	632	42	345	Wuhan University of Technology (武汉理工大学)
18	607	20	492	North China Electric Power University (华北电力大学)
19	605	23	469	Southwest Jiaotong University School of Electrical Engineering (西南交通大学电气工程学院)
20	595	25	459	Huazhong University of Science and Technology (华中科技大学)

Source: William C. Hannas, Huey-Meei Chang, Daniel H. Chou, and Brian Fleeger, "China Advanced AI Research," CSET, June 2022.

Who funds AI research in China and worldwide?

Data on project sponsorship can also be gleaned from the metadata of most Chinese academic journal articles. Where available, we tabulated aggregate statistics of top funding organizations, taking account of sub-units and variant names reported in the metadata both for Chinese papers and for international academic literature. This information is shown in Table 5.3, which ranks

TABLE 5.3 Funder-supported AI scholarly publications[27]

2020 rank	2020 papers	2015 rank	2015 papers	Funding source
1	37,596	1	12,954	National Natural Science Foundation of China
2	10,199	5	2,899	Ministry of Science and Technology (China)
3	8,318	26	315	National Key Research and Development Program of China
4	8,265	3	3,385	National Science Foundation (USA)
5	7,245	2	3,485	European Commission
6	5,649	4	3,029	Ministry of Education (China)
7	4,873	6	1,746	National Institutes of Health (USA)
8	3,556	7	1,297	Fundamental Research Funds for the Central Universities (China)[28]
9	2,453	11	599	National Research Foundation of Korea
10	1,896	13	518	China Postdoctoral Science Foundation
11	1,822	8	1,041	Japan Society for the Promotion of Science
12	1,704	19	415	Ministry of Science ICT and Future Planning
13	1,644	12	565	Natural Sciences and Engineering Research Council
14	1,626	10	618	Engineering and Physical Sciences Research Council
15	1,571	18	429	Chinese Academy of Sciences
16	1,565	14	513	German Research Foundation
17	1,339	15	509	European Research Council
18	1,331	29	303	China Scholarship Council
19	1,185	17	490	National Council for Scientific and Technological Development
20	1,167	24	351	Coordenação de Aperfeiçoamento de Pessoal de Nível Superior (Brazil)

Source: Daniel H. Chou. "Counting AI Research," CSET, June 2022.

funder-supported AI scholarly publications worldwide in 2020; 2015 stats are added for comparison.

There are gaps in funding information, some presumably deliberate, others an artifact of journal policy, so the sum of all paper counts in Table 5.3 is lower than the paper counts for 2020 illustrated in Table 5.1. Nonetheless, the data show PRC funding sources dominating other countries' funding sources in the number of AI publications supported in 2020 and 2015.

The increases in PRC-funded AI research output from 2015 to 2020 correlate with national AI initiatives over the same period. Table 5.3 does *not* include CNKI funding information, where the National Natural Science Foundation of China is also the dominant source, so the distribution in absolute terms is likely even more skewed. Bear in mind that the table shows concentrations of funding sources by paper, not funding amounts, for which we lack data.

CNKI MPS AI Output Trend

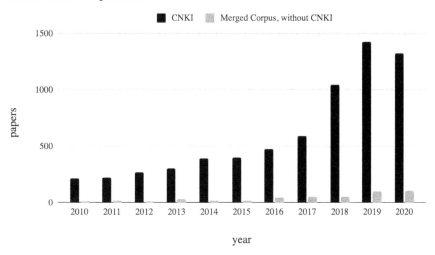

FIGURE 5.3 MPS AI output trend

Source: Daniel H. Chou, "Revisiting China's Security Forces AI Research Output," CSET, June 2022.

AI research by China's security services

How important is AI research to the PRC's domestic security apparatus? Earlier, we registered our and others' observations that China's embrace of AI is driven in part by its contributions to what in Beijing's terms pass for "public security" and what other countries and human rights groups regard in part as the technology of political repression. This matter is explored in detail in the present volume's Chapter 12 and in prior research by colleagues.[29] Our goal here (Figure 5.3) is to show the value of bibliometrics in identifying (confirming) trends, and hammer home a point about the relative importance of Chinese vs. English-language literature.

Consistent with reports of increasing adoption of surveillance and facial recognition technology by China's Ministry of Public Security (公安部, MPS), Figure 5.3 shows an upward trend in MPS AI publications. Perhaps unsurprisingly, MPS-affiliated researchers published more AI papers in Chinese-language CNKI journals than in the (predominantly English-language) journals collected by other aggregators (Web of Science, Dimensions Publications, Microsoft Academic Graph) in the CSET Merged Corpus.[30]

China and worldwide research hubs

China and the United States are the leaders of AI scholarly research output judging by raw publication counts. Their rankings for 2020, along with other countries, are shown in Figure 5.4a.

Countries with most AI scholarly publications in 2020

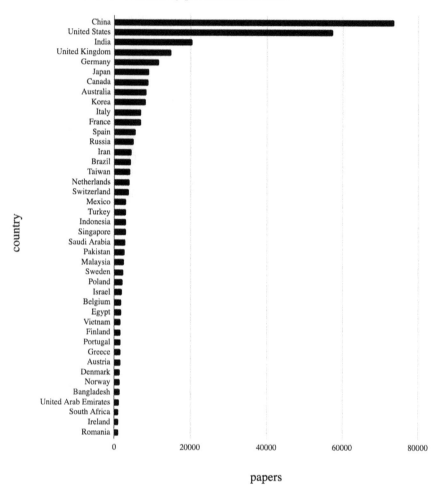

FIGURE 5.4a   Countries with the most AI scholarly publications in 2020

Source: Daniel H. Chou. "Counting AI Research," CSET, June 2022.

    Figure 5.4a shows the CSET Merged Corpus *without* CNKI. Accordingly, the comparison vastly underestimates the number of publications for China, because not all or even most AI articles gathered by CNKI, which focuses on Chinese-language papers, are captured by these other aggregators, and the true number of what is missing is almost impossible to fathom.[31]

    To continue the comparison, Figure 5.4a shows records for 2020 only, the most recent year for which we have data. Figure 5.4b, based on the CSET Merged Corpus (*without* CNKI), tracks AI publication over the past decade.

    These data, derived from keyword searches that also cover what researchers considered AI/ML prior to the advent of deep learning, demonstrate that China

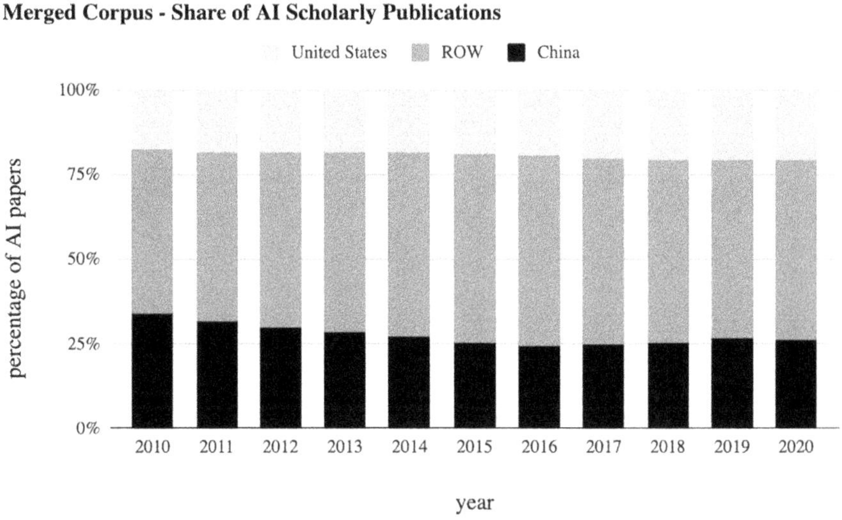

Merged Corpus - Share of AI Scholarly Publications

FIGURE 5.4b   Share of AI scholarly publications

Source: Daniel H. Chou. "Counting AI Research," CSET, June 2022.

has been the global leader in terms of AI publications for at least a decade and, based on incomplete data, probably longer.

How do these distributions map globally? Figure 5.5 illustrates AI research hubs around the world. Each bubble denotes a city whose organizations produced more than 500 AI scholarly articles in the aggregate during 2020, based on the CSET Merged Corpus (*without* CNKI).

Figure 5.6 zooms in on China, based on CNKI journals. There are overlaps with Figure 5.5, but more hubs are distinguishable, because the CNKI record is more inclusive of the Chinese output: Baoding (1,207 vs. 108), Wuxi (1,488 vs. 354), and Guiyang (900 vs. 316). Cities that overlap in both figures (e.g. Beijing, Shanghai, and Hangzhou) in 2020 produced more AI research articles in Chinese than in English, supporting our argument that seeking information about China from English is akin to looking for one's lost keys under the lamppost.

China and international research collaboration

How collaborative is China in AI? Figure 5.7 shows that PRC researchers collaborated most with colleagues in the United States, Great Britain, Australia, and Canada.[32] For China's top ten collaborators, the percentages of collaborated papers and country ranks are nearly unchanged from 2015.[33]

Cross-country comparisons are one measure of AI collaboration. Another measure looks at collaboration between different organizations (irrespective of country). Figure 5.8 shows the share of organizational collaboration in English-language AI scholarly papers between 2010 and 2020. The digits on the figure's

503   17649

FIGURE 5.5 Global AI research hubs in 2020

Source: Daniel H. Chou. "Counting AI Research," CSET, June 2022.

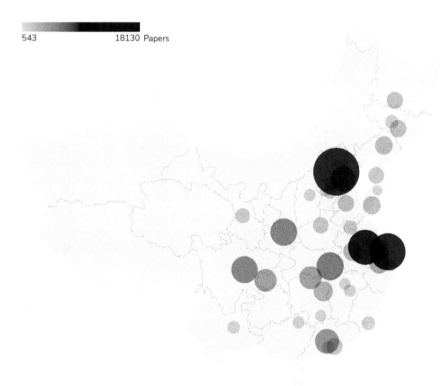

543   18130 Papers

FIGURE 5.6 China AI research hubs

Source: Daniel H. Chou. "Counting AI Research," CSET, June 2022.

Merged Corpus - PRC International Collaboration in AI - 2020

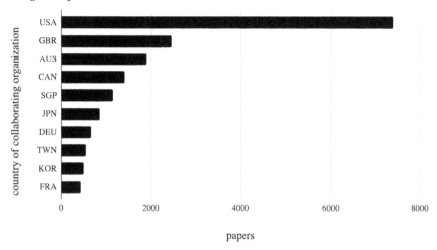

FIGURE 5.7 PRC international collaboration in 2020

Source: Daniel H. Chou. "Counting AI Research," CSET, June 2022.

right show numbers of contributing organizations. A steady increase in the number of institutions contributing to an AI paper is evident based on these sources, which is extraordinary, given the challenging conditions in 2020.[34] A similar trend in the English-language record of increasing AI collaboration between authors from different *countries* is noted for the same time period.[35]

Share of Organization AI Research Collaborations - Merged

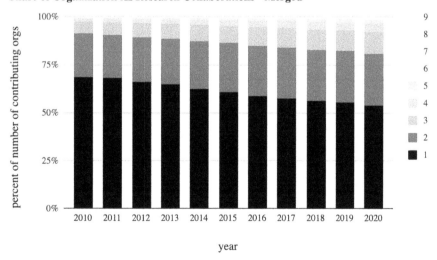

FIGURE 5.8 Share of organization AI research collaborations - merged

Source: Daniel H. Chou. "Counting AI Research," CSET, June 2022.

Share of Organization AI Research Collaborations - CNKI

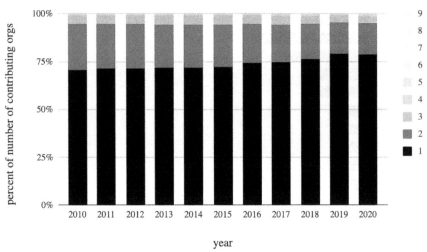

year

FIGURE 5.9   Share of organization AI research collaborations - CNKI

Source: Daniel H. Chou. "Counting AI Research," CSET, June 2022.

However, this trend takes a different turn when we perform the same analysis for CNKI publications. Figure 5.9 shows the share of organizational collaboration among Chinese-language AI scholarly papers from 2010 to 2020. In contrast to Figure 5.8, we discover that *fewer and fewer* papers have authors affiliated with different organizations. This likely reflects, in part, the inaccessibility of Chinese-language journals to the wider research community,[36] although there may be other factors that warrant further investigation.[37]

We summarize the preceding sections with the following observations:

- China and the United States—in that order—are the world's leaders in the number of AI academic publications.
- China's AI scholarly output, both journal and conference papers, is highly cited by the world scientific community.
- Chinese researchers publish more AI scholarly articles in Chinese than in English, and the two source types reveal different, even contrasting trends.
- China's AI/ML scholarly publications show consistently high growth compared to all research topics among Chinese-language scholarly publications, and compared to AI publications from the United States.
- Bibliometric analyses of published AI research reveal data on institutional contributions to the national effort not apparent in other types of open sources.
- To understand the China vs. U.S. story for AI research, we need to study both English and Chinese academic publications.

Interpreting bibliometric results: the path from research to applications

There are important nuances to interpreting bibliometrics. Paper counts and citations may—or may not—make Chinese researchers look more competitive in AI than they are in reality, since they have faced acute incentives to improve their publication records.[38] In addition, publications reflect earlier stages of the research and development pipeline, and may not represent the work necessary to adapt AI systems to practical use.[39]

Publication data is an incomplete proxy for research progress

Publish-or-perish incentives are universal, and not inconsistent with high-quality research. However, Chinese researchers have faced strong pressures: their employers often made hiring, promotions, and bonuses contingent on journal publications and citations.[40] These incentives led researchers to bolster their output by various means, from inflating citation counts to publishing fraudulent results.[41] According to an analysis of scientific publications retrieved in 2019, some three times more papers per output volume were retracted for China (0.039%) than for the United States (0.012%), although absolute numbers remained small in all cases.[42]

Importantly, the PRC took steps to resolve the problem in February 2020, by enacting policies requiring that academic organizations not provide bonuses for publications, nor make publication statistics the sole qualification for hiring.[43] Moreover, just as we cannot take Chinese publication counts themselves as a metric of high-quality research, neither can we do so for other countries. Known cases of malfeasance and academic fraud have occurred elsewhere, such as in South Korean stem cell research and U.S. psychology research (giving rise to the "replication crisis").[44]

We should not doubt China's ability to produce valuable research, given its growing resources in human capital and R&D funding. As we have seen, when we select for elite metrics of quality such as publications in a few highly regarded Western research venues or citations from international sources, China's publication record is impressive and improving over time.

AI technologies may have a difficult path from research to deployment, particularly in highly complex, safety-critical application domains

In practice, perhaps the most important gap between publications and impact is the amount of work required to implement AI systems in complex, messy real-world environments. AI, like steam power and electricity, is a general-purpose technology,[45] one that enables progress across a wide variety of domains.[46] Such technologies can lead to incredible economic growth, but there is often a gap of decades between when the technology is created and when improvements are realized. This lag time is explained by the work required to implement the technology in a useful form, and to optimally restructure industry to take advantage of the technology.[47] Historical examples include the electrification of factories and the use of computers in the workplace, both of which took decades to yield net productivity gains.[48] Economists argue that AI deployment will see a similar trajectory: AI applications will eventually lead to significant productivity gains, but may take decades to do so.[49]

Barriers to deploying AI, such as in autonomous vehicles,[50] reflect one of the major weaknesses of modern deep learning systems: they can be brittle, failing unexpectedly in novel situations. And because they are so complex, their failures are hard to anticipate. This problem is especially acute in safety-critical applications such as air traffic control, where minimizing accident rates is essential.[51] Likewise, AI systems deployed for natural security purposes must be robust not just to natural perturbations, but to adversarial attacks.

To curb these weaknesses and enable the useful deployment of AI, researchers and policymakers are increasingly interested in the emerging research field of AI safety. In brief, AI safety research aims to make AI systems more robust, interpretable, and aligned with human goals; we discuss this area in further detail in Chapter 14. Publications in all areas of AI safety have grown rapidly since 2015.[52] Yet while China is a leading publisher of AI research in general, it trails the United States in most areas of AI safety research.

China's AI focus areas could mean that it is early to deploy brittle AI in many areas of interest, but late to deploy reliable AI in safety-critical situations. The large scale of Chinese R&D funding and China's traditional focus on applied research may drive Chinese AI research toward short-term practical applications. Chinese research efforts may be active and fruitful in areas of interest to PRC funders and have straightforward application pathways, such as computer-vision-based surveillance. But more complex applications may prove difficult, unless Chinese organizations prove adept at adopting the latest Western advances in AI safety—as they have in other technical areas—or develop homegrown talent in this area.

China is a rising contributor to AI, particularly in practical application areas

China's growing R&D spending and talent pool are reflected in its increasing competitiveness with the United States for the top spot in academic research. This competitiveness extends to high-quality AI research. In the short term, China will likely be especially prominent in the areas where it has historically excelled, as these areas reflect government funders' priorities and Chinese researchers' talents. These include computer vision research, where China leads even in the top 1% of highly cited papers. While some of this research is targeted at specific applications like surveillance or autonomous vehicles, a large portion is directed at general-purpose research tasks which could improve many computer vision systems. We have also seen that Chinese AI research covers some application areas that could prove important in the near future, including remote sensing, unmanned vehicle flight, and industrial applications.

Perhaps more important, but far less certain, are the prospects for impactful basic AI research in China. So far, the flow of major algorithmic innovations in AI has mostly been from West to East. Even in computer vision, where Chinese researchers rival their U.S. counterparts in highly cited research,[53] key architectures like the convolutional neural network, generative adversarial network, and the transformer were developed in the West. A 2018 Tsinghua University report noted that while China was strong in AI overall, its strengths were more focused on applications than on algorithmic innovation.[54] China may have the talent and funding to develop major new ideas in AI, but so far has directed those resources toward more incremental advances.[55] This may change over the coming decade, as China's resources continue to grow.

Notes

1 Licensed data used in this chapter are reproduced from prior CSET analytic production with authors' permission.
2 Stanford Institute, Human-centered Artificial Intelligence (HAI), *AI Index Report*, 2021, Chapter 1.
3 Melissa Flagg, "Global R&D and a New Era of Alliances," Georgetown University, Center for Security and Emerging Technology, June 2020.
4 Holly Chik. "China Set to Pass U.S. on Research and Development Spending by 2025." *South China Morning Post*, July 16, 2021.
5 Remco Zwetsloot et al., "China Is Rapidly Outpacing U.S. STEM PhD Output," Georgetown University, Center for Security and Emerging Technology, August 2021.
6 William C. Hannas and Huey-Meei Chang, "China's Access to Foreign AI Technology," Georgetown University, Center for Security and Emerging Technology, September 2019.
7 Unpublished analyses of the Chinese- vs. English-language records by this volume's editors demonstrate that the more interesting papers in terms of their value to national security and commercialization opportunities tend to appear in Chinese only.
8 Tim Culpan, "China Isn't the AI Juggernaut the West Fears," *Bloomberg*, October 11, 2021.
9 PRC State Council. 国务院关于印发新一代人工智能发展规划的通知 (The New Generation AI Development Plan), SC 35, 2017.
10 See, e.g., HAI, *AI Index Report*, 2021.
11 Cady, Field and Oren Etzioni, "China May Overtake U.S. in AI Research," Allen Institute for AI, March 13, 2019.
12 Ibid.
13 These observed trends in the two countries' share of AI publications and the precise years of Chinese parity with the United States vary moderately, due to different academic datasets and definitions of AI.
14 Murdick, Dewey, James Dunham, and Jennifer Melot. "AI Definitions Affect Policymaking." Georgetown University, Center for Security and Emerging Technology, 2020.
15 HAI, *AI Index Report*, 2021.

16 CSRankings.org.
17 CSET's merged corpus (referred as "CSET Merged Corpus") of scholarly literature includes Digital Science's Dimensions, Clarivate's Web of Science, Microsoft Academic Graph, China National Knowledge Infrastructure, arXiv, and Papers with Code. All CNKI content is furnished as machine-readable data files for off-platform use by East View Information Services, Minneapolis, MN. Use of these data here and in other chapters derives from their primary, licensed application to previously published GU/CSET papers, acknowledged in the narrative.
18 Acharya and Dunn, 2022.
19 These figures include all publications in which any author had an affiliation with a Chinese/U.S. institution at the time of publication. In 2019, 900 papers in these venues—making up roughly a quarter of the Chinese publications and a sixth of the U.S. publications—were the U.S.-Chinese collaborations.
20 CSRankings AI rankings, 2011–2015, https://perma.cc/AXS2-26RG; CSRankings AI rankings, 2016–2020, https://perma.cc/B23T-B3VW.
21 For Figures 5.1 and 5.2, we define AI papers based on the CSET Map of Science, following previous research. For an explanation of this methodology, see Ilya Rahkovsky et al., "AI Research Funding Portfolios and Extreme Growth," *Frontiers in Research Metrics and Analytics*, 2021.
22 Ibid.
23 Catherine Armitage. "Fresh Twists in China's Bid for Research Dominance," *Nature Index*, May 6, 2021.
24 Yuki Okoshi. "China's Research Papers Lead the World in Cutting-edge Tech." *Nikkei Asia*, January 6, 2019.
25 "Superpowered Science: Charting China's Research Rise," *Nature Index*, May 26, 2021.
26 Our datasets were partitioned into four subsets for comparison, as specified: CNKI only (Journals only or Journals and Conferences) and the CSET Merged Corpus (with and without CNKI).
27 Based on available funding information.
28 中央高校基本科研业务费资助.
29 Murdick, Dewey, Daniel Chou, Ryan Fedasiuk, and Emily Weinstein, "The Public AI Research Portfolio of China's Security Forces," Georgetown University, Center for Security and Emerging Technology, March 2021.
30 See endnote 16.
31 Combining these two measures of Chinese publications, unfortunately, is not as simple as adding two figures, since many papers by Chinese researchers have English-language analogs (translations and *near* translations), or were published originally in English and reappear in a Chinese-language version. Deduplicating the variants is a Herculean task even with smart algorithms, since the titles often do not match, the co-authors' order of appearance may be jumbled, and the Anglicized names of Chinese authors in English-language papers vary in important ways from the pinyin representation of their true (Chinese character) names—assuming the journal editors get even that detail right. On top of it all, there is deliberate obfuscation—similar content published in multiple venues to inflate resumes. One can spend—we have spent—weeks compiling non-duplicative corpora on narrowly defined topics.
32 Countries are represented using ISO 3166-1 alpha-3 codes.
33 Data and chart omitted here.
34 Papers with six or more contributing organizations all share the same shade, because actual percentages of more than six collaborating units require shading an area close to the grid line width.
35 Data and chart omitted here.
36 Many Chinese-language journals include English titles and abstracts to improve the chance of inclusion in English scholarly literature aggregators. Clarivate's Web of Science and Elsevier's Scopus both require a journal article to have an English abstract

regardless of source language. Here, we include Chinese-language journals without English abstracts when we measure overall publication counts as a proxy of research interest.

37 Some Chinese-language journals are just the publishing outlet for a specific organization. *Modern Radar* (现代雷达), for instance, mainly publishes articles by researchers from the CETC 14th Research Institute. These journals include both classified and unclassified articles. Analogous publications are CIA's *Studies in Intelligence* and NSA's *Cryptology* and *Cryptologic Quarterly*.

38 Editorial comment: one can argue that these incentives *drive* legitimate research. Many of us in our present and former careers, where publishing is expected, are motivated by the carrot *and* by the stick.

39 By the same token, the absence of high-quality basic research, in China's case especially, may have no bearing on a country's ability to field successful applications. This point is argued by Chinese AI entrepreneur Kai-Fu Lee and by the present book's authors and editors here and elsewhere.

40 Eva Xiao. "Red Flags Raised over Chinese Research Published in Global Journals." *The Wall Street Journal.* July 5, 2020.

41 Li, Sonia Qingyang. "The End of Publish or Perish? China's New Policy on Research Evaluation." *Observations: A Short Paper Series*, Max Planck Institute for the History of Science, November 19, 2020. Plagiarism also remains a problem as evidenced in the BAAI survey report "A Roadmap for Big Model" (third edition uploaded April 2, 2022), which included passages from a dozen other papers without attribution (https://nicholas.carlini.com/writing/2022/a-case-of-plagarism-in-machine-learning.html). BAAI quickly acknowledged their editorial oversight and pledged to redress the issue (https://www.baai.ac.cn/portal/article/index/cid/4/id/404.html).

42 Tang, Li. "Five Ways China Must Cultivate Research Integrity." *Nature* Comment, November 26, 2019. For Japan, the figure was 0.019%.

43 PRC Ministry of Education, Ministry of Science and Technology, 教育部,科技部 印发"关于规范高等学校SCI论文相关指标使用树立正确评价导向的若干意见"的通知 (Notice of the Ministry of Education and the Ministry of Science and Technology on Issuing the "Several Opinions on Regulating the Use of Related Indicators of SCI Papers in Colleges and Universities to Establish Correct Evaluation Orientation"), MOE/MOST 2, February 2020; Mallapaty, Smriti. "China Bans Cash Rewards for Publishing Papers," *Nature* 579, 2020, 18–19.

44 Shrout, Patrick E., and Joseph L. Rodgers. "Psychology, Science, and Knowledge Construction: Broadening Perspectives from the Replication Crisis." *Annual Review of Psychology* 69, 2018, 487–510.

45 Brynjolfsson, Erik, Daniel Rock, and Chad Syverson, "Artificial Intelligence and the Modern Productivity Paradox: A Clash of Expectations and Statistics," *The Economics of Artificial Intelligence*, eds. Ajay Agrawal et al., University of Chicago Press, 2019.

46 Bresnahan, Timothy F., and Manuel Trajtenberg, "General Purpose Technologies: 'Engines of Growth'?" *Journal of Econometrics* 65.1, 1995, 83–108.

47 Brynjolfsson, Erik, Daniel Rock, and Chad Syverson, "The Productivity J-curve: How Intangibles Complement General Purpose Technologies." *American Economic Journal: Macroeconomics* 13.1, 2021, 333–372.

48 Ibid.

49 Ibid.

50 Seamans, Robert. "Autonomous Vehicles as a 'Killer App' for AI." *Brookings Institute Report*, June 22, 2021.

51 Will Hunt, "The Flight to Safety-Critical AI: Lessons in AI Safety from the Aviation Industry," UC Berkeley Center for Long-Term Cybersecurity, August 11, 2020.

52 See Toner, Helen, Ashwin Acharya, and Autumn Toney, "Exploring AI Safety Research in CSET's Map of Science." Georgetown University, Center for Security and Emerging Technology, January 2022.

53 Murdick, Dunham, and Melot, 2020.

54 China Institute for Science and Technology Policy at Tsinghua University, "China AI Development Report 2018," July 2018.
55 Steven W. Popper et al., "China's Propensity for Innovation in the 21st Century: Identifying Indicators of Future Outcomes." *RAND Corporation Research Report,* 2020.

Bibliography

Acharya, Ashwin, and Brian Dunn, "Comparing U.S. and Chinese Contributions to High-Impact AI Research," Georgetown University, Center for Security and Emerging Technology, January 2022.

Bresnahan, Timothy F., and Manuel Trajtenberg, "General Purpose Technologies: 'Engines of Growth'?," *Journal of Econometrics* 65.1, 1995, 83–108.

Brynjolfsson, Erik, Daniel Rock, and Chad Syverson, "Artificial Intelligence and the Modern Productivity Paradox: A Clash of Expectations and Statistics," *The Economics of Artificial Intelligence*, eds. Ajay Agrawal et al., University of Chicago Press, Chicago, Illinois, 2019.

Brynjolfsson, Erik, Daniel Rock, and Chad Syverson, "The Productivity J-curve: How Intangibles Complement General Purpose Technologies," *American Economic Journal: Macroeconomics* 13.1, 2021, 333–372.

Cady, Field and Oren Etzioni, "China May Overtake U.S. in AI Research," Allen Institute for AI, March 13, 2019.

Chik, Holly, "China Set to Pass U.S. on Research and Development Spending by 2025," *South China Morning Post,* July 16, 2021.

China Institute for Science and Technology Policy at Tsinghua University, "China AI Development Report 2018," July 2018.

Culpan, Tim, "China Isn't the AI Juggernaut the West Fears," Bloomberg, October 11, 2021.

Flagg, Melissa, "Global R&D and a New Era of Alliances," Georgetown University, Center for Security and Emerging Technology, June 2020.

Hannas, William C. and Huey-Meei Chang, "China's Access to Foreign AI Technology," Georgetown University, Center for Security and Emerging Technology, September 2019.

Hunt, Will, "The Flight to Safety-Critical AI: Lessons in AI Safety from the Aviation Industry," UC Berkeley Center for Long-Term Cybersecurity, August 11, 2020.

Li, Sonia Qingyang, "The End of Publish or Perish? China's New Policy on Research Evaluation." Observations: A Short Paper Series, Max Planck Institute for the History of Science, November 19, 2020.

Mallapaty, Smriti, "China Bans Cash Rewards for Publishing Papers," *Nature* 579, 2020, 18–19.

Murdick, Dewey, James Dunham, and Jennifer Melot, "AI Definitions Affect Policymaking." Georgetown University, Center for Security and Emerging Technology, 2020.

Murdick, Dewey, Daniel Chou, Ryan Fedasiuk, and Emily Weinstein, "The Public AI Research Portfolio of China's Security Forces," Georgetown University, Center for Security and Emerging Technology, March 2021.

Popper, Steven W., et al., "China's Propensity for Innovation in the 21st Century: Identifying Indicators of Future Outcomes." RAND Corporation Research Report, 2020.

PRC Ministry of Education, Ministry of Science and Technology, 教育部, 科技部印发 "关于规范高等学校SCI论文相关指标使用树立正确评价导向的若干意见"的通知 (Notice of the Ministry of Education and the Ministry of Science and Technology on Issuing the "Several Opinions on Regulating the Use of Related Indicators of SCI Papers in Colleges and Universities to Establish Correct Evaluation Orientation"), MOE/MOST 2, February 2020.

PRC State Council, 国务院关于印发新一代人工智能发展规划的通知 (The New Generation AI Development Plan), SC 35, 2017.

Seamans, Robert, "Autonomous Vehicles as a 'Killer App' for AI." Brookings Institute Report, June 22, 2021.

Shrout, Patrick E. and Joseph L. Rodgers, "Psychology, Science, and Knowledge Construction: Broadening Perspectives from the Replication Crisis." *Annual Review of Psychology* 69, 2018, 487–510.

Stanford Institute, Human-centered Artificial Intelligence (HAI), AI Index Report, 2021.

Tang, Li, "Five Ways China Must Cultivate Research Integrity," *Nature* Comment, 575 (7784) November 26, 2019, pp. 589–591. For Japan, the figure was 2019.

Xiao, Eva, "Red Flags Raised over Chinese Research Published in Global Journals." *The Wall Street Journal.* July 5, 2020.

Zwetsloot, Remco, et al, "China Is Rapidly Outpacing U.S. STEM PhD Output," Georgetown University, Center for Security and Emerging Technology, August 2021.

6

The balance sheet

China's AI advantages and challenges

Zachary Arnold and Anna B. Puglisi

The development of AI is reaching a key juncture, with investments in foundational technologies, talent, and supporting infrastructure being made now that will impact who leads in the future. China's rise as an AI power challenges long-held assumptions about innovation, growth, and governance. Understanding its current and future trajectory requires a clear-eyed look at where China's present growth is, what its strengths are, and the assumptions about China's capacity to innovate.[1] Equally important will be to look past this snapshot in time and examine China's capacity to drive future discovery through policies, programs, and key investments, considered together rather than individually. It is this broad, integrated capacity building that will in many ways have the biggest impact on the "balance sheet."

This chapter discusses myths surrounding China's ability to succeed and reviews China's successes and failures to date in the key domains on which progress in AI relies, such as talent, business and market conditions, institutional quality, and enabling technologies. We first focus on contextual factors, or *structural inputs*, that shape how AI systems are created, deployed, and used, before turning to *direct inputs* that result in large part from the successful application of these contextual, structural factors.

Addressing some common myths

Despite building a growing foundation for both AI research and manufacturing capability to apply that research, commentators continue to hold doubts and assumptions related to China's ability to innovate. Many question whether China, with its inefficiencies, non-market economy, and authoritarian leadership, can lead in a technology like AI. These myths impact not only our understanding of

DOI: 10.4324/9781003212980-8

current and future capabilities, but also the risk calculations that countries make in relation to China. Here are a few of the main ones:

"China just copies"[2]

This is an oversimplification of reality and ignores the multi decade effort China has put in place to support not only AI, but other emerging technologies and strategic industries.

The debate on whether China is creative or "innovative"—as if this were an all-or-nothing measure—ignores the hard reality that China has excelled in many facets of development and research that do not resemble or require the "eureka moment" innovation idealized in the West. Also overlooked in this debate is that science everywhere is mostly iterative, and that "good enough" is often adequate.

Moreover, the balance sheet is not only about what is happening now but also about what capacity is being built for the future. China is laying the foundation—through investments, strategic policies, and technological know-how leveraged from international collaboration and theft that will enable future discovery. It is this future capacity with which we should be concerned, particularly in multi-disciplinary research, where universities, companies, and the military together work on hard problems, fueling far-reaching innovation and applications.

Whether China "copies" or follows the same path as its strategic competitors is less important than whether its strategies work. China's hybrid approach that combines indigenous R&D with multiple venues of foreign access is highly successful and already fueling its AI development. It is and will continue to be technologically and geopolitically consequential, and therefore must be taken seriously, whatever blind epithets one attaches to it.

"Picking winners doesn't work"[3]

The development of 5G and Huawei point unequivocally to China's success at picking winners, as well as the long list of successful industrial policies throughout the last 50 years.

By word and action, it is clear that an efficient Western-style macroeconomy is not the CCP's end-goal. The argument against "picking winners" assumes that a techno-authoritarian approach is doomed to fail in the long run. But even if China's policies do not ultimately produce globally competitive national champions, they can still create long-lasting distortions in markets and supply chains that shift developmental timelines of technologies, causing U.S. researchers and firms to fall behind their Chinese competitors. It can also cause the hollowing out of parts of the U.S. innovation base, as has happened in the pharmaceutical industry. These dynamics further China's technological and geopolitical ambitions. In that sense, they "work" for China, even if they are not conducive to efficient competition and maximum global innovation.

If China's goal is to suppress competition and eventually dominate in AI, it will be willing to accept inefficiencies in the short-term in order to win the advantage. In any event, "picking winners" may be more compatible with innovation than many assume. China's leaders have made their "Strategic Emerging Industries" (战略性新兴产业) a priority and look beyond return on investment. China has also shown an ability to shift strategies and focus areas when its bets do not work out. There is strength in playing the long game in new technology areas that gives an advantage to those willing to sustain funding for research before there is a commercially viable product. It also demonstrates a willingness to accept risk.

Finally, dismissing China's strategy as "picking winners" ignores the layered approach China actually takes in fostering competition. Restricting the domestic market to foreign competition does not mean that Chinese companies cannot compete with each other. This is the essence of China's strategic emerging industry policy. Nor does it imply that the decision to dominate certain key areas means China will micro-manage every layer of the national innovation base.

"Only democracies can innovate"⁴

> This myth—a Cold War legacy contradicted by history—has permeated policy discussions and scholarship for decades. A close examination of a broad landscape of research in China, especially those areas its government has determined to be priorities, highlights the gains and recognition Chinese scholarship has garnered and strides it has made in many fields.

A key assumption underlying this myth is that the lack of ability to challenge the government undermines the ability to find unique solutions to technical problems. It also assumes that the desire to be politically active—or express contrarian views—is a priority for most scientists. It ignores the lure of elite status, better housing and schooling for children, consistent funding, world-class facilities to work in, and challenging problems to work on.

Not only is there no demonstrable link between IQ and moral consciousness, an argument can also be made that the absence of venues for political expression may cause scientists to double down in those areas of life where "free expression" is encouraged. One only has to look to the numbers of scientists willing to refrain from politics in the West—as a condition of employment or because they are simply uninterested —to see that politics is not a dominant factor for many scientists. Since China has made research in artificial intelligence a priority, it provides funding, support, world-class facilities, and status. These resources will override political and even ethical considerations both domestically and as concerns the willingness of international experts to help build China's indigenous capabilities, democracy or not.

The democracy myth also ignores the well-documented hierarchies, bias, and parochialism of academic institutions in America and other developed nations. In the United States, scientists face inconsistent funding, a culture that does not always value their work, and industry that is increasingly risk-averse and driven by short-term thinking. Private wealth generation and commercial success do not always entail the development of foundational concepts, principles, and technologies that will drive future industries.

These common myths about China's abilities and shortcomings gloss over a panoply of more complex metrics that better reflect the true nature of China's AI development trajectory. A full and faithful accounting of these metrics allows observers to better judge the advantages and challenges China faces as an emerging AI power.

Structural inputs

One useful analytic framework for assessing China's advantages and challenges in developing AI emerges from the literature on innovation, which suggests that high-level structural inputs to a country's ability to innovate include[5]:

- Business and market conditions, such as capital and credit availability, ease of starting businesses, and ease of market access.
- Human capital, particularly in STEM fields and universities.
- Institutional quality and capacity.

This section explores these broad categories in the context of AI and assesses how they fit into an overall "balance sheet" for China's competitiveness and future prospects. We capture several specific structural inputs in our analysis, including financial capital, human capital, scientific and technological institutions, and institutions focused on commercialization. We then identify additional inputs that are especially characteristic of China's AI development trajectory, including technology transfer and ethical asymmetries.

Financial capital

Assessment: *Chinese AI researchers and firms have plenty of money. Capital overabundance may even be a problem.*

China's AI sector needs capital to develop, commercialize, and deploy new tools and technologies, and it apparently has plenty. Funds from the government or commercial buyers and investors are flowing steadily into AI and related technologies, at times overwhelming the sectors' abilities to absorb them.[6] More recently, hybrid public-private funding channels have proliferated, further blurring the already uncertain line between public and private in China's economy.[7]

The Chinese government is a massive funder and purchaser of AI R&D. One recent high-level estimate suggests that Chinese and U.S. public investments were both on the order of several billion dollars per year as of 2018.[8] It is possible that China could be spending more than these estimates suggest, since its public budgets are not fully transparent. But even if China is "merely" keeping pace with the United States, this is a huge change. For decades, America dominated nearly every category of R&D spending; by all indications, China has now vaulted into peer status, including in AI.[9]

Further along the technology development cycle, the Chinese government, at the central, provincial, and local levels, is also buying AI systems and services in tremendous quantities, with surveillance, smart city technologies, and the criminal justice system among the leading areas for deployment. This rush to deploy, alongside similarly massive investments in AI-related infrastructure and manufacturing capacity, has fueled the Chinese AI sector's rapid expansion, but has also prompted concerns about sustainability and overcapacity.[10] But given the strategic priority China's leaders assign to these domains, the spigot of public money will probably stay open.

Even larger funding channels exist outside the state budget. In R&D, Chinese AI firms have historically spent less than their foreign counterparts, but the sums are still huge in the absolute. Baidu, Alibaba, and Tencent (referred to as the BAT companies) spend billions a year on research and development, with large amounts dedicated to AI research.[11] Together with the rest of China's non-state companies and state-owned enterprises, the BAT companies also comprise an enormous domestic market for AI products and services, supporting thousands of smaller AI-focused companies.

Finally, state and non-state investors fuel Chinese AI activity through the capital markets. Chinese AI companies are publicly traded in New York, Hong Kong, and increasingly on the mainland. Chinese AI start-ups received tens of billions of dollars in disclosed private-market investment between 2015 and 2019 and continue to attract investors from around the world.[12] Many of these investors, including a rapidly growing body of public-private "guidance funds" (引导基金), have Chinese government backing.[13] Others are purely commercial, including multinational investment funds, pensions, and private equity investors.[14]

Human capital

Assessment: *A mixed bag. China has a strong domestic AI workforce, but less ability to recruit non-Chinese researchers and engineers.*

The AI talent market is global, especially for roles in research and engineering that require higher education. Nations' capabilities in AI depend both on nurturing native-born workers and on attracting and retaining talent from abroad. Today, China's domestic AI workforce is impressive and rapidly growing. However, China is less able than the United States to attract experts from other countries, especially non-ethnic Chinese, despite the proliferation of recruitment programs designed to do exactly that.

By numbers, China's domestic AI workforce is almost certainly unrivaled. China produces huge numbers of STEM graduates every year, including many more AI PhDs than the United States.[15] AI-focused university programs and specializations have proliferated, and government-mandated curricula at the primary, secondary, and post-secondary levels feature AI-related subjects such as Python coding, robotics, and data analysis.[16]

But quality matters as much as quantity in domestic workforce development, and China has steadily improved its showing on this front as well. There have long been concerns about the actual content and quality of Chinese STEM degrees, especially at the undergraduate and master's levels; about whether torrents of Chinese graduates can be usefully incorporated into the economy; and, at the doctoral and postdoctoral levels, about whether enough talent is directed to basic research.[17] But these concerns have less force today than they did a decade or two ago, and arguably less in AI than other fields. China's leading universities now boast AI programs that rival any foreign competitor, and there is evidence that these top schools are producing a larger share of the domestic talent pool than before.[18]

China's prospects in the international competition for AI talent are more mixed. Relatively few foreign-born AI students and professionals express interest in moving there, given linguistic, cultural, and political differences, and government-sponsored recruitment programs, such as the now-notorious "Thousand Talents" initiative, do not seem to have had much success attracting workers who are not ethnic Chinese.[19] However, for Chinese-born AI specialists studying or working abroad, China is clearly much more attractive today than it was even ten years ago. These so-called "sea turtles" (海龟) have played an important role in developing China's AI industry, and the momentum they have helped build will attract many more returnees in the coming years.

On balance, the best evidence suggests that China has gained ground in the global competition for talent, but still lags overall.[20] The future, however, is nevertheless uncertain: rising U.S.-China tensions, pandemic-related travel disruptions, and restrictive U.S. immigration policies may direct more talented AI researchers, engineers, and developers to China. And countries other than the United States, such as Canada, the United Kingdom, and Australia, may absorb more of those who choose to go elsewhere.

Institutional infrastructure: universities and State Key Labs

Assessment: *China's universities and State Key Lab* (国家重点实验室) *infrastructure have benefited from sustained investment and an influx of Western-trained talent.*

Revitalizing universities remains a core piece of China's long-term science and technology (S&T) development strategy and is a focus of multiple development plans. The Chinese government has significantly increased higher education and research funding over the last decade in support of this goal, with the average elite university budget amounting to 1.3 billion USD in 2019.[21] The previous chapter highlighted the gains China has made in AI research, as measured by papers, with China leading scholarly output in 2020. Much of this output came from universities which traditionally have not been the drivers of basic research. As a way to grow the next generation of AI professionals, a recent study on AI education in China highlights that China has instituted a standardized AI major at 345 universities in March 2021, up from 215 the year before, and has founded AI institutes at 34 of those universities.[22]

In addition to universities, China's State Key Labs (SKLs) system supports strategic basic research that requires extensive, long-term investment. Comprising hundreds of the country's most elite research facilities, the SKL ecosystem is inherently collaborative and integrative: prominent Chinese entrepreneur Liu Ruopeng (刘若鹏) described SKLs as having a similar mission and focus as Bell Labs had in the United States, which was to integrate different aspects of the development cycle in such a way as to have researchers and developers working together to solve difficult problems.[23] While often compared to U.S. national labs, SKLs are fundamentally different: they bring together and leverage the strengths of existing universities, research institutes, and enterprises to facilitate the development of new disciplines such as AI. Although most SKLs are managed by departments of the Chinese government, including the Chinese Academy of Sciences (CAS), an increasing number of laboratories are run by private companies. Their mission is cutting-edge research, attracting and training domestic and foreign talent, and conducting academic exchanges inside and outside China.

China's SKLs have benefited prominently from Western-trained talent. The aforementioned Liu Ruopeng is not only the founder of China's Kuang-Chi (光启) Group—a leader in China's advanced materials industry—but also an alumnus of Duke University, where he helped Chinese researchers access critical research data in a technology transfer effort that ultimately helped establish the Kuang-Chi Group.[24]

Commercialization infrastructure: strategic emerging industries and industrial clusters

Assessment: *Along with deficits in basic science, China's ability to commercialize technology has long been an Achilles heel. While it has put in place policies, programs, and administrative rules to leverage its market as a way to rectify this shortcoming, it still has work to do.*

China has sought to address S&T commercialization since the mid-1990s by creating midway facilities in every nook and cranny of the country, including "incubators" (孵化器), "innovation service centers" (创业服务中心), "overseas scholar pioneering parks" (留学人员创业园), and "technology transfer centers" (技术转移中心) for both innovations done domestically and "imported" from abroad, with limited success.[25] This is still a weakness in AI-related start-ups.

Beginning with the Medium- and Long-Term Plan for S&T Development in 2006 and continuing with its most recent policy on what China calls its strategic emerging industries, China has tried to create a more entrepreneurial environment to foster indigenous companies. China's newest effort promotes "industrial clusters" (产业集群), where the state offers funding, space, talents, and other resources to promote the development of commercial enterprises. These clusters cover 12 areas, including AI, AI manufacturing, and key adjacent industries.[26]

Technology transfer

Assessment: *China is a leader in technology transfer, and gains significantly from having its own ideas to work with as well as ideas from the rest of the world.*

As documented in earlier chapters and previously cited work by several of this book's authors, China most frequently targets technologies—such as AI—that align with goals set out under major policies like the Medium- and Long-Term Development Plan (MLP), strategic emerging industries strategy, and Made in China 2025. In pursuing these technologies, China's lack of transparency with collaborators and aggressive technology acquisition practices pose increasing concerns. China stands to benefit from the openness of university collaborations and commercial agreements without being held to the same standards.

Xi Jinping's views on AI development highlight this lack of collaborative reciprocity. In 2018 remarks, Xi noted that "artificial intelligence is a vital driving force for a new round of technological revolution and industrial transformation. China must control AI and ensure it is securely kept in our own hands."[27] While China's dependence on foreign transfers for much of its S&T development is usually regarded as a "weakness," we view China's ability to merge both sources of inspiration, whatever else one thinks of it, as an enduring strength.

Ethical asymmetries

Assessment: *China has demonstrated a willingness to test and deploy new AI systems and explore new areas of AI research unrestrained by Western-style ethical and safety concerns.*

Ethical flexibility may allow China to rapidly deploy new systems and exploit new "small data" areas of AI such as transfer learning, data labeling, artificial data generation, Bayesian methods, and reinforcement learning. China's willingness to "push the envelope" in certain technology areas—as seen historically with stem cells or more recently with chimera embryos—forces us to contemplate whether an authoritarian government with different freedoms and protections has an inherent advantage in AI development. Examples of this ethical flexibility have already been applied to AI development, especially in the field of AI-powered facial recognition software as part of the country's ongoing campaign of repression against its Uighur minority population.[28]

Direct inputs: building an innovation base[29]

Structural inputs are the foundation for the development of direct inputs that have immediate bearing on the growth, innovative capacity, and success of China's AI industry. Ample funding, capable human capital, collaborative research ecosystems, a favorable commercial environment, infusions of foreign technology transfer, and permissive ethical standards all serve the development of direct inputs like software, data, and computing equipment. The quality and availability of these direct inputs are critical determinants of technical success in AI development and application.

Software

Assessment: *China is not quite at the cutting edge, but this should not be an obstacle for the foreseeable future.*

The best-known direct input to AI technology is software—the algorithms, models, and basic software toolkits that process data and return outputs. Generally, U.S. researchers and multinationals are thought to be ahead of their Chinese competitors in this domain.[30] Chinese researchers have yet to publicly demonstrate fundamental advances on par with the work that produced today's dominant AI algorithms, or novel applications rivaling DeepMind's Alpha series.

But even if it trails the leading edge, China's development of AI-related software is likely advanced enough to sustain and possibly accelerate its current trajectory of AI innovation. China's world-class AI researchers and engineers can and do replicate, adapt, and refine innovations from abroad. Chinese researchers regularly reproduce foreign AI software innovations, such as the computationally massive language models introduced recently by American firms, in a matter of months.[31] In other words, China is well positioned to exploit a "fast follower" strategy—at a minimum.[32]

Heavy investment in core AI software capabilities could yield breakthrough innovations in software development, though funding is a necessary but not sufficient condition of innovative success. Chinese firms Baidu, Huawei, and other Chinese AI leaders have all introduced general-purpose AI software platforms meant to compete with Google's TensorFlow and Facebook's PyTorch, the current leaders in the space. None of the Chinese upstarts had meaningful market share within or outside China as of 2019, but this could change as geopolitical and technological winds shift.[33] China's massive public funding of R&D, and the growing share of funding earmarked for basic research, could also fuel algorithmic breakthroughs at home.[34]

Data

Assessment: *China's AI sector has unparalleled access to many types of data, providing a real but easily overstated advantage.*

Current machine learning models are data-hungry. In development, training data are used in massive quantities to calibrate the models' internal parameters; in deployment, models ingest real-world data in an ever-increasing variety of forms. In both cases, the old maxim "garbage in, garbage out" applies with force, making access to sufficient quantities of relevant, high-quality data a critical asset.

With its huge population, increasingly digitized economy, embrace of mass surveillance, and authoritarian system of government, China has copious data to draw on. These perceived data advantages are often argued to give China's AI sector a broad competitive advantage.[35] There is some truth to these arguments: China's economy generates huge amounts of data that could be used in AI models, and privacy restrictions on its use have been loose. Moreover, the Chinese government is better equipped than its democratic counterparts to commandeer data and data processing capabilities from the nominally private sector.[36]

On balance, though, China's "data advantage" is frequently overstated.[37] First, and most fundamentally, most AI systems rely on domain-specific data— that is, data directly related to the intended application of the system—which suggests that China's aggregated quantitative advantage in data is perhaps less useful than it first appears. For example, Alibaba's troves of mobile payment data could help fuel advances in AI-enabled financial services but would probably be useless for developing autonomous vehicles or facial recognition tools. Second, data siloing among non-state AI industry competitors is a problem in China just as elsewhere. Unlike the government, Chinese AI firms cannot force competitors—or in some cases, even their own departments and subsidiaries—to share data.[38] Third, data sharing with or compelled by the government may be easier under China's authoritarian system, but it is not yet frictionless.[39] Fourth, the notion that Chinese companies can freely exploit whatever data they may have for whatever purpose is increasingly outdated today, as regulations tighten amidst a broader reining in of the Chinese tech sector. Fifth, the future may bring AI innovations that neutralize today's data imbalances—AI luminary Zhu Songchun's (朱松纯) famous adoption of a "small data" paradigm is indicative.[40] Disciplines such as transfer learning are maturing quickly, opening the door to new AI tools that require much less real-world data than current technology.[41]

Compute and compute production

Assessment: *China's weakness in high-end computing hardware could constrain its AI ambitions.*

Developing advanced machine learning models generally requires specialized, cutting-edge computing hardware.[42] At present, there is no production of state-of-the-art AI chips in China. Even the most advanced Chinese chip manufacturers are several "nodes" (roughly, technological generations) behind market leaders in other countries, most notably Taiwan. Firms in Taiwan, the United States, Europe, South Korea, and Japan also dominate the market for most advanced chip inputs, such as semiconductor manufacturing equipment, chip design, and specialized optics.[43] As a result, Chinese AI developers buy large amounts of high-end computing hardware from abroad, and Chinese manufacturers largely rely on foreign equipment and expertise to make their (non-leading edge) AI chips.[44]

China's government is acutely aware of this dependence and is pouring tens of billions of dollars in direct investment, plus massive indirect subsidies, into the domestic semiconductor sector.[45] It is not clear where this push will end up. Natural monopoly dynamics and high capital intensity characterize many critical stages of the semiconductor supply chain, and much of the relevant knowledge is "know-how" embodied in skilled individuals—not formalized intellectual property that can straightforwardly be bought and assimilated. All these factors favor incumbent producers. China's government is currently trying to overcome them with subsidies, recruitment campaigns targeting semiconductor engineers and technicians, and other top-down efforts, but the challenge is formidable.[46] Many of the government's efforts have already faced setbacks.[47]

In the near and medium terms, then, China is unlikely to achieve independence in AI hardware. But for now, this is to some extent a theoretical weakness: China can still buy high-end chips from abroad to fuel its AI sector. If tensions escalate, producer nations could theoretically cut off China's supply but may not have the political will to do so. Revenues from the Chinese market help sustain the semiconductor industry and an effective blockade would require coordination among diverse nations. Absent extreme geopolitical circumstances, the most that can reasonably be expected is surgical controls on key manufacturing inputs that are concentrated in relatively few countries, such as cutting-edge photolithography machines.[48]

There are other caveats. As with data, developments in machine learning such as more compute-efficient training methods may make foreign computing hardware less important for China's industry.[49] New hardware paradigms could also lead to AI chips that can be produced with fewer foreign inputs. Another caveat is geopolitical. Taiwan currently controls a huge share of cutting-edge AI chip manufacturing. If Taiwan and China are reunified, peacefully or by force, mainland China could quickly gain access to world-leading AI hardware manufacturing capabilities.

Chinese views on strengths and the challenges ahead

China's self-assessment of its own strengths and weaknesses in AI development largely falls into similar categories as the ones described in the preceding sections of this chapter, though few Chinese experts explicitly cite innovation literature in arriving at their conclusions. Nevertheless, many of their judgments echo the observations we make above, suggesting a degree of consensus about China's AI "balance sheet."

China's top AI luminaries generally agree on their country's AI advantages. In an exclusive interview with Peking University after he briefed the Politburo on China's AI development in 2018, Academician Gao Wen (高文) of the Chinese Academy of Engineering (CAE) credited strong policy support, massive amounts of data derived from China's large population, rich application scenarios, and high levels of investment for advancing China's AI development.[50] A year later, CAS Academician Tan Tieniu (谭铁牛) echoed these same factors and added market scale and widespread cellphone adoption as decisive reasons for

China's current success in remarks to the Standing Committee of the National People's Congress.[51]

Established leaders and technical researchers also concur on China's most glaring weaknesses in AI development, citing insufficient breakthroughs in basic research, dependence on foreign hardware, reliance on foreign open-source software, and a comparative shortage of human capital as obstacles to China's rise as an AI power. Gao in particular noted in his 2018 interview that China lacked influential home-grown software platforms,[52] and he and Tan both complained that China still lagged behind the United States in an aggregate number of top AI researchers, even though China ranked second only to the United States.[53] These problems (and more) persist today: in May 2021, a team of researchers led by CAE Academician Liao Xiangke (廖湘科) reiterated China's deficiencies in basic research and dependencies on foreign hardware and software, and wrote that intellectual property protection, standardization, and other necessary conditions for commercialization remained underdeveloped.[54]

China's experts are quick to caveat these weaknesses, arguing either that they can be remediated as domestic capabilities improve or that these deficiencies will be addressed through stronger policy support. Liao's research team, for instance, regards China's smart chip design capabilities to be "nearly on-par with those of world powers," but that the actual manufacturing of these chips is reliant on foreign tool chains.[55] The group calls for increased investment from the highest levels of China's S&T establishment and intensified recruitment and cultivation of elite talent, arguing that these measures (among others) will break the "ingestion-emulation" (引进-模仿) cycle that has bedeviled China's AI development.[56]

Conclusion

Considering successes in industries like robotics,[57] biotechnology (see Chapter 8), and surveillance (see Chapter 12), we assess that China's AI "balance sheet" shows real strengths, but also continued gaps and areas for improvement. China benefits from ample financial capital, robust institutional infrastructure, extensive and effective technology transfer efforts, and substantial ethical flexibility, all of which have contributed to strength in direct inputs like software and data.

In other areas, however, China faces headwinds of varying force. From a structural standpoint, China's human capital is a mixed bag but improving in quality, while its commercialization infrastructure and capacity to develop the requisite computing equipment for AI development remain major weaknesses. China's researchers, firms, and governments are working to close these gaps. As these efforts unfold over the coming years, it will be essential to remember that China, as always, will follow its own path.

While China's AI development balance sheet shows a mixed record so far, China's support for emerging and foundational technologies unfolds over time, as it puts into place the building blocks of a specific industry.[58] These market "interventions" will benefit chosen national champion companies *at the same time* they help lay out a national infrastructure. Existing weaknesses and caveats notwithstanding, China's emergence as an AI power indicates that its combination of domestic innovation, foreign importation, state investment and support, and world-class talent appears to be working.

Notes

1 William C. Hannas and Didi Kirsten Tatlow, eds., *China's Quest for Foreign Technology: Beyond Espionage,* London: Routledge, 2021.

2 See, e.g., Peter Guy, "China Never Really Stopped Being a Copycat, and That's Why Its Tech Companies Aren't Changing the World," *South China Morning Post*, April 10, 2016.

3 See, e.g., James Pethokoukis, "America Dreams of Chinese State Capitalism," *The Week*, January 12, 2020; 167 Cong. Rec. S3481, daily ed. May 26, 2021, statement of Senator Mike Lee, China "has held a tight, cronyist, command-and-control grip over its economy—heavily subsidizing industries and constantly picking winners and losers. While China has picked up some steam through some of these actions, we cannot ignore that whatever momentum it may have acquired is of dubious success and minimal sustainability in the long run."

4 See, e.g., Regina M. Abrami et al., "Why China Can't Innovate," *Harvard Business Review*, March 2014; James Pethokoukis, "5 Questions for Matt Ridley on Innovation and Freedom," *AEIdeas*, June 9, 2020.

5 Mariana Mazzucato, "The Entrepreneurial State: Debunking Public vs. Private Sector Myths," *Public Affairs*, 2015; Organisation for Economic Cooperation and Development, "Science, Technology and Innovation in the New Economy," September 2000; Sabrina Howell, "Financing Innovation: Evidence from R&D Grants," *American Economic Review*, 107.4, 2017, pp. 1136–1164; Yun Liu, et al., "S&T Policy Evolution: A Comparison between the U.S. and China (1950-Present)," *IEEE Xplore*, September 2011; Richard P. Suttmeier, Cong Cao, and Denis Simon, "Knowledge Innovation and the Chinese Academy of Sciences," *Science*, 312, May 2006 pp. 58–59; Anna B. Puglisi et al., "Building the S&T Drivers of the Future: The National Innovation Base," July 2022.

6 Ngor Luong, Zachary Arnold, and Ben Murphy, "Understanding Chinese Government Guidance Funds: An Analysis of Chinese-Language Sources," Georgetown University, Center for Security and Emerging Technology, March 2021.

7 Curtis J. Milhaupt and Wentong Zheng, "Beyond Ownership: State Capitalism and the Chinese Firm," *Georgetown Law Journal*, March 2015.

8 Ashwin Acharya and Zachary Arnold, "Chinese Public AI R&D Spending: Provisional Findings," Georgetown University, Center for Security and Emerging Technology, December 2019.

9 Giuliana Viglione, "China Is Closing Gap with United States on Research Spending," *Nature*, January 15, 2020.

10 Fei Dian (斐典), "投资人逃离人工智能" (Investors Flee Artificial Intelligence), *36Kr*, September 25, 2019.

11 Zhao Xiaochun, "Baidu CEO Robin Li: We Spend 15% of Annual Revenue on AI," *KrASIA*, July 4, 2018.

12 Zachary Arnold, Ilya Rahkovsky, and Tina Huang, "Tracking AI Investment: Initial Findings from the Private Markets," Georgetown University, Center for Security and Emerging Technology, September 2020.

13 Ngor Luong, Zachary Arnold, and Ben Murphy, "Understanding Chinese Government Guidance Funds: An Analysis of Chinese-Language Sources," Georgetown University, Center for Security and Emerging Technology, March 2021; Hao Chen and Meg Rithmire, "The Rise of the Investor State: State Capital in the Chinese Economy," *Studies in Comparative International Development* 55, July 29, 2020.

14 See, e.g., Zeyi Yang, "Everything You Need to Know about the SenseTime IPO," *Protocol*, August 31, 2021.

15 Remco Zwetsloot et al., "China Is Fast Outpacing U.S. STEM PhD Growth," Georgetown University, Center for Security and Emerging Technology, August 2021.

16 Dahlia Peterson, Kayla Goode, and Diana Gehlhaus, "AI Education in China and the United States: A Comparative Assessment," Georgetown University, Center for Security and Emerging Technology, September 2021.

17 Remco Zwetsloot, "China's Approach to Tech Talent Competition: Policies, Results, and the Developing Global Response," *Global China*, April 2020.

18 Zwetsloot et al., 2021.

19 Hepeng Jia, "China's Science Ministry Gets Power to Attract More Foreign Scientists," *Nature Index*, March 23, 2018.

20 Remco Zwetsloot and Dahlia Peterson, "The US-China Tech Wars: China's Immigration Disadvantage," *The Diplomat*, December 31, 2019.

21 Fedasiuk, Ryan et al., "A Competitive Era for China's Universities: How Increased Funding Is Paving the Way," Georgetown University, CSET, March 2022.

22 Ibid. 16.

23 "Building a Consortium of State Key Laboratories to Develop Cutting-Edge Technologies in Nanniwan," *ChinaNewsWeb*, March 5, 2021.

24 "Kuang-Chi Group: A PRC Technology Acquisition Platform," *Pointe Bello*, February 2021; PRC Ministry of Science and Technology, 科技部关于组织申报企业国家重点实验室的通知 (Notice of the Ministry of Science and Technology on Organizing the Application of Enterprise State Key Laboratories) MOST 228, 2014; Wang Na (王纳), "光启刘若鹏:组建国家重点实验室联合体, 推广'贝尔实验室'群创新模式" (Kuang-Chi Liu Ruopeng: Establish a Consortium of State Key Laboratories to Promote the Innovation Model of 'Bell Laboratories' Group), *Guangzhou Daily* (广州日报), March 4, 2021.

25 Hannas, William C., James Mulvenon, and Anna B. Puglisi, *Chinese Industrial Espionage*, Routledge, London, 2013.

26 PRC National Development and Reform Commission, 加快推进战略性新兴产业产业集群建设有关工作通知 (Notice on accelerating the construction of industrial clusters in strategic emerging industries), NDRC 1473, 2019.

27 Xi Jinping (习近平), "推动我国新一代人工智能健康发展" (Promote the Healthy Development of China's New Generation of Artificial Intelligence), *Xinhuanet*, October 31, 2018.

28 Patrice Taddonio, "How China's Government Is Using AI on Its Uighur Muslim Population," *PBS*, November 21, 2019.

29 Anna B. Puglisi et al., "Building the S&T Drivers of the Future: The National Innovation Base," July 2022.

30 Zhang Jia (张佳), "清华孙茂松:中国AI最缺的是世界级科研领军人物" (Tsinghua University's Sun Maosong: The Biggest Deficiency of Chinese AI is the Lack of World-Class Scientific Research Leaders), QQ Net, accessed October 19, 2021.

31 See, e.g., Jack Clark, *ImportAI* 247, May 3, 2021.

32 "A few years ago, Chinese researchers were seen as fast followers on various AI innovations, but ERNIE [a Baidu language processing model] is one of a few models developed primarily by Chinese actors and now setting a meaningful SOTA [state-of-the-art result] on a benchmark developed elsewhere. We should take note." Jack Clark, *ImportAI* 259, July 26, 2021.

33 Lorand Laskai and Helen Toner, "Can China Grow Its Own AI Tech Base?"

34 Smriti Mallapaty, "China's Five-year Plan Focuses on Scientific Self-reliance," *Nature*, March 11, 2021.

35 See Kai-Fu Lee interview at *Frontline*, "In the Age of AI," https://www.pbs.org/wgbh/frontline/film/in-the-age-of-ai/transcript/.

36 Zach Dorfman, "Tech Giants Are Giving China a Vital Edge in Espionage," *Foreign Policy*, December 23, 2020.

37 Husanjot Chahal et al., "Messier than Oil: Assessing Data Advantage in Military AI," Georgetown University, Center for Security and Emerging Technology, July 2020.
38 Li Guofei (李国飞), "全面反思腾讯的战略已暴露了非常严重的问题" (A Total Rethinking of Tencent's Strategy Has Exposed Very Serious Problems), *Sina Finance*, August 14, 2018.
39 Sun Yu, "Jack Ma's Ant Defies Pressure from Beijing to Share More Customer Data," *Financial Times*, March 1, 2021.
40 Wu Xin (吴昕), "朱松纯:强认知AI的领路人" (Zhu Songchun: the Leader of Strong AI), *Jiqizhixin* (机器之心). January 29, 2021.
41 Husanjot Chahal et al., "Small Data's Big AI Potential," Georgetown University, Center for Security and Emerging Technology, September 2021.
42 Dario Amodei and Danny Hernandez, "AI and Compute," OpenAI, May 16, 2018; Saif M. Khan, "AI Chips: What They Are and Why They Matter," Georgetown University, Center for Security and Emerging Technology, April 2020.
43 Saif M. Khan, 2020; Saif M. Khan, "The Semiconductor Supply Chain: Assessing National Competitiveness," Georgetown University, Center for Security and Emerging Technology, January 2021.
44 Wei Sheng, "China Spends More Importing Semiconductors Than Oil," *TechNode*, April 29, 2021; Wency Chen, "Alibaba Ramping up TSMC Orders as Huawei Moves to Mainland for Chips," *KrASIA*, May 8, 2020.
45 Will Hunt et al., "China's Progress in Semiconductor Manufacturing Equipment," 2012; Organisation for Economic Cooperation and Development, "Measuring Distortions in International Markets: The Semiconductor Value Chain," OECD Trade Policy Papers 234, December 12, 2019.
46 Ibid.
47 David Manners, "China Falling Badly Short of 'Made In China 2025' Chip Target," *Electronics Weekly*, May 22, 2020; Kevin Xu, "China's 'Semiconductor Theranos': HSMC," *Interconnected*, March 4, 2021.
48 Hunt et al., 2012.
49 Dario Amodei and Danny Hernandez, "AI and Compute," *OpenAI*, May 16, 2018.
50 "高文院士在中共中央政治局讲解人工智能发展后首次接受专访" (Academician Gao Wen's First Interview after Briefing on AI Development to CCP Politburo), November 28, 2018, http://www.ciotimes.com/Information/163989.html.
51 "谭铁牛院士人大常委会讲座: 人工智能的创新发展与社会影响" (Academician Tan Tieniu's Remarks at the National People's Congress Standing Committee: Development of Innovation in Artificial Intelligence and Its Societal Impact), October 29, 2019, https://www.secrss.com/articles/14992.
52 Gao Wen, op. cit.
53 Tan Tieniu, op. cit.
54 Gao Lei (高蕾), Fu Yongquan (符永铨), Li Dongsheng (李东升), and Liao Xiangke (廖湘科), "我国人工智能核心软硬件发展战略研究" (Development Strategy for the Core Software and Hardware of Artificial Intelligence in China) in *Strategic Study of Chinese Academy of Engineering* (中国工程科学) 23.3, March 2021.
55 Gao et al. "我国人工智能核心软硬件发展战略研究"
56 Ibid.
57 Sara Abdulla, "China's Robotics Patent Landscape," Georgetown University, Center for Security and Emerging Technology, August 2021; Margarita Konaev and Sara M. Abdulla, "Trends in Robotics Patents: A Global Overview and an Assessment of Russia," Georgetown University, Center for Security and Emerging Technology, November 2021; Sara Abdulla, "Concentrations of AI-Related Topics in Research: Robotics," Georgetown University, Center for Security and Emerging Technology, September 2021.
58 Alex Rubin, Alan Omar Loera Martinez, Jake Dow, and Anna B. Puglisi "The Huawei Moment," Georgetown University, Center for Security and Emerging Technology, July 2021.

Bibliography

Chen, Hao, and Meg Rithmire. "The Rise of the Investor State: State Capital in the Chinese Economy." *Studies in Comparative International Development* 55, 2020.

Gao Lei (高蕾), Fu Yongquan (符永铨), Li Dongsheng (李东升), and Liao Xiangke (廖湘科), "我国人工智能核心软硬件发展战略研究" (Development Strategy for the Core Software and Hardware of Artificial Intelligence in China), *Strategic Study of Chinese Academy of Engineering* (中国工程科学) 23.3, March 2021, pp. 90–97.

Hunt, Will, Saif M. Khan, and Dahlia Peterson. "China's Progress in Semiconductor Manufacturing Equipment." Georgetown University, Center for Security and Emerging Technology, March 2021.

Laskai, Lorand, and Helen Toner. "Can China Grow Its Own AI Tech Base?" New America Cybersecurity Initiative, November 4, 2019.

Luong, Ngor, Zachary Arnold, and Ben Murphy, "Understanding Chinese Government Guidance Funds: An Analysis of Chinese-Language Sources," Georgetown University, Center for Security and Emerging Technology, March 2021.

Milhaupt, Curtis J., and Wentong Zheng. "Beyond Ownership: State Capitalism and the Chinese Firm." *Georgetown Law Journal* 103 (3), March 2015, 665–722.

Naughton, Barry. *The Rise of China's Industrial Policy*, 1978 to 2020. Universidad Nacional Autónoma de México, Centro de Estudios China-México, Mexico, 2021.

Organisation for Economic Cooperation and Development. Main Science and Technology Indicators 1, 2020.

Organisation for Economic Cooperation and Development. "Measuring Distortions in International Markets: The Semiconductor Value Chain." OECD Trade Policy Papers 234, December 12, 2019.

PRC Ministry of Science and Technology. 科技部关于组织申报企业国家重点实验室的通知 (Notice of the Ministry of Science and Technology on Organizing the Application of Enterprise State Key Laboratories), MOST 228, 2014.

Stanford Institute for Human-Centered Artificial Intelligence. AI Index Report, 2021.

Xi, Jinping (习近平). 推动我国新一代人工智能健康发展 ("Promote the Healthy Development of China's New Generation of Artificial Intelligence"), *Xinhuanet*, October 31, 2018.

Zwetsloot, Remco. "China's Approach to Tech Talent Competition: Policies, Results, and the Developing Global Response." Georgetown University, Center for Security and Emerging Technology, April 2020.

PART III

Impact on cutting-edge disciplines

7

Chinese AI and neuroscience

William C. Hannas and Huey-Meei Chang

The preceding chapters outlined China's AI strengths. We now examine the impact of Chinese AI on three cutting-edge disciplines—neuroscience, biology, and quantum computing—that will shape humanity in the coming decades.

The present chapter expands earlier research by its authors on China's efforts to merge human and artificial intelligence and realize a first-mover advantage in AI competition.[1] China was doing brain-inspired AI research before it recognized AI as a standalone discipline. Its influence on Chinese AI today is apparent in the Chinese language literature—less so in English sources, where little information on this part of China's AI program is available.

We introduce the technologies, review statutory support, analyze key documents defining the project, sketch its infrastructure, and review the associated scholarship that leads us to conclude that China is actively pursuing the challenges characteristic of AI-brain research worldwide.[2]

Why "AI + brain"?

AI's dirty secret is that it began as an effort to replicate human thought.[3] As the magnitude of building artificial *general* intelligence (AGI) sank in, and other early hopes—such as fostering a superhuman "intelligence explosion"—faded,[4] AI specialists retreated from these broad themes toward "narrow" AI focused on more limited, achievable tasks,[5] where it succeeded grandly.

Despite this progress, AI faces a crunch because its development[6] remains tied to needs driven by human cognition. Next-generation tasks such as decision-making, planning, and computer vision, not to mention continual learning, metalearning, and creativity—all innate features of our "three pound universe"[7]—have proven to be devilishly difficult to emulate on silicon, prompting new interest, in China and universally, in computationally modeling real cognitive processes.

DOI: 10.4324/9781003212980-10

We start by reviewing efforts to bring AI and brain science into alignment. Scientists worldwide distinguish three broad categories of AI-brain research: brain-inspired artificial intelligence (BI-AI, 类脑智能), connectomics (人脑连接组), and brain-computer interfaces (BCIs, 脑机接口).

- BI-AI seeks mathematical descriptions of brain processes that contribute to behavior. This is understood literally, not as a metaphor—the models match the actual "computation performed by biological wetware."[8]
- Connectomics involves empirical and computational efforts to replicate brain structure and functioning. The link with AI derives from a need to invoke AI to test simulations, and from AI's role in interpreting (aligning) images of brain sections.
- BCIs acquire electrical signals from the brain, interpret them, and optionally transform the signals into actions. Their link with AI is two-fold: AI is used to process brain signals and, potentially, support direct access to computing resources.

Although many goals of AI-brain research parallel mainstream AI, the difference is that the latter, at best, mimics human behavior, while the former replicates the neuronal functions that give rise to behavior. While not aimed necessarily at rehabilitating the AGI paradigm, the likelihood of this research ending up there is believed by Chinese experts to be higher or inevitable.[9] A review of the technologies is illustrative.

Brain-inspired AI addresses the limitations of traditional AI—its narrowness, slowness, and cost—by modeling real brain features and functions (see Box 7.1). The artificial neural networks (ANNs) used in most types of machine learning (ML) ignore most of what happens inside the brain:

> (F)or a particular neuron in the brain, only 5% to 10% of the input is actually coming from the previous layers. On the other hand, a[n artificial] neural network is almost 100% learning from a previous layer.[10]

For brain-like AI to succeed, one must look beyond traditional AI architectures to other aspects of brain function, such as firing rates, local field potentials, co-firing of neurons, system oscillations, and non-binary events happening outside the synaptic cleft—not to mention links with other cortical areas and subcortical structures needed for sensory integration and higher order functions.

Other key areas of AI research of relevance to BI-AI are as follows:

- **Sparse coding**, namely, the ability to represent things by strongly activating a small subset of the available neurons, achieved by modeling a network's hidden states.
- **Metalearning**, or learning how to learn—in this context, teaching a system to make sense of a task, rather than learning a brittle representation of the data.

BOX 7.1

SOME (ASPIRATIONAL) FEATURES OF BI-AI THAT DISTINGUISH IT FROM AI IMPLEMENTED ON STANDARD NEURAL NETWORKS[11]

- Structure and function follow those of a brain
- Data and information are encoded and processed as spikes over time
- The system can scale to trillions of connections and is highly parallel in operation
- It allows (in theory) for "one pass" learning based on little prior knowledge
- It is computationally inexpensive

- **Transfer learning**, whereby knowledge gained in one domain is transferred to new domains, reducing learning time and potentially enabling planning and creativity.
- **Context-dependent learning** meant to eliminate catastrophic forgetting, an endemic problem in ANNs, where new information erases previously learned patterns.

Connectomics or "brain-mapping" is a physical process that relies on the observation of actual brain tissues for its data. It is hard for a discipline to be any less artificial. Connectomics aims at discovering the brain's structural linkages, functional correlations, and causal interactions.[12] The term mimics "genomics" by design, which belies its goal of creating a detailed map of the human brain.[13] It is based on a commonsense belief that the brain's physical wiring affects (but does not determine) the computations it can perform.

Connectomics uses three mapping scales. Macro-scale investigates links between cortical and subcortical areas at the millimeter scale. Micro-scale connectomics maps individual neurons, synapses, and sub-cellular parts visible at micrometer[14] resolution using electron-microscopy. "Meso-scale" (hundreds of micrometers) is an intermediate level that can be acquired and exploited with current tools.

Data are collected non-invasively (outside the skull) by imaging in vivo tissue, and by section preparation of deceased brain tissue into 20-40-micron slices, stained, imaged, and aligned in the original 3D configuration. AI supports these reconstructions, which are skewed by inaccuracies in the tools. Owing to its complexity, there is no connectome yet of the human brain, although experts believe that it will eventually be assembled.[15]

BCIs are mechanisms that link the central nervous system with a computational device. Information is exchanged between the two without invoking the sensory receptors through electrodes planted on or under the scalp, inside the skull but outside the brain, or in direct contact with living brain tissue. Historically, neuroprosthetics—devices that supplant or supplement the input/output of the nervous system—has been the main purpose of BCI. More recently, opportunities for cognitive enhancement have captured the attention of commercial[16] and military[17] investors and the imaginations of others, who foresee telepathic communication, virtual life experiences, and unlimited knowledge.[18]

Chinese statutory support for AI-brain research

China's interest in brain science, and in brain-AI research especially, is reflected in statutes that predate its focus on "AI" alone. The following chronology is indicative:

- The "National Medium- and Long-term S&T Development Plan (2006-2020)"[19] counted "brain science and cognition" (脑科学与认知) among its top eight research topics.
- The "12th Five-year Plan for National S&T Development"[20] issued in July 2011 listed "brain science and cognitive science" (脑科学与认知科学) as "important research topics."
- In May 2015, a Shanghai notification put the *composite term* "brain science and artificial intelligence" (脑科学与人工智能) among its "first priorities" for S&T development.[21]
- The China Brain Project (中国脑计划), a 15-year project approved in March 2016 as part of the 13th Five-year Plan, also "prioritized brain-inspired AI over other approaches."[22]

By contrast, "AI" appeared as late as 2015 in state notifications as a catalyst for other types of research only.[23] On May 30, 2016, President Xi Jinping in a speech titled "Striving to Build a World S&T Superpower" referenced "connectomics" without referencing AI.[24]

On July 28, 2016, a "State Council Notification on National S&T Innovation Programs for the 13th Five-year Plan" was issued.[25] The document is relevant here mostly for what it does not emphasize: although AI is mentioned, it is not a major project. "Brain-inspired computing" (类脑计算) and "brain-computer intelligence" (脑机智能) are.

By the end of 2016, China was moving to accept AI in its own right. On November 29, 2016, the State Council released another notification related to the 13th Five-year Plan.[26] Among 21 projects listed, the fifth called for "innovative engineering in artificial intelligence" although the link with brain is still apparent:

> Promote basic theoretical research and core technology development, realize the commercialization of *neuromorphic computing chips*, intelligent robots

and intelligent application systems, embed new artificial intelligence technologies in various fields.[27]

Two events the following year marked China's top-down, formal drive to combine cognitive neuroscience and AI research. On July 8, 2017, the State Council issued "The New Generation AI Development Plan"[28] with its goal of worldwide AI hegemony.[29] Buried in the plan is what we regard as its most significant aspect, namely, an effort to "merge" (混合) human and artificial intelligence.

As stated in its introduction, the goal of the 2017 plan is "a *first-mover advantage* in artificial intelligence."[30] "Brain science research" and "brain intelligence" are key elements of a program aimed at "major breakthroughs" and the "commanding heights of AI technology." Specifically:

> Brain-like intelligent computing theory focuses on breakthroughs in brain-like information coding, processing, memory, learning, and reasoning theories; on forming brain-like complex systems, brain-like control, and other theories and methods; and on establishing new models of large-scale brain-like intelligent computing and brain-inspired cognitive computing models.

"AI-brain" occupies two of the plan's eight "basic theory" categories, specifically "(3) hybrid enhanced intelligent theory" and "(7) brain intelligent computing theory," further defined as follows:

> Research theories and methods of brain-like perception, brain-like learning, brain-like memory mechanisms and computational fusion, brain-like complex systems, and brain-like control.

Later in the document under "intelligent computing chips and systems," the plan states:

> Focusing on breakthroughs in energy-efficient, reconfigurable brain-like computing chips and brain-like vision sensor technologies with computational imaging capabilities, we shall research and develop high-performance brain-like neural network architectures and hardware systems with autonomous learning capabilities to achieve multimedia-aware information understanding and intelligent growth, brain-like intelligent systems with *common sense reasoning* ability. (our italics)

On August 2, 2017, a "National Natural Science Foundation of China Artificial Intelligence Basic Research Urgent Management Project Guide"[31] solicited proposals for 25 AI projects. Its first section outlined three areas of support for AI's "new stage"—all are brain-related. Ten "research areas" (研究方向) were

---

BOX 7.2

CHINA NNSF COG-NEURO-INSPIRED AI FUNDING SUBCATEGORIES

- F060701 computational modeling of cognitive mechanisms (基于认知机理的计算模型)
- F060702 modeling attention, learning, and memory (脑认知的注意、学习与记忆机制的建模)
- F060703 audiovisual perception modeling (视听觉感知模型)
- F060704 neural information encoding and decoding (神经信息编码与解码)
- F060705 neural system modeling and analysis (神经系统建模与分析)
- F060706 neuromorphic engineering (神经形态工程)
- F060707 neuromorphic chips (类脑芯片)
- F060708 brain-like computing (类脑计算)
- F060709 BCI and neural engineering (脑机接口与神经工程)

---

nominated, most falling under AI-brain fusion.[32] In January 2018, the NNSF followed up with "project guidelines," which for the first time named AI as a standalone category—with *nine subcategories* for "cognitive and neuroscience-inspired AI"[33] (see box 7.2).

Besides NNSF, China's Ministry of Science and Technology (MOST), Chinese Academy of Sciences (CAS), and local municipalities also announced grants for AI-brain research.[34] Other funding is provided by the Central Military Commission's Science and Technology Committee (中央军事委员会科学技术委员会), other relevant ministries, universities, enterprises, and private foundations.[35] In terms of scholarship and support, it is clear that China has committed to this alternative paradigm.

Finally, a September 2021 MOST document "Science and Technology Innovation 2030—'Brain Science and Brain-like Research' Megaproject 2021 Annual Project Application Guidelines" hints at China's future BI-AI research.[36] Funded areas, besides "principles of cognition" and interventions to heal cognitive impairments, include "brain-like computing and brain-computer intelligence" with a focus on advanced BCI, neuromorphic chips for nano-devices (presumably implants), and deep reinforcement learning aimed at a "higher level of AGI" (人工通用智能).

Our argument is not that China has ignored AI itself. Papers on neural nets and foundational AI technologies have appeared in Chinese journals since the turn of the century. Rather, the claim is that China sees AI more as a means to practical ends (the "AI +" formula) and less as a solitary endeavor. To cite a popular Chinese techno-novel: "In China, any detached thoughts will crash to the ground. The gravity of reality is too strong."[37]

Chinese scientists' goals and understanding

Besides these state notifications, a review of Chinese technical papers suggests that China fully embraced AI-brain research around 2016. We examine a few examples.[38]

- "Retrospect and Outlook of Brain-inspired Intelligence Research" (类脑智能研究的回顾与展望).[39]

  The paper describes BI-AI as AI's future, and defines China's near-term goals as semantic recognition of perceptual information; collaborative and continuous autonomous learning; efficient big data computing; and brain-like language processing. Autonomous decision-making and control will also be explored. In short:

  > The goal is to realize various human cognitive functions as well as their coordination mechanisms by machine through brain-inspired principles, and eventually reach and go beyond human-level intelligence. (最终达到或超越人类智能水平).

- "Brain Science and Brain-inspired Intelligence Technology-an Overview" (脑科学与类脑研究概述).[40]

  The brain's structure and functional connectivity provide models to solve intransigent problems in traditional AI, which is "not well adapted to real needs." It "lacks generalizability" (缺乏通用性) and learned capabilities cannot be easily extended. While deep learning has made successes, they are shallow and expensive.

- "Progress and Prospect on the Strategic Priority Research Program of 'Mapping Brain Functional Connections and Intelligence Technology'" ("脑功能联结图谱与类脑智能研究"先导专项研究进展和展望).[41]

  The goal "is not to describe all the connections and electrical activities of all nerve cells" but "the functional connections and operation between special types of nerve cell groups in various brain regions" as a precondition for computer-based perception, learning and memory, artificial emotion, decision-making, and self-awareness (自我意识).

- "Neuroscience and Brain-inspired Artificial Intelligence: Challenges and Opportunities" (神经科学和类脑人工智能发展: 机遇与挑战).[42]

  This is a clarion call from the Shanghai-area institutes. The paper celebrates the inclusion of BI-AI in China's top-down planning and urges state support for AI-brain fusion. Its authors foresee "major breakthroughs in brain-like computers and brain-inspired artificial intelligence" by 2025.

- "China Brain Project: Basic Neuroscience, Brain Diseases, and Brain-inspired Computing" (全面解读中国脑计划: 从基础神经科学到脑启发计算).[43]

  "Brain-inspired computing methods and systems are essential to achieve stronger artificial intelligence (AI) and harness the ever-increasing amount of information." China will research alternative brain-inspired "infrastructures" such as neuromorphic chips and model the brain's ability to combine computation and storage. Other research includes concept formation, "cognition of self and non-self, empathy, and theory of mind." In particular:

> Learning from information processing mechanisms of the brain is clearly a promising way forward in building stronger and more general machine intelligence. (通用的机器智能).

> The goal is to simulate in principle the mechanisms and architecture of the brain at multiple levels to meet the grand challenge of making a general AI (更具有普遍性的AI) capable of multitasking, learning, and self-adapting.

- "The Strategic Option of Neuroscience and Brain-inspired Artificial Intelligence in China: Based on a Hundred Experts' Insights" (神经科学和类脑人工智能发展: 未来路径与中国布局——基于业界百位专家调研访谈).[44]
  The authors consulted "over a hundred experts" on a roadmap for Chinese brain-inspired AI. The results are captured in a proposed "3 + 2 + 2" model for brain science, brain-inspired research, and AI that addresses both practical and theoretical areas.
- "Current Situation and Prospect of the Basic Translational Application of Brain and Brain-inspired Intelligence in Shanghai" (上海市脑与类脑智能基础转化应用研究的现状及展望).[45]
  Brain-inspired AI systems are a "core breakthrough point for next generation AI." Although China's focus has been on practical applications, attention will be given to cutting-edge research in theory, algorithms, simulation, and the creation of data standards.
- "Brain-like Machine: Thought and Architecture" (类脑机的思想与体系结构综述).[46]
  The paper reviews worldwide developments as evidence that BI-AI will lead over the next 20 years to "machines with structure close to the brain and performance far beyond the brain."

These policy papers are a window into China's overall research directions. Chinese language AI-brain *technical* papers also evidence a sharp rise in 2016, as shown in Figure 7.1.[47]

Pronouncements by leading scientists underscore this trend. Pu Muming (Poo Mu-Ming), the Shanghai-based, Chinese-American neuroscientist, noted:

> The Chinese government approved a major 2030 S&T Project on Brain Science and Brain-Inspired Technology, also known as the 'China Brain Project' (中国脑计划), "aiming in part to apply neuroscience knowledge for the development of next-generation AI with human-like intelligence and

CNKI Papers Per Year - BI-AI

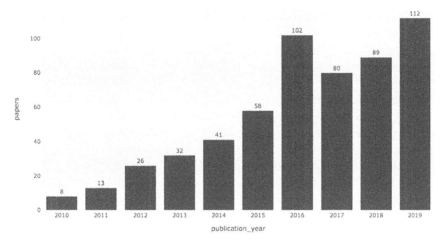

FIGURE 7.1 Brain-inspired AI papers in China's CNKI database (reprinted with permission from GU/CSET "China AI-brain Research")

brain–machine interface technology. Thus we expect an accelerated development of brain-inspired AI technology in China in the coming decade.[48]

Pu went on to state: "*If the ultimate goal of AI is to achieve human intelligence*", then it would be useful to introduce structural and operational principles of the brain into the design of computing algorithms and devices." (our italics)

Zhang Xu (张旭) and seven other BI/connectomics researchers also reference the 2016 launch of the Brain Science and Brain-Inspired Technology project as a game-changer for China AI, noting as does Pu:

> Using the functional connectome big data, computational neuroscientists will build theoretical models of perception and cognition, to *establish a basis for developing a simulated brain, and the corresponding AI algorithms and hardware*.[49] (our italics)

AI-brain research centers and personalities

China's brain-inspired approach to AI is also evidenced in its organizations and distribution of talent. We identified 31 institutes in China doing BI-AI, connectomics, or BCI *as a primary line of research*.[50] Here are six:

1. Fudan University's Institute of Science and Technology for Brain-Inspired Intelligence (复旦大学类脑智能科学与技术研究院) in Shanghai, launched in 2015, studies cognitive neuroscience, computational biology, biomedical

imaging, neural engineering, and brain-inspired chips.[51] Run by Feng Jianfeng, it has the world's largest brain science database with access to the U.S. Human Connectome Project, England's Biobank, and the "largest number of MRI devices in Asia."[52]

2. The Chinese Academy of Science's Center for Excellence in Brain Science and Intelligence Technology (中国科学院脑科学与智能技术卓越创新中心), launched in 2016 in Shanghai, draws on "resources from 20 research institutions and 80 top laboratories" nationwide.[53] Directed by Pu Muming, CEBSIT explores the neural basis of cognitive functions, neuron-inspired chips, connectomics, image recognition, brain-inspired robotics, and semantic comprehension.[54] It also does primate research.[55]

3. The HUST-Suzhou Institute for Brainsmatics (华中科技大学苏州脑空间信息研究院), founded in 2016 in Wuhan, is managed by Luo Qingming with a staff of 120. The institute explores "multi-scale temporal-spatial characteristics of brain architectural and functional connectivity." Its commitment to mesoscale connectomics is based on Micro-Optical Sectioning Tomography aimed at building "a high-resolution mammalian brain atlas."[56]

4. Hefei's University of Science and Technology of China has a National Engineering Laboratory for Brain-inspired Intelligence Technology and Application (类脑智能技术及应用国家工程实验室), founded in 2017 with government and industry participation. Research areas include cognition and neural computing, brain-inspired multimodal sensing, neuromorphic chips, brain-inspired intelligent robotics, and quantum AI.[57]

5. The Chinese Institute for Brain Research (北京脑科学与类脑研究中心) was "deployed" in 2018 as a cooperative framework for local universities, the PLA Academy of Military Science (军事科学院), and others.[58] It "coordinates research institutes and manages research programs under the China Brain Initiative" to make Beijing the "world epicenter for neuroscience and brain-inspired computation."[59]

6. The Beijing Academy of Artificial Intelligence (北京智源人工智能研究院) was established in 2018 under Huang Tiejun to integrate neuroscience, cognitive science, and information science, on its way to building "strong artificial intelligence" (强人工智能) and "super-brain" (超脑) intelligent systems.[60]

Twelve more institutes demonstrate China's diverse commitment to the BI paradigm:

- Beijing Key Laboratory of Human-Computer Interaction (人机交互北京市重点实验室), since 1999.
- CAS Institute of Automation, Research Center for Brain-inspired Intelligence (中科院自动化研究所,类脑智能研究中心) established in Beijing in 2015.[61]
- CAS Institute of Psychology, Key Laboratory of Behavioral Science (行为科学重点实验室), established in 2009 in Beijing, and certified in 2014.

- International Mesoscopic Connectome Project (国际介观连接体项目) within CAS's Institute of Neuroscience (中国科学院神经科学研究所), since 1999.
- Shanghai Jiaotong University Center for Brain-like Computing and Machine Intelligence (仿脑计算与机器智能研究中心), since 2002.
- Shanghai Research Center for Brain Science and Brain-inspired Intelligence (上海脑科学与类脑研究中心), since 2018.[62]
- Shanghai's G60 Brain Intelligence Innovation Park (G60脑智科创基地), another Pu Muming venture, established in 2018.
- State Key Laboratory of Brain & Cognitive Science (脑与认知科学国家重点实验室) in Beijing, 2005.
- State Key Laboratory of Cognitive Neuroscience and Learning (认知神经科学与学习国家重点实验室) founded at Beijing Normal University in 2005.
- Tsinghua University BCI Lab (清华大学脑机接口研究组) in Beijing, in operation since 2004.
- Tsinghua University's Center for Brain-inspired Computing Research (类脑计算研究中心), established in 2014.
- Tsinghua University's Institute for Brain and Cognitive Sciences (脑与认知科学研究院), since 2019.

In Chapter 13, we discuss China's AGI facilities, whose goals surpass those listed here. The 12 provincial institutes cited in our 2020 paper[63] are omitted for lack of space. Their research includes BCI, cognitive computing, computer vision and learning, connectomics, mammalian brain modeling, NLP, neural coding, neuromorphic chips, and neuro-robotics.

Staffing these organizations is a cadre of world-class scientists. We identified 390 specialists in all,[64] sampled below. Candidacy for the following list is based on leadership, publications, and international standing.

- **Feng Jianfeng** (冯建峰) is the chair of the Shanghai National Center for Mathematical Sciences, the dean of ISTBI at Fudan University, and a professor at the Centre for Scientific Computing and Computer Science at Warwick University.
- **Huang Tiejun** (黄铁军) is the vice-chair of Peking University's Institute for Artificial Intelligence, the dean of the Beijing Academy of Artificial Intelligence, and is on the New Generation Artificial Intelligence Governance Expert Committee.
- **Liu Jia** (刘嘉) is a professor in Tsinghua's Department of Psychology and the Tsinghua Laboratory of Brain and Intelligence. He is also the chief scientist at the Beijing Academy of Artificial Intelligence.
- **Luo Minmin** (罗敏敏) is an investigator at the National Institute of Biological Sciences, Beijing, a professor at Tsinghua University's School of Life Sciences, and the director of the Chinese Institute for Brain Research in Beijing.

- **Luo Qingming** (骆清铭) is the president of Hainan University, the dean of the Wuhan Optoelectronics National Research Center of HUSTechnology, and the founder of the HUST-Suzhou Institute for Brainsmatics.
- **Ming Dong** (明东) is the director of the Tianjin Key Laboratory of Brain Science and Neuroengineering, the head of its Brain Science and Brain-inspired Research Center, and the developer of the "Brain Talker" chip.
- **Pan Gang** (潘刚) is a professor at Zhejiang University's College of Computer Science and Technology, the vice-director of the State Key Lab of CAD&CG, and an associate editor of several international journals.
- **Pu Muming** (蒲慕明) is the founder of the Institute of Neuroscience and CEBSIT, and the head of the Laboratory of Neural Plasticity. Pu is a foreign member of the CAS (he became a PRC citizen in 2018), and a member of the U.S. National Academy of Sciences.
- **Rao Yi** (饶毅) is the president of Capital Medical University in Beijing, the founding director of the PKU-IDG/McGovern Institute for Brain Research, and the founding director of the Chinese Institute for Brain Research in Beijing.
- **Shi Luping** (施路平) is the director of Tsinghua University's Center for Brain-inspired Computing Research. Shi earned a PhD at Cologne University and was the program manager at Singapore's Academy of Science for AI and memory projects.
- **Xu Bo** (徐波) is the director of CAS's Institute of Automation, the associate director of CEBSIT, and the chair of the "Next Generation Artificial Intelligence Strategic Advisory Committee." He also serves as the director of USTC's Department of Automation.
- **Zeng Yi** (曾毅) is a professor and deputy director of CASIA's Research Center for Brain-inspired Intelligence, a principal investigator at CEBSIT, a Berggruen Institute fellow, and serves on the 2019 New Generation Artificial Intelligence Governance Expert Committee.

Biographies of these and other AI-brain luminaries are in our 2020 paper.[65] Two diaspora scholars also bear mention for their contributions to China's BI programs: **Xiao-Jing Wang** (汪小京), director of the Schwartz Center for Theoretical Neuroscience at New York University, and **Jianwei Zhang** (张建伟) at the University of Hamburg.[66]

Review and appraisal of Chinese AI-brain research

Three methods were used to assess China's research in this field: (1) a keyword-based literature review, (2) expert evaluation, and (3) a scientific survey of the principles.

1. Literature review

To determine how well Chinese research matches international goals, we compiled a short-list of BI-AI "hot" topics from standard references,[67] as shown in Box 7.3.

BOX 7.3

SOME GOALS OF AI-BRAIN RESEARCH

object/scene vision A nearly intractable problem in computer science, in part caused by the lack of data to build algorithms of the brain's intermediate vision processes

attention modeling Biological attention mechanisms work to prioritize and isolate information relevant at a given moment

continual learning Another name for the "catastrophic forgetting" problem, i.e. learning new tasks without forgetting old ones

episodic memory Recording of and access to personal (autobiographical) events that can be explicitly stated along with their associated context

intuitive understanding Including core concepts abstracted by the brain from experience or, by some accounts, present from birth

imagination Recombining elements familiar in one context into a new context on the basis of analogy (see "transfer learning" above)

planning Closely related to imagination: the ability to run simulated outcomes based on internalized models

sensemaking Identifying relationships that situate new or ambiguous data in a familiar context

effective BCI Linking intact brains directly with computing resources to cure/manage illness, enhance human performance, or augment cognition

neuromorphic computing Chips based on mixed digital/analog—or entirely analog—designs, meant to emulate functioning neuronal structures

---

We then examined the 561 BI-AI papers in Table A[68] and found 352 or 63% binning into one or more of these advanced categories, suggesting that the Chinese research aligns well with global scientific aspirations.

2. SME assessment

A cognitive neuroscientist was retained with a grounding in ML, fluent Chinese, field experience at American labs, and acquaintance with leading Chinese AI-brain principals. Here are some takeaways from our interviews[69]:

- There is a core of scientists genuinely interested in BI-AI research, who are deriving generalizable computing schemes and data representation principles from brain data. This group coincides with the leadership at the Beijing and Shanghai institutes.
- China is rapidly gaining footing in the BI-AI research community on par with Western institutes, as indicated in part by the quantity of accepted

papers at International AI conferences and by cover articles in prominent journals over the last five years.

- China is actively developing software and algorithms for studying connectomes. The CAS Institute of Automation (CASIA) ranks in the top ten internationally, alongside Princeton and MIT, showing that they are invested in this field and are excelling.[70]
- The most cutting-edge BCI work has been conducted on macaque monkeys. China's brain initiative expanded primate facilities in and around China to house thousands of macaques and marmoset monkeys.
- China's political and scientific leaders increasingly recognize BI-AI as a worthy investment, as they believe that this will lead to the next generation of AI. The AI-brain project will be an abiding feature of China's AI landscape.

3. Survey of principals

We also surveyed two groups of PRC scientists—BI-AI specialists and AI generalists—directly on their views about China's AI-brain project.[71] Here are the stats:

- Researchers are split in their views of BI-AI: 39% see it as a normal progression of AI research, 35% see it as "transformational," and 27% regard BI-AI as one of many parallel approaches. More specialists (42% to 28%) see it as transformational.
- A large majority of respondents (88%) consider foreign collaboration to be important to their research. Specialists were more likely to indicate foreign collaboration as extremely important (63%), while generalists selected somewhat important (48%).
- Both groups believe that BI-AI will have more impact over the next five years than other competing approaches; about 84% selected this option. Only 40% of the generalists see neuromorphic computing as having an impact, compared to 79% of the specialists.
- A majority of researchers (74%) think that brain-inspired AI will someday lead to AGI. This prediction is more common among specialists (83%) than generalists (64%). Of those who predicted AGI at all, a majority (63%) believe that AGI is more than 10 years out.
- 92% of generalists and specialists agree that inadequate basic research is an "obstacle" to the success of China's next-generation AI program.[72] Only 16% of all respondents regard inadequate funding as a factor.

In sum, China's AI-brain program has wide support within its scientific community, addresses international benchmark challenges, and is integrated into the R&D infrastructure. *We assess it to be a credible effort that merits attention and respect*. What are some potential roadblocks?

Basic research has been a stumbling block in China and AI is no exception. Best-selling AI author Kai-Fu Lee argues that China's forte is its ability to create practical AI products, not revolutionize the field.[73] His point is supported by China's top scientists. Here is a sample[74]:

- Sun Maosong (孙茂松), Tsinghua University professor of computer science, argues that China lacks leaders in world-class scientific research and falls behind other countries in training "top talent in the basic sciences."[75]
- Tan Tieniu (谭铁牛), former deputy director of CAS, claims, "At present, China is still in the 'follow-up' position in terms of frontier theoretical innovation of artificial intelligence. Most of the innovations are focused on technology applications."[76]
- Xu Kuangdi (徐匡迪), former head of the Chinese Academy of Engineering (CAE), said, "The cornerstone of artificial intelligence is mathematics, and the key element is algorithms. But China's investment in this field is far behind the United States."[77]
- Yau Shing-Tung (丘成桐), Harvard professor and Fields Medal winner, concludes that China "is still some distance from the United States and Britain in terms of basic theory and algorithm innovation."[78]
- Zheng Nanning (郑南宁), another CAE academician, believes that it will take China 5–10 years to reach world levels in basic theoretical and algorithmic research. Hardware design is also an issue.[79]

These complaints are valid but mostly irrelevant. Theory cannot be embargoed and there is no will to do so by governments or scientists. Accordingly, China is addressing this problem as it always has, by a robust program of foreign interaction, cooperation, co-option, incentives, and—like everyone else—by monitoring publicly available information.

One can also question the role that theory—or, at least, its indigenous construct—must play in achieving China's goal of a "more comprehensive"[80] union of human and artificial intelligence. Many of the obstacles to realizing this merger, such as better equipment, application of human and computing resources, data storage and accessibility, and availability of lab animals, do not depend on radical scientific "breakthroughs."

The key is will, which China seems not to lack, driven by the prospect of commercialization and a "first-mover advantage" (先发优势).[81]

Notes

1 Hannas and Chang, et al., "China AI-Brain Research," Georgetown University, Center for Security and Emerging Technology, September 2020.
2 Licensed data used in this chapter are reproduced from prior CSET analytic production with authors' permission.
3 Ben Goertzel and Cassio Pennachin, eds., *Artificial General Intelligence*, New York: Springer, 2007, p. 1.

4 I. J. Good, "Speculations Concerning the First Ultraintelligent Machine," *Advances in Computers*, no. 6, 1966, pp. 31–88.

5 https://en.wikipedia.org/wiki/AI_winter.

6 That is, human-engineered exogenous development. "Self-bootstrapping" AI that rewrites its own algorithms, a staple of the AI safety literature, is discussed in Chapters 13 and 14.

7 Judith Hooper and Dick Teresi, *The 3-Pound Universe*, New York: Tarcher, 1991.

8 IARPA, "IARPA Seeks Partners in Brain-Inspired AI Initiative," January 22, 2015, www.iarpa.gov/index.php/research-programs/microns.

9 Hannas and Chang, et al., "China AI-Brain Research," 2020.

10 Nand Kishor, "IARPA Project Targets Hidden Algorithms of the Brain," *House of Bots*, June 28, 2017, houseofbots.com/news-detail/712-1-iarpa-project-targets-hidden-algorithms-of-the-brain.

11 Adapted from Nikola Kasabov, *Time-Space, Spiking Neural Networks and Brain-Inspired Artificial Intelligence*, Berlin: Springer, 2019, p. 228.

12 Farahani et al., "Application of Graph Theory for Identifying Connectivity Patterns in Human Brain Networks: A Systematic Review," *Frontiers in Neuroscience*, June 6, 2019, pp. 1–27.

13 In 2005, Olaf Sporns and Patric Hagmann independently suggested the term "connectome" to refer to a map of the neural connections within the brain. The term was inspired by the human gene sequencing project. *Wikipedia*, May 5, 2020, https://en.wikipedia.org/wiki/Connectome#Origin_and_usage_of_the_term.

14 Millionth of a meter, also called "micron."

15 "A connectivity atlas of one post-mortem human brain for the larger axons … is probably feasible within ten years." Christof Koch, personal communication, July 9, 2020.

16 Elon Musk (Neuralink), "An Integrated Brain-machine Interface Platform with Thousands of Channels," *bioR$_x$iv*, August 2, 2019.

17 DARPA, "DARPA and the Brain Initiative," https://www.darpa.mil/program/our-research/darpa-and-the-brain-initiative.

18 Ming Dong (明东), "'脑语密码' 破译者" (Decipherer of 'Brain Language Code'), *S&T Daily*, December 25, 2019, http://digitalpaper.stdaily.com/http_www.kjrb.com/kjrb/html/2019-12/25/content_437388.htm.

19 PRC State Council, 国家中长期科学和技术发展规划纲要(2006-2020年) (National Medium- and Long-term S&T Development Plan (2006-2020)), February 9, 2006.

20 PRC State Council, 国家"十二五"科学和技术发展规划 (12th Five-year Plan for National S&T Development), July 14, 2011.

21 Shanghai CCP Municipal Committee, 关于加快建设具有全球影响力的科技创新中心的意见 (Opinions on Accelerating the Construction of an S&T Innovation Center with Global Influence), May 27, 2015.

22 Mu-ming Poo, "Towards Brain-inspired Artificial Intelligence," *National Science Review* Volume 5, Issue 6, November 2018, p. 785.

23 PRC State Council, 国务院关于积极推进"互联网+"行动的指导意见 (State Council Guiding Opinions on Positively Promoting 'Internet +' Action), SC 40, July 1, 2015.

24 "脑连接图谱研究是认知脑功能并进而探讨意识本质的科学前沿，这方面探索不仅有重要科学意义，而且对脑疾病防治、智能技术发展也具有引导作用。" http://www.xinhuanet.com/politics/2016-05/31/c_1118965169.htm.

25 PRC State Council, 国务院关于印发"十三五"国家科技创新规划的通知 (State Council Notification on National Science and Technology Innovation Programs for the 13th Five-year Plan), SC 43, 2016.

26 PRC State Council, 国务院关于印发"十三五"国家战略性新兴产业发展规划的通知 (National Strategic Emerging Industry Development Projects), SC 67, 2016.

27 Ibid. Our emphasis.

28 PRC State Council, 国务院关于印发新一代人工智能发展规划的通知 (New Generation AI Development Plan), SC 35, 2017.

29 Roberts, H., Cowls, J., Morley, J. et al. "The Chinese Approach to Artificial Intelligence: An Analysis of Policy, Ethics, and Regulation," *AI & Society* 36, 2021, pp. 59-77. Sarah O'Meara, "Will China Lead the World in AI by 2030?," *Nature*, Vol. 572, August 21, 2019, pp. 427-428.

30 "构筑我国人工智能发展的先发优势" Our italics.

31 PRC National Natural Science Foundation, 国家自然科学基金人工智能基础研究应急管理项目指南, August 2, 2017, http://www.nsfc.gov.cn/publish/portal0/tab452/info69927.htm.

32 Ibid.

33 http://www.research.pku.edu.cn/docs/2018-07/20180702201045167492.pdf

34 https://www.sciping.com/21237.html; http://www.cebsit.ac.cn/xwdt/202007/t20200722_5639392.html; http://news.sciencenet.cn/htmlnews/2021/1/452104.shtm; https://www.yicai.com/news/100028706.html.

35 Zhang Hongliang (张洪亮), Wang Liping (王立平), Zhang Xu (张旭), "我国神经科学发展现状和未来战略思考" (Neuroscience in China: Status Quo and Strategic Thinking for the Future), 中国科学基金 (*Bulletin of National Natural Science Foundation of China*), 35.2, 2021, 328–338.

36 MOST, 科技创新2030—"脑科学与类脑研究"重大项目2021年度项目申报指南, MOST 265, 2021.

37 在中国, 任何超脱飞扬的思想都会怦然坠地的, 现实的引力太沉重了; Liu Cixin (刘慈欣), *The Three-Body Problem* (三体), Taipei: Owl Press (繁体版), 2011, p. 71.

38 Chinese research on BCI and neuromorphic computing are discussed in Chapter 13.

39 Zeng Yi (曾毅), Liu Chenglin (刘成林), Tan Tieniu (谭铁牛), *Chinese Journal of Computers* (计算机学报), 39.1, January 2016, 212–222.

40 Pu Muming (蒲慕明), Xu Bo (徐波), Tan Tieniu (谭铁牛), *Bulletin of Chinese Academy of Sciences* (中国科学院院刊), 31.7, July 2016, 725–736.

41 Zhang Xu (张旭), Liu Li (刘力), Guo Aike (郭爱克), *Bulletin of Chinese Academy of Sciences* (中国科学院院刊), 31(7), July 2016, 737–746.

42 Han Xue (韩雪), Ruan Meihua (阮梅花), Wang Huiyuan (王慧媛), Yuan Tianwei (袁天蔚), Wang Chaonan (王超男), Fu Lu (傅璐), Chen Jing (陈静), Wang Xiaoli (王小理), Xiong Yan (熊燕), Zhang Xu (张旭), *Chinese Bulletin of Life Sciences* (生命科学), 28.11, November 2016, 1295–1307.

43 Pu Muming (蒲慕明), Du Jiulin (杜久林), Nancy Y. Ip (叶玉如), Xiong Zhiqi (熊志奇), Xu Bo (徐波), Tan Tieniu (谭铁牛), *Neuron*, Volume 92, Issue 3, November 2016, pp. 591–596. The Chinese version of the paper, issued separately, omits "Brain Diseases" from the title.

44 Ruan Meihua (阮梅花), Yuan Tianwei (袁天蔚), Wang Huiyuan (王慧媛), Wang Chaonan (王超男), Fu Lu (傅璐), Chen Jing (陈静), Han Xue (韩雪), Wang Xiaoli (王小理), Xiong Yan (熊燕), Yu Jianrong (于建荣), Zhang Xu (张旭), *Chinese Bulletin of Life Sciences* (生命科学), Volume 29, Issue 2, February 2017, pp. 97–113.

45 Xie Xiaohua (谢小华), Feng Jianfeng (冯建峰), *Psychological Communications* (心理学通讯), February 2019.

46 Huang Tiejun (黄铁军), Yu Zhaofei (余肇飞), Liu Yijun (刘怡俊), *Journal of Computer Research and Development* (计算机研究与发展), 56.6, June 2019, 1135–1148.

47 The authors retrieved some 22,000 documents (2010–2019) from the China National Knowledge Infrastructure database of academic journals that reference BI-AI. The table is based on a curated subset that addresses the topic directly and specifically.

48 Mu-ming Poo, "Towards Brain-inspired Artificial Intelligence."

49 Zhang Xu et al., "Brain Science and Technology: Initiatives in the Shanghai and Yangtze River Delta Region," *Nature*, July 2019, pp. 1–5.

50 We exclude neuroscience and neuroimaging facilities with no declared link to AI.

51 https://istbi.fudan.edu.cn/.

52 David Cyranoski, "Beijing Launches Pioneering Brain-science Centre," *Nature*, 556, April 12, 2018, pp. 157–158.

53 http://www.xinhuanet.com//world/2016-04/28/c_128942147.htm.
54 http://www.ion.ac.cn/. CEBSIT and CAS-ION share a website. "CAS-ION" (CAS Institute of Neuroscience) appears in parentheses after "CEBSIT" on the site's masthead, and both are under Pu Muming's directorship.
55 Through Dr. Nikos Logothetis, co-director of the International Center for Primate Brain Research (国际灵长类脑研究中心).
56 http://en.jitri.org/yanjiuyuan72.html.
57 https://braindata.bitahub.com/.
58 www.cibr.ac.cn/.
59 https://jobs.sciencecareers.org/employer/513965/the-chinese-institute-for-brain-research-beijing-cibr-/.
60 https://www.aminer.cn/research_report/5f44cbf13c99ce0ab7bc8db9?download=false.
61 Home of the "Brainnetome Center (脑网络组研究中心). http://www.brainnetome.org/.
62 In collaboration with the CAS Kunming Institute of Zoology.
63 "China AI-Brain Research," pp. 32–33.
64 Ibid., p. 42.
65 "China AI-Brain Research," pp. 35–39.
66 https://www.crossmodal-learning.org/home.html.
67 Olaf Sporns, *Discovering the Human Connectome*. The MIT Press, Cambridge, MA, 2012; Nikola Kasabov. *Time-Space, Spiking Neural Networks and Brain-Inspired Artificial Intelligence*, Springer, UK, 2019. Also, Intelligence Advanced Research Projects Activity, "Machine Intelligence from Cortical Networks (MICrONS)" Project, "Proposers' Day Briefings" (https://www.iarpa.gov/index.php/research-programs/microns/microns-baa).
68 The search was based on Chinese language documents in the CNKI database for 2010–2019, the last year for which we had complete data. The English language record was not examined to avoid contamination with foreign co-authorship.
69 "China AI-Brain Research," pp. 50–53.
70 http://brainiac2.mit.edu/SNEMI3D/leaders-board.
71 Fielded online through Qualtrics January 5–March 4, 2020. "China AI-Brain Research," pp. 41–45.
72 Written comments included calls for greater integration of basic and applied BI-AI research in China, to offset the application-driven research that characterizes most Chinese AI development.
73 https://www.voachinese.com/a/kai-fu-lee-on-ai-development-2018116/4662278.html.
74 Adapted from Hannas and Chang, **"China's 'Artificial' Intelligence,"** William C. Hannas and Didi Kirsten Tatlow, eds., *China's Quest for Foreign Technology: Beyond Espionage*, Routledge, London and New York, 2021.
75 https://mp.weixin.qq.com/s/YtXW8HlWlRGGxQn5aOeabA.
76 *Qiushi* (求是), April 2019. https:// www.kunlunce.com/llyj/fl11111/2019-02-28/131480.html.
77 http://www.caeshc.com.cn/news_view.php?id=7997.
78 http://news.stcn.com/2019/1017/15436849.shtml.
79 https://www.nature.com/articles/d41586-019-02360-7.
80 "更为全面" Pu Muming, in "专家揭秘'中国脑计划'脑科学成大国'必争之地'" (Expert Reveals 'China Brain Project' and Brain Science Are Becoming a 'Field that Will Inevitably Be Contested by the Great Powers'). http://www.xinhuanet.com//world/2016-04/28/c_128942147.htm.
81 As stated in the introduction to China's "New Generation AI Development Plan."

Bibliography

Goertzel, Ben and Cassio Pennachin, eds., *Artificial General Intelligence*, New York: Springer, 2007.

Hannas, William C. and Huey-Meei Chang, Jennifer Wang, Catherine Aiken, Daniel Chou, "China AI-Brain Research," Georgetown University, CSET, September 2020.

Kasabov, Nikiola. *Time-Space, Spiking Neural Networks and Brain-Inspired Artificial Intelligence*, Berlin: Springer, 2019.

PRC Ministry of Science and Technology, 科技创新2030—"脑科学与类脑研究"重大项目 2020 年度项目申报指南 (Science and Technology Innovation 2030—'Brain Science and Brain-like Research' Megaproject 2020 Annual Project Application Guidelines), 2021.

PRC National Natural Science Foundation, 国家自然科学基金人工智能基础研究应急管理 项目指南, (National Natural Science Foundation of China Artificial Intelligence Basic Research Urgent Management Project Guide), 2017.

PRC State Council, 国家中长期科学和技术发展规划纲要(2006-2020年) (National Medium- and Long-term S&T Development Plan (2006-2020)), SC 9, 2006.

PRC State Council, 国务院关于印发"十三五"国家战略性新兴产业发展规划的通知 (National Strategic Emerging Industry Development Projects), SC 67, 2016.

PRC State Council. 国务院关于印发新一代人工智能发展规划的通知 (The New Generation AI Development Plan), SC 35, 2017.

Sporns, Olaf. *Discovering the Human Connectome*, Boston: MIT Press, 2012.

8

Chinese AI and biology

Anna B. Puglisi and Daniel H. Chou

This book's previous chapters highlighted China's robust research across a wide range of AI disciplines, including its efforts to synthesize human and artificial intelligence.[1] While AI-brain research inherently has a biological nexus, what is often overlooked is the growing importance of AI in biological discovery. The exponential growth of data from biological research in medicine, agriculture, and genomics has necessitated the development of new AI algorithms for analysis and understanding. Examples of how AI is impacting biological discovery include elucidating the structure of molecules such as protein and RNA structures, screening novel drug candidates, and the ability to combine weather and soil data with a knowledge of plant genomics to enhance crop yields. AI is also becoming a key enabler for designing more effective experiments.

This chapter explores how AI now underpins specific aspects of China's biotechnology research, including bioinformatics. We describe the programs and policies China has in place to foster these fields, examine whether research intensity and growth match China's stated goals, and explore the elements of China's system—including its willingness to forgo certain ethical considerations—that give China a potential advantage as others debate the way to move forward.[2]

AI's impact on biotechnology research

China and the world in general are on the cusp of game-changing discoveries in biotechnology driven by advances in AI. These applications include identifying drug targets, image screening, and predictive modeling of proteins and nucleic acids. The use of AI in basic research promises to shorten research timelines, enable analysis that was previously impossible, and open new fields of research, given AI's ability to process the vast amounts of experimental health and environmental

DOI: 10.4324/9781003212980-11

data generated by today's researchers and support an understanding of these data. The following areas are drivers of this change.

Bioinformatics

Bioinformatics can be described as using computation and statistics to understand biology, allowing scientists to better understand the function of genes and proteins, three-dimensional shapes of proteins and nucleic acids, and the evolution of parts of the genome. AI takes this field to the next level by enabling more efficient data processing and analysis, expediting the translation of experimental science to real-world applications. China has prioritized bioinformatics, fostering the national champion BGI, as well as establishing key enabling infrastructure. Bioinformatics is inherently interdisciplinary in scope, which comprised engineering, statistical, biological, and other subdisciplines. As a way to enable this development, China is promoting "industrial clusters" to bridge these gaps and bring together different disciplines.

Synthetic biology

Described by the U.S. National Institutes of Health (NIH) as "a field of science that involves redesigning organisms for useful purposes by engineering them to have new abilities,"[3] synthetic biology offers new ways to harness nucleic acids for a wide range of applications. The use of AI to find ways to connect genotypes with phenotypes—basically understanding what genes do and what they code for—has implications for understanding human disease, genome manipulation, and designing life-saving therapies, not to mention increasing the probability of lab accidents, violating ethical boundaries, and creating new or enhancing existing biological weapons. We will explore China's research intensity in this key area where there is overlap with its AI research.

Gain of function research

Research that purposefully or not has the effect of enhancing the virulence or transmissibility of pathogens has direct national security implications. While there are valid reasons for concern, there are also important questions this research can answer that help the biomedical sector prepare for future pandemics. The ability to better understand how pathogens and their hosts interact on the molecular level, and how proteins and other biomolecules function in the cell, will be enabled by AI, yielding potential implications for this line of research.

Agricultural biotechnology

Food security will likely become more of a national security issue as countries worldwide grapple with ways to feed their citizens. Better understanding of genomic factors that impact growth, disease resistance, and the nutritional value of plants and livestock has the potential to impact world hunger and to become a key economic driver. AI is already being used to manage fields for increased yields. Its use to study plant and animal genomics will affect our ability to grow resources for livestock and modify livestock in ways that facilitate ease of handling (e.g. hornless cows)—not to mention replacing them with plant-based substitutes. China's AI and biotechnology plans and programs emphasize the use of AI to improve plants and livestock.

Data privacy, data security, and population surveillance[4]

While not a facet of biotech research itself, as more genomic and other biological information becomes available, AI's impact on our ability to store, analyze, and protect it is increasingly important. The United States and like-minded countries will need to explore whether current procedures governing data privacy are sufficient, or if there are special considerations unique to genomic data. Key among these considerations will be how to maximize discovery while protecting this resource vis-à-vis other countries that do not play by the same rules for sharing and collaboration. It will be important to consider not only what is possible now, but what may become possible in the future. As the field matures, what is not necessarily alarming now—access to a wide range of genomic data—may provide an advantage to researchers who have it.

In addition, China has shown a willingness not only to use genomic data to surveil its own population, but also to export this technology, enabling other authoritarian regimes. Once science fiction, advances in genomics make it easier to track individuals and their families based on genetic information. These advances also create the opportunity for longitudinal studies, making it easier to combine genomic data with other forms of surveillance that, taken together, may lead to a dystopian future.

State policy and the AI-biology nexus

Over the last two decades, China has put in place policies to support biotechnology and its bioeconomy,[5] intended to foster Big Science facilities, national "champions" (i.e. favored companies), talent recruitment, and basic research. This support goes far beyond traditional industrial policies implemented in Europe and other parts of Asia. It is comprehensive and represents an alternative blueprint for the development of emerging technologies and industries. China's all-embracing approach highlights how governments can play a key role in fostering technology areas that rely on longer-timelines, multi-disciplinary coalitions, or Big Science facilities—such as advanced computing, high-end gene sequencing, and colonies of non-human primates (NHPs). These measures increasingly incorporate AI as a key driver.

China's National Medium- and Long-term Plan (MLP) for S&T development (2006–2020)[6]

This S&T blueprint lays out a development strategy that relies on overseas return-ees,[7] foreign collaboration, and the R&D laboratories of international companies that have flocked to China as venues to acquire needed skills. The MLP focuses on both the *process* of science and the specific topic areas it seeks to develop.[8] It regards the development of Chinese biotechnology as "the new revolution of the 21st century" and emphasizes the "importance of genomics, proteomics, sequencing, and discovery of the functions of genes," all aspects that stand to be enhanced by contributions from AI.

China's Precision Medicine Initiative[9, 10]

China's Precision Medicine Initiative (精准医疗计划) seeks to leverage the coun-try's sequencing capacity and access to biomedical data to design unique and tailored therapeutics for individuals, and explore diseases endemic to China. This effort brings together IT and biotech companies with Chinese government sup-port to design and apply new AI-enabled tools that analyze genomic, health, environmental, and behavioral data for insights into human health and therapeu-tics. It is modeled after the U.S. precision medicine initiative.

AI innovation action plan for institutes of higher education[11]

This plan outlines China's efforts to build capacity for AI-Bio research and a tech-nically proficient workforce to support it. Its interdisciplinary aspects are laid out:

- "Promote the deep integration of information technologies such as the Internet, big data, cloud computing, and the Internet of Things with mod-ern biotechnology, health and nutrition, and smart device technology. Make breakthroughs in key technologies such as farm animal and plant informa-tion perception, analysis and smart identification, cross-media data mining analysis in agriculture, hybrid human-computer intelligent interaction and virtual reality in agriculture, swarm intelligence decision-making in agri-culture, and human-computer-animal (人机物) coordination."[12]

13th Five-year Plan for S&T Innovation[13]

The 13th Five-year Plan clearly recognizes the relevance of AI to biotechnology, experimental design, and precision medicine. It further emphasizes the impor-tance of interdisciplinary research and computing power:

- "Build high-throughput calculation, high-throughput experiment, and dedi-cated database platforms, research and develop the four key technologies of multi-level and cross-scale design, high-throughput preparation, high-throughput characterization and service evaluation, and material big data, achieve the transition of new materials R&D from the traditional 'experience-guided experiment' model to the 'theoretical prediction, experimental verification' model."[14]

The plan underscores the importance of genomic data to biotechnology and reiterates government plans for national-level genome databases:

- "Establish a national bioinformatics and sample resource database, research and develop a number of suitable basic technologies and innovative products, comprehensively improve the level of birth defect prevention and control technology, safeguard the reproductive health of the reproductive age population, and improve the quality of the birth population."
- "Accelerate breakthroughs in cutting-edge key technology in life sciences such as new genomics technologies, synthetic biotechnology, biological big data, 3D bioprinting technology, brain science and artificial intelligence, gene editing technology, and structural biology.... improve the originality of cutting-edge biotechnology in China, and seize a commanding position in international biotechnology competition."[15]

China sees the importance of combining AI and biotechnology as the future of medicine:

- "Seize the opportunity for the integrated development of biotechnology and information technology, establish a prospective cohort of millions of healthy people and patients with key diseases, establish a multi-level precision medical knowledge base system and a national biomedical big data sharing platform," etc.[16]

13th Five-year Plan for Military and Civil Fusion[17]

This plan was established in 2017 and focuses on emerging technologies. It calls specifically for a cross-pollination of military and civilian technology in areas not traditionally viewed as "national security issues," such as neuroscience and brain-inspired research, as well as biotechnology. The military-civilian fusion plan states that such projects will be supported by foreign outreach initiatives.

14th Five-year Plan[18]

China's latest Five-year Plan continues to emphasize interdisciplinary research and the use of AI for biological discovery and precision medicine. The plan underscores the importance to China of merging of AI and biotechnology, and its need for both political and financial support.

- "We will promote the integration and innovation of biotechnology and information technology, accelerate the development of biomedicine, bioengineered breeding, biomaterials, bioenergy, and other industries and increase the size and strength of the bio-economy."[19]

Supporting "strategic emerging industries"

China has designated several fields as "Strategic Emerging Industries" (战略性新兴产业, SEI), to foster a more entrepreneurial environment and grow indigenous companies. The effort began at the top, spear headed in 2009 by Wen Jiabao and the State Council,[20] and included preferential tax treatment, subsidies, and government procurement initiatives. AI and biotech are both considered to be SEIs and factor heavily into China's efforts.[21] In 2021, China doubled down on its SEI policy to emphasize "key investments in strategic areas, create 'industrial clusters,' and accelerate the pace of innovation and development in the biotechnology industry."[22]

In a nutshell, China has left no doubt about the role for AI in biotechnology as it seeks to "deepen the integration of biomedical engineering technology with information technology."[23]

AI + biology: a convergence of disciplines

This section introduces some statistical techniques to demonstrate the confluence of biomedical and AI research in China and their increasing interdependence.

AI-Bio industrial clusters

China's recent focus on "industrial clusters" (产业集群) opens a new front for building an innovation ecosystem that promotes multi-disciplinary research which integrates researchers, developers, and government entities. China's central government offers funding, space, talent, and other resources to clusters that focus on strategic emerging industries. They consist of small- and medium-sized enterprises in the same or related industry as well as universities, state key labs (similar to the U.S. national labs), and larger state enterprises such as BGI, described as areas of "flexible specialization" (软性专业化). There are 17 such biomedical clusters located in Beijing (2), Chengdu, Chongqing, Guangzhou, Hangzhou, Harbin, Linyi, Shanghai, Shijiazhuang, Suzhou, Tianjin, Tonghua, Wuhan, Xiamen, Yantai, and Zhuhai.[24] Each location also houses a BGI-associated company or laboratory.

A closer look at these clusters reveals some correspondence between China's artificial intelligence and biotechnology-related efforts. Figure 8.1 shows an overlay of bio-clusters (dark gray) with known AI concentrations (light gray) and their overlap (gray). As expected, Beijing and Shanghai show considerable overlap. The Guangzhou-Shenzhen-Zhuhai region in the south, where many of China's leading biomedical facilities are located, is another such area. In fact, each of the aforementioned cities hosts several to several hundred AI companies, labs, university programs, and government research facilities.

Geographical proximity is one indicator that China's plans are having an impact.[25] Research paper output is another. The following sections compare AI and Bio research hubs on the basis of their Chinese-authored publications.[26]

FIGURE 8.1 AI and bio industrial clusters in selected PRC cities

Source: Puglisi and Chou, "China's Industrial Clusters: Building AI-Driven Biodiscovery Capacity."

AI-Bio research hubs: synthetic biology and bioinformatics

As described earlier, synthetic biology is a key area of biotechnology that will benefit from the application of AI. In Table 8.1, we tabulate the growth of Chinese papers on synthetic biology from 2015 to 2020 by authors' location, to analyze trends and assess any geographical correspondence.

Figure 8.2 maps the geographical distribution of these locations (affiliations) claimed by authors of synthetic biology papers published in 2020.

Compare this with the distribution of AI hubs in Figure 8.3, based on 2020 CNKI publications.[27] While the correspondence is not exact, the co-location in larger municipalities of hubs for both research disciplines is evident. Although not a direct measure of cross-fertilization, it points to its potential, as well as a concerted effort by the Chinese government to foster these synergies. A similar correspondence was generated for bioinformatics (not shown).

These two types of analysis present an initial accounting of cross-disciplinary collaboration—backed by known examples, such as WuXi NextCode and Huawei working together to develop a cloud computing infrastructure to support China's precision medicine initiative, and iCarbonX's use of AI and data mining tools to formulate drugs and therapeutics.

TABLE 8.1 Synthetic biology papers—Average Y2Y Growth—2015–2020

City	2015	2016	2017	2018	2019	2020	AVG Y2Y Growth
Wuxi	14	20	20	22	26	48	31%
Wuhan	14	30	24	31	38	35	28%
Shenzhen	14	12	15	14	27	38	28%
Hangzhou	15	15	10	23	20	28	25%
Tianjin	48	63	62	55	79	122	23%
Chengdu	15	19	19	15	27	35	23%
Nanjing	30	36	28	35	42	68	21%
Guangzhou	19	17	22	23	44	38	20%
Beijing	78	96	111	138	145	179	18%
Dalian	14	15	13	19	19	24	13%
Qingdao	17	19	13	23	13	19	12%
Shanghai	60	50	87	70	74	75	9%
Xi'an	11	12	11	10	13	15	7%
Changsha	12	13	17	14	16	12	2%

Source: Puglisi and Chou, "China's Industrial Clusters: Building AI-Driven Biodiscovery Capacity."

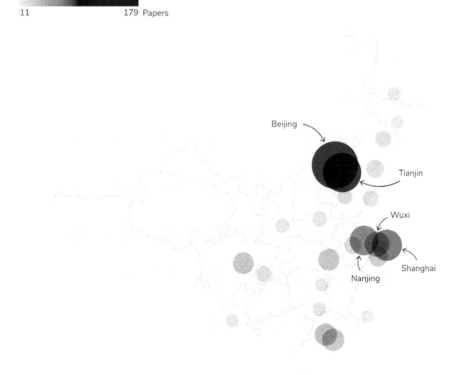

FIGURE 8.2 Research hubs—synthetic biology—2020 (CNKI)

Source: Puglisi and Chou, "China's Industrial Clusters: Building AI-Driven Biodiscovery Capacity."

543   18130 Papers

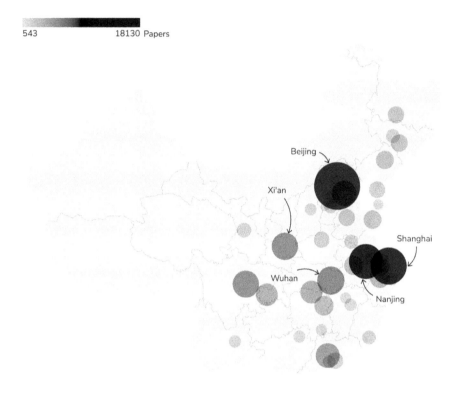

FIGURE 8.3   China AI research hubs – annotated

Source: Puglisi and Chou, "China's Industrial Clusters: Building AI-Driven Biodiscovery Capacity."

CRISPR and AI

CRISPR[28] refers both to a family of DNA sequences found in certain bacteria and to a novel biotechnology for editing the genomes of all organisms in precise ways which capitalizes on specific enzymes that recognize these sequences. Here again, AI has the potential to serve as a key enabler. We examine this specific intersection of genomics and AI by searching for papers containing both "CRISPR" and "learning."[29] "Learning" is used as a proxy for "AI" to match "machine/deep/reinforcement learning," which in today's terms are AI near-synonyms. Our aim is to trace both the baseline growth of CRISPR papers and the growth of AI+CRISPR papers for the sake of comparison.[30]

Figure 8.4a shows continuing growth of CRISPR publications in China and elsewhere since its introduction around 2010. Figure 8.4b shows *accelerated* growth in CRISPR+AI around 2017.

CRISPR - China vs ROW

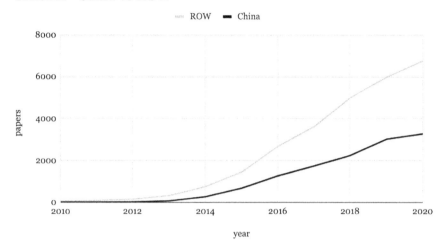

FIGURE 8.4a   CRISPR—China vs. ROW

Source: Puglisi and Chou, "China's Industrial Clusters: Building AI-Driven Biodiscovery Capacity."

Evidence from technical publications

Finally, we extend our analysis by examining correspondences in technical publications between two *full sets* of keywords identified with AI and biology-related disciplines as a measure of their growing interdependence (see Figure 8.5).

CRISPR + Learning - China vs ROW

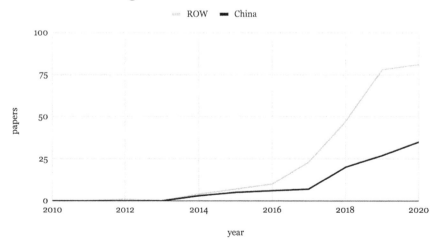

FIGURE 8.4b   CRISPR + learning (AI)—China vs. ROW

Source: Puglisi and Chou, "China's Industrial Clusters: Building AI-Driven Biodiscovery Capacity."

AI + Bio - China vs ROW

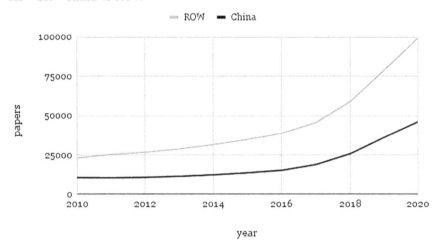

FIGURE 8.5   Academic journal articles containing both bio- and AI-related keywords

Source: Puglisi and Chou, "China's Industrial Clusters: Building AI-Driven Biodiscovery Capacity."

Keywords in both cases were generated from restricted lists to avoid false positives. While the upward trends are expected, the absolute numbers themselves, co-location of facilities, and joint publications suggest that China's programs are having an impact on the growth of this nascent field. As this research is in its early stages, impact is yet to be determined. However, these examples illustrate China's efforts in this area, and highlight the fact that access to both Chinese and English records is needed to evaluate China's capabilities. Here are some samples published in PKU Core Journals taken from our research.[31]

- Sun Daiwen (孙黛雯) et al., "Review of Multimer Protein-protein Complex Topology and Structure Prediction," *Chinese Physics B*, 29.10, 2020.
  - Reviews methods of predicting protein complexes from the protein–protein interactions (PPI) network, predicting missing links in the PPI network, and applying machine/deep learning models in protein structure prediction.
- Pan Xiaoyong (潘小勇) et al., "ToxDL: Deep Learning Using Primary Structure and Domain Embeddings for Assessing Protein Toxicity," *Bioinformatics*, 36.21, 2021.
  - Proposes a deep-learning-based approach for *in silico* prediction of protein toxicity from sequence alone. They used these predictions to model *in silico* modification of a protein sequence.
- Liu Haijie (刘海杰) et al., "Predicting the Disease Genes of Multiple Sclerosis Based on Network Representation Learning," *Frontiers in Genetics*, 11, 2020.
  - Proposes a framework to identify multiple sclerosis-related genes. Their deep-learning-based framework analyzes global topological information

of the whole PPI network and has the potential for identifying other disease biomarkers.

- Zeng Tao (曾涛) et al., "Editorial: Machine Learning Advanced Dynamic Omics Data Analysis for Precision Medicine," *Frontiers in Genetics*, 10, 2020.

    Surveys state-of-the-art progress to integrate multi-scale "omics" datasets to distinguish the novel individual-specific disease causes from conventional cohort-common disease causes. Applications in precision medicine and drug discovery.

- Long Shiyang (龙施洋) and Tian Pu (田圃), "Protein Secondary Structure Prediction with Context Convolutional Neural Network," *RSC Advances*, 9.66, 2019.

    The researchers built a context convolutional neural network for predicting protein secondary structure and compared its performance with popular models (e.g. convolutional neural network, recurrent neural network, and conditional neural field) under similar training procedures.

- Zhong Qi (钟琦) et al., "基于位点特异性打分矩阵的卷积神经网络预测SARS-CoV-2核衣壳蛋白的蛋白质二级结构" (Prediction of the Protein Secondary Structure of SARS-CoV-2 Nucleocapsid Protein through the Convolutional Neural Network Based on a Position-Specific Scoring Matrix), 云南民族大学学报(自然科学版) (*Journal of Yunnan Minzu University* (*Natural Sciences Edition*)), 30.01, 2021.

    Reports on deep learning algorithms for predicting the secondary structure of eight proteins of SARS-CoV-2. Illustrates the depth of talent in China for AI+Bio interdisciplinary research outside the more well-known research hubs.

- Wang Xianfang (王鲜芳) et al., "深度神经网络蛋白质溶解性预测模型设计" (Design of Protein Solubility Prediction Model Based on Deep Neural Network), 河南师范大学学报(自然科学版) (*Journal of Henan Normal University* (*Natural Science Edition*)), 49.02, 2021.

    Describes the design of multiple convolutional neural network models with 6-dimensional sequence features and 51-dimensional structural features to predict protein solubility based on feature extraction and deep learning technology.

- Pan Yue (潘越) et al., "基于卷积神经网络的蛋白质折叠类型最小特征提取" (Extraction of Minimal Representation of Protein Folds Based on Convolutional Neural Networks), 南京大学学报(自然科学) (*Journal of Nanjing University* (*Natural Science*)), 56.05, 2020.

    A deep convolutional neural network (DCNN) was trained to study the shortest feature vectors that were able to recognize different protein folds correctly. Their results improved the understanding of similarity between protein classes.

- Wang Shuijie (王水介) et al., "基于深度学习的第三代基因测序一致性序列生成" (DLCC: Deep-Learning-Based Consensus Construction from Long

Error-prone Reads), 智能计算机与应用 (*Intelligent Computer and Applications*), 10.08, 2020.

> Proposes a consistent sequence generation model based on deep learning to extract the structural characteristics of gene multiple sequence alignment results and generate high-quality consensus for third-generation sequencing data.

• Wang Quan (王荃) et al., "基于深度学习和组织形态分析的肺癌基因突变预测" (Prediction of Gene Mutation in Lung Cancer Based on Deep Learning and Histomorphology Analysis), 生物医学工程学杂志 (*Journal of Biomedical Engineering*), 37.01, 2020.

> Uses Conditional Generative Adversarial Networks to study correlations between lung cancer histomorphological features (phenotype) and epidermal growth factor receptor (EGFR) gene mutations (genotype).

AI+Bio in practice: research and commercial units

Perhaps no better example can be found of AI's synergism with biomedical research than the creation in November 2021 of Isomorphic Labs, an Alphabet (Google) company that builds on the success of AlphaFold2[32] to reimagine the entire drug discovery process from first principles based on an AI-first approach.[33] Just as AlphaZero[34] (2017) sparked AI+Bio research collaboration among Chinese researchers, the PRC government will continue to nurture a policy-friendly R&D ecosystem for AI organizations, biotech industries, and venture capitalist joint ventures that seeks to emulate—and eventually surpass—these globally operating models.

Evidence in China of the hybrid paradigm whereby biotech prospers through AI input while, conversely, AI advances from the availability of biodata can be found in public and private enterprises working in this cross-disciplinary area. Here are some notable examples of companies and institutes:

• BGI Group (华大集团)[35] is a Shenzhen-based gene sequencing company with a global network of more than 100 subsidiaries. The growth and success of BGI demonstrate not only the holistic nature of China's S&T system, combining private and public sectors and the military, but also how sustained support can impact a key emerging industry. Its collaborations give BGI—and China—access to genomic data worldwide.[36]

• Novogene (诺禾致源科技) is a genomic services provider that claims to have the world's largest sequencing capacity.[37] Its founder, Li Ruiqiang (李瑞强), was a senior executive at BGI and is an expert in genomics. Novogene received investments from state-owned entities, including CMB International Capital Corporation, China Merchants Bank, and the State Development and Investment Corp.[38]

• Hong Kong-based Insilico Medicine, whose motto is "artificial intelligence for every step of pharmaceutical research and development,"[39] has emerged as another major player of AI+Bio research in China. The company claims that its use of AI in pharmaceutical development reduced a multi-year hundreds of millions of dollars discovery process to 18 months at a fraction of the cost.[40]

- NeoX—a Beijing-based company—is another example of a multi-disciplinary approach to AI-Bio. Co-founded by MIT and Caltech graduates, it seeks to use AI to shorten the timeline for pre-clinical drug design.[41] The company has what it describes as a unique and cutting-edge platform to screen candidates and simulate the directed evolution of biomolecules.

- The Chinese Academy of Sciences Institute of Computing Technology (ICT) combines AI and medical research at its Bioinformatics Research Group (生物信息课题组) housed under ICT's Advanced Computing Research Laboratory,[42] and the Medical Imaging, Robotics, Analytical Computing Laboratory & Engineering (医疗影像机器人与分析计算研究组), a subdivision of ICT's Key Laboratory of Intelligent Information Processing.[43]

- Shanghai Jiaotong University's Artificial Intelligence Institute houses a Center for Smart Healthcare (智慧医疗研究中心), which "aims to empower clinical medicine and medical services with AI technology," researches "new paradigms of human-machine interaction," and develops "deep learning services for clinical diagnosis." The center applies AI to disease prediction and a variety of health-related tasks.[44]

- Nankai University College of Artificial Intelligence (南开大学人工智能学院) hosts the Tianjin Municipal Key Laboratory of Intelligent Robotics (天津市智能机器人技术重点实验室). R&D conducted at this laboratory includes medical and service robotics (surgery and rehabilitation support), brain-computer interfaces, and micro and nano detection for life sciences.[45]

Biotechnology in the crosshairs: technology acquisition

No treatment of Chinese S&T is complete without an examination of state and corporate efforts to acquire foreign technology. While China has made great strides in its domestic capabilities in both biotechnology and AI, its development strategies, as articulated in policy documents and their implementation notifications, invariably incorporate *technology transfer* as a key component. Since biotechnology and biomedical research have not been considered national security issues, however, discussing these strategies and their mitigation has been more problematic.

In particular, the nexus of AI and biotechnology is a relatively immature area. Much cutting-edge work takes place in academia or in corporate labs, and is early in its development cycle, beyond the scope of traditional counterintelligence. As it happens, China's "Achilles heel" is precisely here: in the early, foundational stages of high-tech development, where mitigation is especially challenging. As one wag aptly put it, "You can't embargo Newton's Laws."

Here follows a few examples and case studies in the AI-biotech sector that demonstrate how China leverages its talent programs, domestic funding, and market access to acquire technology in the short term, and to grow its domestic capabilities. Taken individually they are anecdotal, however, they fit squarely into the programs and policies that China has implemented to build this prioritized field, and they have unfolded over a period of decades not years. A fuller treatment can be found in this volume's chapters three, four, and their associated bibliographies.

- ZhenFund (真格基金) is an early stage investor, whose leadership partners with PRC state-sponsored talent programs and start-up contests.[46] ZhenFund has invested in numerous AI companies, some of which are in the biotech space such as SYNYI-AI (森亿医疗科技), a smart hospital solutions provider; Deep Intelligent Pharma (深度智耀科技), a firm pursuing pharmaceutical discovery and development through AI; and CareAI Co. Ltd (恺尔生物), a bioinformatics technology and high performance computing company.[47]
- AI-biotech firm XtalPi Technology (晶泰科技) based in China with a Boston branch also received investments from ZhenFund after winning a cash prize at the Harvard-China Forum Pitch Competition.[48] XtalPi provides drug R&D services for pharmaceutical firms using computational physics, quantum chemistry, AI, and cloud computing.[49] All three of its co-founders were former MIT postdoctoral researchers, subsequently recruited through PRC talent programs.[50]
- China's National Genomics Data-Center (国家基因组科学数据中心) founded in 2019 benefits from returned talent that have direct experience in leading U.S. universities and NIH.[51] The Center acts as a clearing house for China's genetic data, with a genome sequencing archive and branches with portfolios in precision medicine and agriculture. Many of its leading scientists have trained abroad and are members of China's various talent programs, often while still employed by their Western university. One of its leading scientists was selected as a CAS 100 Talent member while still working at the NIH.
- Li Xiaotao (李晓涛), who was a postdoctoral researcher at MIT, founded BIAI Inc. (必爱智能生命科技) with the assistance of the Shenzhen municipal government's talent program known as the Peacock Plan. BIAI, which stands for "biological intelligence and artificial intelligence," has offices in Massachusetts and Shenzhen and "relies on the technology platform of MIT and the Chinese Academy of Sciences." The company develops brain-computer interactions and supports treatment of brain disorders using data algorithms and smart wearable devices.[52]
- Rao Yi (饶毅) is an example of an early returnee who has influenced how newer Chinese researchers are being trained. Rao's lab investigates molecular and cellular mechanisms underlying behavior and cognition. He credits the importance of interdisciplinary work for his success.[53] Rao was a member of the inaugural group of Thousand Talent recruits, returning in 2007. He is currently the president of Capital Medical University in Beijing, the former Dean of Sciences at Peking University, the founding director of the PKU-IDG/McGovern Institute for Brain Research, and other high posts.

Finally, a recent CSET study highlights how China's technology transfer professionals, the so-called "S&T Diplomats" (科技外交官), broker technology transfer deals and coordinate with overseas experts to fulfill technology wish lists for Chinese entities. More than half of the 642 projects examined were biotechnology or AI projects.[54]

Analysis and recommendations

China is banking on applying AI to biomedical research to achieve a "transformation of China from a biotech power (生物技术大国) to a biotech superpower (生物技术强国)."[55] It is laying the groundwork to do this—much like its strategy to develop 5G—by having a long-term commitment, building an innovation base that includes industrial clusters and interdisciplinary research labs, attracting talent, and leveraging its collaborations with foreign entities. During the latter half of the 20th century, corporate labs were crucial globally for combining basic research—usually the province of academia—with the commercial drivers of industry.[56] Notable examples in the United States included Bell Labs, GE Research Labs, and Xerox PARC. The roles that such corporate labs played—and their ultimate value—were larger than simply profit and return on investment: they drove key aspects of innovation. China appears to be trying to conjure up analogous synergies in the development of AI and biotechnology.

A lot is at stake in the application of AI to biological discovery. On the one hand are the economic considerations. The global "AI in Drug Discovery" market was valued at $230 million in 2021 and is projected to reach a market value of over $4 billion by 2031.[57] The bioinformatics market alone is expected to grow to $13.50B by 2023 with a 14.5% compound annual growth rate.[58] These technologies will impact economic growth, public health, and, as a consequence, national security.

On the other hand are the ethical considerations. China has shown that it is willing to push ethical boundaries in biology especially, with its less-regulated use of human embryos,[59] mass production of NHPs,[60] and genomic surveillance.[61] The implications of China exporting these technologies and setting the tone for discovery challenge global norms on many levels and have a direct impact on human and animal rights worldwide.

Then, there is the matter of how China uses access to genomic data and the knowledge gained in global collaboration for its military and security apparatus. Advances in the use of AI as applied to biotech research will have a direct impact on items such as human performance modification, population surveillance, and the further design of biological weapons. China has said that it will use any knowledge or technology it acquires for its military.[62, 63] This is not conjecture, profiling, or analysis, but China's stated position. We should believe them.

The rapid growth of Chinese vendors such as BGI, iCarbonx, and WuXi NextCode underscores the need for the United States and its partners to forge a common agenda for the development and governance of biotechnologies and use of genomic data. This agenda must go beyond defensive and restrictive measures by fostering the strategic investments needed for foundational technologies and the platforms that enable growth in this field. We offer the following additional recommendations:

Invest in strategic infrastructure

To ensure data and knowledge discovery are not outsourced and lost to strategic competitors, democratic nations should invest strategically in infrastructure that supports the use of AI in biological discovery and the bioeconomy, such as sequencing capabilities, diagnostics, and associated computing infrastructure. The ability to drive medical research, provide medicines, and ensure adequate food supplies will become more dependent on genomic data, specifically designed computing power, and access to animal models.

Shore up supply chains

Policymakers should undertake a detailed survey of the human capital and supply chains needed to support biotechnology R&D. Too often, policy recommendations and research projects are focused on a snapshot in time and therefore fail to take account of foundational—not necessarily the most cutting-edge—aspects of an industry. The ability to support biotechnology discovery, as well as human and animal health, is a key part of leading in this area.

Choose our partners carefully

Ensuring that the United States and its allies benefit from our strategic decisions should be a part of our funding and investments from the outset. If we truly believe that biotechnology is a national security issue, we should decide which partners we want to work with, establish parameters for sharing information, and build cyber-security into all sponsored projects. While we reaffirm the importance of open science, we must also acknowledge the costs to the global norms of science of IP theft, a lack of transparency, and violations of existing agreements on the global norms of science. This includes holding U.S. scientists and companies to these global norms regardless of where they are conducting the research.

Take the long view

The disturbing reality that China presents today is inconvenient to those benefiting in the short term. This includes those companies seeking short-term profits, academics who benefit personally from extra funding or relatively inexpensive (but highly educated) labor in their labs, and former government officials who cash in as lobbyists for China's state-owned or state-supported companies. China is masterful at implementing tactics such as divide-and-conquer, identity politics, controlling the narrative, and falsely presenting lopsided engagements as "win-win." The reality is that we are not competing on an equal field—not in biotech and not in other S&T disciplines.

Notes

1 Chapter 7 in this volume. See also Hannas and Chang, et al., "China AI-Brain Research," Georgetown University, Center for Security and Emerging Technology, September 2020.
2 Licensed data used in this chapter are reproduced from prior CSET analytic production with authors' permission.
3 https://www.genome.gov/about-genomics/policy-issues/Synthetic-Biology.
4 Here, "population surveillance" means collecting DNA samples from humans, not genomic surveillance of pathogens to identify emerging diseases.
5 See narrative below.
6 PRC State Council, 国家中长期科学和技术发展规划纲要(2006–2020年), SC 9, 2006.
7 "New Policies to be Issued to Lure Overseas Students Home," *People's Daily*, July 29, 2000; "China Allotted 200 Million Yuan for Students Returned from Overseas," *People's Daily*, January 22, 2002.
8 Cao et al., *China's 15-year Science and Technology Plan, Physics Today*, December 2006.
9 Brian Wang, "China's $9.2 Billion Precision Medicine Initiative Could See about 100 Million Whole Human Genomes Sequenced by 2030 and More If Sequencing Costs Drop," NextBIGfuture.com, June 7, 2016.
10 Cyranoski, D. "China Embraces Precision Medicine on a Massive Scale," *Nature* 529, 2016, 9–10.
11 PRC Ministry of Education, 教育部关于印发高等学校人工智能创新行动计划的通知, MOE 3, 2018.
12 CSET translation at https://cset.georgetown.edu/research/ai-innovation-action-plan-for-institutions-of-higher-education/.
13 PRC State Council, 国务院关于印发"十三五"国家科技创新规划的通知, SC 43, 2016.
14 CSET translation at https://cset.georgetown.edu/publication/state-council-notice-on-the-publication-of-the-national-13th-five-year-plan-for-st-innovation/.
15 Ibid.
16 Ibid.
17 PRC Ministry of Science and Technology, "十三五"科技军民融合发展专项规划 (13th Five-year Special Plan for S&T Military-Civil Fusion Development), MOST 85, 2017.
18 PRC National People's Congress and Chinese People's Political Consultative Conference,中华人民共和国国民经济和社会发展第十四个五年规划和2035年远景目标纲要 (The 14th Five-year Plan for the National Economic and Social Development of the People's Republic of China and the Outline of Long-Term Goals for 2035), March 2021.
19 Ibid., https://cset.georgetown.edu/publication/china-14th-five-year-plan/.
20 Office of the PRC State Council, "温家宝主持召开三次新兴战略性产业发展座谈会" (Wen Jiabao Hosted Three Emerging Strategic Industry Development Symposiums), September 22, 2009; PRC State Council, 国务院关于加快培育和发展战略性新兴产业的决定 (State Council Decision on Accelerating the Cultivation and Development of Strategic Emerging Industries), SC 32, 2010.
21 PRC National Development and Reform Commission, 关于扩大战略性新兴产业投资培养壮大新增长点增长极的指导意见 (Guiding Opinions on Expanding Investment in Strategic Emerging Industries, and Cultivating New Growth Points and Poles), NDRC 1409, 2020.

22 https://cset.georgetown.edu/publication/china-14th-five-year-plan/.
23 PRC State Council, 国务院关于印发"十三五"国家战略性新兴产业发展规划的通知, (National 13th Five-year Plan for the Development of Strategic Emerging Industries), SC 67, 2016.
24 PRC National Development and Reform Commission, 加快推进战略性新兴产业产业集群建设有关工作通知 (Notice on Accelerating the Construction of Industrial Clusters in Strategic Emerging Industries), NDRC 1473, 2019.
25 Unpublished analysis by this book's editors of Google Maps, Street View, and public imagery of China's so-called "science towns" (科学城) has shown a correlation between physical proximity and cross-disciplinary collaborative work units generally.
26 All China National Knowledge Infrastructure (CNKI) content furnished as machine-readable data files for off-platform use by East View Information Services, Minneapolis, MN, USA.
27 Figure 8.3 is reproduced from this volume's Chapter 5.
28 "Clustered regularly interspaced short palindromic repeats."
29 We compiled Chinese and English search terms for "CRISPR" and "learning" to query against both Chinese and English titles and abstracts.
30 If a paper had co-authors claiming both Chinese and ROW organizations, it was counted once in each for ROW and China.
31 PKU Core Journals (北大核心期刊), also known as Core Journals of China (中文核心期刊), include publication venues curated as high impact by Peking University. PKU Core Journals' curation process incorporates more than ten measures of impact. For details, see http://hxqk.lib.pku.edu.cn/.
32 https://deepmind.com/blog/article/putting-the-power-of-alphafold-into-the-worlds-hands.
33 Demis Hassabis, "Introducing Isomorphic Labs," November 2021, https://www.isomorphiclabs.com/.
34 https://deepmind.com/blog/article/alphazero-shedding-new-light-grand-games-chess-shogi-and-go.
35 BGI华大in Chinese. The Beijing Genomics Institute, forerunner of the BGI Group, began life in 1999 and continues some of its earlier activities in the Chinese Academy of Sciences as the Beijing Institute of Genomics (北京基因组研究所, BIG). We use the term "BGI" interchangeably to refer to the composite entities.
36 *Reuters* reported that BGI used a military supercomputer to analyze genetic data obtained from its sales of prenatal tests to map the prevalence of viruses in Chinese women, look for indicators of mental illness, and genetically identify Tibetan and Uyghur minorities. BGI published at least 12 joint studies on the tests with the PLA since 2010. Kirsty Needham and Clare Baldwin, "Special Report: China's Gene Giant Harvests Data from Millions of Women," *Reuters,* July 7, 2021.
37 https://en.novogene.com/about/about-novogene/.
38 "Novogene," https://www.crunchbase.com/organization/novogene-corporation/company_financials.
39 https://insilico.com.
40 https://techcrunch.com/2021/06/22/a-i-drug-discovery-platform-insilico-medicine-announces-255-million-in-series-c-funding/.
41 https://www.chinamoneynetwork.com/2020/07/06/ai-driven-biotech-company-neox-raises-10m-pre-a-round.
42 http://bioinfo.ict.ac.cn/.
43 "About Us," http://miracle.ict.ac.cn/.
44 https://ai.sjtu.edu.cn/center.
45 https://ai.nankai.edu.cn/xszx/tjsznjqrjszdsys.htm.
46 https://www.lieyunwang.com/archives/131950.
47 http://en.zhenfund.com/Case/?id=3.
48 http://harvardchina.org/pitch-en/.

49 https://www.xtalpi.com/en/about/.
50 https://zhuanlan.zhihu.com/p/141693312; https://www.jingtaikeji.com/zh-hans/about/.
51 https://ngdc.cncb.ac.cn/about.
52 https://www.liepin.com/company/12926211/.
53 https://newsen.pku.edu.cn/news_events/news/focus/9857.htm.
54 Ryan Fedasiuk, Emily Weinstein, and Anna B. Puglisi, "China's Foreign Technology Wish List," Georgetown University, Center for Security and Emerging Technology, May 2021.
55 13th Five-year Plan for S&T Innovation (op. cit.).
56 Jon Gertner, *The Idea Factory: Bell Labs and the Great Age of American Innovation*, Penguin Press, London, 2012.
57 https://www.globenewswire.com/en/news-release/2021/06/21/2250298/0/en/AI-in-Drug-Discovery-Market-Worth-US-4-056-2-Million-by-2031-Visiongain-Research-Inc.html.
58 "Bioinformatics Market Worth $13.50 Billion in 2023," *Inter Press Service News Agency*, August 5, 2020.
59 Liang Puping et al., "CRISPR/Cas9-mediated Gene Editing in Human Tripronuclear Zygotes." *Protein Cell* 6.5, 363–372, 2015; David Cyranoski, "The Crispr-Baby Scandal: What's Next for Human Gene Editing" *Nature* 566, 2019, 440–442.
60 There are marmoset colonies in the United States; however, US regulatory hurdles and expenses give China an edge.
61 James Leibold and Emile Dirks, "Genomic Surveillance: Inside China's DNA Dragnet," Australian Strategic Policy Institute: *The Strategist*, June 17, 2020.
62 Alex Joske, "Hunting the Phoenix: The Chinese Communist Party's Global Search for Technology and Talent," Australian Strategic Policy Institute, August 2020.
63 Anna B. Puglisi, "Testimony before the Senate Select Committee on Intelligence," August 4, 2021, https://www.intelligence.senate.gov/sites/default/files/documents/os-apuglisi-080421.pdf.

Bibliography

Auslander, Noam, Ayal B. Gussow, and Eugene V. Koonin, "Incorporating Machine Learning into Established Bioinformatics Frameworks," *International Journal of Molecular Science*, 22.6, March 2021, pp. 1–19.
Bhaskar, Harish, David C. Hoyle, and Sameer Singh, "Machine Learning in Bioinformatics: A Brief Survey and Recommendations for Practitioners," *International Journal of Molecular Science*, 36.10, October 2006, pp. 1104–25.
Braw, Elisabeth, "How China Is Buying Up the West's High-Tech Sector," *Foreign Policy*, December 3, 2020.
Camacho, Diogo M. et al., "Next-Generation Machine Learning for Biological Networks," *Cell*, 173.7, June 2018, pp. 1581–1592.
Cyranoski, David, "AI Drug Discovery Booms in China," *Nature Biotechnology* 39, 2021, pp. 900–902.
Frazer, Jonathan et al., "Disease Variant Prediction with Deep Generative Models of Evolutionary Data," *Nature* 599, October 2021, pp. 91–95.
Inza, Iñaki et al., "Machine Learning: An Indispensable Tool in Bioinformatics," *Methods of Molecular Biology*, 593, 2010, pp. 25–48.
Mitchell, Melanie et al., "Gathering Strength, Gathering Storms: The One Hundred Year Study on Artificial Intelligence," (AI100) 2021 Study Panel Report," Stanford University, 2021.
Narayanan, Ajit, Edward C. Keedwell, and Björn Olsson, "Artificial Intelligence Techniques for Bioinformatics," *Applied Bioinformatics*, 1.4, 2002, pp. 191–222.

O'Brien, John T., and Cassidy Nelson, "Assessing the Risks Posed by the Convergence of Artificial Intelligence and Biotechnology," *Health Security*, 18(3) June 2020, 219–227.

PRC National Development and Reform Commission, 加快推进战略性新兴产业产业集群建设有关工作通知 (Notice on Accelerating the Construction of Industrial Clusters in Strategic Emerging Industries), NDRC 1473, 2019.

PRC National Development and Reform Commission, 关于扩大战略性新兴产业投资培养壮大新增长点增长极的指导意见 (Guiding Opinions on Expanding Investment in Strategic Emerging Industries, and Cultivating New Growth Points and Poles), NDRC 1409, 2020.

PRC National People's Congress and Chinese People's Political Consultative Conference, 中华人民共和国国民经济和社会发展第十四个五年规划和2035年远景目标纲要 (The 14th Five-year Plan for the National Economic and Social Development of the People's Republic of China and the Outline of Long-Term Goals for 2035), March 2021.

PRC State Council, 国务院关于印发"十三五"国家科技创新规划的通知 (State Council Notice on the Publication of the National 13th Five-year Plan for S&T Innovation), SC 43 2016.

PRC State Council, 国务院关于印发"十三五"国家战略性新兴产业发展规划的通知, (National 13th Five-year Plan for the Development of Strategic Emerging Industries) SC 67, 2016.

Puglisi, Anna, and Daniel H. Chou, "China's Industrial Clusters: Building AI Driven Bio-discovery Capacity," Georgetown University, Center for Security and Emerging Technology, June 2022.

Smalley, Eric, "AI-powered Drug Discovery Captures Pharma Interest," *Nature Biotechnology*, 35.7, July 2017, pp. 604–605.

Zampieri, Guido et al., "Machine and Deep Learning Meet Genome-scale Metabolic Modeling," *PLoS Computational Biology*, 15(7), July 11, 2019, pp. 1–24.

9

China at the nexus of AI and quantum computing

Jonathan Ray

The convergence between artificial intelligence (AI) and quantum computing has global economic and security implications, with applications ranging from advancing pharmaceuticals to breaking traditional encryption. In its national and local state plans, China's policymakers clearly seek global leadership in both of these domains, and encourage synergies between them. Traditional research institutions, namely universities and laboratories, are leading theoretical work and basic research and development for quantum computers to power AI applications, quantum machine learning (ML), and other foundational work. Additionally, China's premier cloud service providers are advancing the two technologies with quantum simulators and online platforms for ML and algorithm development. These companies are driving the commercialization of quantum technologies for industries like pharmaceuticals, materials science, and chemistry. China's investments and rapid advancements warrant analytic attention to avoid technological surprise and inform U.S. policymakers and leaders in these fields. To that end, this chapter identifies key entities pursuing research on the nexus between the two technologies, assesses technology paths and obstacles, and provides indicators for future analyses.

Introduction

Convergence between China's ambitions for AI and quantum computing could accelerate the country's advancements in both fields and disrupt commercial industries and the security of modern Internet, communications, and tele-communications (ICT) technologies. The rapidity of recent developments in AI has been linked to advances in computing, although computational power remains a bottleneck for ML. This challenge has prompted massive Chinese state and private investments at the national and provincial levels to accelerate the

DOI: 10.4324/9781003212980-12

development of specialized computing technologies that transcend traditional computing models, including quantum computers. At the forefront of this development, long-established state science and technology (S&T) research institutions like the Chinese Academy of Sciences (CAS) and academic institutions like Tsinghua University are joined by newer commercial champions such as Baidu, Huawei, and others.

Quantum computing machines use qubits, typically subatomic particles such as electrons or photons, as opposed to traditional "bits"—binary digits—in classical computers "corresponding to an electrical value of off or on."[1] While bits can only represent ones or zeroes, a qubit can represent both at the same time, a state called "superposition." Currently, researchers are generating groups of qubits to exist in a single quantum state, called "entanglement," with every additional qubit providing exponential increases in computing power as opposed to the linear increase per bit in classical computers. "Quantum supremacy" refers to the point at which a quantum computer can complete a mathematical calculation beyond the capability of any traditional supercomputer, and "quantum advantage" emphasizes quantum computers "doing *some* useful things *somewhat* faster or more efficiently—enough to make them economically worthwhile."[2] Google's quantum computer *Sycamore* used superconducting materials to achieve the supremacy milestone in December 2019, and *Jiuzhang* (九章) at the University of Science and Technology of China (中国科学技术大学, USTC) used photons to achieve the same a year later. While computing power increases exponentially per qubit, quantum states are incredibly fragile and consequently the machines are error-prone and require highly controlled environments. The slightest "noise," such as vibration or temperature change, can cause qubits to come out of superposition.

AI and in particular its subfield ML can benefit quantum computing, especially in experiment design and implementation. By examining photographs of the *Jiuzhang* experiment, a leading quantum computing expert observed that the large number of hand-aligned optical elements would demand a tremendous amount of manual labor to align with micrometer precision, whereas experiments with this many components are natural fits for AI algorithms to automate processes and reduce labor.[3] Quantum physicist Michael Krenn's teams at the University of Vienna and later the University of Toronto demonstrated the benefit of ML for experiments with their MELVIN and THESEUS algorithms. In 2016, Krenn used MELVIN to design a quantum experiment, and in 2021 collaborated with the USTC researcher Lan-Tian Feng (冯兰天) to fabricate the proposed setup on a single photonic chip and carry out the designed experiment.[4]

In the opposite direction, a growing list of technology companies aspire to utilize quantum computers and algorithms for ML and algorithm development for AI applications. U.S. technology leaders like Google and IBM as well as China's Baidu, Alibaba, and others described below hope that quantum computing will power AI ML algorithms to ingest, classify, and analyze greater amounts of data. For this goal, they are promoting open-source ML libraries (such as Google's TensorFlow, IBM's Qiskit, and Baidu's Paddle Quantum) to develop and improve algorithms for quantum computers. If successful, these service providers may reap economic benefits from pharmaceuticals, new materials, and other industries.

While evaluating timelines for one—let alone two—leading edge technology is difficult, it is clear that China's leadership intends to leverage its strengths in both technologies and be a first mover on the combined output. As one of China's leading quantum scientists Pan Jianwei (潘建伟)[5] views it, "AI is a type of software technology, and quantum computing is a hardware technology." By combining the two humankind would create its own "non-biological 'child'."[6] Assessing the current state and future trajectory of both is essential for U.S. policy planners to avoid technological surprise in security applications and maintain economic competitiveness.

AI and quantum computing in Chinese leadership statements, state and local plans

China's Paramount Leader Xi Jinping regularly demonstrates strong support for prioritizing emerging technologies, and has shown particular interest in AI and quantum computing. In October 2017, his work report to the 19th Party Congress highlighted the new technological revolution that is emerging, including rapid breakthroughs in AI and quantum science.[7] It is also notable that since Xi assumed power in 2012, among the 70-odd[8] Politburo study sessions, only three have been on specific technologies—AI (2018), blockchain (2019), and quantum computing (2020).[9] During the AI study session, Xi stated, "Accelerating the development of a new generation of AI is an important strategic starting point for China to gain the initiative in global science and technology competition."[10] Similarly, at the quantum science session, he said that the two technologies are "of great scientific significance and strategic value."[11]

China's state plans and long-term S&T goals similarly emphasize the two technologies' strategic value and offer more specific objectives. In 2017, the "New Generation Artificial Intelligence Development Plan" issued by the State Council explicitly linked the two by calling for advances in theoretical research in quantum intelligence computing, specifically methods for quantum-accelerated ML, the establishment of models for convergence between AI and quantum computing, and the formation of high-efficiency, accurate, and autonomous quantum AI system setups.[12] The 14th Five-year Plan (2021–2025) lists AI and quantum information as the first two technologies in a list of "forward-looking and strategic national megascience projects" and calls for the development of general-purpose quantum computing prototypes, quantum simulators, and quantum precision measurement technology.[13]

At a more local level, provinces and major cities are including both in their plans for S&T investments.

- In 2019, Jinan, China's "Quantum Valley," included AI in its "Jinan Quantum Information Industry Development Plan (2019-2022)." In 2021–2022, the plan calls for exploring "the commercial value of quantum computing in material simulations, cloud computing, big data, ML, AI, high-performance computing, and other applications."[14]
- In 2021 Beijing, Guangdong, and Shanxi identified quantum technologies and AI as investment priorities for the "new infrastructure development" (新基建) program China launched in 2020 in response to COVID-19 to advance job creation and innovative industries.[15]
- Among provincial and municipal recommendations for implementing the 14th Five-year Plan (2021–2025), 11 included AI and quantum technology: Beijing, Shanghai, Chongqing, Tianjin, Guangdong, Zhejiang, Jiangsu, Shanxi, Guangxi, Anhui, and Sichuan).[16]

Current status, potential synergies, and limits of AI and quantum computing

It is notable that when China's experts in quantum computing discuss timelines for that technology's development, they often list AI as a key beneficiary of such advances. Conversely, some of China's AI experts note that quantum computing is one of a handful of technologies worth pursuing to power AI applications and subfields. In December 2020, *Qiushi* magazine, the CCP's leading theoretical journal, published commentary by Pan Jianwei on Xi's study session on quantum computing discussed above. Pan lays out the three phases and timelines below for quantum computing's development, including applications to AI:

Phase 1 should achieve "quantum superiority" (2020–2025)

In this stage, quantum computers solve specific problems that demonstrate superiority over traditional supercomputers, and require about 50 qubits (e.g. Google's *Sycamore* in 2019 and *Jiuzhang* at the USTC in December 2020). China's traditional S&T institutions and universities feature prominently in this basic R&D stage for quantum computing as well as the mathematical and theoretical progress for AI subfields like ML.

Phase 2 should achieve entanglement of hundreds of qubits and produce a specialized quantum simulator (2025–2030)

This stage, projected to run from 2025 to 2030, should see the entanglement of hundreds of qubits (compared to the current tens of qubits) and quantum simulators that can be applied to applications like ML, material design, and drug development.[17] China's leading cloud computing providers, as discussed below, are emerging as leaders for this stage of applications and seeking industry partnerships.

Phase 3 should achieve a "general-purpose quantum computer" (estimated 2040)

A "general-purpose quantum computer" should manipulate at least millions of qubits and play a role in applications like classical cryptanalysis, big data searches, and AI. Technological challenges make any timeline unclear, and without committing to his own prediction, Pan quotes "international computing experts" as saying that such a computer is approximately 20 years away.[18] This chapter does not speculate that far out but provides some indicators to look for.

Quantum computing is not China's sole approach to greater computational power, nor is its future necessarily guaranteed. In September 2020, Dai Qionghai (戴琼海), Director General of the Chinese Association for Artificial Intelligence (中国人工智能学会, CAAI), Chinese Academy of Engineering academician, and Dean of Tsinghua University's School of Information Science and Technology (信息科学与技术学院), identified three other emerging technologies potentially offering greater computational power for AI[19]:

- In-memory computing (存算一体架构);
- Neuromorphic computing (类脑计算); and
- Photoelectronic intelligent computing (光电智能计算).

The Tianjic chip, "the first neuromorphic chip enabling scalable configurations of both artificial and spiking neural networks"[20] (see Chapter 13), is an example of these technologies.

Dai opined that quantum computing's large footprint and complexity make it useful for specific applications, but not necessarily AI/ML.[21] In addition to bottlenecks already described, quantum computers face tremendous challenges with error correction, which will hinder the technology's development for general use and limit it to computing approximate solutions. China's research into this problem appears more limited, likely indicating early stages of research instead of a lack of interest.[22]

China's research institutes lead basic R&D in quantum computing with AI applications

Since at least 2013, Chinese universities and state laboratories have led basic research and development for quantum computing and preliminary investigations of how to apply quantum computing to AI applications like ML. CAS is a lead player here, notably through laboratories at its subordinate university USTC. Tsinghua University, another leading university in this field, has international collaborations (described below) focused on the nexus of quantum computing and AI, and its alumni include the director for quantum computing at Baidu.

University of Science and Technology of China (USTC)

USTC, a leading public S&T university in China subordinate to CAS, hosts at least five of China's leading laboratories researching the nexus between quantum computing and AI. The university's home city of Hefei is a central node in the network of laboratories and commercial startups dedicated to quantum research. One street is colloquially known as "quantum avenue" (量子大道) with over 20 quantum technology companies.[23]

> Hefei National Laboratory for Physical Sciences at the Microscale (合肥微尺度物质科学国家研究中心) and CAS Center for Excellence in Quantum Information and Quantum Physics (中国科学院量子信息与量子科技创新研究院) led the development of the *Jiuzhang* quantum computer.[24] The former is one of six national research centers established in 2017 by the Ministry of Science and Technology, and supports interdisciplinary focuses across physics, chemistry, materials, biology, and information sciences.[25] The latter, formally led by Pan Jianwei, is a CAS entity that pulls expertise from across the country, with operations in Beijing, Shanghai, Shenzhen, and Jinan. It draws support from at least nine other CAS entities and at least ten of China's leading technical universities.[26] After the *Jiuzhang* test in December 2020, its developers claimed that it can process at a rate 10 *billion* times faster than Google's quantum computer. While the comparison may not be appropriate, given the two systems' differences, the significance of beating America's champion conveys propagandistic value in its own right.[27] *Jiuzhang* may be only a "champion in one single area" for now, but researchers see potential applications in graph theory, ML, and quantum chemistry going forward.[28]
>
> National Engineering Laboratory for Brain-inspired Intelligence Technology and Application (类脑智能技术及应用国家工程实验室, NEL-BITA). In 2017, China's National Development and Reform Commission appointed USTC as the leading partner for NEL-BITA, China's first national-level scientific research entity in the field of brain-inspired intelligence.[29] As a national endeavor, this joint laboratory brings in resources from academia and industry, including Fudan University, four CAS-affiliated institutes,[30] iFlytek, Microsoft Asia Research Institute, and Datatang (Beijing) Technology Co., Ltd.[31] This laboratory has six subordinate units, including a Quantum Artificial Intelligence Laboratory (量子人工智能研究所) focused on quantum simulation and parallel computing structures to enable AI and subfields such as deep learning.[32]
>
> Key Laboratory of Quantum Information (量子信息重点实验室). The lab is China's first provincial-level key laboratory for quantum information,

and focuses on semiconductor quantum chips, quantum entangled networks, quantum integrated optical chips, practical quantum cryptography, and quantum theory.[33] To commercialize these endeavors, the lab has a commercial-facing company, Origin Quantum (本源量子), that is China's first full-stack quantum developer enterprise. Founded in 2017, they launched a platform in 2019 called VQNet that uses a variational quantum circuit (VQC) aimed at enabling ML with more near-term quantum computers.[34]

CAS Key Laboratory of Microscale Magnetic Resonance (中科院微观 磁共振重点实验室), formerly the Spin Magnetic Resonance Laboratory of USTC. This key lab focuses on spin quantum control and its applications in quantum technologies, including nuclear magnetic resonance (NMR), electron spin resonance (ESR), optically detected magnetic resonance (ODMR), magnetic resonance force microscopy (MRFM), and electrically detected magnetic resonance (EDMR).[35] In an example of AI helping advance quantum technology, the lab recently combined deep learning and sparse matrix completion to accelerate an NMR spectroscopy and suppress observation noise.[36]

Tsinghua University

Tsinghua University's work on the synergies between AI and quantum computing is exemplified by Andrew Yao (姚期智, Yao Qizhi), a technical expert and a leader in developing new talent for both technologies. Professor Yao received the Turing Award in 2000 after over two decades of work at U.S. institutions that made "fundamental contributions to the theory of computation, including the complexity-based theory of pseudorandom number generation, cryptography, and communication complexity."[37] In 2004, Yao joined Tsinghua's faculty, and in 2011 became the dean of the Institute for Interdisciplinary Information Sciences, and the founding director of its Center for Quantum Information (CQI).[38] In 2021, he received the Kyoto Prize for his theoretical work and influenced "cutting-edge computer science in multiple fields, including security, privacy, parallel computing, big data processing, and quantum computing."[39]

Yao is a source of national pride as the first Chinese scholar to receive the Turing Award—and for renouncing his U.S. citizenship.[40] Besides his technical accomplishments, Yao focuses on cultivating new talent. His "Yao Class" (姚班) educational model for computer science[41] led to a "Smart Class" (智班) for AI at Tsinghua in 2019 and a Quantum Information Class in 2021.[42] While innovative in these training programs, Yao is no stranger to traditional talent recruitment: after founding CQI, Yao stated, "our immediate step was to recruit high-quality researchers, such as Professor Duan Luming (段路明), a physics professor at University of Michigan, through the Thousand Talents Program."[43]

Duan himself, while at Tsinghua in 2018, proposed a quantum ML algorithm with Michigan PhD students based on generative adversarial models.[44] This research reportedly "offers a remarkable example where a quantum algorithm shows exponential improvement over classical algorithms in an important application field."[45] The following year, Tsinghua scientists used adversarial learning to train a quantum-state generator that replicates a quantum channel simulator's output with 98.8% fidelity. They claim that such an advance could enable ML tasks with noisy intermediate-scale quantum devices.[46] In 2021, Tsinghua researchers published a literature review on neural-network quantum states, and described the approach as having potential breakthroughs for the representation of quantum states and ML.[47]

In 2013, Tsinghua University and the University of Technology, Sydney (UTS) formed a Joint Research Centre for Quantum Computation and Artificial Intelligence.[48] At least six of the 14 key members within its Centre for Quantum Software and Information are Tsinghua graduates. Another, Ying Mingsheng (应明生), served on the editorial board of *Artificial Intelligence Journal* and maintains a dual affiliation. Duan Runyao (段润尧), a Tsinghua graduate and former UTS professor, became the Director of the Baidu Quantum Computing Institute in 2018.[49]

Quantum BATH: the role of China's cloud computing companies in AI and quantum computing development

Four of China's leading providers of cloud computing services (Baidu, Alibaba, Tencent, and Huawei) are at the forefront of deploying platforms that advance quantum computing and AI, notably quantum simulators and online platforms for ML and algorithm development. If successful, they will be the go-to providers for commercial adoption of quantum computing and AI applications for industries, including pharmaceuticals, materials development, and others with demanding computational requirements. The combination of quantum computing simulators and mature cloud computing enables users to develop and verify quantum algorithms and software, including models that support the development of quantum computers and circuits, before the actual hardware is mature. The China Academy of Information and Communication Technology (中国信息通信研究院, CAICT) breaks down the taxonomy of quantum cloud computing as follows[50]:

- **Quantum Infrastructure as a Service (Q-IaaS)**, in which cloud computing services provide quantum simulators and eventually actual quantum equipment for calculations.
- **Quantum Platform as a Service (Q-PaaS)**, which provides a software development platform for quantum computing and quantum ML calculations.
- **Quantum Software as a Service (Q-SaaS)**, which provides programs appropriate to specific applications and to accelerate algorithms for AI.

Table 9.1, based on CAICT's report and augmented by the author's own research, summarizes the leading companies around the world for the above services:

TABLE 9.1 Leading companies in quantum services worldwide

Quantum service	Leading Chinese companies		Leading international companies	
Q-IaaS	Alibaba, Huawei	Full Stack: Origin Quantum	Intel, Honeywell, IonQ, D-Wave,	Full Stack: Rigetti, QuTech, IBM, Google
Q-PaaS	Alibaba, Baidu		Microsoft, Strange Works, AWS	
Q-SaaS	Huawei, Tencent		1Qbit, Q-Ctrl, Quantifi, Avanetix, QxBranch, QunaSys, HQS, D-Wave	

Baidu Institute for Quantum Computing

In 2018, Baidu established the Baidu Institute of Quantum Computing and recruited Duan Runyao, a professor from the University of Technology Sydney, to lead the team. The institute has three technology focuses: "Quantum AI, Quantum Algorithm, and Quantum Architecture (QAAA for short) to provide a comprehensive quantum computing environment known as the Baidu Quantum Plan (BQP)."[51] Discussing *Paddle Quantum* (量桨), Baidu's "bridge connecting quantum computing and AI," Duan said, "researchers in the quantum field can use Paddle Quantum to develop quantum artificial intelligence, and our deep learning enthusiasts have a shortcut to learning quantum computing."[52] At Wave Summit 2020, co-hosted by Baidu and the National Engineering Laboratory for Deep Learning Technology and Applications (深度学习技术及应用国家工程实验室), Duan claimed that *Paddle Quantum* was the first and only deep learning platform for quantum ML in China, and that it has a growing user base.[53]

Alibaba Cloud (Aliyun)

Alibaba Cloud (阿里云, Aliyun), the cloud computing and data backbone for e-commerce giant Alibaba Group, is heavily involved in quantum simulators and has at least two simulators with AI applications.

In July 2015, Aliyun and CAS established the "CAS-Alibaba Quantum Computing Laboratory" (中国科学院–阿里巴巴量子计算实验室) combining Aliyun's classical computing methods, structures, and cloud computing technology with CAS's quantum computing and simulations and "quantum artificial intelligence technologies" to make advances in quantum information sciences and develop a quantum computer.[54] The laboratory hosts an 11-qubit quantum simulator.[55]

In 2017, Aliyun established the Aliyun Quantum Laboratory as one of its X-Labs in the Alibaba Dharma (达摩, Damo) Academy, the e-commerce giant's future technology development unit. The lab's founding director is Shi Yaoyun (施尧耘), formerly at the University of Michigan.[56] A year later, the laboratory claimed to have the world's most powerful quantum simulator, *Tai Zhang* (太章),

powered by the Alibaba Cloud Quantum Development Platform (AC-QDP), and in 2020 debuted *Tai Zhang* 2.0 by simulating Google's 2019 quantum supremacy demonstration with the *Bristlecone* processing unit.[57] *Tai Zhang* 2.0's applications include ML, discovery of particles and materials, and optimization problems.[58]

Tencent Quantum Lab

In 2018, Tencent launched the Tencent Quantum Lab (腾讯量子实验室) and announced its "ABC2.0" technology roadmap (AI, RoBotics, Quantum Computing) that includes quantum AI research.[59] The lab's 2018–2019 research included quantum algorithms for neural networks and ML models for chemistry and material science.[60] The lab collaborates with Iordanis Kerenidis, a researcher at the University of Paris and the Paris Centre for Quantum Computing (PCQC), on neural networking and helped develop a quantum acceleration algorithm that is reportedly suitable for applications. Another international partner is Canada's Vector Institute of Artificial Intelligence, which co-hosted the Tencent Alchemy 2019 competition for advancing ML models useful for chemistry and materials science.[61] In February 2021, the laboratory signed a cooperation agreement with Joincare Pharmaceutical (健康元) to apply quantum and AI in fields of microbial synthetic biology research and related drug research.[62]

Huawei

In October 2018, Huawei released HiQ, a cloud-based platform for quantum computing simulations adapted for use with NUDT's "Tianhe 2" (天河二号) supercomputer. According to Huawei's Chief Quantum Computing Software and Algorithm Scientist Dr. Man-hong Yung (翁文康), "Quantum algorithms provide a new perspective to AI algorithms, inspiring better classical AI algorithms and offering more powerful computing capability."[63] At the 2019 China National Computer Conference, Dr. Yung said that the quantum hardware is insufficient to keep up with the quantum algorithms being developed.[64]

Advanced applications
Cryptographic uses of AI and quantum

In Chinese media, there is great interest and commentary on the implications of quantum computing and AI for encryption standards that undergird global ICT infrastructure. The technical literature on using quantum and AI against encryption is more limited but alarming in its implications. Wang Chao (王潮) at Shanghai University's Key Laboratory of Specialty Fiber Optics and Optical Access Networks (上海大学特种光纤与光接入网重点实验室) has led research on using AI algorithms with the D-Wave quantum annealer.[65] Gate-based quantum computers (such as the *Jiuzhang* and *Sycamore* prototypes and their successors) will likely use Shor's algorithm[66] to factor large numbers and attack encryption like RSA. Wang's group, however, writes that because these computers are in their early development, "D-Wave using quantum annealing may be closer to cracking practical RSA codes than a general-purpose quantum computer (IBM) using Shor's algorithm."[67] Also at Shanghai University, a research group led by Wan Wanggen (万旺根) claims to have received national funding in 2012 to research the use of quantum AI algorithms for encryption and decryption, and in that research achieved the best results internationally in using quantum computing against RSA encryption public keys.[68]

Quantum chips

As of 2021, the global development of quantum computing processors is still in R&D stages, with Chinese labs and companies behind on numbers of quantum processors compared to IBM, Google, Rigetti, and others. To catch up, that year Chinese companies Origin Quantum and NexChip Semiconductor Corp. agreed to develop a quantum chip facility in Hefei, Anhui Province. The partnership is a natural fit between intellectual property and infrastructure. From 2016 to Summer 2021, Origin Quantum has been awarded nearly half (50 of 115) of China's patents with "quantum chip" in the title; conversely, NexChip holds no patents mentioning quantum but has expertise in semiconductor design and manufacturing.[69] The *Global Times* managed expectations in its coverage of the agreement, noting that all quantum chips are in the R&D stage and that lab to market will take at least eight to ten years.[70]

Conclusions and indicators

China is clearly seeking global supremacy in AI, quantum computing, and nexus applications, as demonstrated by the country's policies, investments, and growing network of state and private entities. The country's research institutions and technology companies have made significant and highly publicized accomplishments and are dedicated to talent recruitment and development to ensure continued advances. China's progress in these fields and the potential for disruptive breakthroughs warrant continued analytic attention to indicators from technological, commercial, and security perspectives.

Indicators of China's progress on quantum AI will come from traditional S&T institutions like CAS and universities, which are researching and prototyping quantum computing systems, as well as advancing the math and theory behind quantum ML. Chinese media will likely publicize high-profile tests like *Jiuzhang*; instead of adding to the hype, analysts can work with technical experts to evaluate the relevant literature and assess the utility of such achievements for AI applications, as well as identify other useful indicators of progress. For example, advances in error correction for quantum computing are essential for AI, but will likely appear in technical publications and not media puff pieces. Other useful indicators are corporate announcements, patents, and technology media.

For commercial applications, China's cloud technology champions have embraced the use of their platforms for quantum and AI advances, but indicators of adoption and utilization are too early to quantify. From a technical perspective, they have succeeded in running quantum simulators that can provide some value to applications, and they are trying to incorporate true quantum computing into their traditional computational frameworks. If successful, these firms could gain enormous commercial advantage in pharmaceutical development, material design, and other fields with high-computational requirements. The agreement between Tencent and Joincare Pharmaceutical is a case study worth following to assess the commercial potential of such applications.

The security implications of China's work in quantum and AI are more secretive but necessary to track. While gate-based computers appear to be years away from entangling enough qubits to attack RSA encryption, the use of existing quantum annealers with AI for this purpose is a more immediate threat warranting further technical analysis. Additionally, national standards bodies, such as those participating in quantum-related work under the National Science and Technology Council, may need an expedited timeline to choose and deploy post-quantum cryptography standards.

Notes

1 University Information Technology Services, "What Are Bits, Bytes, and Other Units of Measure for Digital Information, https://kb.iu.edu/d/ackw.
2 Martin Giles, "Explainer, What is a Quantum Computer?" *MIT Technology Review*, January 29, 2019; Gideon Lichfield, "Inside the Race to Build the Best Quantum Computer on Earth," *MIT Technology Review*, February 26, 2020.
3 Jake Taylor, "Learning from the Automation of Physics Experiments," *Perspectives on Public Purpose*, December 16, 2020.
4 Anil Ananthaswamy, "AI Designs Quantum Physics Experiments beyond What Any Human Has Conceived," *Scientific American*, July 2, 2021.
5 Pan Jianwei's role in technology transfer is described in Jeffrey Stoff, "China's Talent Programs," Hannas and Tatlow, eds., 2021, p. 19.
6 Hu Dingkun, "Pan Jianwei Reveals the Three Stages of Quantum Computing Development," *People's Daily Online*, January 15, 2020, http://scitech.people.com.cn/n1/2020/0115/c1007-31549405.html.
7 "Full Text of Xi Jinping's Report at 19th CPC National Congress," *China Daily*, November 4, 2017.
8 See full lists under Xi at "中央政治局集体学习十八届" (Politburo Collective Study Sessions (18th Congress)), 中国共产党新闻网资料库 (Chinese Communist Party News Online Database), http://cpc.people.com.cn/n/2012/1119/c352109-19621672.html; and "中央政治局集体学习十九届" (Politburo Collective Study Sessions (19th Congress)), 中央领导机构资料库 (Central Leadership Organizations News Online Database), http://cpc.people.com.cn/n1/2017/1025/c414940-29608670.html.
9 At "Politburo collective study sessions" (中共中央政治局集体学习), an expert may be invited to present on their area of expertise, normally on policy issues. This count does not include more strategy-oriented study sessions on becoming a cyber great power (2016), big data (2017), or "green development" (2017).

10 "Xi Jinping: Promote the Healthy Development of China's New Generation of Artificial Intelligence," *Xinhua Online*, October 31, 2018, http://www.xinhuanet.com/politics/leaders/2018-10/31/c_1123643321.htm.

11 "Xi Jinping at 24th Study Session of the Politburo Collective Study Session Emphasized the Great Significance of Deep Understanding of the Promotion of Quantum Science Development as well as the Strengthening of Strategic Plans and Systems for Quantum Science Development," *Xinhua Online*, October 17, 2020. Xi's assessment was informed by Beijing Academy of Quantum Information Sciences director Xue Qikun (薛其坤), who likened the role of quantum to semiconductors in the 1950s. See Zhang Yu (张瑜), "专家:未来10年专用中等规模量子计算机或将出现" (Expert: Specialized Medium-Scale Quantum Computers May Appear in the Next 10 Years), *Di Yi Caijing* (第一财经), May 26, 2021.

12 PRC State Council. 国务院关于印发新一代人工智能发展规划的通知 (The New Generation AI Development Plan), SC 35, 2017.

13 "中华人民共和国国民经济和社会发展第十四个五年规划和2035年远景目标纲要" (Outline of the People's Republic of China 14th Five-year Plan for National Economic and Social Development and Long-Range Objectives for 2035), *Xinhua News Agency*, March 12, 2021.

14 "Jinan City Quantum Information Industry Development Plan (2019-2022)," issued by the Jinan Science and Technology Bureau on March 8, 2019, text published by the Jinan Institute of Quantum Technology on September 23, 2020, http://www.jiqt.org/index/show/action/policy/id/1.

15 "Local National People's Conferences Describe New Infrastructure Investment Plans to Push for Breakthroughs in Computer Chips, Quantum Science and Other Technologies," *China Securities Journal*, January 25, 2021, https://sme.miit.gov.cn/xwzx/jdxw/art/2021/art_6c0eec3b7573408a99cb7c6c417d1c75.html.

16 "各省市量子信息"十四五"发展线路图:争相布局 抢占发展制高点" (Diagrams of Individual City and Provincial Quantum Information '14th Five-year Plan' Development Paths: Competing to Lay Out and Seize the Commanding High Grounds for Development), reposted from AskCI Consulting Corporation (中商产业研究院), January 20, 2021, https://www.163.com/dy/article/G0PRDG2305198SOQ.html.

17 This timeline matches a prediction from Professor Xue Qikun, the expert invited to the Politburo's study session on quantum technology, who in 2021 believed that a quantum computer could support machine learning within ten years.

18 Pan Jianwei, "Promote Better China's Quantum Technology Development," *Red Flag Manuscripts*, 23, 2020, http://www.qstheory.cn/dukan/hqwg/2020-12/08/c_1126835704.htm. *Red Flag Manuscripts* is a semi-monthly publication of political theory published by Qiushi magazine for internal and international propaganda work.

19 Dai Qionghai, "Deep Learning Has Encountered Bottlenecks, Comprehensive Neural Observations Inspire the Next Generation of AI Algorithms," Remarks at the 2020 International Conference on Computer Communication and Artificial Intelligence, reposted on the Tencent AI Discussion Forum, September 4, 2020, https://cloud.tencent.com/developer/article/1692341.

20 Jing Pei et al., "Towards Artificial General Intelligence with Hybrid Tianjic Chip Architecture," *Nature*, 572, 2019, 106–111.

21 Dai Qionghai, "Deep Learning Has Encountered Bottlenecks, Comprehensive Neural Observations Inspire the Next Generation of AI Algorithms."

22 Ling Hu et al., "Quantum Error Correction and Universal Gate Set Operation on a Binomial Bosonic Logical Qubit," *Nature Physics* 15, 2019, 503–508.

23 Zhou Chang (周畅), Chen Nuo (陈诺), "'量子大道'上的青年探险者" (The Young Pioneers on 'Quantum Avenue'), *Xinhua*, December 5, 2020.

24 Leading scientists Pan Jianwei and Lu Chaoyang (陆朝阳) listed these two laboratories as their main affiliation when publishing on *Jiuzhang*. See Zhong, Han-Sen et al. "Quantum Computational Advantage Using Photons," *Science* 370.6523, 2020, 1460–1463.

25 "Center Introduction" (中心简介), Hefei National Laboratory for Physical Sciences at the Microscale, https://www.hfnl.ustc.edu.cn/page?catid=2, last accessed July 26, 2021.

26 Supporting CAS entities include Shanghai Institute of Technical Physics, Institute of Semiconductors, Institute of Optoelectronics, Institute of Physics, Shanghai Institute of Microsystems and Information Technology, Institute of Microsatellite Innovation, Wuhan Institute of Physics and Mathematics, University of Chinese Academy of Sciences, and National Time Service Center. "Collaborative innovation units" outside of CAS include Peking University, Tsinghua University, Fudan University, Shanghai Jiaotong University, Nanjing University, National University of Defense Technology, Zhejiang University, Beijing University of Aeronautics and Astronautics, East China Normal University, and Beijing Computing Science Research Center.

27 Hu Dingkun, "Pan Jianwei Reveals the Three Stages of Quantum Computing Development."

28 "China Focus: Chinese Scientists Achieve Quantum Computational Advantage," *Xinhua*, December 4, 2020.

29 "实验室简介" (Laboratory Introduction), National Engineering Laboratory for Brain-inspired Intelligence Technology and Application (NEL-BITA), http://leinao.ustc.edu.cn/25885/list.htm, last accessed July 26, 2021.

30 Shenyang Institute of Automation, Institute of Microelectronics, Institute of Electronics, and the Institute of Neuroscience.

31 "Laboratory Introduction," NEL-BITA.

32 "组织机构" (Organization Structure), NEL-BITA, http://leinao.ustc.edu.cn/25887/list.htm, last accessed July 26, 2021. The other laboratories are Brain Cognition and Neural Computing, Neuromorphic Multimodal Perception and Information Processing, Neuromorphic Chips and Systems, Neuromorphic Computing Systems, and Neuromorphic Intelligent Robots.

33 "实验室简介" (Laboratory Introduction), CAS Key Laboratory of Quantum Science, USTC, http://lqcc.ustc.edu.cn/index/lists/001001, last accessed July 26, 2021.

34 Chen, Zhao-Yun et al. "VQNet: Library for a Quantum-Classical Hybrid Neural Network." arXiv preprint arXiv:1901.09133 (2019).

35 "Laboratory Introduction" (实验室简介), CAS Key Laboratory of Microscale Magnetic Resonance, https://lmmr.ustc.edu.cn/sysjj/list.htm, last accessed July 26, 2021.

36 Kong Xi, Zhou, Leixin, Li, Zhijie et al., "Artificial Intelligence Enhanced Two-Dimensional Nanoscale Nuclear Magnetic Resonance Spectroscopy," *npj Quantum Information*, 6.79, 2020.

37 Bruce Kapron, "Andrew Chi-Chih Yao, China - 2000," A.M. Turing Award Laureates, https://amturing.acm.org/award_winners/yao_1611524.cfm, last accessed July 26, 2021.

38 Mu-ming Poo and Ling Wang, "Andrew Chi-Chih Yao: The Future of Quantum Computing," *National Science Review*, 5, 2019, 598–602.

39 "2021 Kyoto Prize Laureates: Andrew Chi-Chih Yao," Inamori Foundation, https://www.kyotoprize.org/en/en/laureates/andrew_chi-chih_yao/.

40 "'对话'杨振宁、姚期智:我为什么放弃外国国籍?" (Dialog—Chen Ning Yang and Andrew Yao: Why Did I Give Up My Foreign Citizenship?"), *Xinhua News Agency*, February 21, 2017.

41 Poo and Wang, "Andrew Chi-Chih Yao: The Future of Quantum Computing."

42 "清华大学姚期智获2021年度"京都奖"" (Tsinghua University Professor Andrew Yao Wins 2021 'Kyoto Prize'), *Sina*, June 22, 2021.

43 Poo and Wang, "Andrew Chi-Chih Yao: The Future of Quantum Computing."

44 Shuai Sun, "Prof. Duan's Group Discovered a Quantum Machine Learning Algorithm Based on Generative Models," Tsinghua University Center for Quantum Information, December 9, 2018.

45 Gao, X., Z-Y. Zhang, and L-M. Duan. "A." *Science Advances*, 4.12, 2018.

46 Ling Hu et al., "Quantum Generative Adversarial Learning in a Superconducting Quantum Circuit," *Science Advances*, 5.1, January 25, 2019.

47 Jiang Wenjie (蒋文杰) and Deng Dongling (邓东灵), "神经网络量子态及其应用" (Neural Network Quantum States and Their Applications), *Physics* (物理), 50.2, 2021.

48 "Academic Report on the Opening of the Tsinghua University – University of Technology Sydney Quantum Computing and Artificial Intelligence Joint Research Center," Department of Computer Science and Technology, Tsinghua University, June 8, 2013, https://www.cs.tsinghua.edu.cn/info/1034/1557.htm.

49 Analysis of QSI leadership page conducted in June 2021. "QSI Research Team," University of Technology, Sydney, https://www.uts.edu.au/research-and-teaching/our-research/centre-quantum-software-and-information/qsi-team/qsi-research-team; Prof Mingsheng Ying. https://profiles.uts.edu.au/Mingsheng.Ying.

50 "Research Report on Development Trends in Quantum Cloud Computing (2020)," Technology and Standards Research Institute of China Academy of Information and Communications Technology, October 2020.

51 "Baidu Quantum Computing Institute" (百度量子计算研究所), Baidu, https://quantum.baidu.com/.

52 "Introducing Paddle Quantum: How Baidu's Deep Learning Platform PaddlePaddle Empowers Quantum Computing," Baidu Research, May 27, 2020, http://research.baidu.com/Blog/index-view?id=137.

53 "'Wave Summit 2020'深度学习开发者峰会" ('Wave Summit 2020' Deep Learning Developer Summit), National Engineering Laboratory for Deep Learning Technology and Applications, May 28, 2021, http://www.dlnel.org/news/details_3?id=214.

54 "中国科学院—阿里巴巴量子计算实验室挂牌" (CAS-Alibaba Quantum Computing Lab Opens"), Bureau of Science Communication CAS (中国科学院科学传播局), September 2, 2015.

55 "Platform Introduction" (平台介绍), CAS Center for Excellence in Quantum Information and Quantum Physics, (中国科学院量子信息与量子科技创新研究院) https://quantumcomputer.ac.cn/index.html.

56 Mos Zhang, "Alibaba Says Its New 'Tai Zhang' Is the World's Most Powerful Quantum Circuit Simulator," *Medium*, May 9, 2018; "X Laboratory - Quantum Lab," Alibaba, https://damo.alibaba.com/labs/quantum.

57 "阿里开源量子模拟器'太章2.0', 支持量子算法和纠错探索" (Aliyun Open Source Quantum Simulator 'Tai Zhang 2.0' Supports Quantum Algorithm and Error Correction Exploration), Aliyun, December 23, 2020, https://developer.aliyun.com/article/780439.

58 Ibid.

59 "腾讯量子实验室亮相全球数字生态大会, 公布三大核心研究成果" (Tencent Quantum Laboratory Unveils Its Three Core Research Results at the Global Digital Ecosystem Summit), Tencent Technology (腾讯科技), May 22, 2019, https://tech.qq.com/a/20190522/007599.htm.

60 "Research - Tools" (研究 - 工具), Tencent, https://quantum.tencent.com/research.

61 "Tencent Quantum Laboratory Unveils, op. cit.

62 "Joincare Pharmaceutical and Tencent Quantum Lab Reach Strategic Cooperation Agreement to Jointly Promote Quantum + AI Medicine Research and Development," *National Business Daily*, February 3, 2021, http://www.nbd.com.cn/articles/2021-02-03/1620185.html.

63 "Huawei Unveils Quantum Computing Simulation HiQ Cloud Service Platform," News & Events at Huawei, October 12, 2018; and "华为发布HiQ 3.0 量子计算模拟器及开发者工具" (Huawei Releases HiQ 3.0 Quantum Computing Simulator and Developer Tools), Qtumist, https://www.qtumist.com/post/12516.

64 "阿里、华为、百度、腾讯 '苏州论剑', 四巨头量子计算进展及未来规划究竟如何?" (Alibaba, Huawei, Baidu, and Tencent "Suzhou Swordfight" – What Is the Progress and Future Plans of the Four Giants in Quantum Computing?), 163.com.

65 Quantum annealing is a process used to discover a global minimum in optimization problems, such as the famous traveling salesman problem.
66 Shor's algorithm is used in quantum computing to find prime factors of large numbers, normally considered an intractable problem. The process is relevant to cryptography.
67 Wang Chao et al., "Shaping the Future of Commercial Quantum Computer and the Challenge for Information Security," *Chinese Journal of Network and Information Security*, 2.3, 2016, pp. 17–26; Wang Chao et al., "量子计算密码攻击进展" (Progress in Quantum Computing Cryptography Attacks), *Chinese Journal of Computers* (计算机学报), 43.9, 2020, pp. 1691–1707; and Wang Baonan et al., "从演化密码到量子人工智能密码综述" (From Evolutionary Cryptography to Quantum Artificial Intelligent Cryptography), *Journal of Computer Research and Development* (计算机研究与发展), 56.10, 2019, p. 2112–2134.
68 Chen Jie (陈杰), "万旺根－虚拟现实与大数据学术团队" (Wang Wanggen – Virtual Reality and Big Data Academic Team), November 17, 2020, https://scie.shu.edu.cn/info/1312/5868.htm.
69 Authors' analysis based on patents from Google and CNKI from 2016 to June 2021.
70 Chi Jiungyi, "Chinese Firms to Set Up Quantum Chip R&D Lab to Catch Up with Global Leaders," *Global Times*, April 11, 2021.

Bibliography

"济南市量子信息产业发展规划 (2019-2022 年)" (Jinan City Quantum Information Industry Development Plan (2019–2022), Jinan Science and Technology Bureau (济南市科技局), March 8, 2019.

"地方两会描绘新基建投资施工图 推动芯片、量子科技等技术突破" (Local National People's Conferences Describe New Infrastructure Investment Plans to Push for Breakthroughs in Computer Chips, Quantum Science and Other Technologies), *China Securities Journal* (中国证券报), January 25, 2021.

China Academy of Information and Communications Technology, "量子云计算发展态势研究报告 (2020)" (Research Report on Development Trends in Quantum Cloud Computing 2020), Technology and Standards Research Institute, China Academy of Information and Communications Technology (中国信息通信研究院技术与标准研究所), October 2020.

Dai Qionghai (戴琼海), "深度学习遭遇瓶颈, 全脑观测启发下一代AI算法" (Deep Learning Has Encountered Bottlenecks, Comprehensive Neural Observations Inspire the Next Generation of AI Algorithms), Remarks at the 2020 International Conference on Computer Communication and Artificial Intelligence reposted on the Tencent AI Discussion Forum (AI科技评论), September 4, 2020.

Giles, Martin, "Explainer, What Is a Quantum Computer?" *MIT Technology Review*, January 29, 2019.

Hu Dingkun (胡定坤), "潘建伟揭示量子计算发展三阶段" (Pan Jianwei Reveals the Three Stages of Quantum Computing Development), *People's Daily Online (*人民网*)*, January 15, 2020.

Pan Jianwei, "更好推进我国量子科技发展" (Promote Better China's Quantum Technology Development), *Red Flag Manuscripts (*红旗文稿*)*, 23, 2020.

PRC State Council. 国务院关于印发新一代人工智能发展规划的通知 (The New Generation AI Development Plan), SC 35, 2017.

Tsinghua University, "清华大学－悉尼科技大学量子计算与人工智能联合研究中心开展学术报告" (Academic Report on the Opening of the Tsinghua University – University of Technology Sydney Quantum Computing and Artificial Intelligence Joint Research Center), Department of Computer Science and Technology, Tsinghua University, June 8, 2013.

Wang Chao (王潮), Wang Yun-jiang (王云江), and Hu Feng (胡风), "量子计算机的商业化进展及对信息安全的挑战" (Shaping the Future of Commercial Quantum Computer and the Challenge for Information Security), *Chinese Journal of Network and Information Security (*网络与信息安全学报*)*, 2.3, 2016, 17–26.

Xi Jinping, "习近平:推动我国新一代人工智能健康发展" (Xi Jinping: Promote the Healthy Development of China's New Generation of Artificial Intelligence), *Xinhua Online*, October 31, 2018.

Xi Jinping, "习近平在中央政治局第二十四次集体学习时强调 深刻认识推进量子科技发展重大意义 加强量子科技发展战略谋划和系统布局" (Xi Jinping at 24th Study Session of the Politburo Collective Study Session Emphasized the Great Significance of Deep Understanding of the Promotion of Quantum Science Development as well as the Strengthening of Strategic Plans and Systems for Quantum Science Development), *Xinhua Online*, October 17, 2020.

PART IV

AI in the shadows

10

AI in the Chinese military

Ryan Fedasiuk and Emily Weinstein

The Chinese People's Liberation Army (PLA) believes that AI will fundamentally change the character of warfare, transforming its current approach of "informatized" (信息化) warfare to one of "intelligentization" (智能化). This chapter provides an assessment of where and how AI fits into the PLA's concept of operations, as well as its progress in research and procurement of AI up through the first half of 2021. It first describes the PLA's views on the importance of AI in its overall modernization effort, especially AI's utility in improving battlefield intelligence, surveillance, and reconnaissance (ISR) and command and control. The chapter then examines AI research and procurement, describing several key research areas and procurement trends, before concluding with an overview of the ecosystem powering these developments.

Why AI?

The PLA recognizes a wide range of potential military applications for AI. At the lower end of the spectrum, as in the United States, the PLA is using AI for back-office tasks—including health monitoring, personnel management, and predictive maintenance. Although notions of "AI weapons" inspire popular fear, the reality is that the technology is novel, breaks easily, introduces new vulnerabilities, and demands vast troves of data and expensive computational power to make any meaningful difference in productivity. For these reasons, militaries worldwide are beginning their adoption of AI with many of the same applications as Fortune 500 businesses: to automate mundane tasks and simplify logistical support on the back-end. The PLA Army, for instance, is procuring autonomous tanker trucks, munitions packaging systems, and other logistics and supply chain applications.[1] These enterprise AI solutions represent meaningful contributions to the PLA's operational capacity and combat power.

DOI: 10.4324/9781003212980-14

At the same time, much of the PLA's development of AI is driven by its assessment of the evolving nature and future trajectory of war. The PLA believes that warfare will be increasingly cross-domain, rely on weapons capable of achieving effects at ever-greater ranges, use ad hoc and constantly shifting groupings of forces, feature increased deception and obfuscation, and that all of these activities will take place at progressively faster pace. The PLA therefore views AI as essential to increasing the speed and effectiveness of detection, targeting, and strikes against military targets.[2]

This outlook is consistent with the PLA's overarching strategy for defeating a foreign adversary such as the United States, which centers on dominating in a system-of-systems confrontation—a method of warfighting that focuses on disrupting or paralyzing an enemy's integrated command and control system. U.S.-based analysts have described this doctrine as "systems confrontation" and identify AI as a critical means to achieve the desired disruption or paralysis.[3] Importantly, existing analysis indicates that the PLA is starting to develop and, in some cases, deploy AI for a variety of combat applications, including in ISR, command and control, and weapons systems such as autonomous combat vehicles.[4] At its core, however, AI's military promise most fundamentally amounts to the ability to "see" and "decide"—in other words, build an accurate and reliable picture of the operational environment and determine the best course of action based on that picture. Detection and decision are fundamental tasks for military operations of any kind, and accordingly, this chapter will focus on Chinese developments in military AI which support the PLA's growing capacity in each area.

Seeing and acting

In theoretical writings, PLA officers stress the importance of improved ISR for modern warfare, and emphasize the role of AI toward that end. The PLA believes that future warfare will be "unmanned, intangible, and silent,"[5] and has prioritized the research and development of intelligent and autonomous vehicles in addition to functional, cost-effective, and flexible space solutions.[6] In particular, the 2020 *Science of Military Strategy* states that unmanned aerial vehicles (UAVs) are the primary focus of intelligent unmanned systems development.[7] But, at least in principle, Chinese military leaders aim to bring some modicum of "intelligentization" to battlefield sensors in all domains.[8]

Outside observers make more direct assessments of AI's value in improving the PLA's ISR capabilities. According to the 2021 DoD *China Military Power Report*, the PRC seeks to establish a real-time surveillance, reconnaissance, and warning system using various AI-enabled systems, including the BeiDou (北斗) satellite navigation system. In particular, PLA thinkers highlight the role of big data analysis in threat monitoring and early warning, and the use of AI-enabled tools to respond quickly in the case of a conflict in cyberspace.[9] Ultimately, the PLA wants to "separate the wheat from the chaff" in its ISR inputs, especially by overcoming the problems of obfuscation and data corruption, which can undermine the validity of the operational picture.[10] However, it faces a key challenge in effectively using the ever-greater amount of data and intelligence processed by its own C4ISR[11] network. Operational commanders hope to use AI-based decision support systems to comprehend and make use of expanding data reserves in an effective and timely manner.

Beyond applications aimed at detection, the PLA envisions using AI in selecting courses of action. In response to the increasing operational tempo of war, the PLA hopes to enhance its joint command and control systems by incorporating AI throughout the military decision-making process. "As the pace of war accelerates," write two PLA S&T analysts for *PLA Daily*, "combat time will be calculated in seconds. Only by accurately calculating various combat operations can we achieve a consistent pace."[12] In the PLA's view, the key to modern conflict is to get inside the enemy's Observe-Orient-Decide-Act (OODA) loop and press for decision advantage. PLA experts therefore believe that operational decision-making must be both "accurate and precise" (精确决策) and "quicker than the enemy" (快敌决策) to avoid crippling attacks against their own operational command structure.[13]

Machine learning systems are likely to grow in importance for the PLA's command and control infrastructure, as they may provide flexibility for commanders to come up with courses of action and make operational decisions in a reasonable amount of time.[14] The PLA is employing big data analysis techniques and computer-assisted decision-making to automate much of the cognitive work of intelligence analysis, but many of these applications still appear to be in the early stages of development.

In practical terms, Chinese defense industry experts have identified a lack of AI-enabled tools to process the masses of intelligence which the PLA's ISR assets are able to produce as a weakness that must be rectified.[15] Ultimately, this points to a key difference in the shift from informatized to intelligentized operations, in that the former stresses "human-in-the-loop warfare" (人在回路中的战争) and is still largely constrained by the boundaries of human cognition, while the latter emphasizes "data-in-the-loop warfare" (数据在回路中的战争), in which AI-enabled C4ISR platforms increasingly drive the command process, especially lower-level and initial decision-making.[16] Having expended enormous effort and resources over several decades to construct a comprehensive and robust C4ISR system, the PLA now hopes to use AI to make effective use of large datasets under modern operational conditions.

AI research and procurement for military applications

While the U.S. military considers technological investment to be related to either research, development, test, and evaluation (RDT&E) or procurement, the process of technology development and maturation appears much more fluid in China. That said, competing institutional interests and considerations shape the direction of PLA technology research and procurement, including in AI.[17]

Accordingly, the paragraphs that follow are not a comprehensive accounting of all the different avenues of technology development, but rather constitute an overview of the specific AI subfields most immediately relevant to the PLA.

Key research areas

Target identification, discrimination, and tracking are especially popular research topics among PLA engineers, and are relevant across all warfighting domains. The PLA Strategic Support Force (SSF), for example, tends to focus on developing AI systems for "battlefield situational awareness, electromagnetic target reconnaissance, electronic countermeasures, electronic defense, and electromagnetic spectrum management," many of which involve automated pattern or target recognition.[18] Chinese AI researchers are also working on similar methods for improving detection across different domains—including deep-learning-based target recognition algorithms to identify surface warships via both overhead imagery and undersea acoustic sensor networks.[19]

While some of this research has been ongoing for well over a decade, improvements in information technology and access to larger training datasets will greatly accelerate the pace of Chinese military breakthroughs in AI. PLA Air Force (AF) researchers have studied improved target recognition in passive radar systems since at least 2009, but in 2019, new models and better datasets enabled researchers to improve identification accuracy using neural networks.[20] Researchers at the National University of Defense Technology (NUDT) have been using algorithms to improve feature selection for target discrimination in synthetic aperture radar imagery since 2007,[21] but by 2018, researchers were using training sets with thousands of warship images scraped from the internet.[22] Moreover, as the PLA continues to field a larger number of ISR platforms each year, the proliferation of data available to Chinese military AI researchers will steadily improve the performance of new sensors.

Though somewhat less prominent in the public research literature, AI-assisted decision-making tools in command systems are particularly vital for the PLA's modernization strategy. Much of this research is inspired by existing U.S. and foreign decision support systems, which use AI to achieve incremental improvements in performance. One 2018 example from Xidian University and the Key Laboratory of Information Systems Engineering (信息系统工程重点实验室) typifies this approach: after reviewing the role of self-adaptive agent frameworks in U.S. command and control systems, the authors experimented with a search-based self-adaptive decision method and reinforcement learning to better adapt to changing battlefield conditions in a notional decision support system.[23]

Despite its apparent progress in researching and testing AI-assisted decision support systems, evidence suggests that the PLA's efforts in this area are far from fully mature. One 2020 review article describing the state of the field complained about a lack of interpretability and an overreliance on data that cannot be sustained under warfighting conditions. The researchers went on to describe how decisions made by deep learning algorithms are difficult to explain, leading to a "black box" phenomenon and level of uncertainty unacceptable to military commanders. The article also criticized deep learning models for requiring large amounts of data, an undesirable trait in environments restricted by operational security considerations.[24]

A third area of abundant public research with military applications is autonomous vehicle and swarming technology for both ISR and combat. PLA units and defense state-owned enterprises (SOE) regularly award AI-based undersea target recognition contracts to Harbin Engineering University (HEU), one of the Seven Sons of National Defense (国防七子); and HEU researchers at this university publish frequently on unmanned and autonomous undersea vehicles.[25] In a December 2013 interview, an HEU professor noted that the Chinese military was particularly interested in using unmanned undersea vehicles (UUVs) for intelligence gathering and "drawing the fire of enemies in sea battles."[26] Some of this research has evidently progressed to field testing. In July 2021, the Chinese military partially declassified a 2010 paper by the Journal of Harbin Engineering University that discussed how unmanned submarines could use AI to detect and target a mock craft with a torpedo. The 2010 publication was testing this concept in the context of a drone submarine launched in the Taiwan Strait without human intervention.[27]

Notable procurement and development

Trends in research publications are likely the most reliable open-source indicators of Chinese military progress in AI, as the technology is still emerging and most research programs do not go beyond experimentation. But as a supplement to academic output, procurement information may shed light on the Chinese military's mature and maturing AI capabilities. Although some purchases may end up as vaporware, equipment contracts offer a particularly strong signal of both intent and capability with respect to AI, as Chinese military leaders must choose where and how to invest resources for maximum effect.

Publicly available procurement records indicate the PLA is investing in a variety of combat applications, including autonomous combat vehicles, ISR, and information warfare, examples of which are described below. The SSF is the PLA component most active in identifiable public AI procurement, followed by the Navy and Army, while the AF and Rocket Force appear to lag in public AI-related procurement (see Figure 10.1).

Some of these purchases reflect a role for AI in information warfare, specifically in the cyber and electromagnetic domains. In 2020, for instance, SSF units purchased several AI-based vulnerability detection and sentiment analysis systems, representing some of the PLA's most expensive purchases of "intelligent" equipment that year.[28] While some of the Army's outlays have gone to logistics, it has also invested in electronic warfare platforms.[29] Other PLA units awarded AI-related contracts for "automatic frequency modulation, microwave

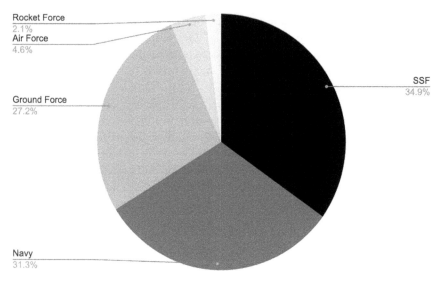

FIGURE 10.1   AI-related contracts awarded by PLA service branches, April–November 2020

Source: 190 procurement notices adapted from Fedasiuk, Melot, and Murphy, 2021.

jamming, broadband automatic gain control, and multi-source signal separation" to improve the speed and adaptability of electronic warfare systems.[30]

The PLA is also working to improve sensing at sea, especially in the under-sea domain. In 2020, PLA Navy units awarded contracts for AI systems to map ocean floor topography and catalog signals into sonar signature libraries—both useful for identifying submarines.[31] Other long-running efforts have yielded more tangible outcomes. For example, in addition to developing the HSU-001 large UUV first unveiled in China's 2019 National Day military parade,[32] HEU researchers developed a series of "Smart Water" (智水) autonomous underwater vehicles (AUVs) for automated target recognition and path-planning missions.[33]

Procurement tenders have also focused on UAVs and adjacent technologies for aerial combat. Airborne systems are common in unmanned and autono-mous vehicle contracts from 2020.[34] The PLA Army appears optimistic about unmanned vehicle swarm technologies,[35] and the PLA AF has published tenders for "developing, producing and testing autonomous intelligent systems for drone clusters."[36] The Rocket Force has committed less to public AI procurement than its sister services, though it has hosted public competitions for AI-based mis-sile guidance, which attracted more than 100 competing teams from Chinese universities.[37]

Companies and research organizations are also developing products that use AI to improve remote sensing capabilities, including spaceborne ISR.[38] PLA units and defense SOEs have equipped experimental satellites with computer vision systems, which can autonomously identify objects from space and send high-fidelity images back to ground facilities.[39] For example, the Chinese firm Chengdu Guoxing Aerospace Technology Co. (成都国星宇航科技) was reportedly working on experimental satellites with embedded AI applications.[40] Other concrete efforts to improve space-based remote sensing are focused on training datasets: in 2021, scientists from the CAS Aerospace Information Research Institute (中国科学院空天信息创新研究院) created a benchmark dataset for fine-grained object recognition in high-resolution remote sensing imagery, also known as FAIR1M, containing 15,000 high-definition images and one million labeled "scenes." The system can reportedly train an AI system to identify the presence of an aircraft, as well as its make and model.[41]

The AI development ecosystem and military-civil fusion

To support military intelligence, decision-making, and combat operations, Chinese leaders aim to translate civilian S&T accomplishments into military advantage—and this is particularly true with respect to AI. Tightening public-private coordination fits under the broader umbrella of China's Military-Civil Fusion (军民融合, MCF) development strategy, a holistic approach to national development that ensures new technological breakthroughs simultaneously advance the country's economic and military development.[42] The 2017 "New Generation Artificial Intelligence Development Plan" (新一代人工智能发展规划), a foundational document for AI development, exemplifies this high-level emphasis on MCF. The Plan calls specifically for the promotion of two-way conversion, transformation, and applications for military and civilian science and technology (S&T) achievements in AI, the sharing of military and civilian innovation resources and platforms, and standardization of communication and coordination among research institutions, universities, enterprises, and the military and defense industry.[43]

In addition to military academies and applied research institutes, the PLA also benefits from the work of civilian universities with direct ties to the military, State and National Defense Key Laboratories (重点实验室), major state-owned defense conglomerates, and private enterprises. Together, these five kinds of entities comprise a vast AI development ecosystem devoted to achieving military-relevant research breakthroughs and supplying the PLA with AI solutions.

PLA academic institutions are deeply involved in AI-related research, though to what extent is hard to quantify. The PLA's public AI-related research output dwarfs that of internal security forces like the People's Armed Police and Ministry of Public Security: one March 2021 CSET study revealed that PLA entities were responsible for 93.5 percent of some 49,105 AI-relevant articles published by Chinese security services.[44] In the aggregate, however, the PLA is a relatively small contributor to China's overall AI research output: as of November 2021, a search in CNKI revealed only one PLA institution (the NUDT) in the top 20 publishers of AI-related articles.[45] Differences in article classification methodologies and search result variability in Chinese academic databases make it difficult to draw definitive conclusions about the PLA's research ecosystem for military AI capabilities.

PLA academies are relatively infrequent AI research publishers, which suggests that they may rely more heavily on the work of civilian universities to develop relevant capabilities. We note that several universities were more prolific publishers than the one PLA entity listed above, including three of the Seven Sons of National Defense (Harbin Institute of Technology, Nanjing Institute of Technology, and Nanjing University of Astronautics and Aeronautics) and Xidian University, itself a former PLA institution with close and continuing ties to the PLA.[46] Institutions like these are key implementers of China's military-civil fusion strategy, and occasionally develop products or bid on procurement contracts, themselves.[47]

The PLA also relies on State and National Defense Key Laboratories for AI research and as hubs for collaboration. Hosted by all manner of PLA institutions, civilian universities, and defense conglomerates, the labs are an indispensable part of China's research ecosystem. Organizations like the Key Laboratory for Information Systems Engineering (信息系统工程重点实验室) and the National Defense Key Laboratory for Near-Surface Detection Technology (近地面探测技术国防重点实验室) are actively working on AI research with direct military applications.[48]

Defense conglomerates are also top players in PLA AI development. These state-owned, civilian-run behemoths are visible examples of military-civil fusion in AI research, drawing on the talent and resources of hundreds of subordinate research institutes, such as those in the China Electronics Technology Group Corporation (CETC) and China Aerospace Science and Technology Corporation (CASC), which contribute to China's AI research and development ecosystem.[49] CASC, China Aerospace Science and Industry Corporation (CASIC), and the Aviation Industry Corporation of China (AVIC) are prominent UAV builders, and are national leaders in developing intelligent AI-enabled unmanned vehicles.[50]

The PLA today also enjoys access to cutting-edge systems and equipment developed by China's private technology sector. By the end of 2020, nearly 25,000 private enterprises (民营企业) were registered to supply the PLA with weapons and equipment, with 22 percent specializing in manufacturing computer, communications, and other electronic equipment.[51] Some 250 companies supply the PLA with AI-related systems and equipment, 60 percent of which are private enterprises.[52] One prominent example is Xi'an Tianhe Defense (西安天和防务技术), the first private military enterprise listed in China.[53] In 2020, the company's maritime subsidiary won China's National Underwater Robot Competition,[54] and procurement records indicate that it went on to supply AUV to the SSF later in the year.[55]

The PLA uses a wide range of resources to ensure the successful research and application of AI as quickly as possible. Policy support for military-civil fusion is likely to intensify. Recent draft legislation emphasizes a need to accelerate the development of intelligent weapons and equipment and deepen MCF collaboration in emerging technologies such as AI,[56] laying the rhetorical groundwork for further funding and incentives to support the R&D ecosystem.[57] From a practical standpoint, MCF presents stark challenges for foreign observers and policymakers. The wide and complex array of academic, corporate, and military actors feeding the Chinese industrial base will be harder to track, and their activities will aggravate long-standing problems with Chinese technology transfer from foreign powers.

Conclusion

PLA advances in a variety of AI subfields have the potential to erode or dramatically reverse U.S. military dominance in critical warfighting domains. PLA researchers are keenly aware that in the context of modern warfare, if the PLA can "see it," then they can almost certainly "shoot it," especially given decades-long investments in kinetic military hardware that are now bearing fruit.

The PLA expects that the accelerated tempo and information overload of future warfare will put its human decision-makers under extreme pressure to not only make decisions quickly, but also to do so in fraught political contexts. AI represents a prized opportunity for the PLA to resolve this apparent paradox by preserving its highly centralized, consensus-driven command culture even in the face of the demands of current and future warfare.

PLA AI researchers need not master "detection" and "decision" problems entirely for their work to yield favorable results. Even partial solutions to the PLA's sensing problem could immediately endanger U.S. military superiority in the air, in space, and at sea by compromising the locations, capabilities, and activities of U.S. military assets operating anywhere in the Western Pacific. Should any future confrontation come to blows, incremental improvements in decision-making brought about by AI could help PLA commanders cope with the pressures of high-speed, information-intensive warfare and enable the PLA to wage war against its peer competitors much more effectively.

Successful development and adoption of AI, then, is a key determinant of successful PLA modernization. Should the PLA prove able to harness AI for detection and decision advantage, it will have made significant progress toward overtaking the U.S. military as the premier fighting force in Asia and perhaps the world.[58]

Notes

1 Fedasiuk, Melot, and Murphy, 2021.
2 Kevin Pollpeter and Amanda Kerrigan, "The PLA and Intelligent Warfare: A Preliminary Analysis," Center for Naval Analyses, October 2021; Fedasiuk, "Chinese Perspectives on AI and Future Military Capabilities," 2020.
3 Michael Dahm, "Chinese Debates on the Military Utility of Artificial Intelligence," *War on the Rocks*, June 5, 2020; Jeffrey Engstrom, "Systems Confrontation and System Destruction Warfare: How the Chinese People's Liberation Army Seeks to Wage Modern Warfare," RAND Corporation, 2018.

4 Fedasiuk, Melot, and Murphy, 2021.

5 Academy of Military Science (军事科学院), 战略学—2013 年版 (*The Science of Military Strategy*—2013 edition), AMS Press (军事科学出版社), Beijing, 2013, p. 120.

6 Xiao Tianlang (肖天亮) et al., 战略学—2020年修订版 (*The Science of Military Strategy*—2020 revised edition), National Defense University Press (国防大学出版社), Beijing, 2020.

7 Xiao Tianlang (肖天亮) et al., op. cit. p. 177; and Fedasiuk, Melot, and Murphy.

8 Zhang Yan (张岩) and Wang Le (王乐), "当无人机拥有群体智能" (When Unmanned Vehicles Have Swarm Intelligence), *PLA Daily*, September 3, 2021, https://www.81.cn/jfjbmap/content/2021-09/03/content_298211.htm.

9 "Military and Security Developments Involving the People's Republic of China," U.S. Department of Defense, 2021.

10 Although the PLA still struggles to acquire certain types of operationally relevant data, such as radar imagery to train intelligent missile seekers, PLA analysts John Chen and Morgan Clemens note that the PLA likely possesses large, non-public datasets used in intelligence analysis (personal communication, December 2021).

11 Command, control, communications, computers, intelligence, surveillance, and reconnaissance.

12 Shi Chunmin and Tan Xueping, "Digital Warfare Requires Data Thinking," 2018.

13 Wang Yinfang (王印芳), "向指挥能力建设要战斗力" (Fighting Strength Needed for Building Command Capacity), *PLA Daily*, April 7, 2016, http://www.81.cn/jwzl/2016-04/07/content_6995272.htm.

14 Some analysts also argue that the PLA's collectivized, consensus-based command model will create added pressure to automate parts of the military decision-making process. For example, see Zhu Haiwen (朱海文), "坚持党委对联合作战的统一领导" (Uphold the Unified Leadership of the Party Committee in Joint Operations), *PLA Daily*, June 9, 2021, http://www.81.cn/ll/2021-06/09/content_10047132.htm.

15 Qiao Hui (乔慧), Su Yun (苏云), and An Jin (安瑾), "面向海量数据的海情数据分析技术研究" (Research on Maritime Intelligence Data Analysis Technologies for Massive Data), in *Command Control and Simulation* (指挥控制与仿真), 40.2, 2018, 48.

16 Li Wei (李伟) and Zhao Zipeng (赵子鹏), "打造未来作战优势链路" (The Path of Building Future Operational Superiority), *PLA Daily*, February 11, 2020, https://www.81.cn/jfjbmap/content/2020-02/11/content_253748.htm.

17 Yoram Evron, *China's Military Procurement in the Reform Era: The Setting of New Directions*, Routledge, London and New York, 2015.

18 Cui Jifeng (崔积丰) and Hu Fuzeng (胡富增), "基于模式识别的自适应有源干扰策略研究" (Research on Adaptive Active Jamming Strategy Based on Pattern Recognition), *Ship Electronics Engineering* (舰船电子工程) 38.10, October 2018, pp. 104–108; Wang Long (王龙), Wang Lijia (王黎佳), Chen Lei (陈雷), Cao Xinglong (曹兴龙), "一种认知雷达信号相关杂波感知方法" (A Cognitive Radar Signal Correlated Clutter Sensing Method), *Ship Electronics Engineering* (舰船电子工程), 40.7, 2020, pp. 85–92; Ji, Zhou, and Liu, 2020, op. cit.

19 See Gu Dongliang (谷东亮), Xu Xiaogang (徐晓刚), and Jin Xin (金鑫), "基于Faster R-CNN的海上舰船识别算法" (Marine Ship Recognition Algorithm Based on Faster-RCNN), *Journal of Image and Signal Processing* (图像与信号处理), 7.3, July 2018, 136–141; and Zhu Hongrui (朱洪瑞), "基于线谱的水下复杂环境目标检测方法研究" (Research on Underwater Complex Target Detection Based on Line Spectrum), Master's thesis, June 2018.

20 Lin Meiqing (蔺美青) and Cai Yi (蔡轶), "无源雷达目标识别的神经网络模型构建" (Building of Neural Networks Model for Target Recognition of Passive Radar), *Radar Science and Technology* (雷达科学与技术), 17.5, October 2019.

21 Gao Gui (高贵) et al., "基于遗传算法的SAR图像目标鉴别特征选择" (Feature Selection for Target Discrimination in SAR Images Based on Genetic Algorithm), *Acta Electronica Sinica* (电子学报), 36.6, June 2008, 1041–1046.

22 Gu Dongliang (谷东亮) et al., 2018, op. cit.

23 Wu Tong (吴桐) et al., "挥控制信息系统动态演化的自适应决策方法" (Self-Adaptive Decision Method for Dynamic Evolution of Command and Control Information System), *Command Information System and Technology* (指挥信息系统与技术), 9.5, October 2018, 43–49.

24 Luo Rong (罗荣) et al., "深度学习研究现状及在海战场指挥信息系统中应用展望" (Research Status of Deep Learning and Its Application Prospect in Command Information System of Sea Battlefield), *Ship Electronic Engineering* (舰船电子工程), 40.11, November 2020, 1–6, 52.

25 Fedasiuk, Melot, and Murphy. Examples of papers examined include: Zhao Yuxin (赵玉新) and Zhao Ting (赵廷), "海底声呐图像智能底质分类技术研究综述" (Survey of the Intelligent Seabed Sediment Classification Technology Based on Sonar Images), *CAAI Transactions on Intelligent Systems* (智能系统学报) 15.3, 2020, 587–600; and Ma Meizhen (马梅真), "水下目标识别技术研究" (Study on Underwater Target Recognition Technique), HEU MS thesis, 2007.

26 Stephen Chen, "After Drones, China Turns to Unmanned Vessels to Boost Its Marine Power," *South China Morning Post,* December 5, 2013.

27 Stephen Chen, "China Reveals Secret Programme of Unmanned Drone Submarines Dating Back to 1990s," *South China Morning Post,* July 8, 2021.

28 Fedasiuk, Melot, and Murphy, 2021.

29 Ibid.

30 Ibid.

31 Fedasiuk, "Leviathan Wakes: China's Growing Fleet of Autonomous Undersea Vehicles," 2021.

32 "HSU-001无人水下潜航器 - 武器百科大全" (HSU-001 Unmanned Underwater Vehicle-Weapon Encyclopedia), http://www.wuqibaike.com/index.php?doc-view-21619.

33 "自治水下机器人，一种具有高度人工智能的系统" (Autonomous Underwater Robot, a System with a High Degree of Artificial Intelligence), *KK News*, October 26, 2017, https://kknews.cc/zh-my/science/nvzax92.html.

34 Fedasiuk, Melot, and Murphy.

35 Ibid.

36 Kartik Bommakanti, "A.I. in the Chinese Military: Current Initiatives and the Implications for India," Observer Research Foundation, February 2020.

37 Clay, Marcus, "To Rule the Invisible Battlefield: The Electromagnetic Spectrum and Chinese Military Power," *War on the Rocks*, January 22, 2021; "百余支军地高校战队对决空工大 '智胜空天-2018'无人机挑战赛" (Hundreds of Military and Local Colleges and Universities Compete against the Aerospace Engineering University in the 'Wisdom Air and Space 2018 UAV Challenge'), *PLA News* rehosted by Ministry of National Defense, December 16, 2018, https://perma.cc/BUJ7-222H.

38 Some of these products may eventually be procured by the PLA even if they are not represented in available procurement sources.

39 "Chinese Commercial Space Startup Develops AI Satellites," *Xinhua News*, November 25, 2018.

40 Ibid.

41 "China Makes 'World's Largest Satellite Image Database' to Train AI Better," *South China Morning Post*, April 30, 2021.

42 Emily Weinstein, "Testimony before the U.S.-China Economic and Security Review Commission on 'U.S. Investments in China's Capital Markets and Military-Industrial Complex'," March 19, 2021, https://www.uscc.gov/sites/default/files/2021-03/Emily_Weinstein_Testimony.pdf.

43 PRC State Council, 国务院关于印发新一代人工智能发展规划的通知 (The New Generation AI Development Plan), SC 35, 2017.

44 Murdick et al., "The Public AI Research Portfolio of China's Security Forces: A High-Level Analysis," 2021. The study considers the People's Armed Police and PLA separately, although as of 2018 the PAP is subordinate to the Central Military Commission, the same military body that controls the PLA.

45 John Chen and Morgan Clemens, private communication, November 26, 2021.
46 Australian Strategic Policy Institute, "Xidian University," updated May 13, 2021, https://unitracker.aspi.org.au/universities/xidian-university/.
47 Australian Strategic Policy Institute, "The China Defence Universities Tracker," November 25, 2019, https://www.aspi.org.au/report/china-defence-universities-tracker; "HSU-001无人水下潜航器 - 武器百科大全" (HSU-001 Unmanned Underwater Vehicle-Weapon Encyclopedia), http://www.wuqibaike.com/index.php?doc-view-21619.
48 Wu Tong (吴桐) et al., "挥控制信息系统动态演化的自适应决策方法" (Self-Adaptive Decision Method for Dynamic Evolution of Command and Control Information System), *Command Information System and Technology* (指挥信息系统与技术), 9.5, October 2018, 43–49; Zhu Huijie (朱会杰) et al., "无人机精确定位中的目标实例分割算法" (Target Instance Segmentation Algorithm in Accurate Location for UAV), *Journal of Command and Control* (指挥与控制学报), 7.2, June 2021, 192–196.
49 Li Hongbiao (李宏彪) and Zhang Yongliang (张永亮), "潜艇在水深底质数据下的航线规划" (Route Plan of Submarine under Bottom Water Quality Data), *Electronic Design Engineering* (电子设计工程), 26.1, January 2018, 70–73; Wang Jie (王杰) et al., "基于Radau伪谱法的SAR末制导成像段弹道优化" (Trajectory Optimization of SAR Imaging Guidance Based on Radau Pseudospectral Method), *Modern Defence Technology* (现代防御技术), 41.5, October 2013, 41–46.
50 See Zhao Lei, "Stealth Drone about to Hit World Market," *China Daily*, November 6, 2018; Liu Yang and Liu Caiyu, "China Unveils New Stealth Drone Prototype at Air Show," *Global Times*, November 5, 2018; Jonathan Ray et al., "China's Industrial and Military Robotics Development," October 2016.
51 "Distribution of Civil-Military Enterprises" (民参军企业分布), PLA Weapons and Equipment Acquisition Information Network (武器装备采购信息网), accessed August 7, 2020, https://archive.vn/aKFBT.
52 Fedasiuk, Melot, and Murphy.
53 Founded in 2001, Xi'an Tianhe Defense Technology Co. Ltd. (西安天和防务技术股份有限公司) claims to be the first private military enterprise established in China, and today operates 14 subsidiaries for different technology areas. "Tianhe Defense," accessed June 2020, https://archive.vn/P9kjL.
54 "2020全国水下机器人(湛江)大赛现场赛获奖结果公示" (2020 National Underwater Robot (Zhanjiang) Competition: Live Competition Winning Results Announcement), *Phoenix Network News*, May 27, 2020.
55 "水下机器人大赛:西安天和海防智能科技有限公司-智慧海洋队简介" (Underwater Robot Competition: Xi'an Tianhe Haiphong Intelligent Technology Co., Ltd.-Introduction to Smart Ocean Team), *Phoenix New Media*, May 16, 2020.
56 National People's Congress and Chinese People's Political Consultative Conference, "规划纲要草案:加快国防和军队现代化 实现富国和强军相统一" (Draft Planning Outline: Speed Up the Modernization of National Defense and the Armed Forces to Realize the Unity of a Prosperous Country and a Strong Military), *Xinhua News*, March 5, 2021.
57 Weinstein, "Don't Underestimate China's Military-Civil Fusion Efforts," *Foreign Policy*, February 5, 2021.
58 The authors thank SOSi analysts John Chen and Morgan Clemens for their support in this chapter's review and preparation.

Bibliography

Beauchamp-Mustafaga, Nathan and Jessica Drun, "Exploring Chinese Military Thinking on Social Media Manipulation against Taiwan," *Jamestown Foundation China Brief*, April 12, 2021.

Bowman, Bradley and Jared Thompson, "Russia and China Seek to Tie America's Hands in Space," *Foreign Policy*, March 31, 2021.

Chase, Michael, Kristen A. Gunness, Lyle J. Morris, Samuel K. Berkowitz, and Benjamin S. Purser III, "Emerging Trends in China's Development of Unmanned Systems," RAND Corporation, 2015.

Clay, Marcus, "The PLA's AI Competitions," *The Diplomat*, November 5, 2020.

Clay, Marcus, "To Rule the Invisible Battlefield: The Electromagnetic Spectrum and Chinese Military Power," *War on the Rocks*, January 22, 2021.

Engstrom, Jeffrey, "Systems Confrontation and System Destruction Warfare: How the Chinese People's Liberation Army Seeks to Wage Modern Warfare," RAND Corporation, 2018.

Fedasiuk, Ryan, "Chinese Perspectives on AI and Future Military Capabilities," Georgetown University, Center for Security and Emerging Technology, August 2020.

Fedasiuk, Ryan, "Leviathan Wakes: China's Growing Fleet of Autonomous Undersea Vehicles," Center for International Maritime Security, August 17, 2021.

Fedasiuk, Ryan, Jennifer Melot, and Ben Murphy, "Harnessed Lightning: How the Chinese Military Is Adopting Artificial Intelligence," Georgetown University, Center for Security and Emerging Technology, October 2021.

Hsu, Kimberly, Craig Murray, Jeremy Cook, and Amalia Feld, "China's Military Unmanned Aerial Vehicle Industry," U.S.-China Economic and Security Review Commission, June 13, 2013.

Ji Weijie (姬伟杰), Zhou Weiping (周伟平), and Liu Tingjun (刘挺君), "Analysis on the Development Characteristics of Modern Electronic Warfare" (现代电子战发展特点浅析), *Optoelectronics (*光电子*)* 10.3, September 2020, pp. 60−65.

Kania, Elsa, "Battlefield Singularity: Artificial Intelligence, Military Revolution, and China's Future Military Power," Center for a New American Security, November 2017.

Kania, Elsa, "The PLA's Unmanned Aerial Systems: New Capabilities for a 'New Era' of Chinese Military Power," China Aerospace Studies Institute, August 2018.

Kania, Elsa, "'AI Weapons' in China's Military Innovation," Brookings Institution, April 2020.

Kania, Elsa and John Costello, "Seizing the Commanding Heights: The PLA Strategic Support Force in Chinese Military Power," *Journal of Strategic Studies* 44.2, May 12, 2020, pp. 218−264.

Liu Peng (刘鹏), "Clarify the Human-machine Relationship in Intelligent Combat Decision-making" (厘清智能作战决策中的人机关系), *PLA Daily*, December 2020.

Murdick, Dewey, Daniel Chou, Ryan Fedasiuk, and Emily Weinstein, "The Public AI Research Portfolio of China's Security Forces: A High-Level Analysis," Georgetown University, Center for Security and Emerging Technology, March 2021.

National People's Congress and Chinese People's Political Consultative Conference, "Draft Planning Outline: Speed up the Modernization of National Defense and the Armed Forces to Realize the Unity of a Prosperous Country and a Strong Military" (规划纲要草案: 加快国防和军队现代化 实现富国和强军相统一), *Xinhua News*, March 5, 2021.

PRC State Council, "Opinions of the General Office of the State Council on Promoting the Deep Development of Military-Civil Fusion in the National Defense Technology Industry" (国务院办公厅关于推动国防科技工业军民融合深度发展的意见), SC 91, December 2017.

Ray, Jonathan, Katie Atha, Edward Francis, Caleb Dependahl, James Mulvenon, Daniel Alderman, and Leigh Ann Ragland-Luce, "China's Industrial and Military Robotics Development," U.S.-China Economic and Security Review Commission, October 2016.

Shi Chunmin (石纯民) and Tan Xueping (谭雪平), "Digital Warfare Requires Data Thinking" (数字化战争需要数据化思维), *PLA Daily*, November 22, 2018.

Stone, Alex and Peter Wood, "China's Military-Civil Fusion Strategy: A View from Chinese Strategists," China Aerospace Studies Institute, 2020.

Weinstein, Emily, "Don't Underestimate China's Military-Civil Fusion Efforts," *Foreign Policy*, February 5, 2021.

Weinstein, Emily, "Testimony before the U.S.-China Economic and Security Review Commission on 'U.S. Investments in China's Capital Markets and Military-Industrial Complex,'" March 19, 2021.

11

Cyber and influence operations

John Chen

The possible use of AI in Chinese information operations prompts pressing questions. How might Chinese actors wield AI in future cyber intrusions and online influence operations, and with what effect? What kind of algorithmic research is underway to support these efforts? This chapter answers these questions by briefly examining the strategic relevance of AI to Chinese information operations, describing key research and development (R&D) centers and AI-enabled information operations techniques, and discussing some implications of Chinese research in AI-enabled information operations. Its primary findings indicate that China's technical experts are researching AI to improve stealth, scale, and adaptability in information operations. Published Chinese research is vast and exploratory, but steadily progressing in maturity and led by organizations with close ties to the People's Liberation Army (PLA), the Ministry of State Security (MSS), or China's defense industrial base. This work may render Chinese AI-enabled information operations more effective, though success is not guaranteed, and deployment may be limited by the regime's fear of losing control over China's domestic information environment.

Introduction

Chinese information operations had a moment in the summer of 2019. Amid a swell of pro-democracy street protests engulfing Hong Kong, hacked Twitter accounts transformed the feeds of ordinary Twitter users into blaring mouthpieces of pro-China geopolitical opinion, while automated "zombie" accounts praised Hong Kong security forces and accused demonstrators of colluding with an American conspiracy.[1] In Taiwan, fake news items flooded social media outlets ahead of an upcoming presidential election. China-friendly Taiwanese content farms churned out fake news items, while public relations firms attempted

DOI: 10.4324/9781003212980-15

to purchase popular Facebook fan pages and recruited local Taiwanese social media influencers to spread pro-China messages.[2] The Chinese party-state was eventually fingered as the culprit behind both campaigns: in Hong Kong, state-run news services affiliated with the Chinese Communist Party's (CCP) United Front Work Department had contracted out efforts to build a presence on foreign social media, while the Taiwan campaign was thought to have been carried out by the PLA Strategic Support Force (SSF).[3]

These online influence campaigns in Hong Kong and Taiwan, along with the 2014 hack of the U.S. Office of Personnel Management, the 2015 attack on health care insurer Anthem, and the 2017 Equifax credit reporting agency breach, are part of a long rap sheet of information operations by the Chinese state that underscores the increasing importance of artificial intelligence (AI). Examples continue to pile up: cybersecurity analysts hypothesize that Hafnium's unusually indiscriminate theft of data from Microsoft Exchange Server systems in 2021 may have been linked to a broader Chinese pursuit of data to support development of AI in information operations.[4] The looming specter of AI in these activities prompts pressing questions. Were any of these campaigns enabled, assisted, or driven by AI, and to what extent? How might Chinese actors wield AI in future cyber intrusions and online influence operations, and what kind of algorithmic research is underway to support these efforts?

Many of these questions are difficult to answer. The complete answers to some, like whether any of these operations were enabled by AI, will likely remain unknown except to the actors that designed and carried out the operations. The answers to others, however, can be derived from publicly available information sources ranging from authoritative books and strategy documents to Chinese academic and technical writings. These sources show that Chinese strategists and policymakers embrace AI development to secure cyberspace as a "cyber great power" (网络强国), while technical experts want to use AI for stealth, scale, and adaptability in information operations, focusing on algorithm classes like generative adversarial networks (GANs), natural language generation, adversarial machine learning, autoencoders, and various kinds of artificial neural networks. Much of this technical research is carried out by universities and research labs with close ties to the PLA, the Ministry of State Security (国家安全部, MSS), or China's defense industrial base. Given current research trends in the field and the strategic concerns of Chinese leadership, Chinese AI-enabled information operations may become even harder to detect and therefore more effective, though that success is not guaranteed, and deployment may yet be restrained by the CCP's fear of disrupting its control over China's domestic information environment.

Although China's larger AI development strategy and its potential application of AI to modern warfare are relevant, this chapter does not directly assess these topics, both of which have been covered skillfully and thoroughly by others.[5] Instead, this chapter first examines the broader strategic relevance of AI to information operations through the writings of authoritative Party officials and

China's foremost technical specialists. Next, this chapter uncovers several R&D centers of excellence and the techniques they are studying to apply AI to information operations like cyber intrusions and online influence campaigns. Finally, the chapter concludes with a discussion of some implications of Chinese research in AI-enabled information operations.

Chinese information operations and the strategic role of artificial intelligence

Cyber intrusion and influence campaigns like the ones described above are part of the CCP's emphasis on cyberspace (网络空间) as an indispensable domain of national security. According to top CCP national security researchers, the networks and information that comprise cyberspace are "important strategic resources and critical infrastructure for a nation's politics, economy, culture, military, science and technology development, ecological environment, and society,"[6] the security of which is inextricably tied to the country's continued modernization.[7] As a vital means of modernization and governance as well as a potential existential threat to national and regime security, cyberspace is viewed as a global commons to be governed by Westphalian customs of national sovereignty and characterized by fierce interstate competition.[8] Only as a cyber great power with "a clear strategy, advanced technology, flourishing industry, and the ability to both attack and defend" can China hope to successfully advance its national interests in cyberspace.[9]

China's cyber intrusions and online influence activities are intended to maximize the political, economic, and social benefits that accrue to the nation with widespread use of the internet while maintaining security and stability. Cyber intrusion campaigns run by the MSS and the forerunners of the current PLA SSF have purloined immeasurably valuable troves of information from foreign computer networks over the past two decades, facilitating a massive transfer of knowledge, intellectual property, and technology to China. At home and increasingly abroad, members of the United Front Work Department, propaganda departments, the PLA SSF, Party and state media, the Chinese People's Political Consultative Conference, and others engage in "online public opinion guidance" (网络舆论引导) intended to prevent color revolutions at home and to shape discourse favorably abroad.

AI is expected to profoundly change these information operations. One recent commentary in the CCP Central Party School's *Study Times* newspaper provided perhaps the most succinct summary of these anticipated changes, arguing that AI's increasing maturity presages the appearance of "super viruses and trojans" capable of "altering boot-disks, harming databases, and destroying data formation channels." It warned that other AI applications will tamper with the views and comments of netizens and enable the proliferation of fake public opinion data and falsified imagery, audio, video, and other media, all of which could ultimately endanger the Party's efforts to secure its online ideological space (网络意识形态).[10]

To combat and harness these effects, China's state economic planning apparatus has prioritized a variety of technologies as part of a sweeping plan to improve China's competitiveness in AI development. In 2017, China's science and technology development bureaucracy was ordered to focus on knowledge computing engines, cross-medium analytic reasoning technology, swarm intelligence, hybrid (human-machine) enhanced intelligent architectures, autonomous unmanned systems, virtual reality intelligent modeling, intelligent computing chips and processors, and natural language processing.[11] Work across these eight focus areas was expected to form systems capable of "strengthening AI cybersecurity technology R&D, products, and system-wide network security defense," among other improvements.[12] Though broad, China's emphasis on these technology areas summarizes the contours of its larger strategic aspirations for AI in information operations.

From aspiration to application: the AI-powered future of information operations

Both established scholars and promising young researchers are working to translate these strategic aspirations into specific applications. The most enlightening research blends detailed technical assessments with policy and strategy prescriptions and is often supported by prestigious, high-wattage Chinese S&T organizations. Consulting efforts from distinguished bodies like the Chinese Academy of Engineering (中国工程院, CAE) have resulted in a growing body of literature describing future development trajectories for AI in both cyber intrusion techniques and online influence operations.[13]

Sitting at one convergence of policy and technical research is Fang Binxing (方滨兴). Dubbed the "Father of the Great Firewall" (中国网络防火墙之父) for his past work,[14] Fang exemplifies the highly interconnected nature of China's AI R&D ecosystem. Among other positions, he is concurrently an academician at the CAE, chief scientist at the state-owned defense conglomerate China Electronics Corporation (中国电子信息产业集团, CEC), and director of the National Engineering Laboratory for Information Security Technologies (信息内容安全技术国家工程实验室) and the Beijing University of Posts and Telecommunications-Ministry of Education Key Laboratory for Trustworthy Distributed Computing Services (北京邮电大学可信分布式计算与服务教育部重点实验室).[15, 16] Aside from high-level policy, industry, and academia, Fang's work and views are likely also influential within the PLA: as of 2017, Fang was advising doctoral students at the National University of Defense Technology's Institute of Computer Science (国防科技大学计算机学院).[17] Fang is among the most prolific authors writing at the intersection of cybersecurity strategy, academic research, and application.

Fang and several younger cybersecurity experts have begun to articulate details of what they term "[AI-]powered attack/defense" (赋能攻击/防御) in information operations. In early 2021, Fang and his colleagues predicted an AI-fueled arms race in cyberspace characterized by intensifying competitive dynamics between AI-powered offense and defense.[18] Other scholars have noted that AI-enabled online influence operations pose a formidable challenge to nation-states and societies, including China's own efforts to maintain social and political stability at home.[19] Together, these writings suggest an emerging consensus among some of China's most prominent cybersecurity, computer science, and AI researchers: AI will usher in unprecedented stealth, scale, and adaptability to both offensive and defensive information operations, and China's S&T ecosystem needs to be at the cutting edge of these developments.

Perhaps the most publicized of AI's myriad applications is to improve attack vector stealth and survivability. Among other cybersecurity applications, AI's comparative advantage in handling large amounts of multi-source, heterogenous data could be harnessed to craft highly realistic social engineering attacks or stealthier, more evasive malware for cyber intrusions.[20] AI-powered malware could benefit from extensive data collection from the operating environment, mimicking environmental features and normal behavioral signatures to avoid detection by the defense.[21] According to these experts, successful integration of AI into new attack vectors could yield code capable of concealing its payloads and intended targets even in the face of reverse malware engineering and rigorous network monitoring efforts.[22] Just as AI can help design cyber intrusion techniques that can elude detection, Chinese experts argue that it can also create fake content for influence operations that is virtually indistinguishable from authentic content.[23] More specifically, algorithms could generate convincing text or even audio and video for both phishing attacks[24] and for mass dissemination across social networks.[25]

AI could also enable cyber intrusion and online influence campaigns at unprecedented scale, especially through improved autonomy and automation. For cyberattacks, decentralized autonomous coordination algorithms could enable autonomous "botnet swarms" capable of large-scale denial-of-service attacks. Using AI for command and control could free these botnets from the numerical limitations (and comparatively easy attribution) of traditional centralized command-and-control infrastructure, while self-learning capabilities could allow botnets to recognize and attack targets of opportunity on their own.[26] Other algorithms are capable of generating vast amounts of realistic content to meet the needs of online influence operations.[27] AI can help with large-scale distribution of this content, too: according to one Chinese researcher, realistic social media bots are already playing a disproportionately large role in spreading disinformation, autonomously targeting influential users to amplify fake content.[28]

A third AI application is to improve attack vector effectiveness by optimizing vulnerability discovery and improving adaptability. Here again, AI's comparative superiority in processing huge amounts of heterogenous, unstructured data could pay off in designing self-adapting cyber intrusion techniques and exploiting (or defending against) ephemeral opportunities for content customization and delivery in influence operations. Using feedback from actual or simulated defenses as training sets for AI-enhanced malware will result in more adaptable attack vectors capable of making adjustments on the fly, either to avoid detection or to strike at precisely the best moment and location.[29] For online influence activities, data-mining algorithms could enable a sentiment analysis in near-real time,[30] and adaptive and responsive social media botnets could selectively deploy

TABLE 11.1 Overview of application areas for AI in cyber and influence operations

Application Area	Presumptive or Aspirational Use Case	Required or Exemplar Technologies
Improved stealth and survivability	Hyper-realistic phishing attacks; more elusive malware	Natural language generation; deep learning methods; adversarial sample generation and insertion
Large-scale attacks	Automated, responsive spambot networks to spread disinformation; large-scale, autonomous denial-of-service botnets	Autonomous command and control algorithms
Improved adaptability	Automated vulnerability discovery; adaptive malware; real-time sentiment analysis; adaptive media content	Machine learning algorithms for fingerprinting operating systems; deep neural networks and reinforcement learning to defeat detection and destruction

or modify content according to changing conditions in the field.[31] These use cases are summarized in Table 11.1.

For Fang and other top cybersecurity scholars, certain classes of AI algorithms are especially promising for achieving desired improvements in intrusion techniques. In 2018, researchers at the China Information Technology Security Evaluation Center (中国信息安全测评中心, CNITSEC), the technical branch of the MSS, focused heavily on recurrent neural networks (RNNs) and Q-learning algorithms, among others, for AI-powered vulnerability discovery techniques.[32] Fang et al. view GANs, deep neural networks (DNNs), and adversarial machine learning as "deep-learning enablers for new types of attacks"[33] relevant to nearly every stage of offensive cyber operations. For their part, researchers at the Chinese Academy of Sciences Institute of Information Engineering (中国科学院信息工程研究所, CAS IIE) emphasized many of the same technologies and identified domain generation algorithms (DGAs) and long short-term memory (LSTM) networks in a June 2021 study published by CNITSEC.[34] Together, these classes of algorithms likely represent the highest priority for Chinese technical research on AI in cyber operations.

The effective use of these algorithm classes for cyber intrusions is likely to alter competitive dynamics between offense and defense in multiple phases of the network attack cycle, sometimes simultaneously. For instance, Fang and several collaborators argue that network traffic mimicry could yield substantial payoffs in both the command-and-control and evasion phases of a network attack.[35] Other researchers see automated penetration testing tools and adaptive malware optimized for evasion as especially impactful across the reconnaissance, vulnerability exploitation, and installation phases of a network attack cycle.[36] Table 11.2 captures these vectors.

TABLE 11.2 Categorization of AI-enabled cyber intrusion techniques described in Fang et al. and Liu et al. [37, 38]

	Preparation	Delivery	Engagement	Presence/Persistence	Effect	Command and Control	Evasion
Evasive malicious code	x						x
Generating malicious data-flow based on GAN framework (IDSGAN)			x	x		x	x
Intelligent password-guessing			x	x			
Novel CAPTCHA solver			x				
Automated high-end spear-phishing		x					
Network phishing email generation		x					
DeepLocker new-type malware					x		
DeepExploit automated pentesting tool			x		x	x	
DeepDGA deep-learning algorithm						x	
AI-enabled vulnerability scanning	x						
Attack intention concealment (black box model)							x
Automated vulnerability exploitation			x				
Automated detour certification				x			
Precision targeting and attack based on deep learning classification					x		

Chinese influence operations experts focus on many of the same classes of algorithms, but for slightly different applications and with different anticipated effects. For topic detection and tracking in online opinion monitoring, clustering algorithms like K-nearest neighbor (KNN), k-means clustering, and ant colony optimization are popular areas of research. For text segmentation, work continues on improving methods using Latent Dirichlet Allocation (LDA) and Vector Space Models (VSMs).[39] For deepfake content generation, a group of researchers at CAS IIE identified GANs, natural language generation models like RNNs, variational autoencoders (VAEs), and convolutional neural networks (CNNs) as critically important algorithms for future study.[40]

For both AI-enabled cyber intrusion methods and online influence operations, many of these specific technical opinions rely heavily upon foreign research. Nevertheless, these writings still shed valuable insight on what top Chinese researchers consider the most important leading-edge developments in the field. Literature reviews frequently cite research from Black Hat and other international work while avoiding mention of corresponding Chinese research. The relative absence of Chinese research citations could indicate that Chinese R&D efforts are either comparatively laggard or not published because of their highly sensitive nature. *This absence of evidence, however, is not evidence of absence*: a substantial amount of relevant foundational and applied research output is concentrated at a handful of research centers within China's AI R&D community.

The academic research and development base

Most of the relevant Chinese academic literature on AI-powered cyber operations comes from a handful of elite research universities with close ties to the PLA and China's defense industrial base, especially the Seven Sons of National Defense (国防七子), a septet of universities with close ties to China's defense industry. Beijing University of Posts and Telecommunications (北京邮电大学, BUPT), Xidian University (西安电子科技大学), University of Electronic Science and Technology of China (电子科技大学, UESTC), and Harbin Institute of Technology (哈尔滨工业大学, HIT) produce the most publicly available technical research on the high-priority methods needed to actualize AI-powered cyber intrusion techniques (see Table 11.3). Among the classes of algorithms that Chinese cybersecurity experts deem most vital, publications on natural language generation using RNN and LSTM algorithms were the most prolific, followed by research on GANs, Q-learning algorithms, adversarial machine learning, and DGAs.

Judging by publication volume, many of the same institutions are also leaders in AI-powered influence operations. Xidian University, BUPT, and HIT are all leading publishers of algorithmic research in the key phases of network public opinion monitoring, especially in areas like topic detection and tracking, text segmentation, and sentiment analysis.[42] These universities are also prolific publishers on algorithms that are increasingly applied to produce deepfakes, including CNNs, GANs, natural language generation algorithms, and autoencoders, in order of publication volume. While not all the articles identified in Table 11.4

TABLE 11.3 Most prolific publishing institutions for AI-powered cyber algorithms[41]

Algorithm Class	GANs (3,815 results)	Natural Language Generation (RNN/LSTM) (12,732 results)	Adversarial Machine Learning (example generation) (545 results)	Domain Generation Algorithms (227 results)	Q-Learning Algorithms (863 results)
Top Five Publishing Institutions (Number of Publications)	Xidian University (206)	BUPT (610)	Xidian University (38)	North China Power University (华北电力大学) (17)	BUPT (63)
	UESTC (203)	UESTC (433)	HIT (26)	UESTC (12)	Xidian University (50)
	BUPT (117)	HIT (426)	BUPT (22)	BUPT (11)	HIT (40)
	HIT (81)	Xidian University (289)	UESTC (22)	Xidian University (7)	Hefei University of Science and Technology (合肥工业大学) (39)
	University of Chinese Academy of Sciences (中国科学院大学) (72)	Beijing Jiao Tong University (北京交通大学) (260)	Shanghai Jiao Tong University (上海交通大学) (18)	NUDT (7)	Nanjing University of Posts and Telecommunications (南京邮电大学) (37)

TABLE 11.4 Most prolific publishing institutions for commonly cited deepfake algorithms[43]

Algorithm Class	GANs (994 results)	Natural Language Generation (including RNN) (268 results)	Autoencoders (including VAE) (261 results)	Convolutional Neural Networks (2,157 results)
Top Five Publishing Institutions (Number of Publications)	Xidian University (55)	BUPT (25)	Xidian University (14)	UESTC (103)
	BUPT (46)	Xidian University (16)	BUPT (13)	Xidian University (98)
	UESTC (45)	UESTC (13)	UESTC (12)	BUPT (88)
	HIT (26)	University of Chinese Academy of Sciences (9)	HIT (9)	South China University of Technology (48)
	South China University of Technology (华南理工大学) (24)	Beijing Jiao Tong University (7)	University of Chinese Academy of Sciences (9)	HIT (48)

are necessarily directly related to AI-enabled deepfakes, the aggregate body of research suggests that these universities have fostered a significant amount of research interest in these algorithms.

In a qualitative sense, specialized research centers led by impeccably credentialed scholars are likely among the most important organizations researching high-priority algorithms for both cyber and influence operations. While these entities publish far fewer articles in public, their layered ties to high-level Chinese S&T bodies, the PLA, and the defense industry make them focal points for cross-pollination and information-sharing in the R&D ecosystem. For instance, Wang Feiyue (王飞跃), one of China's most prominent AI scholars, directs both the State Key Laboratory for Management and Control of Complex Systems (复杂系统管理与控制国家重点实验室) at the Chinese Academy of Sciences Institute of Automation and the NUDT Military Computational Experiments and Parallel Systems Technology Research Center (军事计算实验与平行系统技术研究中心),[44] where he is able to direct resources to GAN research and ensure that both the civilian Chinese Academy of Sciences and the PLA will benefit from any of his further work on GANs in AI-powered cyber intrusion techniques and deepfakes for influence operations.[45]

Other advances in high-priority algorithmic research are notable because of the organizations that undertake the work. Researchers at the PLA Strategic Support Force Information Engineering University (战略支援部队信息工程大学, SSF-IEU), the institution responsible for training the SSF's network warfare officers,[46] are actively studying adversarial machine learning in cyber intrusion techniques, demonstrating increasingly complex uses of the method beginning in 2019. Starting with a survey of adversarial example generation techniques for malware,[47] SSF researchers progressed to a demonstrative technique for spoofing network traffic using adversarial examples,[48] and in March 2021, explored methods for using adversarial example generation in imagery.[49] Other SSF-affiliated organizations like the Jiangnan Computing Technology Research Institute (江南计算技术研究所, also known as the SSF 56th Research Institute)[50] and the State Key Laboratory of Mathematical Engineering and Advanced Computing (数学工程与先进计算国家重点实验室) have assisted in similar research.[51]

SSF researchers and their comrades in other parts of the PLA are also studying an array of AI-enabled technologies for online influence operations, including some with potential offensive applications. Over the last three years, SSF-IEU graduate students have published on various topics related to AI-enhanced exploitation of social media networks, including algorithmic community detection,[52] spambot detection,[53] and user identification across various social networks[54]—all subjects with obvious defensive purposes but also possible offensive utility. Others have begun applying AI-enabled sentiment analysis techniques to foreign languages in a more obvious effort to train algorithms for influence operations abroad. For instance, in March 2021, researchers from the SSF and NUDT's College of Computer Science (计算机学院) built a multi-step sentiment analysis model for analyzing the tweets of U.S. politicians using LSTM, CNN, C-LSTM, and

BERT algorithms for classification,[55] and in May 2021, a computational linguistics graduate student at SSF-IEU's Luoyang Foreign Language Academy (洛阳外国语学院) demonstrated a hybrid sentiment analysis model for Korean text using CNN and Bi-LSTM algorithms.[56]

Perhaps one of the foremost proponents of AI-enabled offensive influence operations is Li Bicheng (李弼程), whose career trajectory and research output exemplify an increasing degree of collaboration among stakeholders in any Chinese online influence campaign executed abroad. After obtaining his PhD from NUDT and a government-sponsored stint as a visiting scholar at Manchester University in the United Kingdom, Li spent 18 years as a lecturer, professor, and PhD advisor at SSF-IEU, where his research interests included intelligentized information processing, online ideological security, network public opinion monitoring and guidance, and big data mining.[57] In 2016, Li was the first of a cadre of specially recruited scholars to move to Huaqiao University College of Computer Science and Technology (华侨大学计算机科学与技术学院), a university directly subordinate to the United Front Work Department,[58] where in June 2019 he co-developed a model for network opinion guidance based on an intelligent agent system[59] with a researcher from the PLA's 61716 Unit, also known as the PLA's 311 Base, which specializes in psychological operations.[60] Li's career pit-stops hint at an ongoing effort to turn technical AI and influence operations expertise into more practical applications.

Like the work of his SSF colleagues researching AI-powered cyber intrusion methods, Li's research also demonstrates progressively more advanced and detailed study. Shortly after Li moved to Huaqiao University, he published a pair of theoretical articles laying out a basic framework for online influence operations[61] arguing that these activities were indispensable components of a joint warfare construct.[62] By 2019, Li had published work identifying key technical aspects of a "network public opinion early warning system"[63] and a demonstrative model for AI-enabled online influence operations using an intelligent agent system.[64] His most recently published work in 2020 focuses on simulations and modeling for AI-enabled network opinion guidance[65] and a means of assessing the effectiveness of AI-enabled online influence operations.[66] This progression from broader theory to specific application to theoretical assessment is likely but one example suggesting steady advancement in academic research related to AI in information operations.

Conclusion and implications

If Chinese researchers succeed in employing AI in the ways described above, China's AI-enabled information operations will become even harder to detect and therefore, even more effective. Spoofed, adaptive network signatures could camouflage malware against even the most vigilant human network defenders, and deepfake videos or imagery produced at scale could overwhelm the already limited ability of social media companies to combat state-run online influence operations. While there is little public evidence that China has already used these AI-enabled techniques, one way to assess which methods are more or less likely to be employed and over what time horizons is to examine testing and simulation environments, though that remains beyond the scope of this chapter. Regardless, China's R&D activities suggest that it certainly has a potent, if possibly latent, capability to use AI for information operations.

Much of this capability will likely accrue to the Chinese military and intelligence services, where it will remain a closely held secret until deployed in the wild. A significant amount of the applied AI research in information operations is carried out by the Seven Sons of National Defense, universities with former ties to the PLA (like Xidian University), or organizations like CNITSEC directly tied to MSS technical espionage operations. In keeping with the missions of these organizations and best practices for information warfare, the most advanced capabilities will only be revealed when unleashed upon a target during actual operations to maximize their effectiveness.

It is possible and even likely that the best defense against these AI-powered offensive information operations will be AI-enabled defense. The integration of AI by both the offense and the defense will accelerate an arms race between the two as researchers increasingly work to build weapons and defenses that can exceed existing human or machine-assisted capabilities.

Among other technical factors, large, accurate training sets will be an important determinant of victory—a factor that has not gone unnoticed by Chinese operators as they pilfer ever larger amounts of data from networks abroad, even as some developers argue that China's domestic datasets are of poor quality.[67]

Chinese success is not inevitable in either offensive or defensive operations. Much of the cutting-edge academic literature described in this chapter relies heavily on research published abroad, especially the United States. Furthermore, Chinese AI researchers openly acknowledge that much of the most widely used development infrastructure are foreign platforms—simulation programs like Netlogo, Anylogic, Matlab, Vensim, and Swarm are all foreign products, and the two most dominant deep learning frameworks, TensorFlow and PyTorch, are made by Google and Facebook, respectively.[68] China's leading researchers in AI-enabled information operations will still have to contend with many of the same dependencies their comrades in other AI industries do—much of the leading work is still done outside of China.

Beyond technical constraints on future success, Chinese planners may also be constrained by strategic considerations that could encourage restraint. China's professed cybersecurity strategy is designed to keep the current regime in power and increasingly resembles a paranoid defensive crouch. For the CCP, the use of AI-powered deepfakes in influence operations may open a Pandora's box of retribution that could result in a dramatically more dangerous domestic information environment. This fear of massively destructive influence operations used in their homeland could deter China's leaders from using the highest quality, indistinguishable deepfakes in an influence campaign, at least until their researchers are sufficiently confident in a technical means of defense.

China's development of AI for information operations, then, should be understood not only as a burgeoning field that could yield extensive improvements to its information operations capabilities, but also as a double-edged sword that could result in significantly increased threat perception, especially in terms of regime stability. The extent to which China's leaders and top AI and cyberspace researchers can reconcile those dualities will determine the future trajectory of China's AI development in information operations.

Notes

1 Jeff Kao and Mia Shuang Li, "How China Built a Twitter Propaganda Machine Then Let It Loose on Coronavirus," *ProPublica*, March 26, 2020.
2 Insikt Group, "Chinese Influence Operations Evolve in Campaigns Targeting Taiwanese Elections, Hong Kong Protests," *Recorded Future*, April 29, 2021.
3 Nathan Beauchamp-Mustafaga and Jessica Drun, "Exploring Chinese Military Thinking on Social Media Manipulation against Taiwan," *China Brief*, 21.7, April 2021.
4 Dina Temple-Raston, "China's Microsoft Hack May Have Had a Bigger Purpose than Just Spying," National Public Radio, August 26, 2021.
5 Among other works, see Gregory C. Allen, "Understanding China's AI Strategy: Clues to Chinese Strategic Thinking on Artificial Intelligence and National Security," Center for a New American Security, February 2019 and Elsa Kania, "Artificial Intelligence in China's Revolution in Military Affairs," *Journal of Strategic Studies* 44.4, May 2021, pp. 515–542.
6 CCP Central Committee Party School International Strategy Research Academy (中共中央党校国际战略研究院), 中国特色国家安全战略研究, p. 182.
7 Ibid., p. 181.
8 CCP Central Committee Office of the Central Cyberspace Affairs Commission, "国家网络空间安全战略" (National Cyberspace Security Strategy), December 27, 2016, http://www.cac.gov.cn/2016-12/27/c1120195926.htm.
9 Jin Jiangjun (金江军), ed., 网络安全和信息化党政领导干部读本 (Network Security and Informatization Party Government Leadership Cadre Reader), Beijing: Central Party School Press, 2015, p. 78.
10 Zeng Xianjie (曾贤杰), "网络意识形态安全工作着重抓什么" (What Online Ideological Security Work Should Emphasize), *Study Times* (学习时报), April 25, 2021.
11 PRC State Council, 国务院关于印发新一代人工智能发展规划的通知 (New Generation AI Development Plan), SC 35, 2017.
12 Ibid.
13 Zhu Shiqiang (朱世强) and Wang Yongheng (王永恒), "基于人工智能的内容安全发展战略研究," pp. 67–74.
14 Lin Lu (林露) and Xiong Xu (熊旭), eds., "北邮校长毕业典礼公开请辞 校方称目前不解释" (BUPT President Asks to Resign at Graduation Ceremony; School Will Not Explain), *Beijing Youth Daily* (北京青年报), June 28, 2013.
15 Liu Hang (刘航) and Shao Wen (邵文), "超过60位国内外院士将出席世界人工智能大会 (Over 60 Domestic and Foreign Experts Will Appear at World Artificial Intelligence Conference), *The Paper* (澎湃新闻), July 6, 2021, https://www.thepaper.cn/newsDetail_forward_13377289.
16 See Fang Binxing (方滨兴) biography at https://www.cae.cn/cae/html/main/colys/71871048.html.
17 "国防科技大学2018年博士研究生招生简章(初步方案)" (National University of Defense Technology 2018 PhD Student Recruitment General Regulations), August 2017, http://www.mod.gov.cn/services/site21/20170920/6c0b8409b7e31b2c05ef0b.pdf.
18 Jia et al., "基于人工智能的网络空间安全防御战略研究," p. 100.
19 Zhu and Wang, pp. 67–74.
20 Jia et al., p. 100.

21 Fang et al., "人工智能赋能网络攻击的安全威胁及应对策略," pp. 64–65.

22 Ibid., pp. 63–64.

23 Shao Chengcheng (邵成成), "在线社会网络中虚假信息传播的研究."

24 Fang et al., p. 63.

25 Zhang Zhiyong (张志勇) et al., "人工智能视角下的在线社交网络虚假信息检测、传播与控制研究综述" (Survey on Fake Information Detection, Propagation and Control in Online Social Networks from the Perspective of Artificial Intelligence), *Chinese Journal of Computers* (计算机学报), 2020, pp. 1–27.

26 Fang et al., p. 63.

27 Hu Shengwei (胡盛伟), "基于深度学习的条件文本生成技术与应用研究."

28 Shao Chengcheng (邵成成), "在线社会网络中虚假信息传播的研究."

29 Fang et al., p. 63.

30 Zhu and Wang, pp. 67–74.

31 Hu Shengwei (胡盛伟), "基于深度学习的条件文本生成技术与应用研究."

32 Zou Quanchen (邹权臣) et al., "从自动化到智能化:软件漏洞挖掘技术进展" (From Automation to Intelligentization: Survey of Research on Vulnerability Discovery Techniques), *Journal of Tsinghua University (Science and Technology)* (清华大学学报, 自然科学版), 58.12, 2018, 1086.

33 Ji et al., "深度学习赋能的恶意代码攻防研究进展," p. 672.

34 Liu et al., "人工智能在网络攻防领域的应用及问题分析," pp. 32–36.

35 Ji et al., p. 672.

36 Liu et al., pp. 32–36.

37 Ji et al., p. 672.

38 Liu et al., pp. 32–36.

39 Cai Wandong (蔡皖东), ed., 网络舆情分析技术 (*Network Opinion Analysis Technology*), Beijing: Publishing House of Electronics Industry, 2018, pp. 119–154, 155–181.

40 Liang Ruigang (梁瑞刚) et al., "视听觉深度伪造检测技术研究综述" (A Survey of Audiovisual Deepfake Detection Technologies), *Journal of Cyber Security* (信息安全学报), 5.2, 2020, pp. 1–17.

41 These searches were carried out in CNKI on August 16, 2021, filtering for results in the information technology field. Keywords used as follows: for GANs: (主题: 生成对抗网络 + GAN) AND (主题: 网络); for natural language generation: (主题: 自然语言生成 + RNN + 循环神经网络 + LSTM + 递归神经网络) AND (主题: 网络); for adversarial machine learning: (对抗样本) AND (主题: 网络); for domain generation algorithms: (主题: DGA + 域名生成算法) AND (主题: 网络); for Q-learning: (主题: Q学习) AND (主题: 网络).

42 CNKI searches dated August 24, 2021.

43 These searches were carried out in CNKI on August 23, 2021, filtering for results in the information technology field. Keywords used as follows: for GANs: (主题: 生成对抗网络 + GAN) AND (全文: 虚假 + 伪造); for natural language generation: (主题: 自然语言生成 + NLG + RNN + 循环神经网络) AND (全文: 虚假 + 伪造); for autoencoders: (主题: 变分自编码器 + VAE + 自编码器) AND (全文: 虚假 + 伪造); for convolutional neural networks: (主题: 卷积神经网络 + CNN) AND (全文: 虚假 + 伪造).

44 Zheng Wenbo (郑文博), Wang Kunfeng (王坤峰), and Wang Feiyue (王飞跃), "基于贝叶斯生成对抗网络的背景消减算法" (Background Subtraction Algorithm with Bayesian Generative Adversarial Networks), *Acta Automatica Sinica* (自动化学报), 44.5, May 2018, 878.

45 Wang in addition was a professor at Arizona State University in the 1990s and the director of both its Robotics and Automation Laboratory and Complex Systems Research Group. In 2011, he was first to be selected by a "high-level talent introduction plan" (Thousand Talents) in the military arena. https://www.kmust.edu.cn/info/1011/4362.htm.

46 Costello and McReynolds, "China's Strategic Support Force: A Force for a New Era," p. 51.

47 Wang Shuwei (王树伟) et al., "基于生成对抗网络的恶意软件对抗样本生成综述" (Review of Malware Adversarial Sample Generation on Generative Adversarial Networks), *Journal of Information Engineering University* (信息工程大学学报), 20.5, 2019, 616–621.

48 Hu Yongjin (胡永进) et al., "基于对抗样本的网络欺骗流量生成方法" (Method to Generate Cyber Deception Traffic Based on Adversarial Sample), *Journal on Communications* (通信学报), 41.9, September 2020, 59–70.

49 Yu Kechen (于克辰), Guo Li (郭莉), and Yao Mengmeng (姚萌萌), "基于空间及能量维度的黑盒对抗样本生成方法" (The Generation of Black Box Adversarial Sample Based on Spatial and Energy Dimension), *Netinfo Security* (信息网络安全), 21.3, 2021, 72–78.

50 https://zh.wikipedia.org/wiki/中国人民解放军战略支援部队网络系统部第五十六研究所.

51 Yu Yingchao (于颖超), Ding Lin (丁琳), and Chen Zuoning (陈左宁), "机器学习系统面临的安全攻击及其防御技术研究" (Research on Attacks and Defenses Towards Machine Learning Systems), *Netinfo Security* (信息网络安全), 18.9, 2018, 10–18.

52 Ma Xiaofeng (马晓峰), "社交网络中的社区检测算法研究" (Research on Community Detection Algorithms in Social Networks), PhD dissertation, PLA Strategic Support Force Information Engineering University (战略支援部队信息工程大学), 2018.

53 Qu Qiang (曲强), "社交网络垃圾用户检测关键技术研究" (Research on Spam User Detection on Social Networks), Master's degree dissertation, PLA Strategic Support Force Information Engineering University (战略支援部队信息工程大学), 2019.

54 Guo Xiaoyu (郭晓宇), "跨社交网络用户身份识别技术研究" (Research on User Identification Across Social Networks), Master's degree dissertation, PLA Strategic Support Force Information Engineering University (战略支援部队信息工程大学), 2020.

55 Chang Chengyang (常城扬), Wang Xiaodong (王晓东), and Zhang Shenglei (张胜磊), "基于深度学习方法对特定群体推特的动态政治情感极性分析" (Polarity Analysis of Dynamic Political Sentiments from Tweets with Deep Learning Method), *Data Analysis and Data Discovery* (数据分析与知识发现), 51.3, March 2021, 121–131.

56 Zhao Tianrui (赵天锐), "基于深度学习的韩国语文本情感分类" (Sentiment Analysis of Korean Text Based on Deep Learning)," *Intelligent Computer and Applications* (智能计算机与应用), 11.5, May 2021, 82–87.

57 Li Bicheng (李弼程), "师资队伍、人工智能系" (Teaching Contingent, Artificial Intelligence), Huaqiao University College of Computer Science and Technology, accessed August 24, 2021, https://cst.hqu.edu.cn/info/1169/1264.htm.

58 "学校简介" (School Overview), School Summary, Huaqiao University, accessed August 24, 2021, https://www.hqu.edu.cn/xxgk/xxjj.htm.

59 Li, Hu, and Xiong, "网络舆情引导智能代理模型," pp. 73–77.

60 Costello and McReynolds, p. 63.

61 Li Bicheng (李弼程), "网络舆论斗争系统模型与应对策略" (Network Public Opinion Struggle System Modeling and Tactics in Response), *National Defense Technology* (国防科技), 37.5, October 2016, 72–75.

62 Li Bicheng (李弼程), "网络舆论斗争的全域一体化联合作战" (Network Public Opinion Struggle in All-Domain Integrated Joint Operations), *National Defense Technology* (国防科技), 38.2, March 2017, 85–88.

63 Chen Gang (陈刚), Li Bicheng (李弼程), Guo Zhigang (郭志刚), Lin Chen (林琛), "网络舆情监测预警系统模型与关键技术" (Key Technologies and Model of Network Opinion Detection and Early Warning System)," *Journal of Information Engineering University*, 20.1, January 2019, 116–121.

64 Li, Hu, and Xiong, pp. 73–77.

65 Li Bicheng (李弼程) et al., "网络舆论智能引导仿真推演模型与系统构建" (Simulation-Deduction Model and System Construction of Intelligent Guidance of Network Public Opinion), *National Defense Technology* (国防科技), 41.5, October 2020, 35–40.

66 Xiong Yao (熊尧), Li Bicheng (李弼程), and Wang Ziyue (王子玥), "基于模糊综合评判的网络舆论引导效果评估" (Assessment of Intelligent Network Opinion Guidance Effectiveness Based on Fuzzy Comprehensive Judgment), *Journal of Modern Information* (现代情报), 40.6, June 2020, 55–67.

67 Jordan Schneider, "Could an 'AI Winter' Be on the Horizon for China?" New America Cybersecurity Initiative, December 4, 2019, https://www.newamerica.org/cybersecurity-initiative/digichina/blog/could-ai-winter-be-horizon-china/.
68 Lorand Laskai and Helen Toner, "Can China Grow Its Own AI Tech Base?" New America Cybersecurity Initiative, November 4, 2019.

Bibliography

CCP Central Committee Party School International Strategy Research Academy (中共中央党校国际战略研究院), eds., 中国特色国家安全战略研究 (*National Security Strategy Research with Chinese Characteristics*), Beijing: Central Party School Press, 2016.

Costello, John and Joe McReynolds, "China's Strategic Support Force: A Force for a New Era," *China Strategic Perspectives* 13, October 2018.

Fang Binxing (方滨兴), Shi Jinqiao (时金桥), Wang Zhongru (王忠儒), and Yu Weiqiang (余伟强), "人工智能赋能网络攻击的安全威胁及应对策略" (AI-Powered Cyberspace Attacks: Security Risks and Countermeasures), *Strategic Study of Chinese Academy of Engineering* (中国工程科学), 23.3, March 2021, 60–66.

Hu Shengwei (胡盛伟), "基于深度学习的条件文本生成技术与应用研究" (Research on Deep-Learning Based Content Generation Technology and Applications), Master's dissertation, Huaqiao University, 2020.

Ji Tiantian (冀甜甜), Fang Binxing (方滨兴), Cui Xiang (崔翔), Wang Zhongru (王忠儒), Gan Ruiling (甘蕊灵), Han Yu (韩宇), and Yu Weiqiang (余伟强), "深度学习赋能的恶意代码攻防研究进展" (Research on Deep Learning-Powered Malware Attack and Defense Techniques), *Chinese Journal of Computers* (计算机学报), 44.4, April 2021, 669–695.

Jia Yan (贾焰), Fang Binxing (方滨兴), Li Aiping (李爱平), and Gu Zhaoquan (顾钊铨), "基于人工智能的网络空间安全防御战略研究" (Artificial Intelligence Enabled Cyberspace Security Defense), *Strategic Study of Chinese Academy of Engineering* (中国工程科学), 23.3, March 2021, 98–105.

Li Bicheng (李弼程), Hu Huaping (胡华平), and Xiong Yao (熊尧), "网络舆情引导智能代理模型" (Intelligent Agent Model for Network Public Opinion Guidance), *National Defense Technology* (国防科技), 40.3, June 2019, 73–77.

Liu Baoxu (刘宝旭), Zhang Fangjiao (张方娇), Liu Jiaxi (刘嘉熹), and Liu Qixu (刘奇旭), "人工智能在网络攻防领域的应用及问题分析" (Analysis of Problems and Applications of Artificial Intelligence in the Network Attack Field), *China Information Security* (中国信息安全), 6, 2021, 32–36.

PRC State Council, 新一代人工智能发展规划 (New Generation Artificial Intelligence Development Plan), July 8, 2017.

Shao Chengcheng (邵成成), "在线社会网络中虚假信息传播的研究" (The Spread of Misinformation in Online Social Networks), PhD dissertation, National University of Defense Technology (国防科技大学), 2018.

Zhu Shiqiang (朱世强) and Wang Yongheng (王永恒), "基于人工智能的内容安全发展战略研究" (Development of Content Security Based on Artificial Intelligence), Strategic Study of Chinese Academy of Engineering (中国工程科学), 23.3, March 2021, 67–74.

12

AI and the surveillance state

Dahlia Peterson

China's artificial intelligence (AI) surveillance applications are meant to provide stability and control, but are not applied equally in society, and are frequently used without regard for human rights. This chapter will examine AI-based surveillance in China with respect to its historical context, the state of data fusion, applications in Xinjiang, how it benefits from new biometric standards, trends in mass control and behavior modification, and attempts to export AI surveillance internationally. Finally, the chapter will consider some technical challenges faced by China as well as U.S. policy responses and their global implications.

AI surveillance in China has evolved iteratively to add capabilities, e.g. predictive policing, along with facial, voice, and other biometric recognition. But China still pragmatically uses community-based policing and AI concurrently in programs such as Golden Shield, Safe Cities, Skynet, Sharp Eyes, and Police Cloud. It relies heavily on data fusion to take the information from these different sources and merge them to produce an actionable analysis. Tools like these are used intensively and oppressively in Xinjiang but are not confined or original to that region.

Much of China's AI surveillance innovation stems from legislative initiatives requiring private firms to cooperate with security organs. As a result, asymmetric monitoring and punitive measures are now daily fare in Chinese life, including finance, healthcare, and education, among others, with the aim of maintaining social order, regime stability, and changing behavior. China actively cultivates global AI governance and exports AI surveillance solutions to authoritarian regimes worldwide. Despite rapid progress, China faces many challenges, especially in data integration, compute, and system vulnerabilities.

DOI: 10.4324/9781003212980-16

Historical overview: manual surveillance aided by advanced technologies

From 1949 to the early 1990s, China shifted from wholly manual surveillance and policing to increasing reliance on advanced technology. Early mechanisms included employment "units" (单位), the residency registration system (户口), and secret political files (档案).[1] As China began to reform and "open up" in 1979, however, these traditional methods lost effectiveness,[2] creating a "need" for a more technological approach, spurred by the 1989 pro-democracy protests and the advent of the Chinese internet. Today, China uses a wide slate of non-AI surveillance methods, including national DNA databases, real-name registration requirements, and analog surveillance cameras; however, this is increasingly assisted by AI-powered censorship of internet and phone communications, facial and voice recognition-based video surveillance, predictive policing, and data fusion.[3, 4]

AI is used today in all of China's major national surveillance programs. These programs can overlap, especially when it comes to advancing earlier programs' goals and using their physical infrastructure. Accordingly, there is no consensus on the number of facial recognition-equipped cameras in China,[5] nor the ratio of private to publicly owned cameras, whether the cameras feed both local and national surveillance systems, or how many serve commercial versus public security applications.

Golden Shield Project (金盾工程)

China's first major modern surveillance program was launched by the Ministry of Public Security (公安部, MPS) in the early 2000s. Designed to increase the Chinese government's control over the entire population, it honed in on political dissidents. The project incorporates technologies now central to China's surveillance apparatus, such as internet censorship and—in the most AI-heavy elements—facial and voice recognition.[6] It was initially rolled out in two main phases: first through population databases, ID tracking systems, and internet surveillance tools, and then through surveillance camera systems.[7] According to state-run media, between 2003 and 2006, the MPS logged personal information for 96 percent (or 1.25 out of 1.3 billion) of China's citizens.[8]

Safe Cities and Skynet: preliminary evidence of data fusion

China achieved greater social control through Safe Cities (平安城市) and Skynet (天网工程), two programs that are sometimes used synonymously, but are in fact slightly different. The Ministry of Public Security and the Ministry of Science and Technology launched Safe Cities in 2004.[9] It provides disaster warnings, urban and traffic management, and public security maintenance through three interlocking systems covering technical, physical, and civil air defense.[10] By 2005, 22 provinces and 21 cities were operational under Safe Cities.[11]

The MPS and the Ministry of Industry and Information Technology (MIIT) launched Skynet in 2005 with similar goals, namely to "fight crime and prevent possible disasters" through a nationwide network of closed-circuit television cameras.[12] It focuses on public surveillance, claiming full-time coverage of major districts, streets, schools, and business areas, and timed surveillance over smaller streets, with footage sent to manned command centers.[13] Although Chinese media often laud Skynet as relying on AI as a "facial recognition system," it is unknown how many cameras are facial recognition-equipped, especially considering that the technology was underdeveloped in 2005.[14] By 2018, Safe Cities' scope still appeared broader than Skynet, which was apparently active in 16 cities, provinces, and municipalities, with 20 million cameras in use.[15]

However, another use of AI in Skynet may be data fusion. Data fusion is the key to how Chinese surveillance systems achieve "visualization" (可视化), "police informatization" (警务信息化), and ultimately "stability maintenance" (维稳) via regional "law enforcement, crime prevention, management, control, and service" (打防管控服).[16] For example, in July 2021, MIIT think tank China Electronics Standardization Institute (中国电子技术标准化研究院, CESI) spotlighted Chinese company Intellifusion, whose human-centered (以人为核心) DeepEye (深海) "multidimensional big data system" integrates video footage from Skynet, vehicle data, mobile phone data, Geographic Information Systems (GIS) data, and Wi-Fi and traffic data.[17] It uses big data tools such as its Tiantu (天图) engine for clustering and archiving, and performs relationship mapping with its Tianpu (天谱) engine. These tools are designed to provide early warnings (预警) to police, and provide a mode of surveillance that integrates images and codes (图码联侦).[18]

Sharp Eyes further pioneers data fusion

Sharp Eyes (雪亮工程) is one of the clearer examples of China's increasing reliance on AI. It is also one of China's latest programs, and the most direct example of an initiative that builds upon the goals and infrastructure used by all aforementioned programs. China's National Development and Reform Commission (国家发展和改革委员会, NDRC), the Central Political and Legal Affairs Commission, the MPS, and six other government bodies launched Sharp Eyes in 2015.[19] The program expanded on a predecessor program from circa 2011 called Village-to-Village Surveillance (村村通视频监控), which had begun integrating Skynet surveillance with civilian cameras, likely mostly non-facial recognition equipped at the time.[20] The apex of Sharp Eyes' goals was to provide full, real-time rural surveillance coverage by 2020.[21] Meeting that larger goal necessitated milestones such as integrating rural-urban surveillance, and alleviating pressure on police, who were sparse in rural areas.[22] It is worth noting that Sharp Eyes is not only a rural project: it also has projects in major metropolises such as Guangzhou and Beijing.[23]

Sharp Eyes' depends on AI for data fusion. While the exact nature of its algorithms is obscure, it is known that Sharp Eyes similarly pulls from a variety of data sources, including traditional CCTVs, facial recognition cameras, and cameras for vehicle and license plate recognition. When combining public and private video data, Sharp Eyes focuses on facial and other attributes from "key" locations, such as hospitals, schools, entertainment businesses, hotels, major road intersections, and storefronts.[24]

Sharp Eyes aggregates citizens' biometrics into "virtual identities" in databases using citizens' digital trails. These include media access control (MAC) addresses of electronic devices, phone numbers, and WeChat social media handles. Data fusion is used to combine this information with GIS data; the merged data are transmitted to "societal resource integration platforms."[25]

Sharp Eyes is interesting not just for its reliance on cutting-edge technologies, but because it explicitly calls for citizen involvement, a marked departure from other programs. Sharp Eyes' methods and even its name are directly inspired by the Cultural Revolution (1966–1976), when the phrase "The people have sharp eyes" (群众的眼睛是雪亮的) was born. Despite its association, Sharp Eyes was not piloted in Xinjiang, but rather Linyi (临沂) in Shandong Province. In Linyi, authorities installed upgraded cable boxes on citizens' televisions, allowing them to view surveillance feeds and report crimes via "one-button press" on special remote controls.[26] One propaganda slogan from the MPS proclaimed: "Remote control in hand, safety in heart" (遥控器在手里,安全感在心里).[27] These TV surveillance feeds became a nationwide staple.

Other examples from Linyi of community-oriented, technology-enabled surveillance are in mobile apps. One project—"Everyone is a Safety Officer" (人人都是平安员)—pushed video surveillance and public security information to citizens' phones. Similarly, the "Neighbors Help Each Other" (邻里互助) project established groups of households to patrol areas, and report public security incidents via their app.[28]

Although Sharp Eyes has made headway integrating advanced technologies, it is far from seamless. From 2020 onward, authorities have slated the program's next goals as improving data integration, since video surveillance data is still siloed, and there is no standard data mining approach.[29] Western analyses of Sharp Eyes also indicate that its first iteration was repeatedly dogged by technical difficulties and inconsistent standards.[30]

Data fusion in predictive policing

Data fusion also underlies predictive policing, or anticipatory and preventative law enforcement. China is pushing to make predictive policing a core aspect of its surveillance model, and that approach features in the nationwide Police Cloud (警务云) program and Xinjiang's Integrated Joint Operations Platform (一体化联合作战平台, IJOP).[31]

In 2015, the MPS launched Police Cloud, a program that linked provincial Police Cloud-computing centers and created a national Police Cloud database.[32] Data fusion is also present here: the initiative merges public and private data such as CCTV footage, medical history, supermarket memberships, IP addresses, social media usernames, delivery records, residential addresses, hotel stays, records of petitioning to the government, and biometric data. In Xuzhou (徐州), Jiangsu, for example, the police also purchase data from third parties.[33] Information is tied to confirmed identities and to government-issued ID cards.[34] Police Cloud helps track individuals' locations and personal relationships, "visualizing" correlations that police officers would not otherwise be able to detect, while claiming that it can predict future actions.[35] Authorities in Harbin claimed that they could anticipate terrorist events by training algorithms on prior data.[36]

These programs target all citizens, but the intensity is magnified for seven categories of "focus personnel." This label includes petitioners, those supposedly involved in terrorism, and persons "undermining social stability," interpreted to include Muslim Uyghur ethnic minorities, who are tracked nationwide.[37] This gives the Chinese police *carte blanche* to surveil and implement "stability maintenance" against individuals who don't conform to the authorities' notion of social stability. Predictive policing systems, for their part, put individuals in a legal gray zone: while citizens cannot be charged for crimes they are suspected of planning to commit, they can be charged for attempting to commit crimes.[38]

AI surveillance in Xinjiang

The northwestern region of Xinjiang has commanded global attention for its intensive levels of AI surveillance. The media narrative on Xinjiang often revolves around it being the "testbed" for Chinese surveillance technology but, as we have shown, many such programs were first fielded in other areas of China. However, it is undeniable that Xinjiang hosts China's highest concentration of repressive surveillance. These run the gamut from house stays by government officials, predictive policing, biometric surveillance under cover of public health, facial and voice recognition, and widespread "convenience police station" checkpoints.[39]

This physical and technological surveillance feeds into a network of nearly 1,200 internment camps, where between one and three million Uyghurs and other Turkic Muslims undergo forced political indoctrination, sterilization, and rape.[40] There is an ongoing debate on whether the Xinjiang crisis is "genocide." As of April 2021, the United States, Netherlands, Canada, and the United Kingdom have declared that genocide is occurring.[41] However, the likelihood of these charges reaching the International Court of Justice is dim.[42]

Within Xinjiang, the IJOP is a clear example of how AI-enhanced hybrid surveillance monitors and punishes what would typically be considered legal behavior.[43] The system remotely monitors excess electricity use, use of WhatsApp and virtual private networks (VPNs), or driving another's car. The platform leverages facial recognition from surveillance camera footage, license plate tracking, phone records, and social media posts.[44] One of its more invasive

technologies "three-dimensional portrait and integrated data doors" (三维人
像综合数据门), manufactured by state-owned defense conglomerate China
Electronics Technology Group,[45] looks like an airport metal detector, but can
perform facial recognition, scan ID cards, and pull electronic device identifier
numbers.[46] Authorities also use what they call the "anti-terrorism sword," which
plugs into phones and downloads contents for analysis.[47] By fusing data obtained
through remote and invasive technologies, authorities scrutinize individuals
with greater accuracy.

The IJOP digests data and sends push notifications to officers, granting them
the ability to pull aside someone walking through a data door or interrogate them
at home. This can result in detainment, imprisonment, or internment. For those
not put behind bars, the IJOP assigns threat levels to different individuals, placing
geofences around where they can and cannot go.[48] However, intensified surveillance of Uyghurs is not constrained within Xinjiang. The increasing nationwide
prevalence of Uyghur face detection means that Uyghurs are placed under a
microscope wherever they may be. The next section will examine how standards
concretize Uyghur surveillance across China.

Standards frameworks for biometric surveillance and data fusion

Chinese standards bodies are actively codifying national and provincial biometric surveillance approaches. In December 2017, the MPS released draft facial
recognition guidelines calling for Uyghur detection.[49] While for unknown
reasons it was never officially published, other standards have since called for
detecting catchall "personal attributes," including "ethnicity" and "skin color."[50]
In practice, this is the same as Uyghur detection, since police have requested
the capability in at least 12 nationwide projects.[51] Furthermore, major Chinese
companies, including Huawei, Hikvision, Dahua, Megvii, Alibaba, Tiandy, and
Sensetime, all claim to provide Uyghur detection.[52]

Separate from ethnicity recognition, Chinese standards bodies—including
the Biometric Recognition Technical Subcommittee (SAC/TC 28/SC37) and
the National Information Security Standardization Technical Committee (SAC/
TC 260)—have more broadly developed or are currently designing standards for
fingerprint, iris, and facial recognition, as well as biometric information protection requirements.[53]

Areas to watch: emotion recognition, social credit, and health surveillance

Widespread AI-based behavior modification is increasingly common in the three
buckets of emotion recognition, social credit, and health surveillance. These are
not tied to one specific public security program, but are nonetheless gaining
traction within China.

Emotion recognition

Emotion recognition is a type of facial analysis technology, which is distinct from facial recognition because it does not identify individuals. While it is seen in some quarters as a natural next step in the evolution of biometric technology applications, struggles to find genuine use cases and may not even be able to correctly detect emotions. The U.S. Transportation Security Authority's Screening Passengers by Observation Techniques (SPOT) program and Europe's iBorderCtrl were discredited for lack of a scientific basis.[54] Chinese scholars claim to have identified several use cases, including "early warning" (预警)[55] and some proposed public security adaptations at the Tibetan border, airports, railways, subways, and for customs inspections.[56] Underlying methods include detecting facial blood flow to determine emotional states, as well as detecting facial feature points to identify calmness, happiness, sadness, anger, surprise, fear, contempt, and disgust.[57]

Social credit

China's social credit system, seen from the government's perspective, is designed to guide persons and especially businesses to follow administrative laws and help establish credit in a traditionally unbanked country. The goal is to address long-standing issues such as food scandals, intellectual property infringement, failure to pay fines, and other types of anti-social activities. The main enforcement mechanism for this is not low scores but court blacklists.

The blacklist mechanism is what scholar Rogier Creemers calls "disproportionate sanctions": failure to comply with the law in one area leads to restrictions everywhere.[58] By limiting access to luxuries and certain comforts, the system induces people to follow administrative rules and avoid repeat offenses. On a more limited and local level, there is also a rewards system that fast tracks government documents processing.[59]

As with most large data integration systems, AI plays a part here; however, the social credit system is not at present an AI surveillance program. One example is its use in supporting business risk management by relying on financial technology (fintech) to identify qualified borrowers and approve loans.[60] In 2018, China Minsheng Bank began using machine learning methods to analyze risk data and screen potentially problematic customers based on training sets of past rule breakers and loan fraudsters.[61] In 2019, the State Council called for the use of AI and big data to create a unified and traceable suite of credit supervision data.[62]

Chinese technology companies such as Alibaba, Tencent's WeChat, and ByteDance's Douyin (抖音, the Chinese version of TikTok) work with the courts to publicize blacklists and solicit public support to locate offenders.[63] Other companies like voice recognition giant iFlytek have worked with China UnionPay and Huishang Bank to launch a "voiceprint + face" authentication process to prevent identity theft.[64]

Health surveillance

The COVID-19 pandemic has given the Chinese government a reason to expand its surveillance architecture. These technologies—including tracking apps, drone surveillance, cameras inside and outside houses, remote temperature scanning, and upgraded facial recognition to identify mask wearers—have gained legitimacy for public health purposes but have a significant risk of mission creep.[65]

For example, Alibaba's and Tencent's Health Code apps provide a color-coded estimate of health risk based on personal information, such as government-issued ID number, residence, and human interactions.[66] Source code analysis revealed that Health Code shares data with the MPS, raising concerns that the tracking will persist after the pandemic.[67] Some human rights activists question if the apps' denial of entry to some places is meant instead to maintain stability.[68]

Exporting AI surveillance technology worldwide

China's AI surveillance has gone global, aided by the Digital Silk Road (DSR) component of Xi Jinping's Belt and Road Initiative.[69] DSR promises positive support for telecommunications, cloud computing, e-commerce, and mobile payments—along with the usual dangers associated with AI-enabled surveillance.[70] Overall, the umbrella risk stemming from these digital projects is that they can erode national sovereignty, since governments buying the equipment may not have full control of the operations, management, digital infrastructure, or the data generated.[71]

Estimates for the spread of Chinese surveillance projects depend on which technologies are included. One estimate put the figure at 80 countries—democracies and repressive regimes alike.[72] The exports include data cameras and whole security solutions involving data fusion analytics that support multiple command and control centers.[73] In Latin America, Chinese companies have spurred the use of surveillance technology and primed the market for further expansion by offering equipment and software either at discounted prices or for free.[74]

Censorship is another area of concern. By one account, Huawei has nearly 2,000 middleboxes across 69 countries[75] that can monitor internet activity and block select websites, and in fact are doing so in 17 countries, including Oman and Burundi,[76] and at least 13 Safe Cities projects from Kenya to the Philippines.[77]

China's technological challenges

Despite the dominant media narrative that China's surveillance state is omnipresent and operates seamlessly, behind the scenes the reality is less perfect: it faces significant hurdles with compute limitations and information integration, which authorities have long called "information islands" (信息孤岛). One Chinese industry watcher noted: "The legacy of China's 'omnipotent government' is that it 'oversees too much,' behind which invisible entanglements of power and interests have formed."[78] In other words, swallowing such massive amounts of data may impede authorities' ability to improve urban governance and maintain its vision of stability. The Chinese surveillance state as it stands today is not effortlessly and automatically keeping the pulse on every individual. Rather, fundamental issues remain, including police inefficiency, unreliable and incomplete basic data, and incompatible datasets or systems.[79]

China's data integration approach also curtails Sharp Eyes' and other surveillance programs' effectiveness. The current approach inefficiently involves both horizontal and vertical axes, i.e. across departments and regions, and from the bottom up within the same bureaucratic entity.[80] *ChinaFile* analysis of procurement notices indicates that authorities want to improve integration in both directions,[81] for example, a citywide Sharp Eyes Video Sharing and Exchange Platform in Beijing, which would integrate footage from different departments. Similarly, by the end of 2017, Linyi had 4,611 comprehensive management information platforms (综治信息平台) to achieve "stability maintenance" among vertical and horizontal systems.[82] However, these efforts may result in duplicative data and more of the same issues that already plague the system.

Other reforms attempted to tackle the "information island" challenge structurally, including the 2017–18 reorganization of the People's Armed Police and passing of the 2017 National Intelligence Law, aimed at integrating disparate intelligence and national security authorities.[83] The 13th Five-year Plan for National Informatization (2016–2020) detailed problems with "information islands," and called for integrating systems across ministries and departments.[84] In 2017, the Party asked local governments to establish comprehensive information platforms, likely similar to those established under Sharp Eyes.[85]

Chinese portrayals of their surveillance state seem to gloss over computational limitations. For example, Chinese state media has claimed that Skynet can scan the entire Chinese population in one second with 99.8 percent accuracy.[86] However, vice president of Chinese AI facial recognition company Megvii said that the technology cannot run 24/7 and would need a supercomputer to viably scan more than 1,000 faces at a time.[87] Connecting to supercomputing capabilities over the cloud is also considered unviable from a security perspective, meaning that systems may have to rely on slower, limited options.[88] There are tradeoffs as well, and upgrading legacy video surveillance systems with face recognition often decreases image quality or creates lags in response times.[89]

Chinese surveillance giants Hikvision and Dahua are actively addressing retrofitting challenges. The two companies have the world's largest market shares in video surveillance and are subject to U.S. government usage bans.[90] Both are active in deep learning. Hikvision, which began exploring deep learning applications in 2012,[91] claims that its algorithms can achieve "comparable or even better-than-human pattern recognition accuracy and the ability to classify and recognize thousands of features."[92] Dahua has made similar boasts, stating that systems trained on deep learning algorithms can improve poorer image quality and allow wider angles for image intake.[93]

U.S. policy responses

Scholar Darren Byler estimates that nearly 1,400 Chinese companies were competing for lucrative contracts in Xinjiang by 2018—of these, around 1,000 were Xinjiang-based.[94] It is unclear how many surveillance companies operate nationwide.

A consistent policy throughout both the Trump and Biden administrations has been to take human rights into account in deciding whether to add Chinese firms and security organs to the Department of Commerce Bureau of Industry and Security's (BIS) Entity List. This effectively bars those entities' access to U.S. components. To date, BIS has listed 28 Chinese companies for human rights abuses in Xinjiang. These include video surveillance companies Dahua, Hikvision, Megvii, Yitu, Sensetime, and Yixin Science and Technology Co. Ltd., voice recognition firm iFlytek, and digital forensics firm Xiamen Meiya Pico Information Co. Ltd.[95]

A newer addition to the Entity List, Xinjiang-based Leon Technology, oversaw half of the Safe Cities projects in Urumqi by the end of 2017.[96] The firm also launched a joint venture with Sensetime called Tang Li Technology, increasing surveillance through "convenience police stations" in Kashgar and expanding monitoring to thousands of video access points in the city's rural areas.[97]

Global implications

Due to the opaque nature of supply chains, it is challenging to assess how well U.S. policy is working. It is hard to know if companies on the U.S. Department of Commerce's Entity List are sourcing alternatives, if they are continuing to access U.S. technologies through workarounds, or if homegrown R&D like those described with Dahua and Hikvision's deep learning efforts are succeeding. How to identify data fusion firms that belong on the Entity List is challenging too, as history shows that they do not advertise their roles in the system.

China also benefits immensely from U.S. AI firms lured by Chinese funding to bring product trials and R&D to China, facilitating technology transfer.[98] The China Security Industry Network has praised Intel and NVIDIA's graphics processing units (GPU)—the core of machine learning operations—for "inseparably cooperating" with Chinese security companies.[99] Chinese companies rely heavily on Seagate and Western Digital to provide surveillance hard drives, and more advanced drives that enable AI-powered surveillance used by Hikvision and Dahua.[100] *The Intercept* uncovered Oracle documents from 2010 to 2020 hinting at how to alleviate "information islands" by fusing police and social media data.[101] One document describes removing "barriers and stovepipes" to police "both the physical and digital worlds."

In 2020, the State Department released thorough guidance for companies' export considerations. However, the document is nonbinding, and the pull of commercial interests is hard to resist.[102] The promise of big payout and weak export enforcement mean that it may be difficult to stem the tide of U.S. surveillance inputs and technology exports. Nonetheless, public exposure is turning the tide, and it is increasingly hard for companies to claim ignorance of their involvement in China's surveillance state.

At the global scale, China promotes digital authoritarianism through its Belt and Road Initiative as well as through global norms and standards-setting at bodies such as the UN's International Telecommunications Union. Chinese standards proposals have been criticized for promoting policy recommendations over technical specifications, but they continue to make inroads in developing nations in Africa, the Middle East, and Asia.[103] However, neither companies in the United States nor from other democratic nations have proposed viable alternatives. Focusing media attention on Chinese data fusion practices and boosting R&D spending so companies can provide alternate global tech standards would be a step in the right direction.

In light of China's ongoing passage of vague security laws and propensity for ethically dubious AI programs with weak privacy protections, U.S. policymakers should consider the implications and moral hazards for American firms doing business in China. China's Personal Information Protection Law, its answer to the European Union's General Data Protection Regulation, went live in November 2021, with an anticipated widespread impact on foreign companies.[104] As China's AI surveillance undoubtedly benefits from U.S. AI technology, lawmakers should regularly evaluate how key technologies transferred to China are applied to avoid abetting China's vision of creating an omnipresent, even omnipotent, surveillance state.

Notes

1 Dahlia Peterson, "Foreign Technology and the Surveillance State" in Hannas and Tatlow, eds., *China's Quest for Foreign Technology: Beyond Espionage*, Routledge, 2021.
2 Maya Wang, "China's Dystopian Push to Revolutionize Surveillance," *The Washington Post*, August 18, 2017. See also Zhou Yongkang, "加强和改进社会管理促进社会稳定和和谐" (Strengthen and Improve Social Management to Promote Social Stability and Harmony), *People's Daily*, October 25, 2006.
3 Ryan Gallagher, "How U.S. Tech Giants Are Helping to Build China's Surveillance State," *The Intercept,* July 11, 2019; Li Yuan, "Learning China's Forbidden History, So They Can Censor It," *The New York Times*, January 2, 2019; Samm Sacks and Paul Triolo, "Shrinking Anonymity in Chinese Cyberspace," *Lawfare*, September 25, 2017; "China: Police DNA Database Threatens Privacy," *Human Rights Watch*, May 15, 2017; Paul Mozur, "Inside China's Dystopian Dreams: A.I., Shame and Lots of Cameras," *The New York Times*, July 8, 2018; Lisbeth, "White Paper Outlines Potential Uses of AI," *China Digital Times,* November 19, 2018.
4 "How a Chinese AI Giant Made Chatting—and Surveillance—Easy," by Mara Hvistendahl, *Wired*, May 18, 2020.
5 "中国安装了1.76 亿个监控摄像头, 这市场还在增长" (China Has Installed 176 Million Surveillance Cameras and the Market Is Still Expanding), *Q Daily*, November 21, 2017;"旷视(Face)亮相中国安防服务联盟人脸识别打造立体安防"(Megvii(Face++)Debuts at China Security Service Alliance, Face Recognition Creates Three-dimensional Security) 科学中国 (*Science China*), August 5, 2016, https://web.archive.org/web/20200605002338/https://www.sohu.com/a/109282144_313468.

6 Greg Walton, "China's Golden Shield: Corporations and the Development of Surveillance Technology in the People's Republic of China," International Centre for Human Rights and Development, 2001.

7 Xu Xu, "To Repress or To Co-opt? Authoritarian Control in the Age of Digital Surveillance," *American Journal of Political Science*, 65.2, April 2021, pp. 309–325.

8 "金盾工程数据库包括12亿多中国人的信息" (The Golden Shield Project Database Includes Information on More Than 1.2 Billion Chinese), 博讯新闻 (*Boxun News*), April 9, 2006, https://web.archive.org/web/20160305214310/http://www.boxun.com/news/gb/china/2006/04/200604091432.shtml; "China: The Public Security Bureau (PSB) Golden Shield Project, including implementation and effectiveness; Policenet, including areas of operation; level and effectiveness of information sharing by the authorities (2010-February 2014)," Immigration and Refugee Board of Canada, March 7, 2014, https://www.refworld.org/docid/543ba3824.html.

9 "从源起到未来安防企业共话"平安城市"" (From its Origins to the Future: Security Companies Discuss "Safe Cities") 千家网 (*Qianjia*), May 31, 2011, https://archive.vn/CSixz.

10 "平安城市发展历程回顾及未来发展方向展望" (Development History of Safe Cities and Prospects for Future Development) 千家网 (*Qianjia*), March 20, 2017, https://web.archive.org/web/20200515224631/http://www.qianjia.com/html/2017-03/20_267576.html; "雪亮工程、平安城市、天网工程这三者之间有什么不同" (The Difference between Sharp Eyes, Safe Cities and Skynet), *ASMag*, April 11, 2018.

11 "平安城市" (Safe Cities) 百度百科, (*Baidu Encyclopedia*), accessed May 5, 2020, https://baike.baidu.com/item/平安城市/7737245.

12 Dahlia Peterson, "Designing Alternatives to China's Repressive Surveillance State," Georgetown University, Center for Security and Emerging Technology, October 2020; Zhang Zihan, "Beijing's Guardian Angels?" *Global Times*, October 10, 2012.

13 "天网工程规划大纲" (Skynet Project Planning Outline), accessed May 15, 2020. "天网工程是什么? 有什么作用?" (What Is Skynet and What Is Its Purpose?) 第一监控 (*No. 1 Surveillance Blog*), November 3, 2018.

14 Zhao Yusha, "'Sky Net' Tech Fast Enough to Scan Chinese Population in One Second: Report," *Global Times*, March 25, 2018.

15 Peterson, "Designing"; Zhao Yusha, "'Sky Net' Tech"; Chen Shixian and Li Zhen, "'天网'网什么" (What Does Skynet Capture?) 人民周刊 (*People's Weekly*), November 20, 2017, https://web.archive.org/web/20200515220622/http://paper.people.com.cn/rmzk/html/2017-11/20/content_1825998.htm. For instance, the number of video surveillance probes in Wuhan alone has reached 1 million. See "What Is Skynet and What Is Its Purpose?".

16 Dahlia Peterson, "How China Harnesses Data Fusion to Make Sense of Surveillance Data," Brookings TechStream, September 23, 2021.

17 "人工智能标准化白皮书 (2021版)" (*Artificial Intelligence Standardization White Paper (2021 Edition)*), China Electronics Standardization Institute (中国电子技术标准化研究院), July 19, 2021.

18 Ibid.

19 "全国雪亮工程建设综述" (A Summary of Sharp Eyes Construction), 中国安防行业网 (*China Security Industry Network*), October 13, 2017. See the text of Sharp Eyes plan at "关于加强公共安全视频监控建设联网应用工作的若干意见" (Several Opinions on Strengthening the Construction of Public Security Video Surveillance Network Applications), National Development and Reform Commission, May 6, 2015.

20 "'雪亮工程'农村安防监控建设项目你知多少" (How Much Do You Know about the Construction of the 'Sharp Eyes' Rural Security Monitoring Project?), 中国安防展览网 (*China Security Exhibition Network*), December 19, 2016.

21 "Several Opinions on Strengthening."

22 "安防行业迎来雪亮工程重大机遇" (The Security Industry Welcomes Major Opportunities from Sharp Eyes), 中国安防展览网 (*China Security Exhibition Network*), May 23, 2018. See also "Several Opinions on Strengthening," Dahlia Peterson and Josh Rudolph, "Sharper Eyes: Surveilling the Surveillers (Part 1)," *China Digital Times*, September 9, 2019.
23 Peterson and Rudolph, "Sharper Eyes."
24 "'雪亮'工程解决方案," ("Sharp Eyes" Engineering Solutions), 北京瑞光极远数码科技有限公司 (Beijing Ruiguang Jiyuan Digital Technology Co., Ltd.) accessed June 7, 2021, https://archive.ph/6N6vi.
25 Jessica Batke and Mareike Ohlberg, "State of Surveillance," *ChinaFile*, October 30, 2020.
26 Peterson and Rudolph, "Sharper Eyes."
27 Ibid. The full slogan was: "老百姓把遥控器握在手里, 安全感落在了心里." See "社会治安防控织密'人防网'让群众参与进来越来越多'朝阳群众'守护平安不打烊" (Prevention and Control Weaves "Civil Defense Network" to Let the Masses Participate More in "Chaoyang Masses" Style Safety), MPS, https://archive.vn/QsWW3V.
28 Peterson and Rudolph, "Sharper Eyes."
29 "雪亮工程步入最后一年, 建设现状如何?" (Sharp Eyes Is Entering Its Final Year, What Is Its Construction Status?), 千家网 (*Qianjia*), February 24, 2020.
30 Charles Rollet, "China Public Video Surveillance Guide: From Skynet to Sharp Eyes," IVPM, June 14, 2018.
31 "China: Police 'Big Data' Systems Violate Privacy, Target Dissent," *Human Rights Watch,* November 19, 2017; "How Mass Surveillance Works in Xinjiang, China," *Human Rights Watch*, May 2, 2019.
32 "China: Police 'Big Data.'"
33 Ibid.
34 Echo Huang, "What Do China's Police Collect on Citizens in Order to Predict Crime? Everything," *Quartz*, November 20, 2017; "China: Police 'Big Data.'"
35 For example, the Tianjin Police Cloud, which (at the time of writing) HRW identified as the largest project at 27 million RMB (3.9 million USD) claimed that it could monitor "people of certain ethnicity," "people who have extreme thoughts," "petitioners who are extremely (persistent)," and "Uyghurs from South Xinjiang." See "China: Police 'Big Data.'"
36 Batke and Ohlberg, "State of Surveillance."
37 "China: Police 'Big Data.'"
38 Justin Lee, "Chinese Facial Recognition Firm Developing AI to Predict Crimes," *Biometric Update*, July 25, 2017; Peterson, "Designing."
39 Bethany Allen-Ebrahimian, "Exposed: China's Operating Manuals for Mass Internment and Arrest by Algorithm," *International Consortium of Investigative Journalists,* November 24, 2019; "China's Algorithms of Repression"; "Minority Region Collects DNA from Millions," *Human Rights Watch*, December 13, 2017; Darren Byler, "China's Nightmare Homestay," *ChinaFile* (blog) on *Foreign Policy*, October 26, 2018; Isobel Cockerell, "Inside China's Massive Surveillance Operation," *Wired*, May 9, 2019.
40 James Millward and Dahlia Peterson, "China's System of Oppression in Xinjiang: How It Developed and How to Curb It," Brookings Institution, September 2020; Allen-Ebrahimian, "Exposed"; Sheena Chestnut Greitens, Myunghee Lee, and Emir Yazici, "Counterterrorism and Preventive Repression," *International Security* 44.3, 2019, pp. 9–47; Zamira Rahim, "Prisoners in China's Xinjiang Concentration Camps Subjected to Gang Rape and Medical Experiments, Former Detainee Says," *The Independent*, October 22, 2019; "China Cuts Uighur Births with IUDs, Abortion, Sterilization," *Associated Press,* June 29, 2020.
41 "Uyghurs: MPs State Genocide Is Taking Place in China," *BBC*, April 23, 2021.
42 Eva Dou and Lily Kuo, "China Scrubs Evidence of Xinjiang Clampdown amid 'Genocide' Debate," *Washington Post,* March 17, 2021.
43 "How Mass Surveillance Works."

44 "China's Algorithms of Repression," *Human Rights Watch*, May 1, 2019.

45 Ibid.

46 Ibid.

47 Yael Grauer, "Revealed: Massive Chinese Police Database," *The Intercept*, January 29, 2021.

48 "How Mass Surveillance Works."

49 Charles Rollet, "China Government Spreads Uyghur Analytics across China," IPVM, November 25, 2019.

50 Conor Healy, "Uyghur Surveillance & Ethnicity Detection Analytics in China," Testimony to the Uyghur Tribunal, August 20, 2021, https://uyghurtribunal.com/wp-content/uploads/2021/09/Conor-Healy.pdf.

51 Rollet, "China Government Spreads."

52 Healy, "Uyghur Surveillance."

53 CESI, "Artificial Intelligence Standardization."

54 Vidushi Marda and Shazeda Ahmed, "Emotional Entanglement: China's Emotion Recognition Market and Its Implications for Human Rights," Article 19, January 2021.

55 Ibid.

56 Ibid.

57 Ibid, p. 22.

58 Interview with Rogier Creemers, "The Social Credit System – Part III," Asia Society.

59 Mary Duan, "HAI Fellow Shazeda Ahmed: Understanding China's Social Credit System," Stanford University Human-Centered Artificial Intelligence," August 31, 2020.

60 "'人工智能+信用建设,' 信用算力全面启动双轮驱动战略," ('Artificial intelligence + Credit Construction,' Credit Calculation Power Fully Launched the Two-Wheel Drive Strategy), *China Daily*, March 8, 2019.

61 "高科技为社会诚信构筑新堤防线:人工智能和大数据成重要手段," (High-tech Builds a New Defensive Perimeter for Social Integrity: Artificial Intelligence and Big Data Become Important Means), 东方财富网 (*Eastmoney*), July 4, 2018.

62 PRC State Council, "Guiding Opinions of the General Office of the State Council on Accelerating the Construction of the Social Credit System and Building a New Credit-based Supervisory Mechanism."

63 Duan, "HAI Fellow Shazeda Ahmed."

64 *Eastmoney*, "High-tech builds."

65 Arjun Kharpal, "Use of Surveillance to Fight Coronavirus Raises Concerns about Government Power after Pandemic Ends," *CNBC*, March 26, 2020; Nectar Gan, "China Is Installing Surveillance Cameras Outside People's Front Doors ... and Sometimes inside Their Homes," *CNN Business*, April 28, 2020; Masha Borak, "Chinese Police Now Have AI Helmets for Temperature Screening," *Abacus* (blog) on *South China Morning Post*, February 28, 2020; Martin Pollard, "Even Mask-wearers Can be ID'd, China Facial Recognition Firm Says," Reuters, March 9, 2020.

66 Maya Wang, "China: Fighting COVID-19 with Automated Tyranny," *The Diplomat*, April 1, 2020.

67 Paul Mozur, Raymond Zhong, and Aaron Krolik, "In Coronavirus Fight, China Gives Citizens a Color Code, with Red Flags," *The New York Times*, March 1, 2020.

68 "多位内地維權人士「健康碼」突變紅、程式異常被禁赴北京上海," (Many Mainland Human Rights Activists Banned from Going to Beijing and Shanghai Due to 'Health Codes' Suddenly Turning Red and Program Anomalies") 立場新聞 (*The Stand News*), November 7, 2021.

69 Joshua Kurlantzick, "Assessing China's Digital Silk Road: A Transformative Approach to Technology Financing or a Danger to Freedoms?" Council on Foreign Relations, December 18, 2020.

70 Ibid.

71 Danielle Cave et al., "Mapping China's Tech Giants," Australian Strategic Policy Institute, April 18, 2019.

72 Sheena Greitens, "Dealing with Demand for China's Global Surveillance Exports" (The Brookings Institution, April 2020).

73 Ibid; Cave et al., "Mapping."

74 Gaspar Pisanu and Verónica Arroyo et al., "Surveillance Tech in Latin America Made Abroad, Deployed at Home," *Access Now*, August 10, 2021; Leo Schwartz, "Major Surveillance Firms Are 'Gifting' Tools to Find a Foothold in Latin America," *Rest of World*, August 12, 2021.

75 Valentin Weber and Vasilis Ververis, "China's Surveillance State: A Global Project," Top 10 VPN, August 3, 2021.

76 Ibid.

77 Ibid.

78 "数字化公共治理:重新编码的社会秩序" (Digitalized Public Governance: A Recoded Social Order), 钛禾产业观察 (*Taihe Industry Observer*), translated by Jeffrey Ding, May 19, 2021.

79 Maya Wang, "China's Bumbling Police State," *The Wall Street Journal*, December 26, 2018.

80 Huirong Chen and Sheena Greitens, "Information Capacity and Social Order: the Local Politics of Information Integration in China," *Governance*, 2021.

81 Batke and Ohlberg, "State of Surveillance."

82 "山东临沂创新实施'雪亮工程'成为综治亮点," (Linyi, Shandong's Innovative Implementation of 'Sharp Eyes' Has Become a Highlight in Comprehensive Management), 国安防行业网 (*China Security Industry Network*), October 13, 2017, https://archive.ph/ccKDz.

83 Chen and Greitens, "Information capacity."

84 Ibid.

85 Ibid.

86 Zhao Yusha, "'Sky Net' Tech."

87 Peterson, "Designing"; Harrison Jacobs, "China's 'Big Brother' Surveillance Technology Isn't Nearly as All-seeing as the Government Wants You to Think," *Business Insider,* July 15, 2018.

88 Jacobs, "China's 'Big Brother'."

89 Other issues include non-cooperative users, camera placement, and low/changing lighting conditions. See Eifeh Strom, "Facing Challenges in Face Recognition: One-to-One vs. One-to-Many," *ASMag*, September 19, 2016.

90 John Honovich, "Ban of Dahua and Hikvision Is Now US Gov Law," *IPVM*, August 13, 2018.

91 Wensan Fang, "2019年中国AI+安防行业发展研究报告" (2019 China AI+Security Industry Development Research Report), 安防展览网 (*Security Exhibition Network*), May 10, 2019.

92 Hikvision staff also claim that this is due to their "own excellent algorithm development team and using the most powerful GPUs in our computer platforms." See William Pao, "Applying Deep Learning to Facial Recognition Cameras," *ASMag,* February 21, 2018.

93 William Pao, "Applying deep learning."

94 Darren Byler, "The Global Implications of 'Re-education' Technologies in Northwest China," Washington, DC: Center for Global Policy, June 8, 2020; Danielle Cave, Fergus Ryan and Vicky Xiuzhong Xu, "Mapping More of China's Tech Giants: AI and Surveillance," *ASPI*, November 28, 2019.

95 AFP, "China's Blacklisted AI Firms: What You Should Know," *Bangkok Post,* October 13, 2019.

96 This includes one of the 11 Dahua and Hikvision Xinjiang projects highlighted by IPVM worth 1.2 billion USD. Leon was one of the awardees alongside Dahua in the Qiemo Safe County project in 2017. See Charles Rollet, "Dahua and Hikvision Win over $1 Billion in Government-backed Projects in Xinjiang," *IPVM*, April 23, 2018; Jeffrey Ding, "Complicit - China's AI Unicorns and the Securitization of Xinjiang," *ChinAI*, September 23, 2018.

97 Jeffrey Ding, op. cit.
98 "Harvard University-Backed Startup BrainCo Inc. Gets the Biggest Purchase Order in Brain Machine Interface (BMI) Industry," BrainCo, Inc., May 18, 2017.
99 Peterson, "Foreign Technology."
100 Ibid.
101 Mara Hvistendahl, "How Oracle Sells Repression in China," *The Intercept*, February 18, 2021.
102 Bureau of Democracy, Human Rights, and Labor, "Guidance on Implementing the UN Guiding Principles for Transactions Linked to Foreign Government End-Users for Products or Services with Surveillance Capabilities," U.S. Department of State, September 30, 2020.
103 Peterson, "Designing"; Meng Jing, "Chinese Tech Companies Are Shaping UN Facial Recognition Standards, According to Leaked Documents," *South China Morning Post*, December 2, 2019.
104 Anna Gamvros and Lianying Wang, "PIPL: A Game Changer for Companies in China," Norton Rose Fulbright, August 24, 2021.

Bibliography

Allen-Ebrahimian, Bethany. "Exposed: China's Operating Manuals for Mass Internment and Arrest by Algorithm," International Consortium of Investigative Journalists, November 24, 2019.
Batke, Jessica and Mareike Ohlberg, "State of Surveillance," *ChinaFile*, October 30, 2020.
Bureau of Democracy, Human Rights, and Labor, "Guidance on Implementing the UN Guiding Principles for Transactions Linked to Foreign Government End-Users for Products or Services with Surveillance Capabilities," U.S. Department of State, September 30, 2020.
Byler, Darren. "The Global Implications of 'Re-education' Technologies in Northwest China," Center for Global Policy, June 8, 2020.
Chen, Huirong and Sheena Greitens, "Information Capacity and Social Order: The Local Politics of Information Integration in China," *Governance*, 2021.
China Electronics Standardization Institute, "Artificial Intelligence Standardization White Paper (2021 Edition)," July 2021.
Healy, Conor. "Uyghur Surveillance & Ethnicity Detection Analytics in China," Testimony to the Uyghur Tribunal, August 20, 2021.
Marda, Vidushi and Shazeda Ahmed, "Emotional Entanglement: China's Emotion Recognition Market and Its Implications for Human Rights," Article 19, January 2021.
Millward, James and Dahlia Peterson, "China's System of Oppression in Xinjiang: How It Developed and How to Curb it," Brookings Institution, September 2020.
Peterson, Dahlia and Josh Rudolph, "Sharper Eyes: Surveilling the Surveillers (Part 1)," *China Digital Times*, September 9, 2019.
Peterson, Dahlia. "Designing Alternatives to China's Repressive Surveillance State," Georgetown University, Center for Security and Emerging Technology, October 2020.
Peterson, Dahlia. "Foreign Technology and the Surveillance State" in William C. Hannas and Didi Kirsten-Tatlow, eds., *China's Quest for Foreign Technology: Beyond Espionage*, Routledge, London and New York, 2021, pp. 241–257.
Peterson, Dahlia. "How China Harnesses Data Fusion to Make Sense of Surveillance Data," TechStream (blog) on Brookings Institution, September 23, 2021.

PRC National Development and Reform Commission, "关于加强公共安全视频监控建设联网应用工作的若干意见" (Several Opinions on Strengthening the Construction of Public Security Video Surveillance Network Applications), May 6, 2015.

PRC State Council, "国务院办公厅关于加快推进社会信用体系建设构建以信用为基础的新型监管机制的指导意见" (Guiding Opinions of the General Office of the State Council on Accelerating the Construction of the Social Credit System and Building a New Credit-based Supervisory Mechanism), SC 35, 2019.

Rollet, Charles. "China Public Video Surveillance Guide: From Skynet to Sharp Eyes," IPVM, June 14, 2018.

PART V

AI hazards and safety

13

Future paths and challenges

Huey-Meei Chang and William C. Hannas

China's plan to lead the world in artificial intelligence (AI) by 2030, described in its 2017 "New Generation AI Development Plan,"[1] lays the groundwork for "general artificial intelligence" (通用人工智能),[2] while calling for a merger (混合) of AI and human intelligence.[3] The two goals, while aspirational, are shared by many Chinese scientists, and by state institutes intent on realizing these prizes early enough for a "first-mover advantage."[4] Accordingly, this chapter focuses on China's work in technical areas that support these related projects:

- China's traditional and brain-inspired AI research aimed at a more general-purpose AI that overcomes the time, cost, and capability limits of today's "narrow" AI, and
- China's efforts to enhance human cognition by merging with AI computational resources, achieved through brain-computer interfaces (BCI) and implanted chips.

The former approaches what is known in English as *"artificial general intelligence"* (AGI). The latter ends in "cognitive offloading" or "distributed cognition" (分布式认知).[5] Both are potential springboards for *superintelligence* (超级智能). We also examine China's *neuromorphic chips* (类脑芯片), which some see as enablers of both theoretical outcomes.

Pathways to advanced AI

More than a decade ago, AI pioneer Eliezer Yudkowsky issued a warning as pertinent now as it was then, namely,

> By far the greatest danger of Artificial Intelligence is that people conclude too early that they understand it.[6]

DOI: 10.4324/9781003212980-18

Leaving aside its technical complexity, disagreements on AI's definition and scope, sundry notions of "intelligence," and our own profound ignorance, Yudkowsky argues that it is difficult to set aside human biases to characterize objectively AI's state and potential. How then can we assess the paths China may take, by will or happenstance, in fulfilling its goal of AI dominance?

While acknowledging the difficulty of forecasting, we note that progress in AI—in China or anywhere—is a function of dynamics guiding the discipline since it was conceived, i.e. the drive to *build smarter AI*. "Smarter" implies breaking through the limits of today's narrow AI, which addresses discrete tasks only, to competence in many complex tasks executed by humans.

A glimpse at the future may also be found in what China's leaders, program directors, and scientists plausibly claim to be doing.[7] And indeed, speculation over China's intent to work toward general AI, fueled by statements in 2019 by top scientists,[8] was validated in 2020 by the announcement of a "Beijing Institute for General Artificial Intelligence" and other projects underway elsewhere (see below).

Based on these two measures—AI's inherent dynamic and China's declared intent—our focus will be on Chinese efforts to create advanced AI, understood in China as "AGI" or better. We appreciate that bundling these vectors under one ill-defined term will not by itself shed light on how (and when) these capabilities will be realized. What follows then is a summation of expert views offered as an aid toward understanding China's particular choices.

There are (at least) five principled ways to build "advanced" (human or above) AI[9]:

1. You can try to understand intelligence, i.e. identify its salient features and create functionally equivalent machine algorithms.[10] This is the majority viewpoint, associated with traditional ML/deep learning.[11] Its dependencies are better algorithms, access to big data, and faster compute cycles.

2. Or you can reverse engineer a human brain—its complete physical structure—on the assumption that what emerges is, *ipso facto*, human intelligence,[12] in which case the three dependencies for option 1 are less of an issue. This "neuromorphic" or brain-imitative approach derives function from structure and is the province of "connectomics."[13]

3. One can, in theory, brute force the emergence of human-like intelligence, as Shulman and Bostrom put it, by running "genetic algorithms on computers that are sufficiently fast to recreate on a human timescale the same amount of cumulative optimization power that the relevant processes of natural selection instantiated throughout our evolutionary past."[14]

4. A fourth option plays on our understanding of intelligence.[15] There is no reason to view intelligence as uniquely human.[16] Any "de novo" AI substantially able "to achieve goals in a wide range of environments"[17] would qualify, even if it lacks anthropomorphic elements, such as affect, consciousness, and a theory of mind.

5. Finally, a robust lash-up with computational resources through seamless BCI positions both elements, human and machine, to achieve (overachieve) human goals. Embedded nanoscale chips and high-throughput cognitive "offloading" (partial brain emulation) are hypothetical approaches.

These categories are prototypes culled from the AI literature to illustrate possibilities. In practice, they merge and their boundaries are disputed. Yudkowsky, for example, treats whole brain emulation as outside the AI family,[18] while Hansen views it as the paramount approach to AGI.[19] Baum sees WBEs as "computational entities with general intelligence" and hence within the AI pale,[20] and so on.

Another schema, vetted by China's practitioners,[21] identifies three distinct research areas that lead potentially to advanced general intelligence: brain-inspired artificial intelligence (BI-AI, 类脑智能), connectomics (人脑连接组) or "brain mapping," and BCI (脑机接口).[22] Within BI-AI, three levels of "inspiration" are distinguishable, namely:

- Inspiration by default. Since "intelligence" derives from biological brains, efforts to emulate intelligence on artificial platforms are brain-inspired.[23] AI concepts such as neural nets and connection weights are analogs of these natural phenomena.
- De facto inspiration. Cognitive behavior is simulated by computational algorithms. The "inspiration" is ad hoc and owes less to detailed modeling of brain processes and more to equating machine learning successes with macro-level brain operations.
- Inspiration by design. Accurate mathematical descriptions of real brain processes are run on computers to reproduce the behavior. Functional equivalence is eschewed in favor of neural models that correspond directly to the brain's biological computations.

This schema covers four of the prototypes given above. The remaining category—AGI through genetic (evolutionary) algorithms—is also a topic of research in China and worldwide, if not in the comprehensive manner described by Shulman and Bostrom, then as the product of deliberate efforts to expand the domains within which AI functions.[24]

We cite these multiple pathways to emphasize that no one knows through what venue "AGI" may be realized,[25] how and when someone will achieve it, or for that matter what "it" is, as there are no precedents,[26] no "metrics for measuring progress toward such ambitious forecasting targets,"[27] nor a clear break between advanced AI and what meets the AGI threshold.[28]

Nor is there a consensus among experts whether advanced AI will be an unmitigated boon, our final curse, or simply another milestone in human progress. Whether AI achieves parity, by some common measure, with human intellect, however, is hardly the end of it, as it is highly *unlikely* that intelligence will stall at the human level. On this point, there is widespread agreement:

- "(T)here are no current grounds for expecting AI to spend an extended period in the Homo sapiens sapiens range of general intelligence."[29]
- "The human level is a minor pit stop on the way to the highest level of intelligence allowed by physics, and there is plenty of room above us."[30]
- "(H)umanity occupies only a tiny portion of the design space of possible minds. This space is much larger than what we are familiar with from the human example."[31]

As the indomitable Eliezer Yudkowsky put it:

> It would be the height of biological chauvinism to assert that, while it is possible for humans to build an AI and improve this AI to the point of roughly human-equivalent general intelligence, this same human-equivalent AI can never master the (humanly solved) programming problem of making improvements to the AI's source code.[32]

In fact, there is less disagreement on when *superintelligence* ("any intellect that greatly exceeds the cognitive performance of humans in virtually all domains of interest")[33] will arrive than human-level AI itself. While estimates for AGI vary from years later to never,[34] the leap to artificial superintelligence (ASI) is measured in months, days, or even seconds.

ASI was conceived by Irving J. Good in talks at UCLA in 1962 as an "intelligence explosion," a self-bootstrapping process in which an AI bright enough to manipulate its own code can redesign itself to be more capable again and again.[35] This recursive pathway is joined by other scenarios: BCI-enhanced brain augmentation,[36] computing "overhang," namely, computing power increases faster than the software able to emulate human intelligence, so when advanced AI is realized, it runs everywhere (explosively),[37] etc.

Detailed speculation on what *that* outcome portends is beyond our present scope but its import cannot be overstated.[38] Bostrom, as usual, saw it first—the following passage is from a section titled "Repressive totalitarian global regime" penned two decades ago:

> (O)ne can imagine that an intolerant world government, based perhaps on mistaken religious or ethical convictions, is formed, is stable, and decides to realize only a very small part of all the good things a posthuman world could contain. Such a world government could conceivably be formed by a small group of people if they were in control of the first superintelligence and could select its goals. If the superintelligence arises suddenly and becomes powerful enough to take over the world, the posthuman world may reflect only the idiosyncratic values of the owners or designers of this superintelligence.[39]

Or as Ross Andersen in an interview with AI luminary Zeng Yi (曾毅) warned more recently:

> An authoritarian state with enough processing power could force the makers of such software to feed every blip of a citizen's neural activity into a government database.[40]

Concerns such as these motivate this book's concluding chapters and form the impetus for much of our research.

China's computational approaches to advanced AI

Whether China—or someone in China—achieves "AGI," what that means for the world, and how other countries can hedge against it are subjects worth considering. The more one looks at China's AI development, the more one appreciates the possibility. Standard bromides meant to dispel anxiety, e.g. other countries spend more on research, China lacks the creativity, the threat is light-years away, must be weighed against the uncomfortable truths that this authoritarian state does not need to be at the cusp to access cutting-edge research,[41] does not need to spend through the nose to make decisive gains,[42] and does not share the (public-facing) Western view of AGI's late arrival but sees it happening much sooner.[43]

In terms of number of entities pursuing an AGI agenda, China ranks second only to the United States, according to Seth Baum's painstaking 2017 "first-ever survey of active AGI R&D projects,"[44] updated in 2020.[45] Baum initially credited the United States with 23 programs to China's six[46] based on the open-source record—although we hasten to point out that every foreign technology program of significance has researchers who are Chinese, co-author with Chinese, or whose work in some way is accessible to China due to scientific collaboration and Beijing's tireless efforts to extract IP from its owners "by various means" (以多种方式).

Here is Baum's inventory of China's (known) AGI programs prior to November 2017, when his first paper was published, plus two he placed outside the pale:

- Tencent AI Lab, the AI group of Tencent
- Baidu Research, an AI research group within Baidu
- China Brain Project, led by Mu-Ming Poo (Pu Muming)
- Research Center for Brain-Inspired Intelligence
- SingularityNET, an open AI platform led by Ben Goertzel
- Artificial Brain Laboratory (Hugo de Garis of Xiamen Univ.) ("inactive")
- NARS, led by Pei Wang of Temple University (our attribution)

The first five are active "AGI" programs, then and now: Baidu and Tencent are known players. Pu Muming (蒲慕明) manages several BI-AI projects and openly

CNKI Papers Per Year - AGI

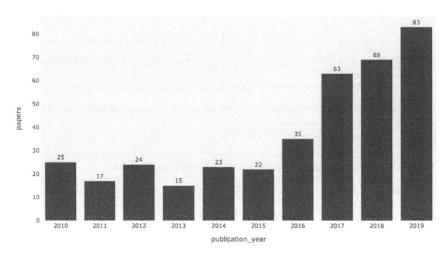

supports AGI.[47] The Research Center for Brain-Inspired Intelligence (类脑智能
研究中心) is a component of the CAS Institute of Automation (中科院自动化研究
所)—a major AGI center.[48] Goertzel's work was reassigned to "Netherlands" in
the 2020 survey with China as a "partner." Although Hugo de Garis' project is
inactive, Xiamen is a major outpost for related AI research and our inclination is
to include it.[49] Pei Wang's (王培) research is connected with China initiatives so
the attribution is a toss-up.[50]

Both surveys are dated.[51] Moreover, the 2017 survey was completed *before*
advanced AI took off in China. Figure 13.1 shows Chinese academic papers on
the AGI theme in the China National Knowledge Infrastructure (CNKI) database between 2010 and 2019. The spike in production that began in 2017 coincides with the first survey's cut-off date, and would not have been captured in
any case as there is no indication that Baum's team examined the Chinese record.

Our study of recent Chinese sources adds some institutions to the count.[52]
Since there is no clear line between advanced AI and "sufficiently advanced AI"
(AGI euphemism), this addendum is almost certainly conservative.[53] We judge
the following to be reliable:

From the "BATH" group of AI powerhouses—Baidu, Alibaba, Tencent, and
Huawei—we add Huawei to the list on the basis of an agreement signed in 2021
with the CAS Institute of Automation, a known AGI actor, to build a "general artificial intelligence" (通用人工智能) platform in Wuhan.[54] Baum looked
at Alibaba in 2017 and found "no indications of AGI projects"[55]; in November
2021, Alibaba's Dharma Institute (达摩院) announced a ten trillion-parameter
"Multi-Modality to Multi-Modality Multitask Mega-transformer" (M6) AI

system, reportedly surpassing both Google and Microsoft's achievements, and billed as the company's "large-scale AGI model."[56]

Tsinghua professors Tang Jie (唐杰) and Liu Jia (刘嘉), and Peking University's Institute for Artificial Intelligence vice-chair Huang Tiejun (黄铁军), besides their advocacy of AGI also have in common leading roles in the Beijing Academy of Artificial Intelligence (北京智源人工智能研究院, BAAI), as clear an example of an AGI-oriented institution as can be found. Here is some recent reporting:

- "In order to explore the possibility of *strong artificial intelligence* (强人工智能), the Zhiyuan Research Institute[57] will successively develop Shenji (神机) 1 (a high-precision fine neural network simulation system), Shenji 2 (large-scale spiking neural networks), and Shenji 3 (a high-precision large-scale *general-purpose* intelligent simulation system) and other simulation platforms."[58]
- "BAAI is not satisfied with realizing general artificial intelligence through the path of deep learning. In the past year, the organization has formed teams focusing on other important directions such as reinforcement learning and brain-inspired computing."[59]
- "BAAI is the home of Wudao (悟道) 2.0, made public in June 2021. It claims to have 1.75 trillion parameters, surpassing Google's 1.6 trillion… The computer is said to be 'close to breaking' a number of Turing tests."[60] Its aim is to "enable machines to think like humans and move toward general AI," according to builder Tang Jie."[61]

Finally, as part of this trajectory, the Ministry of Science and Technology (MOST) and the Beijing city government in 2020 stood up a "Beijing Institute for General Artificial Intelligence" (北京通用人工智能研究院, BIGAI) headed by returned UCLA professor and renowned AI scientist Zhu Songchun (朱松纯, see Box 13.1),[62] in concert with Peking University's Institute for Artificial Intelligence[63] and Tsinghua University's own (planned) AGI institute.[64] The facility will be staffed by 1,000 researchers drawn from China and, as usual, "all over the world."[65] We predict that the move will lead to clones, first in Shanghai and then in provincial centers.[66]

A few Chinese "AGI" start-ups are listed here for completeness. No attempt was made to be exhaustive or to verify particular claims:

- Cyntek (辛特科技) headquartered in Singapore with branches in Beijing and Shanghai is "committed to the theoretical exploration and application of AGI." The company claims to have "an autonomous agent with general intelligence."[72]
- Galaxy Eye Technology (北冥星眸) in Hangzhou seeks to commercialize "human-like intelligence technology."[73] Its goal is to build a "first-generation AGI prototype" (通用人工智能第一代原型机).[74]
- IVFuture (智视科技) in Guangxi's Liuzhou High-tech Zone focuses on "brain-like artificial intelligence technology and applications." The company built a joint laboratory of "general artificial intelligence technology" (通用人工智能技术) in October 2020.[75]

BOX 13.1

ZHU SONGCHUN, DIRECTOR OF "BIGAI"

Zhu Songchun (朱松纯), UCLA professor and director of its Center for Computer Vision, Cognition, Learning and Autonomous Robotics, reportedly is returning to China as a "national strategic scientist" to direct the Beijing Institute for General Artificial Intelligence.[67]

Zhu was also appointed the chair of Peking University's Institute of Artificial Intelligence, future head of Tsinghua's new AGI Institute, and will teach "experimental" AGI classes jointly established by the two universities.[68]

Professor Zhu graduated from USTC (Hefei) in 1991 and was awarded a PhD from Harvard in 1996. He has published more than 300 papers in top international journals and won multiple international awards.[69]

Zhu served twice as the principal investigator for U.S. Department of Defense initiatives in the fields of vision, cognitive science, and AI. His UCLA lab received $40 million in U.S. federal funding, a measure of his value.[70]

Zhu is aware of the strategic significance of AGI, "From the perspective of national security and economic development, I think it is an extremely important field and a battleground for China."[71]

Merging intelligences: brain interfaces, chip implants, neuromorphic computing

China's goal to "merge" (混合) human and artificial intelligence, announced in the 2017 plan[76] and reiterated in enabling edicts, allows three interpretations: (1) the term can be understood figuratively to describe AI that is increasingly indistinguishable from human intelligence; (2) it can also refer to the growing dependency of people on AI-enabled technologies for many or all aspects of life; and finally (3) the term can be understood literally—our focus here.

Once science fiction, whole brain emulation[77] is embraced now by AI theorists[78] who describe two categorical approaches: a mind is replicated by imitating the brain's physical structure in software.[79] Or stable representations of the brain's mental state are run on external media. The latter possibility approaches our view of where China's merged or "hybrid" AI may be headed.

The concept has solid theoretical support. Muehlhauser regards BCIs "that allow direct neural access to large databases" as devices that could accelerate scientific progress, leading, in turn, to advanced AI.[80] Yudkowsky concurs, noting that one could add neurons or "usefully interface" brains with computers to upgrade human brains.[81] Sotala and Valpola expand the thesis, "We propose that one way mind coalescence might happen is via an exocortex, a prosthetic extension of the biological brain which integrates with the brain as seamlessly as parts of the biological brain integrate with each other."[82] In this scenario:

> Physical or software connections are created between the brains housing the minds, similar to the neuronal connections already existing within each brain. The brains begin communicating with each other directly, as if they were different parts of the same brain. Eventually, any stored information that one of the minds can consciously access becomes consciously accessible to the other minds as well.[83]

They conclude by noting that "various brain prostheses are actively being researched, and their development will help in efforts to build an exocortex."[84] In fact, some of what is needed exists in rudimentary form already, and China is not far behind—if at all. Figure 13.2 tallies Chinese language academic papers on BCI that appeared between 2010 and 2019.

Interest in BCI climbed in 2017 a few months after China's Brain Project (中国脑计划) was announced in November 2016. A summary paper that reviewed significant worldwide BCI developments in 2017 credited CAS Institute of Semiconductors' (中国科学院半导体研究所) fast "scalp-brain computer interface system, expected to promote the application of BCI *in the daily life of ordinary healthy people*."[86] A 2019 paper "Miniaturized Design of Implantable Brain-computer Interface System" claimed transfer rates close to that of stationary equipment.[87]

Continuing the trend, in 2019, Tianjin University unveiled its "Brain Talker" (脑语者) chip able to separate signal from noise with great accuracy.[88] The *chip*

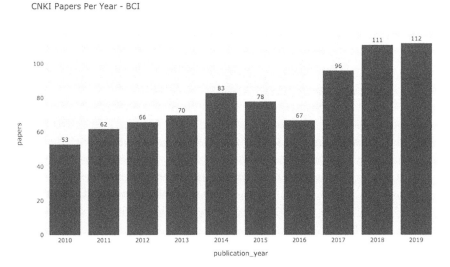

FIGURE 13.2 BCI-related Chinese language academic papers 2010–2019[85] (reproduced with permission)

will "replace traditional computer devices used in BCI," thanks to its portability, greater precision, and faster transmission rates.[89] In early 2021, Fudan University's Institute of Brain-inspired Circuits and Systems (类脑芯片与片上智能系统研究院) announced China's first wireless BCI chip for transmitting information from chip to nerve cells,[90] and Chinese start-up NeuraMatrix (宁矩科技), incubated by Tsinghua, touted an "invasive" (inside the cranium) BCI chip equal to the U.S. company Neuralink's.[91]

On September 16, 2021, China's MOST issued guidelines calling for innovations in "brain-like computing and BCI technology and applications."[92] Among the latter are requirements for:

- "high-density, flexible and malleable brain electrode arrays based on advanced micro-nano processing technology";
- "ultra-high channel number miniaturized wireless BCI circuit structure and optimization (ultra-low noise, ultra-low power consumption, etc.) technology";
- "multi-channel pre-amplification and concurrent real-time sampling, multiplex coding and high-speed wireless transmission."

MOST also mandated development of "neuromorphic chips for novel nanodevices" based on a "storage-computing integrated" (存算一体) chip with neuromorphic components.

MOST's initiatives will almost certainly leverage BCI technologies from the Tianqiao and Chrissy Chen Institute (陈天桥雒芊芊研究院, TCCI), with endowed centers at Caltech and in Shanghai. The latter is a joint venture with the CAS Shanghai Institute of Microsystems and Information Technology (中国科学院上海微系统与信息技术研究所) billed as "China's answer to Neuralink."[93] As one source put it:

> The highlight of this research project is the implantation of an ultra-thin, super flexible, high-throughput neural signal acquisition chip in the brain of mice, which is almost imperceptible to neurons.[94]

Quantum tech aimed at further improving the BCI function may also be on the horizon.[95] Shanghai team leader Tao Hu (陶虎) describes the stakes:

> It is not an exaggeration to say that the brain-computer interface is the main battlefield of the next intersection of life sciences and information technology, and represents a new and potentially disruptive (具有潜在破坏性) technology field.[96]

"Merging" human and machine intelligence is also exemplified in China's efforts to build what are known as "neuromorphic" chips (类脑芯片)—partly analog and partly digital processors that mimic the computational principles of biological

brains. The concept is described by Huang Tiejun, China's outstanding propo-
nent of ASI:

> To achieve AGI, a practical approach is to build the so-called neurocom-
> puter, which could be trained to produce autonomous intelligence and
> AGI. A neurocomputer imitates the biological neural network with neuro-
> morphic devices which emulate the bio-neurons, synapses and other essen-
> tial neural components.[97]

An early realization of the neuromorphic concept is the Tianjic (天机 Chip)
processor developed by a consortium of Chinese researchers at Tsinghua and
UCSB.[98] The development was featured by *Nature* in an article written by Pei
Jing (裴京) et al. titled "Towards Artificial General Intelligence with Hybrid
Tianjic Chip Architecture," where the authors note:

> There are two general approaches to developing artificial general intel-
> ligence (AGI): computer-science-oriented and neuroscience-oriented.
> Because of the fundamental differences in their formulations and coding
> schemes, these two approaches rely on distinct and incompatible platforms,
> retarding the development of AGI. A *general platform* that could support
> the prevailing computer-science-based artificial neural networks *as well as*
> neuroscience-inspired models and algorithms is highly desirable.[99]

A year later, the Tianjic team announced a model of "neuromorphic completeness" consisting of "a Turing-complete software-abstraction model and
a versatile abstract neuromorphic architecture" with toolchain software "to
support the execution of different types of programs on various typical hardware platforms."[100] Developers Pei Jing and Shi Luping (see below) market
the chip through Beijing Lingxi Technology Co. (灵汐科技).[101] They are
joined by SynSense (时识科技), another neuromorphic chipmaker, that claims
to implement "general purpose, real-time neural networks based on spiking
neurons,"[102] and by Zhejiang University's "Darwin II" brain-inspired chips,
792 of which make up its "Darwin Mouse" that can emulate 120 million
spiking neurons.[103]

China's emerging advanced AI potential

These attempts at a unified path to advanced AI find theoretical support in an
essay by (then) Beijing University of Posts and Telecommunications' (北京邮电
学院) professor Zhong Yixin (钟义信), first presented at a 2005 IEEE international conference[104] and later in revised form in 2018.[105] Zhong argued for the
essential unity of "intelligence formation" across biological and artificial platforms. Zhong reiterated these arguments at a 2010 "International Conference on
Advanced Intelligence" that he co-hosted with Goertzel in Beijing.[106]

Such gatherings are now commonplace, exemplified by the annual Conference on Artificial General Intelligence, attended by a core cadre of international AGI mavens and an expanding group of Chinese experts in AI and related disciplines. Sponsored by the AGI Society[107] in cooperation with the AAAI, the conference has run since 2006, twice in China—2013 (Beijing) and 2019 (Shenzhen)—a global testimony to Chinese involvement.

China in addition has hosted its own China AGI Annual Conference (中国通用人工智能年会)[108] since 2016 sponsored by Liu Kai (刘凯),[109] (now) at Liaoning's Bohai University (渤海大学). The conferences run sequentially with a China AGI High-end Forum (中国通用人工智能高端论坛), many of whose attendees are at Wuhan institutes.[110] AGI company IVFuture (see above) presented at the 2020 event.[111]

Chinese participation in AGI conferences is one concrete measure of interest. As a check, the present authors surveyed Chinese AI scientists directly on their attitudes toward AGI.[112] Some 74% responded that the brain-inspired approach alone will lead to general AI. That number rises to 83% among China's specialists. These figures are buttressed by statements from AI principals of standing:

- **Xu Bo** (徐波), director of the CAS Institute of Automation—host to Beijing's Research Center for Brain-inspired Intelligence:

  We believe autonomous evolution (a topic of the institute's research) is a bridge from weak artificial intelligence to general artificial intelligence.[113]

- **Shi Luping** (施路平), director of the Center for Brain-inspired Computing Research, Tsinghua University and head of the Tianjic team:

  Nanodevices have enabled us to develop electronic devices such as neurons and synapses at the level of human brain energy consumption, so now is the best time to develop artificial general intelligence.[114]

- **Tan Tieniu** (谭铁牛), former deputy director of the Chinese Academy of Sciences and deputy chief of the PRC's liaison office in Hong Kong:

  How to make the leap from narrow artificial intelligence to general artificial intelligence is the inevitable trend in the development of the next generation of artificial intelligence. It is also a major challenge in the field of research and application.[115]

- **Zeng Yi** (曾毅), deputy director of CAS's Research Center for Brain-inspired Intelligence:

  The development of narrow (专用) AI does not completely avoid risk, because the system is likely to encounter unexpected scenarios in its application. Having a certain general ability may improve the robustness and adaptiveness of an intelligent system.[116]

• **Huang Tiejun** (黄铁军), vice-chair of Peking University's Institute for Artificial Intelligence and dean of the Beijing Academy of Artificial Intelligence:

> It's impossible for humans to compare to machine-based superintelligence. It will happen sooner or later, so why wait? Even from the perspective of human centrism or human exceptionalism, superintelligence is needed to face big challenges that we can't figure out. That's why I support the idea (Future of Life conference).[117]

True to his word, Huang's Beijing academy announced that its 2020 research would focus on the "cognitive neural basis of artificial intelligence" aiming at "a functional brain-like intelligent system with performance that exceeds a brain" (构建功能类脑、性能超脑的智能系统).[118]

In closing, we can do no better than cite Goertzel's early and prescient belief that China may well "lead the world in advanced AGI." Among the reasons he gives—education, cheaper labor, commitment, and the ability to centralize resources—is this:

> Unlike the U.S., the Chinese research funding establishment has no 'chip on its shoulder' about AI or AGI—it has the same status as any other advanced technology.[119]

Nor, we would add, is there benefit in pretending, ostrich-like, that the genie is still in the bottle.

Notes

1 PRC State Council, 国务院关于印发新一代人工智能发展规划的通知 (New Generation AI Development Plan), SC 35, 2017.
2 Also "强人工智能," i.e. "strong" vs. "weak" or "narrow" AI.
3 Ibid. "Basic Theory. 1. Big Data Intelligence Theory, Data-driven general artificial intelligence mathematical models and theories, etc." (数据驱动的通用人工智能数学模型与理论等).
4 "构筑我国人工智能发展的先发优势" in "New Generation AI Development Plan," paragraph 1, line 2.
5 Defined as "a being with both organic and biomechatronic body parts." https://en.wikipedia.org/wiki/Cyborg.
6 Yudkowsky, 2008. Citations refer to the revised Machine Intelligence Research Institute version.
7 Open-source research on Chinese technical subjects shows unequivocally that the more esoteric the field—or to be totally conspiratorial, the more China cares about a research area—the more likely it is the good information will not be in English.
8 Hannas and Chang, "China's 'New Generation' AI-Brain Project," *PRISM* 9.3, 2021.

9 The discussion is limited to machine-based cognition, and excludes other hypothe-sized ways to artificially elevate intelligence, e.g. drug-induced enhancement, swarm intelligence, gene-editing, and embryo selection (see Shulman and Bostrom, 2014).

10 Yudkowsky argues that one cannot build AI without understanding what "intelli-gence" is. Hansen and Yudkowsky, 2013, p. 347. This formulation corresponds to Pennachin and Goertzel's second and third approaches, namely, those guided by the human brain and mind, with emphasis on the one or the other. Goertzel and Pen-nachin, 2007, p. 22.

11 Huang, 2017.

12 Otherwise known as "whole brain emulation" (WBE, 全脑仿真) or "mind upload." This corresponds roughly to Pennachin and Goertzel's first approach to AGI: "that draw their primary structures and dynamics from an attempt to model biological brains." Ibid., p. 22. Shulman notes, "Regardless of whether we consider such sys-tems to possess mental states, emulations with sufficient functional similarity could substitute for humans in almost any cognitive task." "Whole Brain Emulation and the Evolution of Superorganisms," *Machine Intelligence Research Institute*, 2010.

13 Huang, 2017.

14 Shulman and Bostrom, 2012.

15 This equates to Pennachin and Goertzel's fourth type of AGI project "that have drawn very little on known science about human intelligence in any regard." 2007, p. 22.

16 An "AGI may be built on computer science principles and have little or no resem-blance to the human psyche." Kaj Sotala, 2012, p. 1. Baum et al. argue in the same vein that "many experts do not consider it likely that the first human-level AGI sys-tems will closely mimic human intelligence." Baum, Goertzel, and Goertzel, 2011, p. 191.

17 That is, "efficient cross-domain optimization." Muehlhauser, 2013, p. 43.

18 Hansen and Yudkowsky, 2013, p. 97.

19 Robin Hansen, 2013, and "Whole Brain Emulation: Envisioning Economies and Societies of Emulated Minds," December 2, 2012, https://pswscience.org/meeting/whole-brain-emulation-envisioning-economies-and-societies-of-emulated-minds/.

20 Baum, 2017. p. 8.

21 Hannas and Chang, et al., 2020.

22 See Chapter 7 of this volume for details.

23 "(A)ny computational model of learning must ultimately be grounded in the brain's biological neural networks." Brenden Lake et al., "Building Machines that Learn and Think Like People," *Behavioral and Brain Sciences*, 40, 2017, pp. 1–72.

24 See, e.g., Simon Lucas, Shen Tianyu (沈甜雨), Wang Xiao (王晓), and Zhang Jie (张杰), "基于统计前向规划算法的游戏通用人工智能," (General game AI with statistical forward planning algorithms), *Chinese Journal of Intelligence Science and Technology*, 1.3, 2019, 219–227. Lucas is a British AGI researcher; Shen, Wang, and Zhang are all at the CAS's Institute of Automation (自动化研究所), a leading facility for AGI research.

25 Steve Rayhawk et al., "Changing the Frame of AI Futurism: From Storytelling to Heavy-tailed, High-dimensional Probability Distributions," Machine Intelligence Research Institute, 2009, p. 1.

26 Notwithstanding the "universe as simulation" hypothesis, which seems to have gone mainstream. Fouad Khan, "Confirmed! We Live in a Simulation," *Scientific American*, April 1, 2021.

27 Gruetzemacher et al., 2020, https://arxiv.org/abs/2008.01848.

28 Goertzel and Pitt, 2012.

29 Eliezer Yudkowsky, "Levels of Organization in General Intelligence," in Goertzel and Pennachin, 2007, p. 110 (pagination refers to the MIRI version).

30 Muehlhauser, 2013.

31 Yampolskiy and Fox, 2012.

32 Yudkowsky, op. cit., 2007, p. 105.

33 Bostrom, 2016, p. 3.

34 Everitt et al., 2018. Katja et al., 2018.
35 Good, 1965.
36 "Recursive scenarios are not limited to AI: humans with intelligence augmented through a brain-computer interface might turn their minds to designing the next generation of brain-computer interfaces." Bostrom and Yudkowsky, 2011, p. 14.
37 Luke Muehlhauser interview by George Dvorsky, January 15, 2014, "Can We Build an Artificial Superintelligence that Won't Kill Us?" https://io9.gizmodo.com/can-we-build-an-artificial-superintelligence-that-wont-1501869007.
38 See publications associated with the Machine Intelligence Research Institute (https://intelligence.org/all-publications/) and the Future of Humanity Institute (https://www.fhi.ox.ac.uk/publications/).
39 Bostrom, 2002.
40 Ross Andersen, "The Panopticon Is Already Here," in *The Atlantic*, September 2020.
41 See Chapter 3 of this book.
42 "AGI progress requires theoretical breakthroughs from just a few dedicated, capable researchers, something that does not depend on massive funding." Hence, a Manhattan-scale operation may be less effective than a distributed approach that relies on different methods. Baum, Goertzel, and Goertzel, 2011, p. 190.
43 A survey conducted in 2018 found researchers as a whole giving AGI a 50-50 chance of arriving in 45 years, "with Asian respondents expecting these dates much sooner than North Americans." The aggregates were 30 years vs. 74 years (Katja et al., 2018). CAS Institute of Automation's Zeng Yi predicts its arrival in 2030 (Andersen, 2020).
44 Baum, 2017. The survey includes brain emulation among AGI projects, a practice we follow here.
45 Fitzgerald, et al., 2020. In 2020, Baum et al. added "He4o," an obscure "GitHub project created by Jia Xiaogang," to the China inventory. A description can be found at http://jiaxiaogang.cn/. Jia Xiaogang's (贾晓刚) CV is at http://jiaxiaogang.cn/html/MyResume.html.
46 Baum includes "Real AI," a small "single member company" in Hong Kong focused on AGI safety.
47 "If we want to develop a new generation of artificial intelligence, we must get inspiration from brain science and turn special artificial intelligence into general artificial intelligence, that is, brain-like artificial intelligence." Pu Muming, in 瞭望 (*Outlook*), pp. 6–7, February 8, 2021. http://lw.xinhuanet.com/2021-02/08/c_139729330.htm.
48 CAS Institute of Automation in July 2021 announced a "multi-modal general artificial intelligence" project called "Zidong Taichu" (紫东太初) based on Huawei's "Shengteng" (昇腾) platform, aimed at integrating image, text, and audio data to replicate human semantic processing. Computing support will be via the Wuhan AI Computing Center (武汉人工智能计算中心). https://min.news/en/tech/010e995cff-2998bcd858566a942da080.html.
49 Xiamen University established an Institute of Artificial Intelligence (厦门大学人工智能研究院) in 2020, a major expansion of AI work started in 1988. See this book's Chapter 15 for more detail.
50 Wang ran the First International Summer School for AGI at Xiamen Univ. in 2009 with Goertzel and De Garis, and has engaged with China institutes continuously on AGI, including events in 2012, 2013, and 2016 through 2020.
51 Baum's figure of 45 AGI projects worldwide, expanded to 72 in 2020, is well short of another 2020 estimate of "around 100 groups of people or startups dedicated to creating AGI." Alexey Turchin and David Denkenberger, "Classification of Global Catastrophic Risks Connected with Artificial Intelligence," in *AI & Society* 35, 2020.
52 Future of Life Institute's Brian Tse in 2019 confirmed Baidu's and Tencent's AGI research, and added JD.Com and Horizon Robotics. "Towards A Global Community of Shared Future in AGI," presentation at Beneficial AGI 2019. https://www.youtube.com/watch?v=funu_qgpVWk.

53 Several labs listed in this book's Chapter 7 appear to qualify based on their research but are omitted here for lack of documented intent.

54 https://www.163.com/dy/article/GB1J12NE0514K5HM.html.

55 Baum, 2017, p. 78.

56 通用性人工智能大模型. "超过谷歌 阿里达摩院AI预训练模型M6参数破10万亿" (Ali Dharma Academy AI Pre-training Model M6 Parameters Break 10 Trillion, Exceeding Google), *BJNews* (新京报), November 8, 2021.

57 BAAI is also known as the Zhiyuan Research Institute (智源研究院).

58 https://www.baai.ac.cn/news_article?content_id=48&type=news. Our emphasis. The name "*shenji*" is composed of two morphemes meaning "neural" and "machine."

59 https://www.163.com/dy/article/GBNMEOSQ0511N33R.html?f=post2020_dy_recommends. The article is titled "This Chinese AI research institute, less than three years old, wants to compete technologically on the same level with OpenAI (要和 OpenAI同台竞技)?"

60 http://www.xinhuanet.com/english/2021-06/06/c_139992397.htm.

61 悟道要做的是让机器像一样思考， 迈向通用的人工智能. http://stdaily.com/index/kejixinwen/2021-06/01/content_1149556.shtml. The *Wudao* term translates to "road to awareness."

62 https://www.bigai.ai/about.html.

63 http://www.ai.pku.edu.cn/info/1225/1553.htm.

64 https://www.tsinghua.edu.cn/info/1182/83706.htm.

65 https://www.163.com/dy/article/G3C518KF0511DPVD.html.

66 These latter developments (e.g. Wuhan, Hefei, Harbin, and Chengdu), if they occur, may warrant particular scrutiny.

67 http://www.zidonghua.com.cn/news/tech/41818.html.

68 https://www.tsinghua.edu.cn/info/1182/83706.htm.

69 http://www.zidonghua.com.cn/news/tech/41818.html.

70 https://www.zhihu.com/question/59182074/answer/167219653; http://www.stat.ucla.edu/~sczhu/bio.html.

71 http://www.ai.pku.edu.cn/info/1086/1856.htm.

72 http://www.cyntekcn.com/index.php?c=category&id=4; http://www.cynteksg.com/.

73 https://www.galaxyeye-tech.com/#/aboutUs.

74 https://tech.ifeng.com/c/83JiRVV19Xl.

75 http://www.ivfuture.com/news_cont/page/304.html.

76 PRC State Council, 国务院关于印发新一代人工智能发展规划的通知 ("New Generation AI Development Plan," SC 35, 2017.

77 "(H)ypothetical human minds that have been moved into a digital format and run as software programs on computers." Sotala and Valpola, 2012, p. 1.

78 For example, Salamon and Muehlhauser, 2011.

79 We set aside the philosophical question of whether a representation retains its owners' identity, or as Yudkowsky asks in several places, whether it would even be "sane."

80 Muehlhauser and Salamon, 2012.

81 Eliezer Yudkowsky, 2008, p. 34.

82 Sotala and Valpola, 2012, p. 5.

83 Ibid., p. 1.

84 Ibid., p. 10.

85 Hannas and Chang, et al., 2020, p. 49. Absolute numbers are suppressed by the collection methodology that disallowed non-China co-authored papers or those dealing with the topic tangentially.

86 Zhang Dan, et al., 2018. Our emphasis.

87 Liu Zhaoxu, et al., 2019.

88 Liu Qian (刘茜), et al., "脑语者: 脑科学时代正在走来" (Brain Talker: The Era of Brain Science Is Coming), 光明日报 (*Guangming Daily*), January 18, 2020, http://news.sciencenet.cn/htmlnews/2020/1/434964.shtm.

89 Liang Yu, ed., "China Unveils Brain-computer Interface Chip," *Xinhua*, May 18, 2019, http://www.xinhuanet.com/english/2019-05/18/c_138069590.htm.

90 https://www.yicaiglobal.com/news/china-first-wireless-brain-computer-interface-chip-for-animals-goes-on-display-in-shanghai.

91 https://www.from-the-interface.com/China-BCI-neurotech/.

92 科技创新 2030—"脑科学与类脑研究"重大项目 2021 年度项目申报指南, (Science and Technology Innovation 2030—'Brain Science and Brain-like Research' Megaproject 2021 Annual Project Application Guidelines), MOST 265, 2021.

93 https://www.cheninstitute.org/news/tcci-opens-first-brain-science-frontier-lab-in-shanghai.

94 https://www.rayradar.com/2020/12/29/brain-computer-revolution-musk-left-chen-tianqiao-right/.

95 https://www.yicai.com/news/101092927.html.

96 http://www.xinhuanet.com/techpro/2021-06/03/c_1127524272.htm.

97 Huang, 2017.

98 Lei Deng et al., 2020.

99 *Nature*, 572, July 2019. Our emphasis.

100 Youhui Zhang et al., 2020.

101 http://www.lynxitech.com/index.php/pcproduct; https://zhidx.com/p/156860.html.

102 https://www.synsense-neuromorphic.com/technology.

103 http://www.xinhuanet.com/english/2020-09/04/c_139342858.htm.

104 https://ieeexplore.ieee.org/document/1598796.

105 Zhong Yixin, 2018.

106 http://www.intsci.ac.cn/news/icai2010.pdf.

107 Managed by Ben Goertzel (chair) and Wang Pei (vice-chair). http://www.agi-society.org/.

108 https://blog.csdn.net/cf2SudS8x8F0v/article/details/110675316.

109 Liu Kai was at Huazhong Normal University in 2016, where he collaborated with Wang Pei in a Wuhan AI Working Group (武汉人工智能工作组). https://home.x-in-y.com/course/view.php?id=35.

110 The latter formed the Wuhan group in 2016.

111 http://v.youku.com/v_show/id_XNDM1ODAzNjczMg==.html.

112 Hannas and Chang, et al., 2020. China's AI generalists were split on whether AGI could be achieved in 5–10 years or 10+ years.

113 *S&T Daily*, June 20, 2019, http://www.stdaily.com/qykj/qianyan/2019-06/20/content_773207.shtml.

114 *Tencent Net* (腾讯网), October 31, 2019, https://new.qq.com/omn/20191104/20191104A0BD9U00.html.

115 *Qiushi* (求是), April 2019, http://www.qstheory.cn/dukan/qs/2019-02/16/c_112411 4625.htm.

116 *Guangming Daily* (光明日报), January 24, 2019. http:// www.cas.cn/zjs/201901/t20190124_4678012.shtml.

117 Synthesized from Huang's address to the Future of Life conference on "Beneficial AGI," Puerto Rico, January 5, 2019, session 2 "Should we build superintelligence?" https://www.youtube.com/watch?v=xLYE11yW-hQ&t=17s.

118 http://www.bj.chinanews.com/news/2020/0825/78660.html.

119 http://multiverseaccordingtoben.blogspot.com/2009/07/will-china-build-agi-first.html.

Bibliography

Baum, Seth, "A Survey of Artificial General Intelligence Projects for Ethics, Risk, and Policy," Global Catastrophic Risk Institute Working Paper 17-1, 2017.

Baum, Seth, Ben Goertzel, and Ted Goertzel, "How Long until Human-level AI? Results from an Expert Assessment," *Technological Forecasting and Social Change*, 78, 2011, pp. 185–195.

Bostrom, Nick and Eliezer Yudkowsky, "The Ethics of Artificial Intelligence," William Ramsey and Keith Frankish, eds., *Cambridge Handbook of Artificial Intelligence*, Cambridge University Press, Cambridge, UK, 2011.

Bostrom, Nick, "Existential Risks: Analyzing Human Extinction Scenarios and Related Hazards," *Journal of Evolution and Technology*, 9, March 2002, pp. 1–30.

Bostrom, Nick, *Superintelligence: Paths, Dangers, Strategies*, Oxford University Press, Oxford UK, 2016.

Everitt, Tom, Gary Lea, and Marcus Hutter, "AGI Safety Literature Review," *International Joint Conference on Artificial Intelligence* (IJCAI), arXiv: 1805.01109, 2018.

Goertzel, Ben and Cassio Pennachin, eds., *Artificial General Intelligence*, New York: Springer, 2007.

Goertzel, Ben and Joel Pitt, "Nine Ways to Bias Open-Source AGI toward Friendliness," *Journal of Evolution and Technology*, 22.1, February 2012, pp. 116–131.

Good, Irving J., "Speculations Concerning the First Ultraintelligent Machine," *Advances in Computers*, 6, 1965, pp. 31–88.

Gruetzemacher, Ross et al., "Forecasting AI Progress: A Research Agenda," *Computers and Society*, 170, August 4, 2020, pp. 1–20.

Hannas, William and Huey-Meei Chang, et al., "China AI-Brain Research," Georgetown University, Center for Security and Emerging Technology, September 2020.

Hansen, Robin and Eliezer Yudkowsky, *The Hanson-Yudkowsky AI-FOOM Debate*, Machine Intelligence Research Institute, 2013.

Huang Tiejun (黄铁军), "Imitating the Brain with Neurocomputer: A 'New' Way towards Artificial General Intelligence," *International Journal of Automation and Computing*, 14.5, October 2017, pp. 520–531.

Katja, Grace et al., "Viewpoint: When Will AI Exceed Human Performance? Evidence from AI Experts," *Journal of Artificial Intelligence Research*, 62, 2018, pp. 729–754.

Lei Deng et al., "Tianjic: A Unified and Scalable Chip Bridging Spike-Based and Continuous Neural Computation," *IEEE Journal of Solid-State Circuits*, 55.8, August 2020, pp. 2228–2246.

Liu Zhaoxu (刘朝旭), Wang Minghao (王明浩), Guo Zhejun (郭哲俊), Wang Xiaolin (王晓林), Liu Jingquan (刘景全), "面向植入式脑机接口系统的微型化设计" (Miniaturized Design of Implantable Brain-computer Interface System), *Transducer and Microsystem Technologies* (传感器与微系统), September 2019, pp. 74–76 + 80.

McKenna Fitzgerald, Aaron Boddy, and Seth D. Baum, "2020 Survey of Artificial General Intelligence Projects for Ethics, Risk, and Policy," Global Catastrophic Risk Institute Technical Report 20-1, 2020.

Muehlhauser, Luke and Anna Salamon, "Intelligence Explosion: Evidence and Import," *Singularity Hypotheses: A Scientific and Philosophical Assessment*, Amnon Eden et al., eds., Berlin: Springer. 2012.

Muehlhauser, Luke, "Facing the Intelligence Explosion," *Machine Intelligence Research Institute*, 2013.

PRC State Council. 国务院关于印发新一代人工智能发展规划的通知 (The New Generation AI Development Plan), no. 35, 2017.

Salamon, Anna and Luke Muehlhauser, "Singularity Summit 2011 Workshop Report," *Machine Intelligence Research Institute*, 2011.

Shulman, Carl and Nick Bostrom, "Embryo Selection for Cognitive Enhancement: Curiosity or Game-changer?," *Global Policy*, 5.1, February 2014, pp. 85–92.

Shulman, Carl and Nick Bostrom, "How Hard Is Artificial Intelligence? Evolutionary Arguments and Selection Effects," *Journal of Consciousness Studies*, 19.7–8, 2012, pp. 103–130.

Sotala, Kaj and Harri Valpola, "Coalescing Minds: Brain Uploading-related Group Mind Scenarios," *International Journal of Machine Consciousness*, 4.1, 2012, pp. 293–312.

Sotala, Kaj, "Advantages of Artificial Intelligences, Uploads, and Digital Minds," *International Journal of Machine Consciousness*, 4.1, 2012, pp. 275–291.

Yampolskiy, Roman and Joshua Fox, "Artificial General Intelligence and the Human Mental Model," *Machine Intelligence Research Institute*, 2012.

Yudkowsky, Eleizer, "Artificial Intelligence as a Positive and Negative Factor in Global Risk," *Global Catastrophic Risks*, Nick Bostrom and Milan M. Ćirković, eds., New York: Oxford University Press, 2008.

Zhang Dan (张丹), Chen Jingjing (陈菁菁), Wang Yijun (王毅军), "2017 年脑机接口研发热点回眸" (Looking Back on the Research and Development Hotspots of Brain-computer Interfaces in 2017)," *Science and Technology Review* (科技导报), Volume 36(1), January 2018, pp. 104–109.

Zhang, Youhui et al., "A System Hierarchy for Brain-inspired Computing," *Nature*, 586 October 2020, pp. 378–384.

Zhong Yixin (钟义信), "机制主义人工智能理论: 一种通用的人工智能理论" (Mechanism-based Artificial Intelligence Theory: A Universal Theory of Artificial Intelligence), *CAAI Transactions of Intelligent Systems* (智能系统学报), 13.1, 2018, pp. 2–18.

14

AI safeguards

Views inside and outside China

Helen Toner

For as long as humans have conceived of computers, we have worried about how building thinking machines could go wrong. These worries are not limited to Hollywood depictions of rogue humanoid robots. In a posthumously published essay, no less a mind than Alan Turing speculated that "it seems probable that once the machine thinking method had started, it would not take long to outstrip our feeble powers…At some stage therefore we should have to expect the machines to take control."[1]

As research progress over the last decade has allowed artificial intelligence (AI) systems to evolve from laboratory curiosities to widely used software, conversations about the potential risks these systems might pose have likewise evolved from armchair speculation to technical research directions. In the English-speaking world, heated debates in the mid-2010s about which risks to focus on and why eventually crystallized into a set of technical research directions, including work to make AI systems more reliable, easier to understand, and more aligned with their users' intentions. These subfields of machine learning, collectively referred to as *AI safety*, are now the subject of thousands of published papers each year. In China, public debate about AI risks has been less vociferous, but researcher interest in the underlying technical problems has likewise grown, albeit more rapidly in some areas than others.

Parallel to these developments in technical AI safety research, Chinese policymakers have been grappling with questions of *AI governance*—how to design institutions, laws, and regulations that foster positive applications of AI while preventing harmful uses. Naturally, the Chinese Communist Party (CCP)'s view of which applications count as "positive" vs. "harmful" reflects China's authoritarian model. Nonetheless, the CCP and the Chinese state have made some serious efforts to shape and restrain AI's impacts within China.

DOI: 10.4324/9781003212980-19

This chapter dives into questions foreshadowed by the previous chapter: what do we know about the risks involved in AI development and use, what progress have we seen—particularly in China—in reducing those risks, and what can be done in the future? In what follows, the primary focus is on technical research aiming to make AI safer, beginning by chronicling the emergence of AI safety as a subject of serious research, then describing the research progress made in China and around the world. Next, we touch on some of China's policy and governance efforts to shape AI's development and use, including via regulations, standards, and ethical principles. The chapter closes by exploring some of the transnational safety and security challenges AI presents, the state of international dialogue on these topics, and what might be needed to make more progress on this front.

The rise of "AI safety" research

Prescient quotes by Turing and contemporaries notwithstanding, concerns about the potential risks from AI development began to take hold in the English-speaking world in earnest in the 1990s and 2000s, largely via online discussion boards and email lists. With AI's practical usage still fairly limited, these conversations revolved around abstract, in-principle concerns about the future of intelligence rather than specific instances of AI-induced problems. Early commentators included computer scientist Steve Omohundro—the author of a 2008 paper describing how even a harmless-seeming goal could incentivize an AI to pursue harmful behavior (for example, to acquire resources or defend against attempts to modify its goal)—and researcher Eliezer Yudkowsky, who wrote about the need for "friendly AI" that would not harm humans.[2] In 2009, the Association for the Advancement of Artificial Intelligence ran a panel study to grapple with the challenges and opportunities posed by AI.[3] This ambitiously scoped study concluded that popular fears of a singularity were excessive, but real risks did exist and would need further attention as AI research progressed.

The 2014 publication of *Superintelligence* by Oxford philosopher Nick Bostrom marked the first book-length treatment of risks from AI. The book focused in particular on the dangers of smarter-than-human AI (the titular "superintelligence"), making the case that by the time an AI system is smarter than its creators, it will be too late to steer what that system will do, meaning that it is critical to ensure that powerful AI systems are aligned with human values well in advance. In other words, self-awareness or malicious intent is not necessary in order for a highly capable AI system to pose a threat.

Despite reaching *The New York Times* bestseller list, *Superintelligence* received decidedly mixed reviews. Prominent technologists such as Bill Gates and Elon Musk praised the book, and physicist Stephen Hawking spoke in favor of its core thesis, writing that "the long-term impact [of AI] depends on whether it can be controlled at all."[4] Many AI researchers, however, wrote Bostrom off as an uninformed fearmonger, with machine learning pioneer Andrew Ng famously comparing his concerns with "worrying about overpopulation on the planet

Mars," and roboticist Rodney Brooks attributing the concerns to "fundamental misunderstandings" of how AI works.[5] By this point, a new generation of AI systems based on a type of machine learning called "deep neural networks" or "deep learning" was sweeping the world, showing far better performance than older types of AI on tasks such as image recognition, natural language processing, and playing strategy games such as Go. A common thread in the objections to Bostrom's work was researchers worrying that by focusing on highly capable AI systems, Bostrom was increasing hype about how rapidly AI would advance, which could be bad news for the field. Although *Superintelligence* did not in fact claim that AI research would advance particularly quickly, veterans of previous "AI winters"—in which funding dried up when research failed to meet expectations—saw the book as a risk to their livelihoods, and therefore sought to swat it down. As a result, some of Bostrom's core claims about the potential risks to humanity that highly capable AI could pose *at some point* were largely overlooked. Other critics were concerned that a focus on hypothetical future risks might distract from real, present-day concerns (such as algorithmic bias or privacy), fueling further debates.[6]

Against the backdrop of this ongoing tussle about which risks from AI are worth taking seriously, six up-and-coming young AI researchers published a paper that changed the terms of the debate and seeded a whole new research field.[7] As the title conveys, 2016's *Concrete Problems in AI Safety* converted these long-running discussions about potential future risks from AI into a set of clear, well-specified technical research problems. While most (if not all) of the "concrete problems" drew inspiration from the writings of Bostrom and colleagues, the paper—unlike *Superintelligence*—was written by and for AI researchers. Accordingly, it could neither be criticized on the grounds that it was misleading the general public, nor that it was based on a lack of understanding of real AI research.

The publication of *Concrete Problems*, which would go on to be cited more than 1,000 times, was a key moment in the development of AI safety research. It wasn't that AI researchers had never before concerned themselves with how AI might fail; safety was obviously a primary consideration in the development of autopilot systems, for example. But amidst the boom in deep learning research that had begun a few years prior, most research was focused on finding the newest, sexiest problems that deep learning could solve, with less attention to the pitfalls and potential risks involved. In the months and years after *Concrete Problems* was released, the idea of "AI safety" began to serve as an umbrella for researchers interested not only in pushing the bounds of what AI could do, but also the bounds of how safely and reliably it could do it. Leading AI research labs such as DeepMind (a London-based subsidiary of Alphabet) and OpenAI (an independent research lab based in San Francisco) hired entire teams to work on AI safety; major AI research conferences such as the International Conference on Learning Representations and the International Joint Conference on Artificial Intelligence held dedicated AI safety workshops. Over the course of just a few years, AI safety went from being a philosophical curiosity to an area of computer science research.

In practice, AI safety was—and remains—a loose collection of several related research directions, rather than a single clear field. The throughline connecting the areas to each other is a focus on identifying unintended or undesired behavior in AI systems and developing approaches to ensure these systems work safely and reliably. DeepMind's AI safety team has suggested thinking of the space in terms of three categories of research[8]:

Specification research aims to ensure that an AI system's behavior is aligned with its operator's intentions. This category is closely related to the concerns expressed by Omohundro, Yudkowsky, and Bostrom: like all computers, AI systems do exactly what they're told. This usually works if the task in question is simple, such as predicting the next word in a text. It can go badly wrong, however, when the objective the AI has been told to optimize turns out to differ from our real intentions. Social media companies' focus on user "engagement," for example, is an early example of how specification problems can arise. Because a subset of users finds radicalizing or extremist content highly engaging, it turns out that designing an AI model to optimize for engagement metrics (such as a user's time on site or likelihood of clicking a link) can lead to that content getting boosted. Research into specification aims to design AI systems that can learn to better capture humans' complex values. As we use AI systems in higher-stakes and more complex settings, it will become more important that the objectives we give them capture the nuances and subtleties of what really matters to us.

Robustness research focuses on building AI systems that will stay within safe limits, regardless of the situations they encounter. This includes defending against intentional attempts to meddle with or attack a system, but also incorporates the need for AI systems to behave reliably when used in different contexts from those they were trained for. At present, neural network AI systems are prone to making mistakes that seem incomprehensible from a human perspective, such as mistaking a stop sign for a speed limit sign simply because of a few small stickers.[9] Deep learning models have been shown to be nearly universally vulnerable to these so-called "adversarial examples." What's more, models that seem to perform well in one context may struggle in a slightly different setting. For instance, if an image classifier is trained to detect vehicles or buildings in satellite images of desert terrain, it may do significantly worse if it is later deployed on images of jungle terrain. Until we can ensure that AI systems will reliably work as intended, these kinds of unexpected errors will be a risk.

Assurance research, and the related topic of interpretability research, works to understand and monitor AI systems. Deep learning is famous for being a "black box," in the sense that the internal workings of neural networks are much harder to understand than traditional computer programs. For plenty of applications, this does not matter much. If the system usually works fairly well and failures are not consequential—as in product recommendations from an e-commerce website, say—then there may never be a need to understand in any depth how the model produced its outputs. In other settings, however—such as algorithmic loan decisions, criminal sentencing, or other high-stakes contexts—the ability to understand and challenge an algorithm's conclusions is absolutely necessary. What it even means to "understand" an AI decision is still a contested question: the role and value of a given explanation depend heavily on the sociotechnical context in which the AI system is embedded.[10] Research on assurance, interpretability, and related concepts cannot, on its own, provide answers to complex sociotechnical questions about the appropriate role for AI in different settings. For now, such research aims to build out the technical toolbox available to practitioners and policymakers as they grapple with such questions.

This breakdown is a useful approximation of the space, but "AI safety" remains a fairly nebulous term overall. As discussed further below, phrases such as "beneficial AI" or "trustworthy AI" have also gained some currency, typically referring to a more expansive set of ideas that include AI safety's emphasis on technical problems as well as other relevant issues such as privacy, fairness, and accountability. The language we use for these issues is sure to continue to evolve over time.

AI safety in China

In some ways, discussions of AI safety in China have proceeded similarly to those in English-speaking spaces; in other ways, they have differed. A linguistic quirk is one important source of difference: in Chinese, the word *anquan* (安全) denotes both "security" and "safety." Accordingly, the most natural and obvious way to translate "AI safety" ends up sounding quite different to Chinese ears: "*AI anquan*" is most likely to call to mind cybersecurity or cloud security for the listener—areas that focus more on defending against an adversary than on preventing accidental harm. This can be seen, for example, in the 2019 AI Security Standardization White Paper (人工智能安全标准化白皮书) released by the China Electronics Standardization Institute (中国电子技术标准化研究院), a think tank within the Ministry of Industry and Information Technology.[11] While this white paper mentions a wide range of concerns, including the interpretability and controllability of AI systems, the primary focus is on security issues such as data security, infrastructure security, and "new attack threats" (新的攻击威胁), which overlap most closely with the category of "robustness" described above. By and large, Chinese-language discussions of *AI anquan* tend to focus more heavily on these types of topics than English-language discourse about AI safety.

Of course, linguistic differences do not mean that Chinese researchers do not also discuss the kinds of risks from AI that concern their Western counterparts. While public discussion about the potential dangers of highly capable AI systems does not appear to have been as animated—or begun as early—as that described above, similar topics have certainly received some attention. One of the country's most prominent AI researchers, Nanjing University professor Zhou Zhihua (周志华), wrote in the January 2018 edition of the *Communications of the China Computer Federation* (中国计算机学会通讯) that researchers "should not touch strong AI" (不该去触碰强人工智能).[12] Reasoning that strong AI (an alternate term for human-level AI or artificial general intelligence) would have no reason to agree with human judgments or preferences, Zhou claimed that the day such technology was developed would be the day humanity faces "its greatest survival crisis" (最大生存危机). More recently, a team of researchers at Peking University wrote about the safety risks of strong AI, identifying the "uncontrollability over autonomous consciousness" (自主意识的不可控性) as a key challenge in addition to the need to increase the interpretability and reliability of AI models.[13]

As in the English-speaking world, conceptions of—and language for—AI safety research has changed and developed over time. At the time of writing, it appears that the idea of "trustworthy" (可信) AI is gaining currency, mirroring increasing use of that term internationally to refer broadly to AI that exhibits a range of desirable traits, including robustness, interpretability, fairness, and privacy. In July 2021, the China Academy of Information and Communications Technology (中国信息通信研究院, CAICT), a state think tank, released a white paper on trustworthy AI, proposing an overarching framework that incorporates "supporting technologies" (支撑技术)—such as system robustness/stability, interpretability, privacy, and fairness—alongside laws, regulations, and industry practices. Shortly before the release of this white paper, a full-day session at the 2021 World AI Conference (世界人工智能大会) in Shanghai was dedicated to the topic of trustworthy AI. Even Zhu Songchun (朱松纯)—a superstar AI professor who in 2020 returned to Beijing from UCLA to lead a new research institute working toward artificial general intelligence—is on record on the importance of trustworthiness. In a talk at the annual conference of the China Association for AI in June 2021, Zhu presented a framework for interpretability and claimed that such work would be the key to AI gaining human trust.[14]

One more term to watch is "controllable" AI (可控), used most notably by Xi Jinping himself in a 2018 speech to a Politburo study session.[15] By calling for AI to be "safe, reliable, and controllable" (安全、可靠、可控), Xi—like the Peking University article mentioned above—appears to evince a Bostrom-like interest in the question of how to ensure that humans retain full control of the machines we build. This language has been adopted, for instance, by the Beijing-based startup RealAI (瑞莱智慧), founded in 2018 by researchers affiliated with Tsinghua University's AI research lab.[16] The evolution of safety-focused terminology and organizations like this—both inside and outside China—will be fascinating to observe in the years to come. As AI moves from the laboratory to real world deployment, AI safety will need to move from research papers to large-scale rollout.

Trends in AI safety research output

To take a quantitative look at how basic research on AI safety topics is progressing in China, we can examine trends over time in published research. In previous work, the present author carried out such an analysis, comparing Chinese research output on AI safety topics with progress in the rest of the world.[17] The results, discussed below, were striking.

This analysis drew on work by data scientists at Georgetown's Center for Security and Emerging Technology, who took a corpus of scientific papers covering roughly 90% of the world's scientific literature (including Chinese-language works), then grouped these publications into clusters according to which papers cited each other. The resulting "research clusters" provide a neat way to examine different fields and subfields of scientific research.[18]

To investigate trends in AI safety research, we first used a set of keywords to identify research clusters that appeared to contain papers relating to any of three AI safety subfields that map onto the three categories described above: robustness, interpretability (an important area within the broader category of assurance), and reward learning (a set of approaches aiming to tackle specification problems). This keyword search identified 42 candidate research clusters, which we manually screened to retain only clusters that seemed to revolve primarily around a safety-relevant topic. This left eight clusters containing over 15,000 papers, covering research on topics ranging from how to extract rules from neural networks to how humans can interactively train robots. Having identified these clusters, we could then examine what they showed about Chinese research progress in AI safety compared with other countries and regions. As shown in Figure 14.1, the analysis used country and regional groupings to allow for easier comparison, treating the European Union (EU)

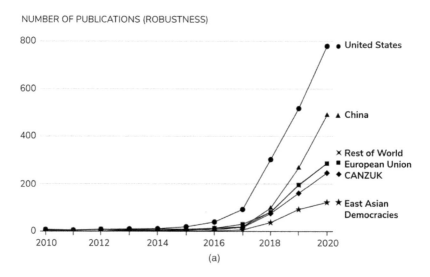

FIGURE 14.1 Papers published in research clusters related to areas of technical AI safety *(Continued)*

Source: Toner and Acharya, "Exploring Clusters of Research in Three Areas of AI Safety."

Note: In the category of robustness, "Rest of World" grew at a nearly identical rate to the EU, so the relevant line is hard to see.

NUMBER OF PUBLICATIONS (INTERPRETABILITY)

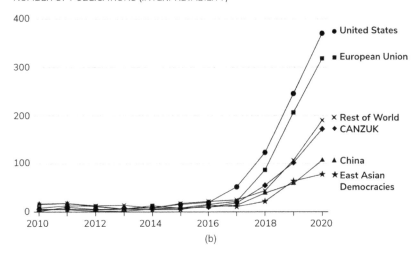

(b)

NUMBER OF PUBLICATIONS (REWARD LEARNING)

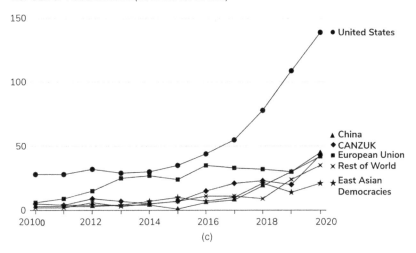

(c)

FIGURE 14.1 *(Continued)*

as a regional bloc, grouping the non-U.S. members of the Five Eyes intelligence alliance—Canada, Australia, New Zealand, and the United Kingdom — together as CANZUK, and consolidating Japan, South Korea, and Taiwan into a group labeled "East Asian Democracies."[19]

Intriguingly, the results were quite different across the three topic areas we considered (robustness, interpretability, and reward learning). China's best showing was in robustness research, which includes work on AI security problems such as defending against adversarial examples. In these clusters, the number of papers published by Chinese researchers was second only to that of U.S. researchers, with both countries showing an uptick in publications starting in 2016–2017, then rapid growth from 2018 onward. In interpretability-related clusters, U.S.-authored papers showed similarly sharp growth from 2016 onward, but China lagged behind the EU and CANZUK, each of which showed notably more growth than in robustness. The picture was most ambiguous when it came to research into specification problems, perhaps reflecting the confusing state of the technical landscape in this area. Here, growth over time was less strong; as in the other areas, U.S. authors had the most publications in 2020, but the characteristic hockey-stick curve seen in the other two areas—and many other areas of AI research—was absent. China, CANZUK, and the EU all lagged behind the United States in this area in recent years. In other words—at least according to this exploratory analysis of research clustered by citation connections—robustness appears to be the area of AI safety research that Chinese scientists have taken up with greatest vigor.

This finding is borne out by an informal look at top publications in robustness-related areas such as adversarial learning, where Chinese research groups are prominent. In 2017, for example, the prominent Neural Information Processing Systems (NeurIPS) conference hosted an adversarial attack and defense competition organized by Google. An international team that included two senior Tsinghua University professors swept the competition: the researchers won not only the defense track (in which participants submitted machine learning models that should be as robust as possible to adversarial examples) but also both attack tracks (which involved generating adversarial examples to attack both unknown and known models).[20] In a similar NeurIPS competition the following year, Tsinghua researchers performed strongly once again, placing second in both the defense and untargeted attack categories.[21]

Why might robustness research have taken off in China so much more rapidly than other types of AI safety work? At this point, we can only speculate. One possible explanation could simply be that Chinese groups are drawn to research areas with competitions like those described above, since winning prizes at such competitions is particularly well-received in China's metrics-dominated academic environment. Chinese researchers have a track record of success in other AI competitions, including in image classification and facial recognition. Robustness research lends itself naturally to the competition format, as there is usually a clear endpoint to compete over—essentially, whether the system did or did not break. In interpretability and specification research, by contrast, it is more difficult to set objective benchmarks, and therefore more difficult to use competitions to push research forward.

A different explanation for the boom in robustness research in China could relate to the linguistic quirk described in the previous section: that AI "safety" in China is synonymous with AI "security." Perhaps this fact leads Chinese researchers to naturally think more in terms of the attack-defense dynamics that are more common to robustness research, and therefore to be drawn more to research in that area.

A final possible explanation, most speculative of all, rests on the different pressures that Chinese and non-Chinese researchers face. In China's controlled information environment, scientists are more constrained in their ability to think and talk about the societal implications of their work, and certainly are discouraged from critical social or political commentary. While robustness research can often focus on crisp, apolitical technical problems, work on interpretability—and perhaps also on specification—tends to grapple more with AI's role as part of a sociotechnical system. Perhaps this, too, can partially explain the lower rates of Chinese publications in this area. We should be cautious, however, not to make this claim too confidently. Western observers have in the past underestimated the extent to which Chinese scholars and consumers alike criticize aspects of China's technology ecosystem, as shown, for example, by China's burgeoning data privacy regime, elaborated below, which has been driven in part by the public's concerns about privacy.

Caution is warranted in interpreting this analysis: while robustness, interpretability, and reward learning are important directions of AI safety research, they are not exhaustive. "AI safety" is still a loose concept that could reasonably be used to refer to a wide range of different work. Future analysis could look for progress in AI safety that is not captured here—perhaps, for example, by identifying research directions pioneered within China, which would be especially likely to slip through the cracks here.

Chinese AI governance

Of course, AI's ultimate effects on society won't depend only on solving the technical problems of how to build safe AI. The commercial, social, and regulatory environments in which AI systems are used—in other words, how AI is governed—will also be critical. To orient the reader to this broader context, a non-exhaustive survey of some relevant developments within China is therefore warranted here.

U.S. commentary often assumes that Chinese governance of AI is practically nonexistent. But outside observers must not confuse the question of whether the CCP will retain its ability to surveil and control its citizens, including using AI (answer: yes) with the question of whether the government will allow tech companies to use AI however they please (answer: no). In reality, Beijing's efforts to shape, promote, and limit the use of AI in China have already been substantial and are only likely to grow. This section explores some of the major contours in Chinese AI governance, both nationally and in international fora.[22]

The area where China has made the most headway is in data governance. Contra the caricatured belief that "Chinese people don't care about privacy," the Chinese public has expressed an increasing concern about how their personal data can be used. In one incident, a comment from Baidu founder Robin Li (李彦宏)—saying that Chinese web users were often willing to exchange privacy for convenience—sparked outrage online, with Chinese state media reporting on the resulting outcry.[23] Then in November 2019, a Chinese law professor sued a wildlife park for forcing him to submit to facial recognition to keep his annual pass. A year later, he won his case, though the park was allowed to continue using biometrics in other settings[24]; several months after that, China's top court ruled that using facial recognition technology without users' consent was an infringement of personal rights and interests—at least for private businesses.[25] Over the same period, the government has been working to build out a data privacy regime that rivals Europe's General Data Protection Regulation in its scope and far outstrips privacy protections enacted in the United States. The passage of the Personal Information Protection Law (个人信息保护法, PIPL) in September 2021 created an overarching framework tying together the flurry of data use regulations and standards that China has released in recent years, including on facial recognition, networked vehicles, data collection by mobile apps, and other areas.[26] The PIPL codifies a set of rights and restrictions, including requiring user consent for any non-essential uses of data, allowing users to opt out from personalized recommendations, and establishing external oversight committees to supervise how platforms handle sensitive data.[27] The law even includes some restrictions on how Chinese government organs can use personal data, although—as is often the case in Chinese legal regimes—significant exceptions are carved out, and it is not yet clear how the restrictions will be enforced.[28] In any event, China now appears to have significantly stronger digital privacy protections than the United States.

If international observers have often underestimated China's efforts on domestic data governance, they may perhaps overestimate China's influence in another area related to AI governance: international standard-setting for AI. The CCP's interest in and commitment to contributing to international technical standards is indisputable. By 2018, China had already published a multi-stakeholder white paper on AI standards, and in April of that year, Beijing hosted the first meeting of an influential AI standards body within the International Organization for Standardization (ISO).[29]

It is not yet clear, however, to what extent this interest translates into a meaningful ability to steer global AI governance. For one thing, AI standardization is currently in its infancy. Many of the technologies in question are not yet widely commercialized, and much of the underlying technical infrastructure that would be needed to reach the consensus required for the development and adoption of standards does not yet exist.[30] For another, China's ability to steer proceedings will depend on the extent to which Chinese organizations have valuable contributions to offer. In the oft-cited case of 5G standards development, the success of Chinese standards organizations and companies rested in large part on the already-established technological superiority of Chinese telecommunications firms, which, in turn, derived from long-term strategic investments by the Chinese government in the telecommunications industry, including via research and development funding, tax incentives, and talent development.[31] In AI, this kind of technological advantage may exist in some areas (e.g. facial recognition), but is unlikely to apply across the board. For these reasons, it is too early to say how technical standards will shape the AI governance playing field, or how China will shape technical standards.

Another area where China's AI governance efforts so far seem more aspirational than actionable is in developing ethics principles. A trend of developing sets of such principles swept the globe from around 2017 to 2020, with organizations from Google to the OECD to the U.S. Department of Defense releasing lists of high-level statements about what it would mean for AI to be ethical. Not to be left out, China entered the fray in May 2019 with the Beijing AI principles, developed by a research group led by Zeng Yi (曾毅) within Beijing Academy of AI (北京智源人工智能研究院, BAAI) and released with endorsement from several other institutions, including Tsinghua and Peking Universities as well as two institutes within the Chinese Academy of Sciences.[32] Like most such documents, the Beijing principles comprise a series of unobjectionable items such as "do good" (造福), "be diverse and inclusive" (多样与包容), and "optimizing employment" (优化就业), with little indication of how these items will influence AI implementation or regulation in practice. More recently, the Chinese government has also endorsed the AI principles released by the G20, with their international recognition extolled in the CAICT white paper on trustworthy AI described above. If nothing else, these and other principles documents may be useful as points of reference in international discussions on AI, as they provide a starting point for broad points of agreement.

International engagement on safety: the path forward

So far, this chapter has introduced a set of risks AI may pose and the technical research directions aiming to solve them, examined Western and Chinese discussions of and progress in those research directions, and outlined some of the policy and regulatory approaches Beijing is using to govern AI. This final section turns to an area that draws these threads together: international discussions of the risks AI poses and what technical and governance tools could be brought to bear on them.

Many of the challenges AI poses can be handled at the national, or even sub-national, level. States can design their own regulatory regimes to handle the risks that come with the rollout of autonomous vehicles, the spread of algorithmic tools to award loans, the use of AI-enabled robots in manufacturing, and other applications whose effects are clearly confined within specific jurisdictions.

Other threats transcend geography. The clearest example is the use of AI in the military domain, where the legality and ethics of autonomous weapons have been subject to widespread debate. But killer robots are just the beginning—the integration of AI into other military systems, such as command and control or intelligence/surveillance/reconnaissance, may jeopardize strategic stability or increase the risk of inadvertent crisis escalation, even in the absence of fully autonomous weapons systems.[33] Beyond the military domain, more speculatively, if the types of more capable and more generalized systems described in the previous chapter are developed, their potential societal ramifications would also certainly cut across borders. For as long as we lack good solutions to the challenges of robustness, specifications, and assurance described at the beginning of this chapter, these challenges will remain especially acute. To effectively manage this category of transnational risks, international engagement will be essential, including engagement between strategic rivals such as the United States and China.

The most prominent multilateral dialogue on AI to date has taken place under the auspices of the United Nations' Convention on Certain Conventional Weapons, where expert meetings to discuss lethal autonomous weapons systems (LAWS) began in 2014. Initially held informally, in 2017, the discussions were formalized as gatherings of a Group of Governmental Experts. Unfortunately, these negotiations have struggled to make substantial headway on the question of how LAWS should be treated under international law. Some basic points of consensus have emerged, for instance, that international humanitarian law applies fully to all weapons systems, including LAWS and that states should consider the risk of proliferation to terrorist groups when developing new weapons systems.[34] Beyond such uncontroversial groundwork-laying, however, there has been little progress on more substantive disagreements, such as whether some types of LAWS should be prohibited by treaty.

On a bilateral basis, China and the United States have so far engaged only informally on AI-related topics. Several institutions have hosted so-called "track II" dialogues to bring Chinese researchers and policymakers together with their U.S. counterparts on an unofficial basis. While most such dialogues stay behind closed doors, one set of talks co-organized by the Center for International Security and Strategy at Tsinghua University, the Brookings Institution, the Berggruen Institute, and the Minderoo Foundation was made public in December 2020. In an article describing the discussions thus far, the U.S. and Chinese delegation heads (retired Marine Corps four-star general John Allen and former vice minister of foreign affairs Fu Ying (傅莹), respectively) describe how AI safety and security problems could threaten international stability, and call attention to the security dilemma dynamic driven by each side's concern that the other might pull ahead in AI capabilities.[35]

If AI capabilities continue to grow, and AI-enabled systems continue to spread to new domains and application areas, international engagement on these topics will only become more important. So far, an important bottleneck on progress has been a lack of tools to monitor and assess AI. What levels of AI capability are strategically and ethically notable, and how could one determine whether another party has reached them? Such tools and concepts, which would be very useful in girding policymakers to develop and enforce a wide range of possible AI-related agreements, are currently almost nonexistent.[36] The next chapter takes up this theme.

Conclusion

How should we expect AI safety and governance within China—and between China and other countries—to develop in the future? A 2020 survey of 49 Chinese AI researchers—distributed, not coincidentally, by the editors of this volume—asked respondents to estimate the "general level of concern in China around AI safety." The results were mixed: 71% described the level of concern as "moderate," 6% as "significant," and 22% believed that there was "no concern."[37] Consensus was greater around a related question—96% of the researchers agreed that "international structures and agreements" would be needed to ensure the safety of future generations of AI.[38] One might speculate that for such agreements to be developed, a higher level of concern might be necessary; if correct, the evolution of Chinese views of AI risk over time will be an important indicator to watch.

Ultimately, managing the assortment of risks that AI poses will require technological advances, thoughtful policy measures, and no small measure of foresight. It remains to be seen whether these ingredients will be realized in sufficient measure, not only in China but across the globe.

Notes

1 A. M. Turing, "Intelligent Machinery, A Heretical Theory," *Philosophia Mathematica*. Series III 4.3, September 1, 1996, 256–60.
2 Omohundro, "The Basic AI Drives"; Eliezer Yudkowsky, "Creating Friendly AI 1.0: The Analysis and Design of Benevolent Goal Architectures," The Singularity Institute, San Francisco, USA, 2001, http://intelligence.org/files/CFAI.pdf.
3 Horvitz and Selman, "AAAI Presidential Panel on Long-Term AI Futures," https://www.microsoft.com/en-us/research/wp-content/uploads/2016/11/panel_chairs_ovw.pdf.
4 Stephen Hawking, "Stephen Hawking: 'Transcendence Looks at the Implications of Artificial Intelligence—but Are We Taking AI Seriously Enough?,'" *The Independent*, October 23, 2017.
5 Andrew Ng, "Is AI an Existential Threat to Humanity?," *Quora*, January 2016; Rodney Brooks, "Artificial Intelligence Is a Tool, Not a Threat," *Rethink Robotics Blog*, 2014.
6 Prunkl and Whittlestone, "Beyond Near- and Long-Term: Towards a Clearer Account of Research Priorities in AI Ethics and Society."
7 Amodei et al., "Concrete Problems in AI Safety," http://arxiv.org/abs/1606.06565.
8 Ortega et al., "Building Safe Artificial Intelligence: Specification, Robustness, and Assurance," https://medium.com/@deepmindsafetyresearch/building-safe-artificial-intelligence-52f5f75058f1.
9 Kevin Eykholt et al., "Robust Physical-World Attacks on Deep Learning Visual Classification," in 2018 IEEE/CVF Conference on Computer Vision and Pattern Recognition (2018 IEEE/CVF Conference on Computer Vision and Pattern Recognition (CVPR), IEEE, 2018), https://doi.org/10.1109/cvpr.2018.00175.
10 Finale and Kortz, "Accountability of AI Under the Law: The Role of Explanation."
11 全国信息安全标准化技术委员会，大数据安全标准特别工作组 (National Information Security Standardization Technical Committee, Big Data Security Standards Special Working Group), "人工智能安全标准化白皮书 (2019 版) " (Artificial Intelligence Security Standardization White Paper (2019 Edition)), 中国电子技术标准化研究院 (China Electronics Standardization Institute), October 2019. http://www.cesi.cn/images/editor/20191101/20191101115151443.pdf. Translation available at https://cset.georgetown.edu/publication/artificial-intelligence-standardization-white-paper/.
12 Zhou Zhihua, "关于强人工智能."
13 Liu Yuqing et al., "针对强人工智能安全风险的技术应对策略."

14 Ma Jian (马剑), "朱松纯:可解释性是人工智能获得人类信任的关键 (Zhu Songchun: Interpretability Is the Key to AI Obtaining Human Trust)," *Qianlong*, June 11, 2021.

15 "习近平:推动我国新一代人工智能健康发展" (Xi Jinping: Promote the Healthy Development of a New Generation of Chinese AI), 新华 (*Xinhua*), October 31, 2018.

16 "关于我们" (About Us), 瑞莱智慧 (RealAI), accessed October 27, 2021, https://realai.ai/about-us.

17 Helen Toner and Ashwin Acharya, "Exploring Clusters of Research in Three Areas of AI Safety," Georgetown University, Center for Security and Emerging Technology, February 2022.

18 Autumn Toney, "Creating a Map of Science and Measuring the Role of AI in It," Georgetown University, Center for Security and Emerging Technology, June 2021.

19 Papers were assigned to countries based on the location of the organization(s) with which the author(s) were affiliated. A paper by authors affiliated with organizations in multiple countries was assigned to each of those countries. For more details on methodology, see Toner and Acharya, "Exploring Clusters of Research in Three Areas of AI Safety."

20 Alexey Kurakin et al., "Adversarial Attacks and Defences Competition," in *The NIPS '17 Competition: Building Intelligent Systems*, Springer International Publishing, 2018.

21 Wieland Brendel, "Results of the NIPS Adversarial Vision Challenge 2018," Bethgelab, November 9, 2018.

22 Local and provincial governance initiatives related to AI are omitted due to length constraints.

23 Liang Jun, "Baidu Chief under Fire for Privacy Comments," *People's Daily*, March 28, 2018; Sacks and Laskai, "China's Privacy Conundrum," *Slate*, February 7, 2019.

24 Jianhang Qin, Tong Qian, and Wei Han, "Cover Story: The Fight Over China's Law to Protect Personal Data," *Caixin*, November 30, 2020.

25 Xinmei Shen, "You Have a Choice: China's Top Court Empowers People to Say 'No' to Facial Recognition Use by Private Businesses," *South China Morning Post*, July 29, 2021.

26 Lee et al., "Seven Major Changes in China's Finalized Personal Information Protection Law," *Digichina*, September 15, 2021.

27 Shen Lu, "China's Privacy Laws Could Be Stronger than America's," *Protocol*, May 8, 2021.

28 Jamie P. Horsley, "How Will China's Privacy Law Apply to the Chinese State?," *New America*, January 26, 2021.

29 Jeffrey Ding, Paul Triolo, and Samm Sacks, "Chinese Interests Take a Big Seat at the AI Governance Table," *New America*, June 20, 2018.

30 Matt Sheehan, "Standards Bearer? A Case Study of China's Leadership in Autonomous Vehicle Standards," *Macropolo*, June 3, 2021.

31 Alex Rubin et al., "The Huawei Moment," Georgetown University, Center for Security and Emerging Technology, July 2021.

32 Interestingly, the endorsements are listed in the English version of the news release, but not the Chinese version. 北京智源人工智能研究院, "Beijing AI Principles," May 2019, https://www.baai.ac.cn/news/beijing-ai-principles-en.html.

33 Michael Horowitz and Paul Scharre, "AI and International Stability: Risks and Confidence-Building Measures," Center for a New American Security, January 12, 2012.

34 "Final Report, Meeting of the High Contracting Parties to the Convention on Prohibitions or Restrictions on the Use of Certain Conventional Weapons Which May Be Deemed to Be Excessively Injurious or to Have Indiscriminate Effects," United Nations, December 13, 2019.

35 Fu and Allen, "Together, The U.S. And China Can Reduce The Risks From AI," 2020.

36 Whittlestone and Clark, "2021."

37 Hannas and Chang, et al., "China AI-Brain Research," 2020.

38 Ibid.

Bibliography

Amodei, Dario, Chris Olah, Jacob Steinhardt, Paul Christiano, John Schulman, and Dan Mané, "Concrete Problems in AI Safety." *ArXiv [Cs.AI]*, June 21, 2016. arXiv.

Beijing Academy of AI (北京智源人工智能研究院), "Beijing AI Principles," May 2019.

Brooks, Rodney, "Artificial Intelligence Is a Tool, Not a Threat." *Rethink Robotics Blog*, 2014.

Ding, Jeffrey, Paul Triolo, and Samm Sacks, "Chinese Interests Take a Big Seat at the AI Governance Table," *New America Cybersecurity Initiative*, June 2018.

Doshi-Velez, Finale, and Mason Kortz, "Accountability of AI Under the Law: The Role of Explanation," Berkman Klein Center for Internet & Society, November 3, 2017.

Fu, Ying, and John Allen, "Together, The U.S. And China Can Reduce The Risks From AI," *Noema Magazine*, December 17, 2020.

Hannas, William C., Huey-Meei Chang, Jennifer Wang, Catherine Aiken, and Daniel Chou. "China AI-Brain Research." Center for Security and Emerging Technology, September 2020.

Horowitz, Michael C., and Paul Scharre, "AI and International Stability: Risks and Confidence-Building Measures," Center for a New American Security, January 2021.

Horsley, Jamie P., "How Will China's Privacy Law Apply to the Chinese State?" *DigiChina*, January 26, 2021.

Horvitz, Eric, and Bart Selman, "AAAI Presidential Panel on Long-Term AI Futures: Interim Report from the Panel Chairs," Association for the Advancement of Artificial Intelligence (AAAI), 2009.

Lee, Alexa, Mingli Shi, Qiheng Chen, Jamie P. Horsley, Kendra Schaefer, Rogier Creemers, and Graham Webster, "Seven Major Changes in China's Finalized Personal Information Protection Law," *DigiChina*, September 15, 2021.

Liu, Yuqing (刘宇擎), et al. "针对强人工智能安全风险的技术应对策略" (Technical Counter-measures Against Safety Risks of Strong Artificial Intelligence), 中国工程科学 (*Chinese Journal of Engineering Science*), 23.3, June 2021, 75–81.

Lu, Shen. "China's Privacy Laws Could Be Stronger than America's" *Protocol*, May 8, 2021.

Omohundro, Stephen M., "The Basic AI Drives," *Artificial General Intelligence 2008: Proceedings of the First AGI Conference*, eds., Pei Wang, Ben Goertzel, and Stan Franklin 171, Amsterdam: IOS Press, 2008.

Ortega, Pedro A., Vishal Maini, and DeepMind Safety Team, "Building Safe Artificial Intelligence: Specification, Robustness, and Assurance." *Medium*, September 27, 2018.

Prunkl, Carina, and Jess Whittlestone, "Beyond Near- and Long-Term: Towards a Clearer Account of Research Priorities," in *AI Ethics and Society*. ArXiv [Cs.CY], January 13, 2020. arXiv.

Sacks, Samm, and Lorand Laskai, "China's Privacy Conundrum." *Slate*, February 7, 2019.

Sheehan, Matt, "Standards Bearer? A Case Study of China's Leadership in Autonomous Vehicle Standards." MacroPolo, June 2021.

Toner, Helen, and Ashwin Acharya. "Exploring Clusters of Research in Three Areas of AI Safety." Center for Security and Emerging Technology, February 2022.

Whittlestone, Jess, and Jack Clark, "Why and How Governments Should Monitor AI Development." *ArXiv [Cs.CY]*, August 28, 2021. arXiv.

Zhou Zhihua (周志华). "关于强人工智能" (On Strong Artificial Intelligence). 中国计算机学会通讯 (*Communications of the China Computer Federation*), 14.1, 2018.

15

Measuring risk and monitoring development

William C. Hannas and Huey-Meei Chang

This final chapter asserts a compelling need for a rigorous AI monitoring regime—a so-called "indications and warning (I&W) watchboard"—focused on potentially problematic AI. The watchboard can be a standalone pilot aimed at validating the use of open-source materials against narrowly defined "high-risk" targets,[1] but eventually it will need to be recast as a component of a much broader science and technology intelligence (STI) network.

China already operates a highly successful model of the proposed system that is worth emulating. That country also offers an insightful aphorism we hope leaders of democratic countries will take to heart, namely: 有备无患 ("forewarned is forearmed").

Existential risks: from NBC to AI and cog-neuro

Many contributors to this volume were drawn to artificial intelligence by enthusiasm for the positive impact AI can have on the human condition, tempered by concern that if mismanaged, or left to run its own course, AI could eradicate liberal human values and humanity itself. The latter outcome, once the province of science fiction, is, as the previous chapter noted, now taken seriously to the point of being ranked with nuclear, biological, and chemical (NBC) annihilation as an "existential risk."[2]

The present authors' thoughts on AI risk are shaped by literature cited in the preceding chapters, and by dialogs with colleagues at two well-regarded technology safety and rights organizations: the Open Philanthropy Project[3] and Columbia University's NeuroRights Initiative.[4] We begin this chapter by summarizing two of their representative papers: "Potential Risks from Advanced Artificial Intelligence"[5] and "It's Time for Neuro-rights: New Human Rights for the Age of Neurotechnology"[6] to build context for a proposal to use China as a proxy for AI risk in general.

DOI: 10.4324/9781003212980-20

"Potential Risks" is a foundational document written in 2015 characterizing the opportunities and, especially, risks of advanced AI. It captures succinctly most of the concerns that motivate the present volume. Under the caption "What is the problem?" the paper explains:

> It seems plausible that sometime this century, people will develop algorithmic systems capable of efficiently performing many or even all of the cognitive tasks that humans perform. These advances could lead to extreme positive developments, but could also potentially pose risks from intentional misuse or catastrophic accidents. For example, it seems possible that (i) the technology could be weaponized or used as a tool for social control, or (ii) someone might create an extremely powerful artificial intelligence agent with values misaligned with humanity's interests. It also seems possible that progress along these directions could be surprisingly rapid, leaving society underprepared for the transition.

Under "Timeline," the document goes on to state:

> It appears possible that the coming decades will see substantial progress in artificial intelligence, potentially even to the point where machines come to outperform humans in many or nearly all intellectual domains, though it is difficult or impossible to make confident forecasts in this area. For example, recent surveys of researchers in artificial intelligence found that many researchers assigned a substantial probability to the creation of machine intelligences 'that can carry out most human professions at least as well as a typical human' in 10-40 years.

The paper draws an analogy between the impact humans have had on other species in a "short geological timescale" and the potential effects of advanced machine intelligence on humanity's role on earth. Related concerns include the following:

- Faster processing speeds may lead to rapid changes in AI capabilities, creating "novel safety challenges in very open-ended domains."
- Deep learning (through hidden layers) may result in humans losing the ability to understand decisions taken by AI.
- "It seems plausible to us that highly advanced artificial intelligence systems could potentially be weaponized or used for social control."
- "In the shorter term, machine learning could potentially be used by governments to efficiently analyze vast amounts of data collected through surveillance."

A 2016 update by OPP co-founder Holden Karnofsky states in part:

> It seems to me that artificial intelligence is currently on a very short list of the most dynamic, unpredictable, and potentially world-changing areas

of science. I believe there's a nontrivial probability that transformative AI will be developed within the next 20 years, with enormous global consequences… Transformative AI could be a very powerful technology, with potentially globally catastrophic consequences if it is misused or if there is a major accident involving it.[7]

If these forecasts are disconcerting, recent developments in cognitive neuroscience are, when considered, positively terrifying. Here are extracts from the NeuroRights paper, penned a year ago by hardcore neuroscientists not prone to hyperbole:

> Technological advancements are redefining human life and are transforming the role of humans in society. In particular, neurotechnology—or methods to record, interpret, or alter brain activity—has the potential to profoundly alter what it means to be human.
>
> Because neurotechnology can be used to stimulate a person's brain, it has the capacity to influence a person's behavior, thoughts, emotions, or memories.
>
> For the first time in history, we are facing the real possibility of human thoughts being decoded or manipulated using technology.

Brain-computer interfaces (BCIs) figure large in this cognitive "revolution." As we noted elsewhere,[8] the relationship between AI and neuroscience—beyond "connectomics" and brain-inspired computational architectures—is one where advances in AI enable gains in the BCI function. Artificial intelligence is used in BCI to digitize brain signals, interpret their coding schema, and resolve contradictory performance vectors. Beyond these (primarily) therapeutic uses, BCI can also be a direct link to digital (AI) resources.

While liberating in one sense (mind augmentation), it takes little imagination to foresee its downsides. For starters, there is scarce hope that this cognitive boon will be more evenly distributed than any of the world's other goods, adding to the gap between the beneficiaries of technological progress and the rest of us. We view it more likely that these benefits will be hoarded by and within nations, leading to the dystopia that AI theorists often describe.

Implausible? The NeuroRights authors cite a host of existing capabilities and features under development with decidedly mixed outcomes:

> Companies and governments are developing devices that would allow people to communicate by thinking, to decipher others' thoughts by reading their brain data, and to have access to all of the internet's databases and capabilities inside their minds.
>
> BCIs can be used to effectively control animals' movement. In addition to reading and analyzing it, non-invasive BCIs may one day be used to *alter* human brain activity. What can be done with mice today could be done with humans tomorrow.

And the hell scenario:

> A neurotechnology revolution has been spearheaded by government bodies in the United States, China, and other countries; they are likely also developing non-medical neurotechnology for military and surveillance uses that are not fully explored or regulated by either national laws or international treaties.

The authors of these documents and members of like organizations have done yeoman's work elaborating measures—collaborative, judicial, institutional, algorithmic—to solve these problems, more than we can list or begin to critique. While such options are being thought through, there is one concrete step that can be taken immediately.

The argument for a China AI monitoring regime

The preceding discussion involves two forms of existential risk: the general problem of "misaligned" artificial intelligence acting—without malice—against human interests; and the special problem of an authoritarian government using AI to suppress dissent, disadvantage competitors, and reshape the world in its likeness. *In terms of risk management, these two threats converge.* Since China ranks among countries able to build potentially unsafe AI, whatever intentions are imputed to its leadership, a commonsense step to mitigating danger of the first type—an I&W regime focused initially on China—also addresses the second problem of hedging against a technically empowered totalitarian state.

It also helps ease the funding problem. Given the reluctance of the United States Intelligence Community (USIC), broadly defined, to build *and maintain* robust foreign technology detection and analysis programs,[9] and the absence of any sustained "outside" effort of adequate scale,[10] the only economically viable way to build a detection mechanism is to begin "small" (one country), test methodologies, establish trust and a user base, and thereby attract additional funds to expand in increments to a full-blown operation able to monitor *all* state and non-state actors.

There are other reasons to begin with China. Measuring AI risk entails the ability to collect and process the right kinds of data. Without diminishing the importance of English sources, the de facto language of international science, a serious I&W regime recognizes the value of exploiting the languages of the target countries. This sounds banal but we assure the reader that this misguided perception—if a paper is not in English, it is not worth examining—thrives within pockets of the USIC and the English-speaking scientific community. This continues despite surveys showing that nearly all papers on sensitive technologies, particularly those weapons-related, are buried in what frustrated analysts call the "soft encryption" of the indigenous language.[11]

In other words, looking for clandestine AI programs in English is the epitome of looking for one's lost keys under the lamppost. Our point is this: the need to treat Chinese sources on a par with English to make any serious headway against the China problem forces the designers of what is intended to become a country agnostic monitoring program to accept in principle the need to process non-English languages. A system weaned on typologically *dissimilar* data—Chinese being the paradigm example—is primed to deal with data from other non-English-speaking countries, where the orthographic gaps are less onerous.

Adding Chinese language to the search space is unlike adding German or Russian not only because of an order of magnitude difference in the difficulty of processing a logographic script but also because of idiosyncrasies in how Chinese proper nouns—the sine qua non of tracking—are represented in scientific literature. On the one hand, this means dealing with the language as it is, and not through English, to reduce ambiguities that arise in transcription, while on the other hand requiring system designers to write code able to deconflict false positives (the homonym problem) and merge disparate representations of the same entity. Putting Spanish or even Korean into the maw gets you little in downstream transitivity, whereas learning how to "do" Chinese—if you can—gets you most of the way to a universal capability.

The argument for focusing on China as an exemplar of AI risk has another dimension. Students of catastrophic risk agree that if the chance of "runaway AI" (or a meteor strike, or fatal pathogen) is very low, the potential adverse consequences may still be great enough to justify strong efforts at mitigation.[12] Similarly, if the risk of China creating or exploiting an asymmetrical advantage in AI is small, *and* confidence in safeguards is high, the results of error, misplaced trust, and bad judgment may be large enough to warrant scrutinizing developments in advance.

Even this calculation may be too facile, as there is no guarantee China—joint conferences and communiqués notwithstanding—will act "reasonably" (do what we want) by acceding to global norms and allowing inspections, with a consequent loss of sovereignty, market share, and first mover advantage, or by eschewing technology that leads to advantages.

- First and obviously, it is hard to ignore a near-existential calamity that did originate in China. Whether one puts the locus of the COVID-19 infection in a Wuhan "wet market" or regional biolab, two datapoints emerge: (1) a massive scourge began in China, despite safeguards, and (2) China responded reluctantly to global calls for information. With this precedent, can one assume that an AI disaster will be treated differently?
- Then, there is Tan Tieniu (谭铁牛), senior CASIA leader, formerly number two at CAS, and *deputy director of the Hong Kong liaison office*. Tan runs several of China's projects on AI's use in biometric recognition and human surveillance. He is involved additionally in four surveillance companies, whose portfolios induce nightmares—that is, a Chinese high official invested totally in what Western analysts regard as AI's malevolent use.[13]
- Tan's case is a microcosm of a larger pattern of technology-enabled abuses captured in this book's Chapter 12. What has become ubiquitous in China is now exported (with the connivance of foreign suppliers) to the world.

Absent any principled move within China to ban AI technology for political control, there is no limit to the types of equipment that can be developed there and deployed anywhere.

- Factory-scale primate farms, scattered throughout China and shunned everywhere else, betray a troubling ambivalence to the moral issues that underlie AI risk. Lower primate DNA is near enough to that order's apex species to give pause to those sensitized to the dangers of AI[14] about the ethics of using (abusing) near cousins to advance a research agenda. Explaining this as a "cultural" difference just strengthens our point.
- Finally, one must ask what China's purpose is in seeking world leadership and a "first mover advantage" (先发优势) in AI. What does "leadership" mean if not to gain a leg up on the rest of humanity? Understood literally, leadership implies staying a step or two ahead of a fast moving target, which may precipitate a headlong "race" into dangerous territory—the very situation AI theorists warn should be avoided.

S&T monitoring: China's model for a worldwide problem

The present authors are equipped to suggest only a few, commonly understood measures to nudge AI research in healthy directions (see this book's Conclusion). We do, however, have decades experience using open sources to track S&T developments, in China especially, and benefit from the counsel of talented colleagues, including some who have built I&W prototypes. We also have a shining model of a monitoring system in China's own highly regarded science and technology intelligence (STI, 科技情报) network.[15]

Our goal is an *indications and warning program* to give policymakers lead time to react to AI developments, but the requirements are the same for any S&T monitoring system, including the operation China uses to detect and transfer foreign technology. We have no interest in the technology appropriation part of that model (that may change someday).[16] Rather, China's STI system is attractive because it demonstrates that I&W via open sources (publicly available information) can be done at all. It also provides clues honed over six decades on how monitoring can proceed. Finally, its existence short-circuits complaints about "spying" unfairly on China.

Accordingly, the following is a much abridged profile of a complex and sprawling system that has proven its value in supporting China's needs. Based on statutes that go back to 1958, the Chinese People's Republic has been using open sources systematically to gauge global progress in S&T for most of its history. Its present structure emerged in 1989, when China's State Science and Technology Commission (today's MOST) defined five organizations responsible for these activities, the main two being the "COSTIND S&T Information Center" (CDSTIC, 国防科委科技情报研究所)[17] for military technologies and the "Institute of Scientific and Technical Information of China" (ISTIC, 中国科技情报研究所), its civilian counterpart. The system has been tweaked continuously, the most recent change being the rebirth of CDSTIC as the Military Science Information Research Center (MSIRC) in 2017.

An informed source estimates the number of "S&T intelligence workers" (科技情报工作人员) that comprise the system at more than 100,000.[18] Even taking into account China's population and the system's other purpose of supporting high-tech appropriation, that figure is large, and exceeds U.S. manpower (USIC, DOD, non-title 50 agencies, and contractors) doing foreign technology analysis by nearly three orders of magnitude. This level of commitment is *not* a function of antiquated data retrieval and analysis; China has used high-tech equipment in STI production for at least four decades.[19] Instead, the number reflects China's appreciation of the value of open source. While we do not recommend—or have any hope of—matching this effort, especially for the limited AI pilot we propose, it is worth knowing how highly America's main strategic competitor thinks of the need to follow global technology trends.

We should dispel another myth—that China needs quantity to make up for quality, hence the big numbers. Table 15.1 shows an abbreviated list of job

TABLE 15.1 2019 AMS/MSIRC military-civilian recruitment form[20]

Job category	Position title	Type of work	Education	Profession
engineer	assistant engineer	software development	Masters or above	computer science and technology, software engineering
science rsch	research intern	comprehensive research on national defense tech	Masters or above	chemical engineering and technology, engineering
science rsch	assistant researcher	big data knowledge mining research	Ph.D.	computer science and technology, software engineering
science rsch	research intern	academic journal editor	Masters or above	design, translation
engineer	assistant engineer	computer network and equipment management	Masters or above	computer science and technology
engineer	assistant engineer	multimedia, animation, film and TV production	undergrad or above	postgraduate: drama and film studies, design
librarian	assistant librarian	website programming and network DB management	full-time undergrad	computer science and technology
science rsch	research intern	data analysis	Masters or above	control science and engineering, computer S&T
engineer	assistant engineer	project management	Masters or above	management science and engineering
librarian	librarian	library file management	Masters or above	management science and engineering

vacancies issued in 2019 by MSIRC, posted here to give a flavor of China's STI operation and the caliber of people staffing it.

Other vacancies are for digital processing and database construction; digital library application technology development and maintenance; intelligence research, electronics research, system demonstration and evaluation; computer network security; software and network engineering; database construction and maintenance; translation and management of foreign-language library materials; "comprehensive research on national defense technology"; and file management.[21]

The table is illustrative of the skills needed in a serious I&W program and compares more than favorably with the slate of talent the present authors could draw on in their former careers.

What does the Chinese system monitor? In their book *Sources and Methods of Obtaining National Defense Science and Technology Intelligence*, Huo and Wang, architects of CDSTIC's main operation, laid out a soup-to-nuts prescription for STI, most elements of which had already been adopted by their organization.[22] The book is humbling to read. Aspects of STI that even today are ignored by other countries' intelligence services are discussed along with quantitative measures and theoretical support.

Chapter 4, for example, dissects sources by type with advice on how each should be used to meet customer requirements. Chapter 8 describes with cookbook-like precision seven "commonly used" analytic methods, including terminology analysis, concept inference, information activation, observation and experimentation, survey statistics, expert appraisal, and mathematical methods, all used to tease out a technology's trajectory from the open-source record.

The authors propose a collection taxonomy based on media type, level of processing, technical nature of the content, field of application, transmission means, user demands, time constraints, level of expectation, and so on.[23] Source evaluation is done through an indexing scheme based on reliability, suitability, timeliness, availability, cost, and ease of decoding.[24] An entire chapter (Chapter 5) is given to studying consumer intelligence needs, which is mostly an afterthought elsewhere (hint: it's not enough just to ask the customer).

China's other main open-source intelligence unit—ISTIC—also provides clues on how I&W should be done in the form of web-based information, journal articles by employees and scholars of STI (that China even *has* such journals says everything), and in an autobiography titled *60 Years of Glory—The 60ᵗʰ Anniversary of the Founding of the Institute of Science and Technical Information of China* (in Chinese),[25] a fact-filled tell all that lacks an English translation.

In 2015, ISTIC, just one element of China's STI architecture, held some 500,000 foreign theses and dissertations, 270,000 foreign-language conference documents, 2.4 million U.S. government S&T reports, more than 4,300 foreign journals, 260,000 foreign search and reference books, and 22 scientific abstract databases and 27 full-text databases.[26] ISTIC also provides "fact-and-data-based decision-making support to government agencies, research institutions, and industry."[27] It actively supports "comprehensive, policy-driven strategic research" on the latest worldwide S&T achievements and trends for leading government departments,[28] and tracks "key industries and S&T fields, providing information for industrial development and corporate decision-making."[29] This last function is outside the scope of our I&W proposition but coincides with thoughts we and other colleagues have for a "National Science and Technology Analysis Center" (below).[30]

No warning system is worth the bother if its output is not communicated. A theme that emerges from our study of China's STI system is the latitude given to its professionals in their interaction with customers,[31] and the PRC government's willingness to take account of their findings in national policy decisions.[32] In part, this is a function of the quality of the messenger, and in part that of the policymaker receiving the information. No matter how timely and well-packaged the message is, if facts are rejected because they clash with politics, ideology, settled views, or one's interpretation of how the world should look, the whole I&W exercise quickly becomes sterile.

Open-source discovery and monitoring AI threats

AI *threat* monitoring means understanding the gap between "normal" AI and truly "dangerous" trajectories. Both can be goals but it is unlikely a comprehensive proposal to track step-by-step technical progress that is not flagged for specific content and thresholds of the sort captured by China's STI network will attract immediate support in the United States, although one can be hopeful. Accordingly, we propose as a preliminary step that the U.S. government—through an executive office outside the USIC or an outsourced contract to vetted performers—undertake monitoring of two areas that cover some (but not all) of the advanced AI threat space as we understand it[33]:

- I&W for technical fundamental advances that somehow alter the research or application landscape by creating a significant enabling advancement or crossing some performance threshold.
- I&W for projection of authoritarian power and/or infringement of ethical norms via collaboration, knowledge transfer, system deployment, or other means by China or other developers of AI and brain-inspired systems.

The first equates—in our schema—to China's efforts to build "general artificial intelligence" via any of several venues described in this book's Chapter 13; the second refers to the creation and export of AI-dependent human rights repression technologies, described in Chapter 12.

These choices were made in appreciation of China's declared intent to achieve *first mover advantage* through general-purpose AI,[34] "merge" human and artificial intelligence, and expand AI's application in all sectors of society (the "AI +" formula), which in a totalitarian context equates to deviance from liberal norms.

Our research into China's use of AI resources suggests that these concerns are real and that data exist to monitor them.

What are—to borrow a term from Huo and Wang—the sources and methods? The present authors compiled a list of source types based on prior success at eliciting Chinese language data on advanced technologies and AI in particular.[35] They include a dozen "general" types accessible to most linguist-researchers and another half dozen "advanced" types that are more resource intensive.

Other methods, including some more technically oriented, are unclassified but outside the public domain. We also created shareable, bilingual lists of indicators and keywords for advanced AI and social control that pass muster locally but need review.[36]

Basic rules of tradecraft apply to open-source collection and analysis just as they do to the classified programs run by governments. Our research on Chinese STI reminds us that the need for discretion is felt by both sides. Be that as it may, there is a *strong case for involving Chinese scientists* in the monitoring process—if not in its operation, then certainly in bilateral discussions of what is and is not dangerous AI, how developments are to be calibrated, what information can or cannot be shared, and in general to sort out misconceptions and establish trust between the world's main AI actors.

Put bluntly, the goal in monitoring foreign developments is *not* to facilitate an "AI arms race," neither directly nor through the back door. This could happen—information is what you make of it—but we believe that accurate data underlies any and all attempts to mitigate risk.

★ ★ ★

While there is more to the problem than what we can describe here, our aim has been to promote a *foundation* for research by experts qualified to do so, and outline a vision of what can be done through open sources. Having done that in the abstract, we need now to demonstrate how such an operation can proceed. The following example illustrates the methodology.

Seth Baum, in his 2017 survey of worldwide AGI programs, de-listed a program at China's Xiamen University (厦门大学) from his watch list,[37] presumably because its founder Hugo de Garis retired. In 2020, however, the university stood up a reinvigorated "Institute of Artificial Intelligence" (人工智能研究院), with a high number of tenure (track) positions (80 full professors, 110 associate professors, and 160 assistant professors making up its "AI-related faculty"),[38] prompting a closer look. The following data were retrieved from Internet searches:

- The AI institute researches machine vision, pattern recognition, and cognitive science, and has teams studying hybrid intelligence and cross-media AI—all AGI precursors.[39]
- The institute has cooperative research relationships with all four of China's "BATH" (Baidu, Alibaba, Tencent, Huawei) companies, each of which has AGI programs.[40]

- AI institute professor Ji Rongrong (纪荣嵘) lamented the inability of AI to deal with the "catastrophic forgetting" problem. Solving it is the "key to AGI (通用人工智能)."[41]

- Xiamen University's AI institute and Tencent, a known AGI developer,[42] announced jointly that "multi-modal fusion," in which the institute specializes, will lead to AGI.[43]

- Ben Goertzel is a visiting professor at Xiamen University's Fujian Provincial Key Laboratory of Brain-like Intelligent Systems (福建省仿脑智能系统重点实验室).[44]

- A high-profile paper by Xiamen University researchers on "Bioinspired Nanofluidic Iontronics" describes brain-like signal processing for neuron-computer interfaces.[45]

- Dean of the College of Humanities Zhu Jing (朱菁, see Box 15.1) and colleagues provided slides at the 2020 China AGI Annual Conference on the definition of AGI.[46]

- Jiang Min (江敏), professor in the university's School of Informatics and a senior IEEE member, co-authors with Goertzel[47] and focuses personally on software and AGI.[48]

Other indicators of a potential AGI program are seen in academic publications and collaboration networks.

BOX 15.1

ZHU JING, DEAN, XIAMEN UNIVERSITY COLLEGE OF HUMANITIES[49]

Zhu Jing (朱菁), Canadian citizen and dean of Xiamen University's College of Humanities, received a BS degree in computer science from Hefei's University of Science and Technology of China in 1991, an MS degree in the philosophy of science from Beijing's Chinese Academy of Sciences University (中国科学院大学) in 1994, and a PhD from Canada's University of Waterloo in philosophy in 2003.

Zhu was an assistant professor at CAS University (2003–2006) before joining the faculty at Sun Yan-Sen University's (中山大学) Institute of Logic and Cognition (逻辑与认知研究所) in Guangdong, where he remained until his posting in Xiamen in 2017. Zhu was also a visiting scholar at Florida State University and London's UCL Institute of Cognitive Neuroscience, and was both a Changjiang Scholar and a 100 Talents Plan awardee.[50]

Professor Zhu's background spans computer science, cognitive neuroscience, psychology, and philosophy—precisely the combination of skills needed to bring AI to full fruition. His work on the cognitive foundation of volition[51] is especially relevant.

Xiamen University AGI Papers

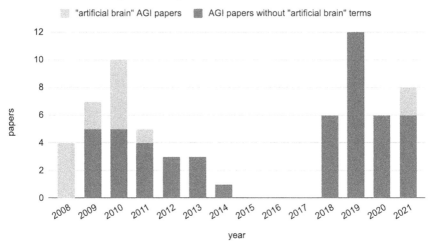

FIGURE 15.1 Papers by Xiamen University researchers on AGI topics

Source: Hannas and Chang et al., "China Advanced AI Research."

Figure 15.1 shows the distribution by year of explicitly AGI-themed papers produced by Xiamen University affiliates beginning in 2008, when de Garis' project began, through its termination in 2011 and on to mid-2021 (data cut-off). The light gray areas are papers retrieved from CNKI and English language databases based on a half-dozen terms aligned with de Garis' China-Brain Project; darker areas represent papers retrieved by searches on Chinese and English expressions for "AGI." In terms of scholarly output, the program's disappearance had a temporary impact only on (overt) AGI research at the university or among its affiliates.

Table 15.2 shows Xiamen University co-author relationships with affiliates of China's big four AI companies and the Chinese Academy of Sciences' Institute of Automation, which all have or will have AGI programs. The papers show the

TABLE 15.2 Papers co-authored by Xiamen University and major Chinese organizations with known AGI programs

Organization	Papers
Baidu	24
Alibaba	11
Tencent	93
Huawei	46
CASIA	16

Source: Hannas and Chang et al., "China Advanced AI Research."

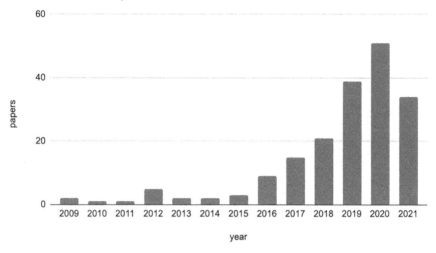

FIGURE 15.2 Xiamen University collaboration with BATH + CASIA

Source: Hannas and Chang et al., "China Advanced AI Research."

existence of collaboration networks only. Figure 15.2 shows the same information expressed over years (2021 is mid-year only).

Finally, we doubt that Professor de Garis failed to bequeath a legacy. His "China Brain Project" involved 20 people, several still there,[52] building their "network of networks" vision of brain function.[53] Although we did not turn up a "hot" AGI program at Xiamen University, this is likely a distinction without a difference, as there is ample evidence that this provincial university is moving (back) toward AGI research, if it ever left it.

From China AI "watchboard" to China STI monitoring

So the question we pose is this: if it makes sense to create on a national (or international) level a mechanism to track aspects of China's AI development, why stop there? Indeed, would such a mechanism even "work" on the limited scale that we proposed? There are several reasons why it may not be possible to restrict the enterprise to a narrowly defined pilot.

First, we have no good idea what form "dangerous" AI will take. On this point, the experts are unanimous. We chose two commonly recognized generic threats—artificial general intelligence (itself badly defined) and AI-enabled devices used for social and political repression, a broad category that keeps expanding. Even if useful work can be done tracking developments in these two areas, success could obscure challenges elsewhere, for example, AI's role in influence operations (propaganda in Cold War terms) or more directly: in understanding the neuronal basis of emotion and motivation (two distinct problems)— and hence controlling people, ant-like, on individual and mass levels.

Second, students of Chinese S&T quickly learn that it is impossible to track China's progress in any field without paying attention to that country's multi-faceted foreign technology access programs, on which it remains highly (but not entirely) dependent. Indeed, the main function of China's STI program is to support the *transfer* of useful technologies it has identified. It and the workings of China's other transfer venues and techniques can fill entire volumes (Chapter 3). Our point is that getting a grip on China's disposition of the AI technologies that inform our pilot means monitoring China's access to U.S. and other foreign developments in these same areas. In other words, expanding the I&W operation.

Finally, AI is an enabling technology—more of a methodology than something that can be tracked in its own right, as China itself understands. Accordingly, the issue needs to be followed not only in terms of what China can theoretically do but also in terms of what implementations may emerge. The present book's chapters on AI + biology and AI + quantum are teasers to alert readers to the possibilities. The real list is as long as the number of S&T disciplines. Moreover, they are interactive: cognitive neuroscience, psychology, linguistics, and nano-technology, to cite just a few more, both benefit from AI developments and hasten the latter's growth. Failure to track China's progress in S&T as a whole puts blinders on the AI effort.

So we are torn between an impulse to proselytize a commonsense, low-budget plan for an I&W watchboard focused on two existential threats, and to promote a larger operation that addresses the issue holistically but at a greater cost—and less chance of being adopted *soon enough to matter*. The fact that we need to do either requires an explanation.

The USIC is structurally and temperamentally indisposed to monitor (i.e. track continuously) foreign S&T developments.[54] It also lacks appreciation for "open source intelligence" (OSINT)—the material best suited to inform our knowledge of S&T developments—as a source with value in its own right, view-ing it instead as an "enabler" of the parochial methods each agency is char-tered (and budgeted) to exploit.[55] These are well-known problems understood inside[56] and outside[57] the community. Our own observations over several dec-ades support these generalizations.[58] The situation is not different within allied and friendly—Australian, British, Canadian, German, Israeli, and Japanese—intelligence services.

The problem is really worse than described, because the existence of *pockets* of OSINT within each of the USIC's major agencies and their foreign analogs, conducted as adjuncts to their primary missions, lends to the impression that useful OSINT on a general scale is being done when it is not. Congressional committees overseeing the USIC are aware of the problem and sympathetic to proposed solutions,[59] but struggle themselves to define a venue and a budget to implement the necessary remedies.[60]

Hence, a vacuum exists in U.S. and allied countries' ability to track Chinese S&T developments (including the role of technology appropriation). As a step toward resolving the general problem, the present authors[61] and colleagues across different sectors of the U.S. government[62] have fleshed out the basics of a proposed National Science and Technology Analysis Center (NSTAC) to monitor and share information on foreign, especially Chinese, technological development, which for reasons given here—and described more fully in the cited sources—would be located *outside* the USIC but with strong allied/friendly country participation.

A comprehensive approach of this sort would necessarily include an "I&W watchboard" for Chinese AI and many other potentially problematic developments. Pending that happy turn of events, we reiterate this book's immediate clarion call for some type of persistent, competently managed mechanism to draw attention, without hype or pretense, to Chinese AI development.

As we and our co-authors have been at pains to demonstrate, the day has long passed when the United States can depend on an unquestioned lead in science to provide technological security. China's progress, commitment, and ambitions in AI compel us to be wary.

Notes

1 Materials used here derive in part from Hannas, Chang, Chou, and Fleeger, June 2022.
2 Future of Life Institute, "Existential risk." https://futureoflife.org/background/existential-risk/.
3 https://www.openphilanthropy.org/.
4 Directed by Rafael Yuste, part of the U.S. BRAIN and International Brain Initiatives. https://nri.ntc.columbia.edu/.
5 OPP, August 2015.
6 Yuste et al., 2021.
7 Karnofsky, 2016.
8 Hannas, Chang et al., "China AI-Brain Research," 2020, pp. 2, 8.
9 "Report of the National Commission for the Review of the Research and Development Programs of the United States Intelligence Community (unclassified version)," 2013. See also Hannas and Chang, "China's STI Operations," January 2021, pp. 1–7.
10 The authors know of just two projects, now defunct, within the USIC to identify and track foreign technological developments on a sustained basis, each focused on different aspects of the problem. Two smaller projects within DOD dried up years ago.
11 Proprietary studies conducted by SOSi's Defense Group Inc. circa 2015.
12 "Even the tiniest reduction of existential risk has an expected value greater than that of the definitive provision of any 'ordinary' good" (Bostrom, 2013).
13 Stoff and Tiffert, 2021. CASIA is the Chinese Academy of Sciences Institute of Automation (中科院自动化所), a major AI institute.
14 It is probably not coincidental that many people affiliated with the Future of Life (Boston) and Humanity (Oxford) Institutes, where existential risk is taken seriously, are principled vegans and animal rights advocates.
15 Hannas and Chang, "China's STI Operations," 2021.
16 See the present book's Chapter 3 on technology transfer.
17 COSTIND expands to "Commission on Science and Technology Industry for National Defense." COSTIND became the State Administration for Science and Technology Industry for National Defense (SASTIND, 国家国防科技工业局) in 2008.

18 Zeng Jianxun, 2019, pp. 227–238.

19 Huo and Wang, 1991.

20 "2019军队文职人员招聘军事科学院军事科学信息研究中心职位表" posted to China's Military-Civilian Personnel Recruitment Network (军队文职人员招聘网), http://jzg. huatu.com/jdwz/zwk/bj/bm25.html. Table adapted from Hannas and Chang, "China's STI Operations," 2021.

21 Ibid.

22 Huo and Wang, 1991.

23 Ibid., Chapter 3.

24 Ibid., Chapter 4.

25 ISTIC, *60 Years of Glory*, 2016.

26 http://digitalpaper.stdaily.com/http_www.kjrb.com/kjrb/html/2016-10/15/content_ 351387.htm?div=0; https://www.istic.ac.cn/isticcms/html/1/151/155/347.html, accessed September 2020.

27 http://www.itxww.com/html/english/istic_e2.htm. Accessed July 2020. Also *60 Years of Glory*, pp. 326, 418. Compare ISTIC's 2016 statement with an August 25, 2021 News Release from our Georgetown center, "CSET has provided a successful model for helping support decision-making with innovative data-driven policy research and recommendations… This model is unique among think tanks."

28 *CIE*, p. 38.

29 https://www.istic.ac.cn/isticcms/html/1/151/155/345.html.

30 Dr. Dewey Murdick, Director, Georgetown University, Center for Security and Emerging Technology, personal communication, 2020.

31 Xia Chengyu, 2001, pp. 104–105.

32 Wu Yishan, 2009, pp. 73–76.

33 Authors' personal consultations with Dewey Murdick, 2021.

34 PRC State Council. 国务院关于印发新一代人工智能发展规划的通知 ("The New Generation AI Development Plan"), SC 35, 2017.

35 William C. Hannas and Huey-Meei Chang, et al., "China AI-Brain Research," Georgetown University, Center for Security and Emerging Technology, September 2020.

36 https://cset.georgetown.edu/contact-us/.

37 Seth Baum, 2017. See this book's Chapter 13.

38 http://www.ucmsr.com/public/uploads/20210419/b5fd69b2c44ada0d8faf70e 6870e1bd0.pdf.

39 Ibid.

40 Ibid.

41 *S&T Daily* (科技日报) interview with Ji Rongrong, April 4, 2020. "学一个忘一个? 人工智能遭遇'灾难性遗忘'解决方案治标不治本" (Learn One and Forget One? Artificial Intelligence Encounters 'Catastrophic Forgetting', and the Solution Treats the Symptoms but Not the Root Cause), http://www.kejie.org.cn/article/detail?id=1404213.

42 "腾讯发布AI开放平台以实现'通用人工智能'" (Tencent Releases AI Open Platform to Realize 'General Artificial Intelligence'), https://tech.huanqiu.com/article/ 9CaKrnKcNfu.

43 https://blog.csdn.net/Datawhale/article/details/117915062.

44 https://m.sohu.com/n/474201345/. Goertzel co-authored some 34 publications with Xiamen University-affiliated persons between 1991 and 2021.

45 Hou Yaqi (侯雅琦) Hou Xu (侯旭), *Science*, 373, August 6, 2021.

46 Zhu Jing (朱菁), Zhan Hao (詹好), Wang Ruoding (王若丁), "浅议AGI的定义和判定标准" (A Brief Talk on the Definition and Standard for Judging AGI), 2020. https:// www.zhihu.com/zvideo/1323402777867595776.

47 https://informatics.xmu.edu.cn/info/1018/6312.htm.

48 https://orcid.org/0000-0003-2946-6974.

49 https://baike.baidu.com/item/朱菁/13982928.

50 State managed talent co-option incentive plans. See Chapter 3.

51 Jing Zhu, *The Conative Mind: Volition and Action*, LAP Lambert Academic Publishing, 2012.
52 Team members Jiang Min (江敏), Shi Xiaodong (史晓东), Zhou Changle (周昌乐), Zhou Jianyang (周剑扬), and Shi Minghui (施明辉) still hold posts at Xiamen University. https://informatics.xmu.edu.cn/szdw/js/3.htm.
53 Hugo de Garis, et al., 2009.
54 The periodic evaluations of this or that foreign technology that do occur fall well short of our understanding of a technology watchboard. This does not even get into the related but more difficult task of forecasting technology.
55 Eliot A. Jardines, "National Open Source Enterprise," April 2006. https://web.archive.org/web/20070928150640.
56 "Report of the National Commission for the Review of the Research and Development Programs of the United States Intelligence Community (unclassified version)," 2013.
57 Florian Schaurer and Jan Storger, "The Evolution of Open Source Intelligence (OSINT)," *The Intelligencer: Journal of U.S. Intelligence Studies*, 19.3, 2013, pp.53–56.
58 Hannas and Chang, "China's STI Operations," January 2021, sections A1 and A2.
59 The present authors, our academic colleagues, and knowledgeable insiders have briefed the Senate and House intelligence committees on this issue and found them to be engaged, concerned, and well-informed.
60 Representatives Castro, Gallagher, Keating, and Fitzpatrick in July 2021 introduced a bipartisan bill to establish an Open Translation and Analysis Center—basically a rebirth of the popular and highly effective Foreign Broadcast Information Service (1941-2005), which had morphed in stages into a closed contingent of the Central Intelligence Agency focused on the latter's own mission. We *applaud this outstanding initiative* but search the bill in vain for "STI," which leads back to the original dilemma of institutions in place obscuring the absence of a needed capability.
61 Hannas and Chang, January 2021, section D.8.
62 Chhabra et al., "Open Source Intelligence for S&T Analysis," 2020.

Bibliography

Baum, Seth, "A Survey of Artificial General Intelligence Projects for Ethics, Risk, and Policy," Global Catastrophic Risk Institute Working Paper, 17-1, 2017.
Bostrom, Nick, "Existential Risk Prevention as Global Priority," *Global Policy* 4.1, February 2013.
Chhabra, Tarun et al., "Open Source Intelligence for S&T Analysis," Georgetown University, Center for Security and Emerging Technology, September 2020. https://cset.georgetown.edu/publication/open-source-intelligence-for-st-analysis/.
de Garis, Hugo et al., "The China-Brain Project: Report on the First Six Months." 2009. https://www.researchgate.net/publication/266642933_The_China-Brain_Project_Report_on_the_First_Six_Months.
Hannas, William C., Huey-Meei Chang, Jennifer Wang, Catherine Aiken, and Daniel Chou. "China AI-Brain Research." Center for Security and Emerging Technology, September 2020.
Hannas, William C. and Huey-Meei Chang, *"China's STI Operations,"* Georgetown University, Center for Security and Emerging Technology, January 2021.
Hannas, William C., Huey-Meei Chang, Daniel Chou, and Brian Fleeger, "China Advanced AI Research," Georgetown University, Center for Security and Emerging Technology, June 2022.
Huo, Zhongwen (霍忠文) and Wang Zongxiao (王宗孝), 国防科技情报源及获取技术 *(Sources and Methods of Obtaining National Defense Science and Technology Intelligence)*, Beijing, Kexue Jishu Wenxuan Publishing Company, 1991.

ISTIC (中国科学技术信息研究所), 甲子辉煌——中国科学技术信息研究所成立60周年纪念 (*60 Years of Glory—The 60th Anniversary of the Founding of the Institute of Science and Technical Information of China*), Beijing, 2016.

Karnofsky, Holden, "Potential Risks from Advanced Artificial Intelligence: The Philanthropic Opportunity," Open Philanthropy, May 6, 2016.

Open Philanthropy Project, "Potential Risks from Advanced Artificial Intelligence," August 2015. https://www.openphilanthropy.org/focus/global-catastrophic-risks/potential-risks-advanced-artificial-intelligence.

Stoff, Jeffrey and Glenn Tiffert, "Eyes Wide Open: Ethical Risks in Research Collaboration with China," Hoover Institution, November 2021.

Wu Yishan (武夷山), "关于我国科技情报工作的几点思考" (Some Thoughts of China's STI Work), 中国科技资源导刊 (*China Science & Technology Resources Review*), 41.6, 2009.

Xia Chengyu (夏承禹), "科技情报部门领导在新形势下的新角色" (A New Role for Leaders of S&T Information Departments under the New Circumstances), 科技进步与对策 (*Science & Technology Progress and Policy*), 2001:1.

Yuste, Rafael, Jared Genser, and Stephanie Herrmann, "It's Time for Neuro-rights: New Human Rights for the Age of Neurotechnology," *Horizons*, 18, 2021.

Zeng Jianxun (曾建勋), "基于国家科技管理平台的科技情报事业发展思考" (Reflection on the Development of the Scientific and Technical Information Industry Based on the National Science and Technology Management Platform), 情报学报 (*Journal of the China Society for Scientific and Technical Information*), 38.3, 2019.

Conclusion

Contributors to this book were asked initially to avoid prescriptions for the issues they write about and focus on *describing* the topics within their purview. This proved to be impossible. Most of us in our daily lives write recommendations for policymakers or whomever else we can cajole for a hearing, so these habits inevitably leak into the narrative. The preceding chapter on monitoring risk is an example of our inability to follow our own rule.

That said, readers outside the U.S. Capital Beltway may be surprised to learn, as we were, that our elected officials, appointees, and their staffs are mostly well-informed on these matters, and agree across party lines that *some things need to be done* to promote our security and prosperity. What we invariably hear in our interactions with policymakers are requests for solutions—ideas on what to do. How can problems be fixed without unnecessarily upsetting the applecart?

Accordingly, we went back to our authors and asked for thoughts on dealing with China's AI challenge. The question supposes that there *is* a challenge and a top-down need to address it. We submit in light of the information in the foregoing chapters that China's AI development does challenge the world. Setting aside malicious intent, China's quest to own this space by 2030 is provocative itself. With stakes this high, one cannot dismiss China's aspirations as hyperbole.

Moreover, as the AI safety literature makes clear, artificial intelligence has risks of its own, independently of its builders' designs. This fact alone argues against a hands-off approach to AI competition and development. While we encourage the work of global consortia in support of AI safety, we also prefer that a guiding hand be exercised by nations with a track record of safety and respect for liberty and human rights. Our recommendations below reflect this bias.

Happily, much of this policy work has been done for us. Three documents in particular win our qualified endorsement. We recommend them as starting points. They are:

DOI: 10.4324/9781003212980-21

- "Asymmetric Competition: A Strategy for China & Technology" (subtitled "Actionable Insights for American Leadership"), China Strategy Group, Fall 2020.[1]

  The paper "advances policies that position the United States to out-compete China without inviting escalatory cycles of confrontation, retaliation, or unintended conflict. While competition is the dominant frame, also essential is considering where cooperation, collaboration, and exchange with China is in our interest, as severing ties and closing off the United States to the ideas, people, technologies, and supply chains necessary to compete effectively will undermine U.S. innovation."[2]

- "Final Report," National Security Commission on Artificial Intelligence, March 2021.[3] A 756-page document released in March 2021 with input from CSET's staff. The study captures our thoughts on the matter completely.

  "AI is part of a broader global technology competition. Competition will speed up innovation. We should race together with partners when AI competition is directed at the moonshots that benefit humanity like discovering vaccines. But we must win the AI competition that is intensifying strategic competition with China. China's plans, resources, and progress should concern all Americans. It is an AI peer in many areas and an AI leader in some applications. We take seriously China's ambition to surpass the United States as the world AI leader within a decade."[4]

- "Proposed Legislative and Institutional Remedies to Mitigate Unwanted Foreign Transfers of U.S. Technology," CSET, September 2021.[5]

  "CSET analysts are often asked about technology transfer—the licit, illicit and grey-zone provisioning of intellectual capital from one nation to another. The matter intersects with 'normal' technology development on multiple levels since nations, often as a matter of state policy, rely on the ingenuity of one another to fashion their futures. While we believe collaboration should be encouraged, the transfer of national security relevant technology—to peer competitors especially—is a well-documented problem and must be balanced with the benefits of free exchange."[6]

These documents address China S&T competition, AI competition in particular, and China's transfer programs that support its AI competitiveness. Among their many propositions, we wish to highlight a few recommendations we believe are particularly important.

1. *Engage China bilaterally and multilaterally in AI safety.*
   China's reticence in public fora to address queries related to biological pandemics coupled with that country's eagerness to achieve a "first mover advantage" in AI raises legitimate concerns about China's commitment on the national level to AI transparency and its ability to enforce prudent AI safety conventions. On the bright side, Chinese AI researchers are acutely aware of the need for caution and sharing best practices and are willing to engage their global counterparts.

Accordingly, the United States and allied countries should identify key AI-related areas of mutual interest for scientific and policy collaboration. Candidates, besides AI safety itself, might include joint development of AI to attenuate common threats ranging from climate change and disease to strategic miscalculations and human relevance in a post-human world.

2. *Get out front in establishing AI standards and practices.*

The United States and liberal democracies should codify international practices and norms in ways that are advantageous to us. Many people dismiss international institutions as idealistic or naïve, but cooperation misses the point. Rules and practices are sticky. We need to ensure that the Chinese government's uses of AI are not accepted as the default.

The U.S. government, and perhaps companies too, need to do more to write AI's rules of the road, especially as Chinese organizations are stepping up. This means contributing to international technology standards drafting and approval, and preempting PRC influence in these standards bodies where inimical to our interests. The task is the easiest when the U.S. government and companies are influential and market-dominant.

3. *Adopt a national strategic view of technology.*

We do not advocate that the United States engage in an AI "race" with China or anyone else, since the risk of escalation is as dangerous (and wasteful) as the Cold War's nuclear threats. Moreover, a technology race per se can easily obscure the importance of factors such as use doctrine, which in the past have been shown to be more decisive than the raw technology. That said, there is no disguising that the competition all parties acknowledge is taking place.

China's support for emerging and foundational technologies unfolds over time, as it puts into place the building blocks of a specific industry. These market interventions benefit chosen national champions at the same time they lay out a national infrastructure. For our part, we surrender nothing by acknowledging, similarly, that laissez faire capitalism works best when the interests of its sponsoring body politic are made its first priority. In this context, we also encourage our multinational corporations to consider the needs of their home country in their technology sharing and stewardship.

4. *Resuscitate American research and manufacturing.*

Quibbling over who gets what share of the world's AI "talent" is a path to failure. Rather, we propose that the U.S. government focus first on building (rebuilding) America's S&T talent and structural foundations to avoid this zero-sum struggle. By the same token, we emphasize that reducing technology loss (our comments below on foreign transfers) by itself is no substitute for positive efforts to create and operationalize new technologies.

We recommend increased federal R&D spending to match or exceed the pace that China and other technologically advanced nations maintain, emphasizing areas that may be neglected by the private sector. Some agencies in addition should boost their budgets for applied research and—taking a cue from China—expand technology commercialization offices at U.S. universities. These offices are typically understaffed and too disconnected from industry to be effective.

5. *Promote, attract, and retain AI talent.*
   Improving the U.S. innovation base has the happy result of simultaneously enhancing our appeal to foreign talent. U.S. policymakers should liberalize current immigration policy, in core AI disciplines especially. Within existing frameworks, lawmakers should address the backlogs in F-1 visa program processing, lift outdated quotas on work and study visas, and improve flexibility in student visa conditions, taking into account the costs they impose on students attempting to study at U.S. institutions.[7]

   Policymakers should also evaluate options for retaining foreign talent, beginning with a clearer path from temporary status to permanent residency and citizenship. We should consider creating a statutory student-to-work pathway, as well as a new visa category for student-entrepreneurs to start companies in the United States.[8] Inclusion by the same token implies a willingness among the newly included to eschew requests (pitches) from their countries of origin for support "while in place."

6. *Mitigate AI technology loss through academic and corporate outreach.*
   Create a public-private institution to promote security throughout America's R&D ecosystem, staffed with experts in technical subjects, counterintelligence, open-source analysis, federal grant processing, and language and area studies pertaining to "foreign countries of concern." Responsibilities should include providing academic and research communities context-specific, data-driven threat assessments that allow them to evaluate risks to research security in any specific situation,[9] with a mandate that includes both government and corporate-funded research.

   Arrest and harassment of (unwittingly) co-opted scientists, who may be unaware of the larger issues, is not the best way to promote patriotism or incentivize compliance with norms that are themselves poorly defined and badly communicated. Better to get in front of the problem with information and support. The U.S. National Counterintelligence and Security Center's 2021 paper "Protecting Critical and Emerging U.S. Technologies from Foreign Threats" is a model of the type of outreach needed.[10]

7. *Create clear and consistent guidelines for "acceptable" sharing practices.*
   Define what transactions are problematic from a national security standpoint, for AI and critical technologies generally. Publicly identify platforms, proxies, and venues inimical to U.S. security. Create consistent, transparent laws and guidelines for the transfer of research and technology to "at risk" countries to eliminate ambiguity, while balancing the benefits the United States accrues from foreign scientific exchange.

   Establish disclosure rules for U.S. government grant recipients researching technical areas. Disallow federal funding to projects linked directly or through performer affiliations to the military establishments and "United

Front" organizations of designated threat countries. Promote transparency through online databases of all overseas funding received by U.S. public universities and their employees, and of foreign entities with a history of improper transfers or intellectual property theft.

8. *Protect U.S. data, key AI technologies from theft and foreign exploitation.*
   China views data as "precious ore" for AI and buys or steals as much as it can. The United States does not have an equivalent to the EU's General Data Protection Regulation and as a result most of our personal identifiable information and pattern-of-life data is floating to be sold by data brokers, monetized by tech companies, or stolen by criminals or nation-states. Passing a U.S. version of GDPR would further balkanize the Internet, but China and Russia are already balkanizing it and it may be time to consider creating an Internet ecosystem for the Free World. A U.S. data privacy law would be a start.

   We devoted a chapter and sections of other chapters to China's AI technology transfers and will not belabor it here, other than to emphasize our findings that the general problem will not disappear as China matures technologically, and that little impact has been made addressing it despite a decade of public disclosure[11] and proselytizing in every corridor of the U.S. government. Progress in mitigating the problem is hampered by American hubris, which refuses to take the threat seriously, and by the lack of any organization, inside or outside government, to detect infractions early enough to matter.

9. *Monitor worldwide AI research, development, deployment.*
   We repeat a standing proposal for a National Science and Technology Analysis Center established directly under the Office of the Director of National Intelligence, or within the U.S. government but outside its intelligence community (IC), to answer technology-related questions, with special emphasis on AI and other critical emerging technologies.[12] The concept is inspired by China's world class S&T open-source monitoring program that has served that country well since 1958.[13] Absent a de novo organization of this sort, the United States has no sustainable means to track China's technology development—not to mention predict its emergence—nor any reasonable hope of stemming technology losses.

   The proposal is for an organization exempt from the proprietary demands of existing U.S. intelligence agencies, whose institutional neglect of open source as a venue in its own right and disregard of foreign science as a collection priority are known problems.[14] Meanwhile, independently of this proposition, we recommend the USIC be mandated to monitor continuously key foreign S&T indicators and provide warnings of potentially hazardous foreign AI development through mission-specific classified venues.

10. *Assess and mitigate risks from worst-case scenarios.*
    Earlier we stated that the level of awareness among U.S. policymakers of many topics we have covered is reassuringly high. One area where this may be less true is in preparing for potential worst-case scenarios related to AI, up

to and including global catastrophic risks. Although the suite of risks posed by AI is not limited to threats of extreme scale, a wise approach to managing the technology must tackle many different types of risks, including scenarios where AI is used deliberately to cause major harm, and scenarios where loss of control spirals into disaster.[15]

Supporting the development of more reliable and trustworthy AI systems, safeguarding against Chinese misuse of AI for authoritarian ends, and monitoring AI development to enable a better-informed U.S. approach are all relevant and valuable. The missing piece is that AI's potential for extreme harm needs to be woven through our thinking about how to promote, protect, and manage this technology. It makes no sense to focus on outpacing China and end up undermining the interests of all humanity. As former Secretary of the Navy Richard Danzig put it, "superiority is not synonymous with security."[16] We must ensure that our efforts to shape AI's development serve our core values and interests.

Notes

1 Signed by 12 persons, including co-chairs Eric Schmidt and Jared Cohen. Marked "Confidential – Not for Distribution" and available publicly at https://s3.document cloud.org/documents/20463382/final-memo-china-strategy-group-axios-1.pdf.
2 Ibid., p. 3.
3 Signed by "a bipartisan commission of 15 technologists, national security professionals, business executives, and academic leaders" and chaired by Eric Schmidt. https://www.nscai.gov/wp-content/uploads/2021/03/Full-Report-Digital-1.pdf.
4 Ibid., p. 2.
5 A composite statement by CSET's management and staff, compiled by William C. Hannas and Huey-Meei Chang. https://cset.georgetown.edu/wp-content/uploads/CSET-Proposed-legislative-and-institutional-remedies-to-mitigate-unwanted-foreign-transfers-of-U.S.-technology.pdf.
6 Ibid., p. 1.
7 Remco Zwetsloot et al., "Keeping Top AI Talent in the United States," Georgetown University, Center for Security and Emerging Technology, December 2019.
8 Ibid.
9 Emily Weinstein and Ainikki Riikonen, "Recommendations to OSTP on National Security Presidential Memoranum-33," Georgetown University, Center for Security and Emerging Technology, November 9, 2021.
10 https://www.dni.gov/index.php/ncsc-newsroom/item/2254-ncsc-fact-sheet-protecting-critical-and-emerging-u-s-technologies-from-foreign-threats.
11 William C. Hannas, James Mulvenon, Anna B. Puglisi, *Chinese Industrial Espionage*, Routledge, London and New York, 2013.
12 William C. Hannas and Huey-Meei Chang, "China's STI Operations," Georgetown University, Center for Security and Emerging Technology, January 2021, pp. 41–43.
13 Hannas, Mulvenon, Puglisi, 2013, pp. 18–49.
14 Hannas and Chang, "China's STI Operations," January 2021, pp. 1–7.
15 Stuart Russell, *Human Compatible*, Viking, New York, NY, 2019; Brian Christian, *The Alignment Problem: Machine Learning and Human Values*, W. W. Norton & Company, New York, NY, 2020.
16 Richard Danzig, "Technology Roulette," Center for a New American Security, May 2018, p. 5.

Appendix

Glossary of terms

211 Program   211工程
863 Program   863计划
973 Program   973计划
985 Program   985工程
AI Industry and Technology Innovation Alliance of China (AIIA)   中国人工智能产业发展联盟
Association of Chinese-American Scientists and Engineers   旅美中国科学家工程师专业人士协会
Aviation Industry Corporation of China (AVIC)   中国航空工业集团
Beijing Academy of Artificial Intelligence (BAAI)   北京智源人工智能研究院
Beijing AI Industrial Alliance (BAIIA)   北京人工智能产业联盟
CCP Central Committee Party School International Strategy Research Academy   中共中央党校国际战略研究院
Changjiang Scholars   长江学者
China Academy of Information and Communications Technology (CAICT)   中国信息通信研究院
China Aerospace Science and Technology Corporation (CASC)   中国航天科技集团
China Aerospace Science and Industry Corporation (CASIC)   中国航天科工集团
China Association for Science and Technology   中国科学技术协会
China Brain Project   中国脑计划
China Defense Science and Technology Information Center (CDSTIC)   中国国防科技信息中心
China Electronics Corporation (CEC)   中国电子信息产业集团
China Electronics Standardization Institute (CESI)   中国电子技术标准化研究所

China Electronics Technology Group (CETC) 中国电子科技集团
China Information Technology Security Evaluation Center (CNIT-SEC) 中国信息安全测评中心
China International Talent Exchange Association 中国国际人才交流协会
China Overseas Exchange Association 中国海外交流学会
China Railway Rolling Stock Corporation (CRRC) 中国中车
China Telecom 中国电信
Chinese Academies of Engineering (CAE) 中国工程院
Chinese Academies of Science (CAS) 中国科学院
Chinese Association for Artificial Intelligence (CAAI) 中国人工智能学会
Chinese Association for Science and Technology USA 中国留美科技协会
Chinese Association of Professionals in Science and Technology 中国旅美专家协会
Chinese Institute of Engineers USA 美洲中国工程师学会
Chinese National Knowledge Infrastructure (CNKI) 中国知网
Chunhui Program (Spring Lights Program) 春晖计划
Comprehensive management information platforms 综治信息平台
Double Innovation Program 双创计划
Education Informatization 2.0 Action Plan 教育信息化2.0行动计划
Federation of Associations of Chinese Professionals in Southern USA 美南中国专家协会联合会
Foreign intellect recruitment innovation bases 创新引智基地
Golden Shield Project 金盾工程
Government guidance funds 政府引导基金
Guangdong Overseas Chinese Innovation and Entrepreneurship Promotion Association 广东省华人华侨创新创业促进会
High-level Overseas Experts Program 海外高层次人才项目
Homeland Serving Action Plan for Overseas Chinese 海外赤子为国服务行动计划
Hundred Talents Program 百人计划
Industrial clusters 产业集群
Ingestion-emulation 引进-模仿
Innovation service centers 创业服务中心
Integrated Joint Operations Platform (IJOP) 一体化联合作战平台
Institute of Automation, CAS (CASIA) 中科院自动化所
Institute of Scientific and Technical Information of China (ISTIC) 中国科技情报研究所
Military-civil fusion (MCF) 军民融合
Ministry of Education (MOE) 教育部
Ministry of Human Resources and Social Security (MHRSS) 人力资源和社会保障部
Ministry of State Security (MSS) 国家安全部
Ministry of Science and Technology (MOST) 科学技术部

Ministry of Public Security (MPS) 公安部

National Fund for Technology Transfer and Commercialization (NFTTC) 国家科技成果转化引导基金

National Basic Research Program (973 Plan) 国家重点基础研究发展规划

National Development and Reform Commission (NDRC) 国家发展和改革委员会

National Engineering Laboratory for Brain-inspired Intelligence Technology and Application (NEL-BITA) 类脑智能技术及应用国家工程实验室

National Natural Science Foundation of China (NNSF) 国家自然基金委员会

National Science Fund for Distinguished Young Scholars 国家杰出青年科学基金

New engineering 新工科

New Century Outstanding Talent Support Program 新世纪优秀人才支持计

New Generation Artificial Intelligence Development Plan 新一代人工智能发展规划

New infrastructure development 新基建

North American Chinese Scholars International Exchange Center 北美洲中国学人国际交流中心

Overseas Chinese Affairs Office (OCAO) 国务院侨务办公室

Overseas scholar pioneering parks 留学人员创业园

Paddle Quantum 量桨

Peacock Program 孔雀计划

Personal Information Protection Law (PIPL) 个人信息保护法

Precision Medicine Initiative 精准医疗计划

Private enterprises 民营企业

Program of Introducing Innovative Talents of Disciplines to Universities (Program 111) 高等学校学科创新引智计划

Seven Sons of National Defense 国防七子

Sharp Eyes 雪亮工程

Shenzhen High-level Talent Association 深圳市高层次人才联谊会

Silicon Valley Chinese Engineers Association 硅谷华人工程师协会

Social capital 社会资本

State Administration of Foreign Experts Affairs (SAFEA) 国家外国专家局

State Development Investment Corporation (SDIC) 国家开发投资集团有限公司

State Grid 国家电网

State Key Laboratories (SKLs) 国家重点实验室

Strategic emerging industries (SEI) 战略性新兴产业

STI workers 科技情报工作人员

Technology Innovation Guidance Fund 技术创新引导专项基金

Technology transfer centers 技术转移中心

Thousand Talents Plan 千人计划
Three-dimensional portrait and integrated data doors 三维人像综合数据门
Tsinghua Alumni Academic Club of North America 北美清华教授协会
United Front Work Department 统一战线工作部
Western Returned Scholars Association (Overseas-educated Scholars Association of China) 欧美同学会(中国留学人员联谊会)
ZGC Innovation Center 中关村硅谷创新中心
Zhangjiang AI Island 张江人工智能岛

Contributors

Ashwin Acharya is an AI Governance Researcher at Rethink Priorities, where he focuses on the long-term impacts of AI progress. Previously, he was a Research Analyst at CSET, conducting bibliometric analyses of research on machine learning, AI safety, and emerging hardware. He holds a Bachelor's in Physics from the University of Chicago and is a Security Studies Master's student at Georgetown University.

Zachary Arnold is an attorney and Analytic Lead for CSET's Emerging Technology Observatory Initiative. His writing has been published in the *Wall Street Journal*, *Foreign Affairs*, *MIT Technology Review*, and leading law reviews. He holds an AB in Social Studies from Harvard College and a JD from the Yale Law School.

Huey-Meei Chang is CSET's Senior China S&T Specialist. She began her career as a data analyst at Taiwan's Academia Sinica, Institute of Biomedical Sciences. She taught document analysis for more than a decade to researchers at U.S. Government agencies, tutored Chinese, and has authored several papers and book chapters on contemporary China topics.

John Chen is a Lead Analyst at SOSi's Center for Intelligence Research and Analysis, where he works on foreign policy, national security, and S&T issues using Chinese-language sources. His research interests include Chinese cyber and information operations. He holds degrees from Dartmouth College and Georgetown University.

Daniel H. Chou is a Data Scientist at Georgetown's Center for Security and Emerging Technology (CSET) where he transforms data into knowledge. Before joining CSET, he supported government clients with analytics of geospatial, unstructured, and text-based data sets. He holds degrees from Caltech and Johns Hopkins University.

Ryan Fedasiuk is a CSET Research Analyst focusing on military applications of AI and China's efforts to acquire foreign technology. He holds a BA in International Studies and a minor in Russian from American University (cum laude, Phi Beta Kappa). He is an MA candidate in the Security Studies Program at Georgetown University.

William C. Hannas is a Georgetown professor and CSET's lead analyst. He was part of the Central Intelligence Agency's SIS cadre and a three-time recipient of its McCone Award. Prior to that, he served in the U.S. Navy and Joint Special Operations Command. He has written and edited several books on Asian security issues. His doctorate is from Penn in Asian languages.

Ngor Luong is a Research Analyst at CSET, focusing on China's industrial policy, AI investment trends, and AI diplomacy in the Asia-Pacific region. She received a BA magna cum laude in International Politics and Economics from Middlebury College and studied abroad at China's Capital Normal University and Zhejiang University of Technology.

Dahlia Peterson is a Research Analyst at CSET, where she focuses on how China uses AI surveillance within China and globally. Her work has been published by the Brookings Institution, Routledge, and *The Diplomat*. She holds a BA in Economics and Chinese Language from UC Berkeley, and is pursuing an MA in Security Studies from Georgetown University.

Anna B. Puglisi is the Director of Biotechnology Programs and Senior Fellow at CSET. She was the National Counterintelligence Officer for East Asia and a CIA senior analyst. She has an MPA and MS in environmental science from Indiana University, and studied and worked in China. She co-authored *Chinese Industrial Espionage* and countless proprietary studies on China.

Jonathan Ray is the Research Director for SOSi's Center for Intelligence Research and Analysis, where he works on national security, foreign policy, and S&T issues using Chinese-language sources. His research interests include semiconductors, hypersonic weapons, nuclear weapons, and emerging technologies.

Jeffrey Stoff is the founder of Redcliff Enterprises, a start-up for public-private partnerships to protect research and intellectual capital. He spent eighteen years as an analyst in components of the U.S. government and is a recognized expert in technology transfer. He has advised the White House, U.S. Departments of Defense, State, NSF, NIH, and multiple academic and corporate entities.

Karen M. Sutter is a specialist in Asian Trade and Finance at the Congressional Research Service. She served as a special advisor at the U.S. Department of Treasury and senior analyst at the CIA and led China research at the US–China Business Council and the Atlantic Council. She worked and studied in Beijing and Taipei and received an MA from the University of Washington.

Helen Toner is CSET's Director of Strategy and Foundational Research Grants. She has advised policymakers and grantmakers on AI policy and as a Senior Analyst at Open Philanthropy. She holds an MA in Security Studies from Georgetown University, and a BSc in Engineering and Diploma in Languages from the University of Melbourne. She is on the board of directors for OpenAI and the Center for the Governance of AI.

Emily Weinstein is a CSET Research Fellow focusing on China's S&T ecosystem, talent flows, and technology transfer issues. She holds a BA in Asian Studies from the University of Michigan and an MA in Security Studies from Georgetown University. Her current research centers around the U.S. export control policy and research security.

INDEX

Note: Page numbers followed by "n" refer to notes; page numbers in **bold** refer to tables; and page numbers in *italics* refer to figures